Computer Science: Theory and Applied Principles

Computer Science: Theory and Applied Principles

Edited by
Fiona Hobbs

WILLFORD PRESS

www.willfordpress.com

Published by Willford Press,
118-35 Queens Blvd., Suite 400,
Forest Hills, NY 11375, USA

ISBN: 978-1-68285-569-0

Cataloging-in-Publication Data

Computer science : theory and applied principles / edited by Fiona Hobbs.
    p. cm.
Includes bibliographical references and index.
ISBN 978-1-68285-569-0
1. Computer science. I. Hobbs, Fiona.
QA76 .C66 2019
004--dc23

For information on all Willford Press publications
visit our website at www.willfordpress.com

Contents

Permissions

List of Contributors

Index

Preface

Computer science studies the principles associated with the design and use of computers. It branches into the study of data structures, algorithms, theories of computation, programming language theory, etc. Studying the theory, engineering and experimentation that are fundamental to the design and usage of computers falls under this area of study. This book presents the contemporary theories and concepts associated with the field of computer science and their practical ramifications across varied industries. The various studies that are constantly contributing towards advancing technologies and evolution of this field are also examined in detail in this book. Scientists and students actively engaged in this field will find the extensive content included herein full of crucial and unexplored concepts.

After months of intensive research and writing, this book is the end result of all who devoted their time and efforts in the initiation and progress of this book. It will surely be a source of reference in enhancing the required knowledge of the new developments in the area. During the course of developing this book, certain measures such as accuracy, authenticity and research focused analytical studies were given preference in order to produce a comprehensive book in the area of study.

This book would not have been possible without the efforts of the authors and the publisher. I extend my sincere thanks to them. Secondly, I express my gratitude to my family and well-wishers. And most importantly, I thank my students for constantly expressing their willingness and curiosity in enhancing their knowledge in the field, which encourages me to take up further research projects for the advancement of the area.

Editor

Fast support vector clustering

Tung Pham[1] · Hang Dang[1] · Trung Le[2] · Thai Hoang Le[1]

Abstract Support-based clustering has recently absorbed plenty of attention because of its applications in solving the difficult and diverse clustering or outlier detection problem. Support-based clustering method perambulates two phases: finding the domain of novelty and performing the clustering assignment. To find the domain of novelty, the training time given by the current solvers is typically over-quadratic in the training size. This fact impedes the application of support-based clustering method to the large-scale datasets. In this paper, we propose applying stochastic gradient descent framework to the first phase of support-based clustering for finding the domain of novelty in the form of a half-space and a new strategy to perform the clustering assignment. We validate our proposed method on several well-known datasets for clustering task to show that the proposed method renders a comparable clustering quality to the baselines while being faster than them.

Keywords Support vector clustering · Cluster analysis · Kernel method

1 Introduction

Cluster analysis is a fundamental problem in pattern recognition where objects are categorized into groups or clusters based on pairwise similarities between those objects such that two criteria, homogeneity and separation, are achieved

✉ Hang Dang
  dthang@hcmus.edu.vn

[1] Faculty of Information Technology, VNUHCM-University of Science, Ho Chi Minh City, Vietnam

[2] Faculty of Information Technology, HCMc University of Pedagogy, Ho Chi Minh City, Vietnam

[21]. Two challenges in the task of cluster analysis are (1) dealing with complicated data with nested or hierarchy structures inside; and (2) automatically detecting the number of clusters. Recently, support-based clustering, e.g., support vector clustering (SVC) [1], has drawn a significant research concern because of its applications in solving the difficult and diverse clustering or outlier detection problem [1,2,8,10,11,15,23]. These clustering methods have two main advantages comparing with other clustering methods: (1) ability to generate the clustering boundaries with arbitrary shapes and automatically discover the number of clusters; and (2) capability to handle well the outliers.

Support-based clustering methods always undergo two phases. In the first phase, the domain of novelty, e.g., optimal hypersphere [1,9,22] or hyperplane [18], is discovered in the feature space. The domain of novelty when mapped back into the input space will become a set of contours tightly enclosing data which can be interpreted as cluster boundaries. However, this set of contours does not specify how to assign a data sample to its cluster. In addition, the computational complexity of the current solvers [3,7] to find out the domain of novelty is often over-quadratic [4]. Such a computational complexity impedes the usage of support-based clustering methods for the real-world datasets. In the second phase, namely clustering assignment, based on the geometry information carried in the resultant set of contours harvested from the first phase, data samples are appointed to their clusters. Several works have been proposed for improving cluster assignment procedure [2,8,11,15,23].

Recently, stochastic gradient descent (SGD) frameworks [6,19,20] have emerged as building blocks to develop the learning methods for efficiently handling the large-scale dataset. SGD-based algorithm has the following advantages: (1) very fast; (2) ability to run in online mode; and (3)

not requiring to load the entire dataset to the main memory in training. In this paper, we conjoin the advantages of SGD with support-based clustering. In particular, we propose to use the optimal hyperplane as the domain of novelty. The margin, i.e., the distance from the origin to the optimal hyperplane, is maximized to make the contours enclosing the data as tightly as possible. We subsequently apply the stochastic gradient descent framework proposed in [19] to the first phase of support-based clustering for achieving the domain of novelty. Finally, we propose a new strategy for clustering assignment where each data sample in the extended decision boundary has its own trajectory to converge to an equilibrium point and clustering assignment is then reduced to the same task for those equilibrium points. Our clustering assignment strategy distinguishes from the existing works of [8, 11–13] in the way to find the trajectory with a start and the initial set of data samples that need to do a trajectory for finding the corresponding equilibrium point. The experiments established on the real-world datasets show that our proposed method produces the comparable clustering quality with other support-based clustering methods while simultaneously achieving the computational speedup.

To summarize, the contribution of the paper consists of the following points:

- Different from the works of [1,2,11,15,23] which employ a hypersphere to characterize the domain of novelty, we propose using a hyperplane to characterize the domain of novelty. This allows us to introduce SGD-based solution for finding the domain of novelty.
- We propose SGD-based solution for finding the domain of novelty. We perform a rigorous convergence analysis for the proposed solution. We note that the works of [1,2, 11,15,23] utilized the Sequential-Minimal-Optimization-based approach [17] to find the domain of novelty wherein the computational complexity is over-quadratic and it requires loading the entire Gram matrix to the main memory.
- We propose new clustering assignment strategy which can reduce the clustering assignment for N samples in the entire training set to the same task for M equilibrium points where M is usually very small comparing with N.
- Comparing with the conference version [16], this paper presents a more rigorous convergence analysis with the full proofs and explanations. In addition, it further introduces new strategy for clustering assignment. Regarding the experiment, it compares with more baselines and produces more experimental results.

2 Stochastic gradient descent large margin one-class support vector machine

2.1 Large margin one-class support vector machine

Given the dataset $\mathcal{D} = \{x_1, x_2, \ldots, x_N\}$, to define the domain of novelty, we construct an optimal hyperplane that can separate the data samples and the origin such that the margin, i.e., the distance from the origin to the hyperplane, is maximized. The optimization problem is formulated as

$$\max_{\mathbf{w},\rho} \left(\frac{|\rho|}{\|\mathbf{w}\|^2} \right)$$

subjects to

$$\mathbf{w}^\mathsf{T} \phi(x_i) - \rho \geq 0, \quad i = 1, \ldots, N$$
$$\mathbf{w}^\mathsf{T} \mathbf{0} - \rho = -\rho < 0$$

where ϕ is a transformation from the input space to the feature space and $\mathbf{w}^\mathsf{T} \phi(x) - \rho = 0$ is equation of the hyperplane. It occurs that the margin is invariant if we scale $(\mathbf{w}, \rho)$ by a factor k. Hence without loss of generality, we can assume that $\rho = 1$ and we achieve the following optimization problem

$$\min_{\mathbf{w}} \left(\frac{1}{2} \|\mathbf{w}\|^2 \right)$$

subjects to

$$\mathbf{w}^\mathsf{T} \phi(x_i) - 1 \geq 0, \quad i = 1, \ldots, N$$

Using the slack variables, we can extend the above optimization problem to form the soft model of large margin one-class Support vector machine (LMOCSVM)

$$\min_{\mathbf{w}} \left(\frac{1}{2} \|\mathbf{w}\|^2 + \frac{C}{N} \sum_{i=1}^{N} \xi_i \right)$$

subjects to

$$\mathbf{w}^\mathsf{T} \phi(x_i) - 1 \geq -\xi_i, \quad i = 1, \ldots, N$$
$$\xi_i \geq 0, \quad i = 1, \ldots, N$$

where $C > 0$ is the trade-off parameter and $\boldsymbol{\xi} = [\xi_1, \ldots, \xi_N]$ is the vector of slack variables.

We can rewrite the above optimization problem in the primal form as follows

$$\min_{\mathbf{w}} \left(J(\mathbf{w}) \triangleq \frac{1}{2} \|\mathbf{w}\|^2 + \frac{C}{N} \sum_{i=1}^{N} \max\left\{0, 1 - \mathbf{w}^\mathsf{T}\phi(x_i)\right\} \right) \tag{1}$$

2.2 SGD-based Solution in the primal form

To efficiently solve the optimization in Eq. (1), we use stochastic gradient descent method. We name the outcome method by stochastic-based large margin one-class support vector machine (SGD-LMSVC).

At tth round, we sample the data point x_{n_t} from the dataset $\mathcal{D}$. Let us define the instantaneous function $g_t(\mathbf{w}) \triangleq \frac{1}{2}\|\mathbf{w}\|^2 + C\max\left\{0, 1 - \mathbf{w}^\mathsf{T}\phi(x_{n_t})\right\}$. It is obvious that $g_t(\mathbf{w})$ is $1 -$ strongly convex w.r.t the norm $\|.\|_2$ over the feature space.

The learning rate is $\eta_t = \frac{1}{t}$ and the sub-gradient is $\lambda_t = \mathbf{w}_t - C\mathbf{I}_{[\mathbf{w}_t^\mathsf{T}\phi(x_{n_t}) < 1]}\phi(x_{n_t}) \in \partial g_t(\mathbf{w}_t)$, where $\mathbf{I}_A(.)$ is the indicator function. Therefore, the update rule is

$$\mathbf{w}_{t+1} = \mathbf{w}_t - \eta_t\lambda_t = \left(1 - \frac{1}{t}\right)\mathbf{w}_t + \frac{C}{t}\mathbf{I}_{[\mathbf{w}_t^\mathsf{T}\phi(x_{n_t}) < 1]}\phi(x_{n_t}) \tag{2}$$

Algorithm 1 Algorithm for solving SGD-LMSVC in the primal form.

Input: C, $K(.,.)$, $\mathcal{D} = \{x_1, ..., x_N\}$
$\mathbf{w}_1 = \mathbf{0}$
for $t = 1$ **to** T **do**
  Sampling n_t from $[N] = \{1, 2, ..., N\}$.
  $\mathbf{w}_{t+1} = \left(1 - \frac{1}{t}\right)\mathbf{w}_t + \frac{C}{t}\mathbf{I}_{[\mathbf{w}_t^\mathsf{T}\phi(x_{n_t}) < 1]}\phi(x_{n_t})$.
endfor
Output: $\mathbf{w}_{T+1}$

Algorithm 1 is proposed to find the optimal hyperplane which defines the domain of novelty. At each round, one data sample is uniformly sampled from the training set and the update rule in Eq. (2) is applied to determine the next hyperplane, i.e., $\mathbf{w}_{t+1}$. Finally, the last hyperplane, i.e., $\mathbf{w}_{T+1}$ is outputted as the optimal hyperplane. According to the theory displayed in the next section, we can randomly output any intermediate hyperplane and the approximately accurate solution is still warranted in a long-term training. Nonetheless, in Algorithm 1, we make use of the last hyperplane as output to exploit as much as possible the information accumulated through the iterations. It is worthwhile to note that in Algorithm 1, we store $\mathbf{w}_t$ as $\mathbf{w}_t = \sum_i \alpha_i \phi(x_i)$.

2.3 Convergence analysis

In this section, we show the convergence analysis of Algorithm 1. We assume that data are bounded in the feature space,

that is, $\|\phi(x)\| \le R$, $\forall x \in \mathcal{X}$. We denote the optimal solution by $\mathbf{w}^*$, that is, $\mathbf{w}^* = \operatorname{argmin}_{\mathbf{w}} \mathcal{J}(\mathbf{w})$. We derive as follows.

Lemma 1 establishes a bound on $\|\mathbf{w}_T\|$, followed by Lemma 2 which establishes a bound on $\|\lambda_T\|$.

Lemma 1 *The following statement holds*

$$\|\mathbf{w}_T\| \le CR, \quad \forall T$$

Proof We have

$$t\mathbf{w}_{t+1} = (t-1)\mathbf{w}_t + C\mathbf{I}_{[\mathbf{w}_t^\mathsf{T}\phi(x_{n_t}) < 1]}\phi(x_{n_t})$$
$$t\|\mathbf{w}_{t+1}\| \le (t-1)\|\mathbf{w}_t\| + CR$$

Taking sum the above when $t = 1, 2, \ldots, T-1$, we gain

$$(T-1)\|\mathbf{w}_T\| \le (T-1)CR$$
$$\|\mathbf{w}_T\| \le CR$$

Lemma 2 *The following statement holds*

$$\|\lambda_T\| = \left\|\mathbf{w}_t - C\mathbf{I}_{[\mathbf{w}_t^\mathsf{T}\phi(x_{n_t}) < 1]}\phi(x_{n_t})\right\| \le 2CR, \quad \forall T$$

Proof We have

$$\|\lambda_T\| \le \|\mathbf{w}_T\| + CR \le 2CR$$

Theorem 1 establishes a bound on regret and shows that Algorithm 1 has the convergence rate $\mathrm{O}\left(\frac{\log T}{T}\right)$.

Theorem 1 *Let us consider the running of Algorithm 1. The following statement holds*

$$\mathcal{J}(\overline{\mathbf{w}}_T) - \mathcal{J}(\mathbf{w}^*) \le \frac{2C^2R^2(\log T + 1)}{T}$$

where $\overline{\mathbf{w}}_T = \frac{1}{T}\sum_{t=1}^{T}\mathbf{w}_t$.

Proof It is apparent that

$$\mathbb{E}[\lambda_t|\mathbf{w}_t] = \mathbf{w}_t - \frac{C}{N}\sum_{n_t=1}^{N} C\mathbf{I}_{[\mathbf{w}_t^\mathsf{T}\phi(x_{n_t}) < 1]}\phi(x_{n_t}) = \mathcal{J}'(\mathbf{w}_t)$$

We have the following

$$\begin{aligned}
\left\|\mathbf{w}_{t+1} - \mathbf{w}^*\right\|^2 &= \left\|\mathbf{w}_t - \eta_t\lambda_t - \mathbf{w}^*\right\|^2 \\
&\le \left\|\mathbf{w}_t - \mathbf{w}^*\right\|^2 - 2\eta_t\lambda_t^\mathsf{T}(\mathbf{w}_t - \mathbf{w}^*) \\
&\quad + \eta_t^2\|\lambda_t\|^2
\end{aligned}$$

Taking conditional expectation w.r.t $\mathbf{w}_t$ the above, we gain

$$\mathcal{J}'(\mathbf{w}_t)(\mathbf{w}_t - \mathbf{w}^*)$$
$$\leq \frac{\mathbb{E}\left[\|\mathbf{w}_t - \mathbf{w}^*\|^2\right] - \mathbb{E}\left[\|\mathbf{w}_{t+1} - \mathbf{w}^*\|^2\right]}{2\eta_t} + \frac{\eta_t}{2}\mathbb{E}\left[\|\lambda_t\|^2\right]$$

$$\mathcal{J}(\mathbf{w}_t) - \mathcal{J}(\mathbf{w}^*) + \frac{1}{2}\|\mathbf{w}_t - \mathbf{w}^*\|^2$$
$$\leq \frac{\mathbb{E}\left[\|\mathbf{w}_t - \mathbf{w}^*\|^2\right] - \mathbb{E}\left[\|\mathbf{w}_{t+1} - \mathbf{w}^*\|^2\right]}{2\eta_t} + \frac{\eta_t}{2}\mathbb{E}\left[\|\lambda_t\|^2\right]$$

$$\mathcal{J}(\mathbf{w}_t) - \mathcal{J}(\mathbf{w}^*) \leq \frac{t-1}{2}\mathbb{E}\left[\|\mathbf{w}_t - \mathbf{w}^*\|^2\right]$$
$$- \frac{t}{2}\mathbb{E}\left[\|\mathbf{w}_{t+1} - \mathbf{w}^*\|^2\right] + \frac{2C^2R^2}{t}$$

Taking expectation again, we achieve

$$\mathbb{E}[\mathcal{J}(\mathbf{w}_t)] - \mathcal{J}(\mathbf{w}^*) \leq \frac{t-1}{2}\mathbb{E}\left[\|\mathbf{w}_t - \mathbf{w}^*\|^2\right]$$
$$- \frac{t}{2}\mathbb{E}\left[\|\mathbf{w}_{t+1} - \mathbf{w}^*\|^2\right] + \frac{2C^2R^2}{t}$$

Taking sum the above inequality when $t = 1, \ldots, T$, we gain

$$\frac{1}{T}\sum_{t=1}^{T}\mathbb{E}[\mathcal{J}(\mathbf{w}_t)] - \mathcal{J}(\mathbf{w}^*)$$
$$\leq \frac{2C^2R^2}{T}\sum_{t=1}^{T}\frac{1}{t} \leq \frac{2C^2R^2(\log T + 1)}{T} \qquad (3)$$
$$\mathcal{J}(\overline{\mathbf{w}}_T) - \mathcal{J}(\mathbf{w}^*) \leq \frac{2C^2R^2(\log T + 1)}{T}$$

$\square$

Theorem 1 shows the inequality for the average solution in the expectation form. In the following theorem, we prove that if we output a single-point solution, with a high probability we have a real inequality.

Theorem 2 *Let us consider the running of Algorithm 1. Let r be an integer randomly picked from $\{1, 2, \ldots, T\}$. Given $\delta \in (0; 1)$, with the probability greater than $1 - \delta$ the following inequality holds*

$$\mathcal{J}(\mathbf{w}_r) < \mathcal{J}(\mathbf{w}^*) + \frac{2R^2C^2(1 + \log T)}{\delta T}$$

Proof Let us denote $X = \mathcal{J}(\mathbf{w}_r) - \mathcal{J}(\mathbf{w}^*) \geq 0$. By definition of r, we have

$$\mathbb{E}_r[X] = \frac{1}{T}\sum_{t=1}^{T}\mathbb{E}[\mathcal{J}(\mathbf{w}_t)] - \mathcal{J}(\mathbf{w}^*)$$

$$\mathbb{E}[X] = \mathbb{E}_{(x_t, y_t)_{t=1}^{T}}[\mathbb{E}_r[X]] \leq \frac{2C^2R^2(\log T + 1)}{T}$$

Using Markov inequality, we gain

$$\mathbb{P}(X \geq \varepsilon) \leq \frac{\mathbb{E}[X]}{\varepsilon} \leq \frac{2C^2R^2(\log T + 1)}{\varepsilon T}$$
$$\mathbb{P}(X < \varepsilon) > 1 - \frac{2C^2R^2(\log T + 1)}{\varepsilon T}$$

Choosing $\delta = \frac{2C^2R^2(\log T + 1)}{\varepsilon T}$, we gain the conclusion. $\square$

We now investigate the number of iterations required if we want to gain an ε-precision solution with a probability at least $1 - \delta$. According to Theorem 2, the number of iterations T must be greater than T_0 where T_0 is the smallest number such that

$$\frac{2R^2C^2(1 + \log T_0)}{\delta T_0} \leq \varepsilon$$
$$\frac{1 + \log T_0}{T_0} \leq \frac{\varepsilon\delta}{2R^2C^2}$$

3 Clustering assignment

After solving the optimization problem, we yield the decision function

$$f(x) = \sum_{i=1}^{N}\alpha_i K(x_i, x) - 1$$

To find the equilibrium points, we need to solve the equation $\nabla f(x) = 0$. To this end, we use the fixed point technique and assume that Gaussian kernel is used, i.e., $K(x, x') = e^{-\gamma\|x - x'\|^2}$. We then have

$$\frac{1}{2}\nabla f(x) = \sum_{i=1}^{N}\alpha_i(x_i - x)e^{-\gamma\|x - x_i\|^2}$$
$$= 0 \rightarrow x = \frac{\sum_{i=1}^{N}\alpha_i e^{-\gamma\|x - x_i\|^2}x_i}{\sum_{i=1}^{N}\alpha_i e^{-\gamma\|x - x_i\|^2}} = P(x)$$

To find an equilibrium point, we start with the initial point $x^{(0)} \in \mathbb{R}^d$ and iterate $x^{(j+1)} = P(x^{(j)})$. By fixed point theorem, the sequence $x^{(j)}$, which can be considered as a trajectory with start $x^{(0)}$, converges to the point $x_*^{(0)}$ satisfying $P(x_*^{(0)}) = x_*^{(0)}$ or $\nabla f(x_*^{(0)}) = 0$, i.e., $x_*^{(0)}$ is an equilibrium point.

Let us denote $B_\epsilon = \{x_i : 1 \leq i \leq N \wedge |f(x_i)| \leq \epsilon\}$, namely the extended boundary for a tolerance $\epsilon > 0$. It follows that the set B_ϵ forms a strip enclosing the decision boundary $f(x) = 0$. Algorithm 2 is proposed to do clustering assignment. In Algorithm 2, the task of clustering assignment is reduced to itself for M equilibrium point. To fulfill cluster assignment for M equilibrium points, we run $m = 20$ sample-point test as proposed in [1].

Algorithm 2 Clustering assignment procedure.

Input: $f(x) = \sum_{i=1}^{N} \alpha_i K(x_i, x) - 1$, B_ε, $\mathcal{D} = \{x_1, \ldots, x_N\}$
$E = \emptyset$.
foreach $x^{(0)}$ **in** B_ϵ **do**
    Find the equilibrium point $x_*^{(0)}$.
    if $\left(x_*^{(0)} \notin E \right)$ **then** $E = E \cup \left\{ x_*^{(0)} \right\}$
endfor
//Assume that $E = \{e_1, e_2, \ldots, e_M\}$
Do m sample point test with for E to find cluster indices for
$e_1, e_2, \ldots, e_M$.
Each point $x^{(0)} \in B_\epsilon$ is assigned to the cluster of its corresponding
equilibrium point $x_*^{(0)} \in E$.
Each point $x \in \mathcal{D} \backslash B_\epsilon$ is assigned to the cluster of its nearest neighbor
in B_ϵ using the Euclidean distance.
Output: clustering solution for $\mathcal{D} = \{x_1, \ldots, x_N\}$

Our proposed clustering assignment procedure is different with the existing procedure proposed in [1]. The procedure proposed in [1] requires to run $m = 20$ sample-point test for every edge connected x_i, x_j ($i \neq j$) in the training set. Consequently, the computational cost incurred is $O(N(N-1)ms)$ where s is the sparsity level of the decision function (i.e., the number of vectors in the model). Our proposed procedure needs to perform $m = 20$ sample-point test for a reduced set of M data samples (i.e., the set of the equilibrium points $\{e_1, e_2, \ldots, e_M\}$) where M is possibly very small comparing with N. The reason is that many data points in the training set could converge to a common equilibrium point which significantly reduces the size from N to M. The computational cost incurred is therefore $O(M(M-1)ms)$.

4 Experiments

4.1 Visual experiment

To visually show the high clustering quality produced by our proposed SGD-LMSVC, we establish experiment on three synthesized datasets and visually make comparison SGD-LMSVC with C-Means and Fuzzy C-Means. In the first experiment, data samples form the nested structure with two

outside rings and one Gaussian distribution at center. As shown in Fig. 1, SGD-LMSVC can perfectly detect three clusters without any prior information while both C-Means and Fuzzy C-Means with the number of clusters being set to 3 beforehand fail to discover the nested clusters. The second experiment is carried out with a two-moon dataset. As observed from Fig. 2, SGD-LMSVC without any prior knowledge can flawlessly discover two clusters in moons, however, C-Means and Fuzzy C-Means cannot detect the clusters correctly. In the last visual experiment, we generate data from the mixture of 4 Gaussian distributions. As shown in Fig. 3, SGD-LMSVC can perfectly detect 4 clusters corresponding to the individual Gaussian distributions. These visual experiments manifest that SGD-LMSVC is able to generate the cluster boundaries in arbitrary shapes as well as automatically detect the appropriate number of clusters well presented in the data.

4.2 Experiment on real datasets

To explicitly prove the performance of the proposed algorithm, we establish experiments on the real datasets. Clustering problem is basically an unsupervised learning task and, therefore, there is not a perfect measure to compare given two clustering algorithms. We examine five typical clustering validity indices (CVI) including compactness, purity, rand index, Davies–Bouldin index (DB index), and normalized mutual information (NMI). A good clustering algorithm should produce a solution which has a high purity, rand index, DB index, and NMI and a low compactness.

4.2.1 Clustering validity index

Compactness measures the average pairwise distances of points in the same cluster [5] and is given as follows

Fig. 1 Visual comparison of SGD-LMSVC (the orange region is the domain of novelty) with C-Means and Fuzzy C-Means on two ring dataset

SGD-LMSVC   C-Means   Fuzzy C-Means

Fig. 2 Visual comparison of
SGD-LMSVC (the orange
region is the domain of novelty)
with C-Means and Fuzzy
C-Means on two-moon dataset

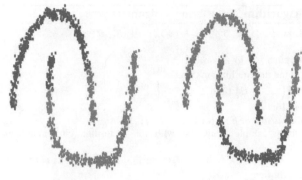

SGD-LMSVC   C-Means   Fuzzy C-Means

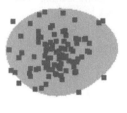

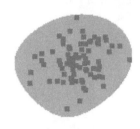

$$\text{Purity} \triangleq \sum_i \frac{N_i}{N} \times p_i$$

The purity ranges between 0 (bad) and 1 (good). This CVI embodies the classification ability of clustering algorithm. A clustering algorithm which achieves a high purity can be appropriately used for classification purpose.

The third CVI used as a measure is rand index [14]. To calculate this CVI for a clustering solution, we need to construct a 2×2 contingency table containing the following numbers: (1) TP (true positive) is the number of pairs that are in the same cluster and belong to the same class; (2) TN (true negative) is the number of pairs that are in two different clusters and belong to different classes; (3) FP (false positive) is the number of pairs that are in the same cluster but belong to different classes; and (4) FN (false negative) is the number of pairs that are in two different clusters but belong to the same class. Rand index is defined as follows

$$\text{Rand} \triangleq \frac{\text{TP} + \text{TN}}{\text{TP} + \text{FP} + \text{TN} + \text{FN}}$$

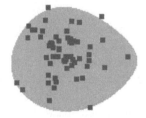

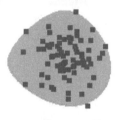

Fig. 3 SGD-LMSVC (the orange region is the domain of novelty) can recognize the clusters scattered from mixture of four Gaussian distributions

$$\text{Compactness} \triangleq \frac{1}{N} \sum_{k=1}^{m} N_k \frac{\sum_{x,x' \in C_k} d(x, x')}{N_k (N_k - 1)/2}$$

where the cluster solution consists of m clusters $C_1, C_2, \ldots, C_m$ whose cardinalities are $N_1, N_2, \ldots, N_m$, respectively.

The clustering with a small compactness is preferred. A small compactness gained means the average intra-distance of clusters is small and homogeneity is thereby good, i.e., two objects in the same cluster have high similarity to each other.

The second CVI in use is purity which measures the purity of clustering solution with respect to the nature classes of data [14]. It is certainly true that the metric purity is only appropriate for data with labels in nature. Let N_{ij} be the number of objects in cluster i that belong to the class j. Again, let $N_i \triangleq \sum_{j=1}^{m} N_{ij}$ be total number of objects in cluster i. Let us define $p_{ij} \triangleq \frac{N_{ij}}{N_j}$, i.e., the empirical distribution over class labels for cluster i. We define a purity of a cluster as $p_i \triangleq \max_j p_{ij}$ and overall purity of a clustering solution as

This can be interpreted as the fraction of clustering decisions that are correct. Obviously, rand index ranges between 0 and 1.

Davies–Bouldin validity index is a function of the ratio of the sum of intra-distances to inter-distances [5] and is formulated as follows

$$\text{DBI} \triangleq \frac{1}{m} \sum_{i=1}^{m} \max_{j \neq i} \left\{ \frac{\Delta(C_i) + \Delta(C_j)}{d(C_i, C_j)} \right\}$$

A good clustering algorithm should produce the solution which has as smallest DBI as possible.

The last considered CVI is normalized mutual information (NMI) [14]. This measure allows us to trade off the quality of the clustering against the number of clusters.

$$\text{NMI} \triangleq \frac{I(\Omega, C)}{[H(C) + H(\Omega)]/2}$$

where $C = \{c_1, \ldots, c_J\}$ is the set of classes and $\Omega = \{\omega_1, \ldots, \omega_K\}$ is the set of clusters. $I(\Omega, C)$ is the mutual information and is defined as

$$I(\Omega, C) \triangleq \sum_k \sum_j P\left(c_j \bigcap \omega_k\right) \log \frac{P\left(c_j \bigcap \omega_k\right)}{P\left(c_j\right) P\left(\omega_k\right)}$$

and $H(.)$ is the entropy and is defined as

$$H(\Omega) \triangleq -\sum_k P\left(\omega_k\right) \log P\left(\omega_k\right)$$

Table 1 The statistics of the experimental datasets

Datasets	Size	Dimension	#Classes
Aggregation	788	2	7
Breast cancer	699	9	2
Compound	399	2	6
D31	3100	2	31
Flame	240	2	2
Glass	214	9	7
Iris	150	4	3
Jain	373	2	2
Pathbased	300	2	3
R15	600	2	15
Spiral	312	2	3
Abalone	4177	8	28
Car	1728	6	4
Musk	6598	198	2
Shuttle	43,500	9	5

It is certainly that the NMI ranges between 0 and 1, and a good clustering algorithm should produce as highest NMI measure as possible.

We perform experiments on 15 well-known datasets for clustering task. The statistics of the experimental datasets is given in Table 1. These datasets are fully labeled and consequently, the CVIs like purity, rand index, and NMI can be completely estimated. We make comparison of our proposed SGD-LMSVC with the following baselines.

4.2.2 Baselines

- *Support vector clustering (SVC)* [1] using LIBSVM [3] for finding domain of novelty and fully connected graph for clustering assignment.
- *Fast support vector clustering (FSVC)* [8] an equilibrium-based approach for clustering assignment.

It is noteworthy that the first phase in our proposed SGD-LMSVC is SGD-based solution for LMOCSVM (cf. Algorithm 1) and the second phase is proposed in Algorithm 2. All competitive methods are run on a Windows computer with dual-core CPU 2.6 GHz and 4 GB RAM.

4.2.3 Hyperparameter setting

The RBF kernel, given by $K(x, x') = e^{-\gamma \|x - x'\|^2}$, is employed. The width of kernel γ is searched on the grid $\{2^{-5}, 2^{-3}, \ldots, 2^3, 2^5\}$. The trade-off parameter C is searched on the same grid. In addition, the parameters p and ε in FSVC are searched in the common grid

Table 2 The purity, rand index, and NMI of the clustering methods on the experimental datasets

Datasets	Purity			Rand index			NMI		
	SVC	SGD	FSVC	VC	SGD	FSVC	SVC	SGD	FSVC
Aggregation	**1.00**	**1.00**	0.22	**1.00**	**1.00**	0.22	0.69	**0.75**	0.60
Breast cancer	0.98	**0.99**	**0.99**	0.82	**0.85**	0.81	0.22	**0.55**	0.45
Compound	**0.66**	0.62	0.13	**0.92**	0.88	0.25	0.51	**0.81**	0.45
Flame	0.86	**0.87**	0.03	0.75	**0.76**	0.03	**0.55**	0.51	0.05
Glass	0.5	**0.71**	0.65	0.77	**0.91**	0.54	**0.60**	0.44	0.53
Iris	**1.00**	**1.00**	0.68	**0.97**	0.96	0.69	0.63	**0.75**	0.71
Jain	0.37	0.46	**0.69**	0.7	0.71	**0.77**	0.53	0.31	**1.00**
Pathbased	0.6	0.5	**1.00**	0.81	0.94	**1.00**	**0.48**	0.43	0.12
R15	0.88	**0.9**	0.37	**0.74**	0.71	0.37	0.67	**0.77**	**0.77**
Spiral	0.09	0.33	**0.53**	0.15	**0.94**	0.75	**0.52**	0.34	0.16
D31	0.94	**0.99**	0.42	**0.88**	0.81	0.54	0.45	**0.50**	0.38
Abalone	0.22	**0.44**	0.03	0.43	**0.86**	0.12	0.22	**0.34**	0.07
Car	0.94	**0.95**	0.70	0.46	0.46	**0.54**	**0.32**	**0.32**	0.24
Musk	0.87	0.68	**0.88**	0.26	**0.28**	0.26	0.21	0.16	**0.23**
Shuttle	**0.06**	0.05	**0.06**	**0.84**	0.83	0.75	0.26	0.41	**0.50**

Table 3 The compactness and DB index of the clustering methods on the experimental datasets

Datasets	Compactness			DB index		
	SVC	SGD	FSVC	SVC	SGD	FSVC
Aggregation	**0.29**	**0.29**	2.84	**0.68**	0.67	0.63
Breast cancer	1.26	**0.68**	0.71	**1.58**	1.38	0.53
Compound	0.5	**0.21**	2.43	**2.45**	0.86	0.67
Flame	0.58	**0.44**	2.28	**1.3**	0.65	3.56
Glass	0.72	**0.68**	1.85	0.53	0.56	**0.93**
Iris	0.98	**0.25**	0.99	**1.95**	1.17	0.77
Jain	0.96	**0.36**	1.16	**1.23**	1.08	0.71
Pathbased	**0.18**	0.3	1.04	0.36	0.73	**1.07**
R15	0.61	**0.13**	1.84	**2.96**	1.42	1.37
Spiral	2	**0.17**	0.18	**1.41**	0.98	0.36
D31	1.41	**0.26**	1.78	**2.33**	1.35	1.21
Abalone	3.88	**0.40**	4.97	3.78	**3.91**	1.29
Car	0.75	**0.74**	14.68	**1.76**	**1.76**	1.57
Musk	**9.89**	30.05	20.00	2.27	**2.83**	0.01
Shuttle	0.50	0.46	**0.26**	**1.86**	1.84	1.32

Table 4 Training time in second (i.e., the time for finding domain of novelty) and clustering time in second (i.e., the time for clustering assignment) of the clustering methods on the experimental datasets

Datasets	Training time			Clustering time		
	SVC	SGD	FSVC	SVC	SGD	FSVC
Aggregation	0.05	**0.03**	0.05	31.42	**2.83**	7.51
Breast cancer	0.18	**0.02**	0.05	19.80	**2.14**	22.86
Compound	0.03	**0.02**	0.10	6.82	**1.17**	7.24
Flame	**0.02**	**0.02**	15.16	1.81	**0.67**	4.31
Glass	0.03	0.03	**0.02**	2.30	**0.53**	10.67
Iris	**0.02**	**0.02**	0.04	1.03	**0.34**	4.33
Jain	**0.02**	**0.02**	0.03	5.80	**0.81**	4.59
Pathbased	**0.02**	**0.02**	0.05	4.02	**0.54**	4.22
R15	**0.02**	**0.02**	**0.02**	4.14	**3.68**	10.43
Spiral	**0.02**	0.03	**0.02**	1.60	**0.99**	7.78
D31	0.17	**0.09**	**0.09**	467.72	**6.56**	33.08
Abalone	2.26	**0.81**	10.94	653.65	**26.58**	242.97
Car	5.62	**0.64**	8.15	67.66	**7.05**	84.47
Musk	55.93	**5.79**	58.49	602.09	**432.58**	510.25
Shuttle	10.03	**0.46**	68.43	1,972.61	**925**	1,125.46

$\{0.1, 0.2, \ldots, 0.9, 1\}$ which is the same as in [8]. Determining the number of iterations in Algorithm 1 is really challenging. To resolve it, we use the stopping criterion $\|\mathbf{w}_{t+1} - \mathbf{w}_t\| \leq \theta = 0.01$, i.e., the next hyperplane does only a slight change.

We report the experimental results of purity, rand index, and NMI in Table 2, compactness and DB index in Table 3, and the training time (i.e., the time for finding

domain of novelty) and clustering time (i.e., the time for clustering assignment) in Table 4. For each CVI, we bold-face the method that yields a better outcome, i.e., highest value for purity, rand index, NMI, and DB index and lowest value for compactness. As shown in Tables 2 and 3, our proposed SGD-LMSVC is generally comparable with other baselines in the CVIs. In particular, our proposed SGD-LMSVC is slightly better than others on purity, rand index, and NMI whereas it totally surpasses others on compactness. Moreover, our proposed SGD-LMSVC is slightly worse than SVC on DB index. Regarding the amounts of time taken for training and doing clustering assignment, our proposed SGD-LMSVC is totally superior than others. For the training time, the speedup is significant for the medium-scale or large-scale datasets including Shuttle, Musk, and Abalone. In particular, the speedup is really significant for the clustering time.

5 Conclusion

In this paper, we have proposed a fast support-based clustering method, which conjoins the advantages of SGD-based method and kernel-based method. Furthermore, we have also proposed a new strategy for clustering assignment. We validate our proposed method on 15 well-known datasets for clustering task. The experiment has shown that our proposed method has achieved a comparable clustering quality compared with the baselines while being significantly faster than them.

References

1. Ben-Hur, A., Horn, D., Siegelmann, H.T., Vapnik, V.: Support vector clustering. J. Mach. Learn. Res. **2**, 125–137 (2001)
2. Camastra, F., Verri, A.: A novel kernel method for clustering. IEEE Trans. Pattern Anal. Mach. Intell. **27**(5), 801–804 (2005)
3. Chang, C.-C., Lin, C.-J.: Libsvm: a library for support vector machines. ACM Trans. Intell. Syst. Technol. **2**(3), 27:1–27:27 (2011)
4. Chu, C.S., Tsang, I.W., Kwok, J.T.: Scaling up support vector data description by using core-sets. In: Proceedings of the 2004 IEEE international joint conference on neural networks, IEEE 2004. vol. 1 (2004)
5. Halkidi, M., Batistakis, Y., Vazirgiannis, M.: Clustering validity checking methods: Part II. SIGMOD Rec. **31**(3), 19–27 (2002)
6. Hazan, E., Kale, S.: Beyond the regret minimization barrier: optimal algorithms for stochastic strongly-convex optimization. J. Mach. Learn. Res. **15**(1), 2489–2512 (2014)
7. Joachims, T.: Advances in kernel methods. In: Schölkopf, B., Burges, C., Smola, A. (eds.) Making Large-Scale Support Vector Machine Learning Practical, pp. 169–184. The MIT Press, Cambridge (1999)
8. Jung, K.-H., Lee, D., Lee, J.: Fast support-based clustering method for large-scale problems. Pattern Recognit. **43**(5), 1975–1983 (2010)

9. Le, T., Tran, D., Ma, W., Sharma, D.: An optimal sphere and two large margins approach for novelty detection. In: The 2010 international joint conference on neural networks (IJCNN), IEEE, pp. 1–6 (2010)

10. Le, T., Tran, D., Nguyen, P., Ma, W., Sharma, D.: Proximity multisphere support vector clustering. Neural Comput. Appl. **22**(7–8), 1309–1319 (2013)

11. Lee, J., Lee, D.: An improved cluster labeling method for support vector clustering. IEEE Trans. Pattern Anal. Mach. Intell. **27**(3), 461–464 (2005)

12. Lee, J., Lee, D.: Dynamic characterization of cluster structures for robust and inductive support vector clustering. IEEE Trans. Pattern Anal. Mach. Intell. **28**(11), 1869–1874 (2006)

13. Li, H.: A fast and stable cluster labeling method for support vector clustering. J. Comput. **8**(12), 3251–3256 (2013)

14. Murphy, K.P.: Machine learning: a probabilistic perspective. The MIT Press, Cambridge (2012)

15. Park, J.H., Ji, X., Zha, H., Kasturi, R.: Support vector clustering combined with spectral graph partitioning. In: Pattern Recognition, 2004. ICPR 2004. Proceedings of the 17th International Conference on, vol. 4, pp. 581–584. IEEE (2004)

16. Pham, T., Dang, H., Le, T., Le, H-T.: Stochastic gradient descent support vector clustering. In: 2015 2nd national foundation for science and technology development conference on information and computer science (NICS), pp. 88–93 (2015)

17. Platt, J.C.: Advances in kernel methods. In: Schölkopf, B., Burges, C., Smola, A. (eds.) Fast Training of Support Vector Machines Using Sequential Minimal Optimization, pp. 185–208. The MIT Press, Cambridge (1999)

18. Schölkopf, B., Platt, J.C., Shawe-Taylor, J.C., Smola, A.J., Williamson, R.C.: Estimating the support of a high-dimensional distribution. Neural Comput. **13**(7), 1443–1471 (2001)

19. Shalev-Shwartz, S., Singer, Y.: Logarithmic regret algorithms for strongly convex repeated games. The Hebrew University, Jerusalem (2007)

20. Shalev-Shwartz, S., Singer, Y., Srebro, N.: Pegasos: primal estimated sub-gradient solver for svm. In. Ghahramani, Z. (ed.) ICML, pp. 807–814 (2007)

21. Shamir, R., Sharan, R.: Algorithmic approaches to clustering gene expression data. In: Current Topics in Computational Biology. pp. 269–300. MIT Press, Cambridge (2001)

22. Tax, D.M.J., Duin, R.P.W.: Support vector data description. Mach. Learn. **54**(1), 45–66 (2004)

23. Yang, J., Estivill Castro, V., Chalup, S K : Support vector clustering through proximity graph modelling. In: Neural information processing, 2002, ICONIP'02, vol. 2, pp. 898–903 (2002)

## 2

Discovering crisis models to help assess coordination plans

A case study of tsunami response plan given by Ho Chi Minh City, Vietnam

Nguyen-Tuan-Thanh Le[1,2] · Chihab Hanachi[3] · Serge Stinckwich[4,5,6] ·
Tuong-Vinh Ho[4,5,7]

Abstract Recently, we have witnessed an increasing number of crises, not only natural disasters but also man-made ones. Coordination among several stakeholders is the key factor to reduce the damage caused by a crisis. However, the plan for coordination can be expressed under various representations, including textual format—the most used one in reality but hard to analyze its efficiency. We consider in this paper a combination of process and organization aspects of a coordination plan. Process models (e.g Petri Net, Business Process Model and Notation) could be used to capture the processes of activities and messages exchanged between the actors involved in a crisis, while organization models (e.g. Role graph, agent-centred multi-agent system, organization centred multi-agent system) are used to highlight the roles, their interactions and the organizational structures. We then describe a proposal that allows performing an automatic transformation from process models to organization models. Our proposal is illustrated with a coordination plan for tsunami response, given by People Committee of Ho Chi Minh City (HCMC), Vietnam.

The work presented in this paper has been funded by the ANR Genepi project.

✉ Nguyen-Tuan-Thanh Le
Nguyen.Le@irit.fr

Chihab Hanachi
hanachi@univ-tlse1.fr

Serge Stinckwich
serge.stinckwich@ird.fr

Tuong-Vinh Ho
ho.tuong.vinh@ifi.edu.vn

1 IRIT Laboratory, University Paul Sabatier Toulouse III, Toulouse, France

2 University of Science and Technology of Hanoi, Hanoi, Vietnam

3 IRIT Laboratory, University Toulouse Capitole I, Toulouse, France

4 IRD, UMI 209, UMMISCO, IRD France Nord, 93143 Bondy, France

5 Sorbonne Universités, Univ. Paris 06, UMI 209, UMMISCO, 75005 Paris, France

6 Université de Caen Basse-Normandie, Caen, France

7 Institute Francophone International, Vietnam National University, Hanoi, Vietnam

Keywords Coordination representation · Business process modelling · Multi-agent system · Organization-centred multi-agent system · Role graph · Mapping process to multi-agent system · Crisis management

1 Introduction

Crisis situations such as natural disasters with environmental consequences impose the coordination of numerous stakeholders: firemen, medical organizations, police, etc. In the context of crisis resolution, coordination plans could be examined under different representations. The mostly used representation in reality is the textual format that has several drawbacks [1]. Its ambiguity makes the coordination among stakeholders difficult. Moreover, it cannot support the direct and autonomous analysis or simulation. Another possible representation of coordination is a process model, e.g. a Business Process Model and Notation diagram (BPMN) as shown in [1]. This diagram, built by analyzing an official textual plan, can support process simulation and analysis [2] due to process complexity, end-to-end process time, resources costs, etc.

Recently, we have witnessed an increasing interest in research aiming at modelling and simulating complex systems (such as Crisis Management) using multi-agent paradigm, i.e the micro aspect. Multi-agent system (MAS) could be separated by agent-centred multi-agent system (ACMAS), i.e. focusing on the individual aspect, and organization centred multi-agent system (OCMAS), i.e. focusing on the social aspect [11]. In our opinion, MAS currently lacks the means to design and visualize the whole system behaviour, i.e the macro aspect. Regarding software engineering, before the implementation, we must perform the design phase to have an overview of studied system. Thus, we argue that multi-agent paradigm should follow this way.

For that reason, the idea of combination between business process and multi-agent system has been raised to improve agent-based design [6] as well as to allow performing divers analysis based on the strong sides of both paradigms (e.g. control-flow complexity metric for process model [14], organizational structure for OCMAS [13], etc.). Process models could be considered as additional components of agent ones, since they can provide means to represent an aggregate view of an MAS behaviour. In addition, process models share several concepts with MAS. Therefore, we believe that the marriage of Process- and Agent models is suitable to design an efficient coordination in complex system [7], such as crisis management, by improving the quality of coordination plan. While stakeholders and their behaviours may be described by agents, the crisis resolution plan is amenable to a process representation.

The work presented in this paper follows a life cycle shown in Fig. 1 to transform from process models (Petri Net, BPMN) to organization models (Role graph, ACMAS and OCMAS). More precisely, we use the Agent-Group-Role (AGR) model proposed by [11] as an OCMAS representation and BDI-Agent as an ACMAS representation.

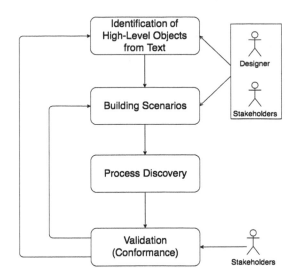

Fig. 2 A scenario-based life cycle for process design and validation from text

Our contribution in this paper consists in the definition of a mapping framework for coordination models in crisis response. We provide the guidelines of transformation among five complementary views (Petri Net, BPMN, Role graph, BDI-agent and AGR). Even if our work examines a concrete case (i.e. the tsunami response plan of Ho Chi Minh City, Vietnam), our approach can be applied to any coordination plan.

This paper is organized as follows. We first give two process representations (Petri Net and BPMN) detected from our tsunami response plan in Sect. 2. Section 3 will present the mappings from process models to organization models (Role graph, ACMAS and OCMAS). Then we provide related works about the process-agent transformation and organizational structure assessment in Sect. 4. Finally, we conclude our work with some perspectives.

2 Design of processes for crisis resolution

We propose a method to design process models of crisis resolution that have the following characteristics (cf. Fig. 2):

1. It is composed of four steps with possible iterations following the validation of stakeholders.
2. The identification of high-level objects take action in support of a meta-model of simple crises (cf. Fig. 2).
3. It is organized around scenarios that correspond to possible plan of crisis resolution.
4. It exploits a process mining technique called α-algorithm [5] to derive the process of crisis resolution (i.e. a Petri Net with special properties) from scenarios.

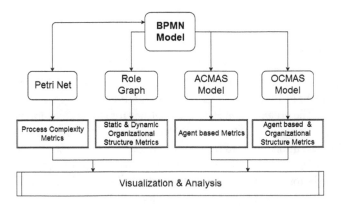

Fig. 1 Life cycle of mapping from process models (Petri Net, BPMN) to organization models (Role graph, ACMAS and OCMAS)

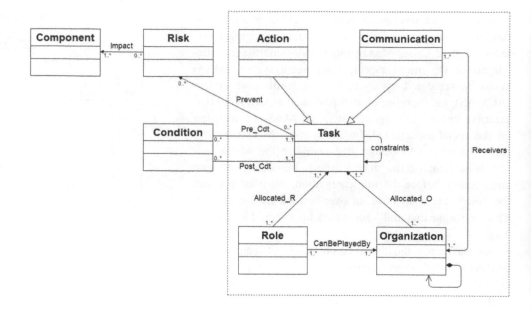

Fig. 3 Meta-model to represent coordination of activities during crisis management

2.1 Identification of high-level objects from text

2.1.1 Principles

The designer must extract from text the top-level objects and the links existing between them. It should be based on the meta-model we propose in Fig. 3. This meta-model is simple enough allowing to extract essential concepts to describe the coordination of activities. There are in the literature more detailed models [3] but the usage may prove to be difficult because it is impossible in reality to dispose of all theoretical information they contain (risk probabilities, gravity factor, etc.).

We prefer here to limit ourselves on high-level concepts, easily identified in the text and that allow derive models of simple processes giving an aggregated view of the plan. The designers, associated with the stakeholders, can then refine the process by proposing scenarios. Although, the analysis of text is supposed here manually but the techniques for automatic text analysis has actually emerged [4] and could be used with profits to extract the elements of our meta-model.

Our meta-model records the tasks and the roles and/or organizations who are in charge of these roles. An organization can contain others and a hierarchy relationship then exists between them. The tasks realize the objectives to reduce or resolve the risks (potential or proven). The tasks may have constraints between them (precedence or choice, etc.) and the causal links: the effect of a task (post-condition) may be exploited by another (pre-condition). The constraints and causal links are given in the Table 1. The tasks can take two forms (communication or action). In the second case, we record the receivers of the communication.

2.1.2 Illustration of identifying organizations, tasks and their relationships from HCMC's Plan

In fact, we have identified in this HCMC's plan over thirty organizations and numerous duties for each one. For legibility reason, we gathered some organizations with similar responsibilities or missions in a more abstract organization. Sometimes organizations share a common role: for example police and military have the first-responder role and as such they have both the mission of evacuating people and informing and transferring injuries people to safe places. We will not detail here the different roles but only the tasks and the organizations.

The organization Local Administration represents actually four organizations: (1) Committee for Flood–Storm Prevention and Search–Rescue of HCMC, (2) People's Committee of Districts, Communes and Towns, (3) Chairman of People's Committee of Districts, Communes and Towns, and (4) Command Center of Program against Flooding of HCMC.

The organization Communication Unit gathers three organizations: (1) Department of Information and Communication, (2) Television station of HCMC, and (3) Radio Voice of HCMC.

The organization Military represents three organizations: (1) High command of HCMC, (2) Border Guard High Command of HCMC, and (3) Border Guard Forces.

The organization Police substitutes for two organizations: (1) Police of HCMC, and (2) Department of Police about Fire Prevention and Fire fighting of HCMC.

The organization Health and Red Cross gathers three organizations: (1) Department of Health, (2) Center for Preventive Medical, and (3) Red Cross of City.

Table 1 Basic relations and constraints between tasks

(C1) Before (A, B)	Means *A* should occur before *B*
(C2) Choice (A, B)	Means we have the exclusive choice between performing *A* or *B*
	A decision procedure is supposed to exist to perform the choice
(C3) Fill (T1, p, T2)	*T1* produces *p* that is used by *T2*, and *T1* should occur before *T2*
	P is a post-condition of *T1* and pre-condition of *T2*
(C4) Parallel (T1, T2)	*T1* could be performed in parallel with *T2*

And finally the organization Local Civil Defence Forces represents two organizations: (1) Local Civil Defence Forces and (2) Young Volunteers Force of HCMC.

As a result, during period of response and search–rescue, seven organizations are considered:

- O1: Institute of Geophysics (Vietnam Academy of Science and Technology)
- O2: Local administration
- O3: Military
- O4: Police
- O5: Local civil defence forces
- O6: Communication unit
- O7: Health and Red cross

We have translated the response plan from Vietnamese into English and produce a summary where we mention the organizations, their tasks and the relations among tasks: an assumed case study of tsunami response plan in HCMC.

When detecting the risk of a tsunami (T1) that may affect the areas of Can Gio (Ho Chi Minh City, Vietnam), the Institute of Geophysics (O1) would inform (T2) the city's Local Administration (O2) about the time, place and predictive level of the tsunami so that it can be well prepared to respond to the disaster depending on the level of tsunami and to minimize the number of victims, the lack of food, etc.

After receiving the message about tsunami warning (T3), the Local Administration (O2) would lead and mobilize possible/available forces, materials, facilities (e.g. car, trucks, canoes, salvage boats, etc.) (T4) to support search and rescue whenever the tsunami happens to minimize the damage and victims. It also directs the evacuation task (T5) with the participation of several functional units such as Military (O3), Police (O4), Local Civil Defence Forces (O5), Communication Unit (O6), Health & Red Cross (O7), etc. The Local Civil Defence Forces (O5) walk along all streets and residential areas to inform citizens using portable loudspeakers (T6), so that people could go to the safe places under the guidance of the Military (O3) and the Police (O4). Meanwhile, if the media infrastructure can work, the Communication Unit (O6) would broadcast the tsunami warning message (T7) on radio and television to inform people on the shore as well as on the vessels about the oncoming risk. The Military (O3) is the core force of evacuating coastal people (T8) to the safe shelters with the cooperation of the Police (O4) (T8'). At the same time, the Military (O3) would whistle alarm, fire the signal (T9) to warn the ships and guide the fishermen (T10) so that they would come back offshore deep waters and keep their boats in safe

locations. The Police (O4) has main tasks of protecting citizens' property (T11) and ensuring the public order and safety (T12) to avoid the disorder situation (e.g. transportation, someone taking advantage from this situation, etc.). The Health & Red Cross (O7) would mobilize the doctors, nurses, rescue teams, facilities, equipment to support the hospitals (T13). During the evacuation, it has a task of performing the first aids (T14) for injured people. For the victims who are in a serious situation, it has to call the ambulance (T15) to transport them to the hospital.

When the Institute of Geophysics (O1) observes the signal about the end of tsunami, it would inform (T16) the Ho Chi Minh City's local administration (O2). After receiving this message (T17), the city's Local Administration (O2) would direct functional units (T18) to overcome the consequences. The Communication Unit (O6) would propose the methods to recover the communication system (T19) after the tsunami. Meanwhile, the Military (O3) and Police (O4) would coordinate to identify the damages (T20) (T20'): collapsed building, dead and/or injured people. The Military (O3) has another task of searching the distress fishermen (T21) on the sea. The Police (O4) also has to ensure the social order and safety (T22) by providing temporary accommodations for the people. The Health & Red Cross (O7) would perform the program of supporting health services, disease prevention (T23) in affected areas. It also verifies the ADN sample of anonymous victims (T24) who were killed or not identified during the tsunami. Finally, after all functional units finish their works, the Local Administration (O2) would close the tsunami response (T25).

Table 2 provides a synthesized view of the tasks and their corresponding performers, extracted from the above case study.

The constraints and causal relations between tasks can be identified in the text by temporal terms such as meanwhile, so that, after, finally, at the same time. We obtained the results reported in Table 3.

2.2 Process discovering and representation by means of Petri nets

The constraints and causal relationships between tasks allow us to generate and then select scenarios' response to the crisis. They are linear and then the objective is able to synthesize all of these scenarios in a single process capable of playing each scenario and explaining clearly the choices and the parallelism between tasks. We will use for this the α-algorithm [5] which allows to deduce a Petri net from a log file.

Table 2 Tasks and their corresponding performers (actors) in tsunami response plan

Tasks	Org.
T1: Detect the risk of tsunami	O1
T2: Inform tsunami warning	O1
T3: Receive tsunami warning	O2
T4: Mobilize forces, materials, facilities	O2
T5: Direct evacuation task	O2
T6: Inform people using portable speakers	O5
T7: Broadcast tsunami info	O6
T8: Evacuate people	O3
T8': Help to evacuate people	O4
T9: Fire signal to warn the ships	O3
T10: Inform the fishermen to safe places	O3
T11: Protect people's property	O4
T12: Ensure the order and safety	O4
T13: Mobilize doctors, nurses, rescue teams, facilities, equipments	O7
T14: Perform the first aid	O7
T15: Call ambulance for serious cases	O7
T16: Inform end of tsunami	O1
T17: Receive end of tsunami	O2
T18: Direct to overcome the consequences	O2
T19: Recover communication system	O6
T20: Identify damages	O3
T21: Search distress fishermen	O3
T20': Help to identify damages	O4
T22: Ensure the public order and safety	O4
T23: Support health services, disease prevention	O7
T24: Verify ADN sample of anonymous victims	O7
T25: Close tsunami response	O2

Table 3 Relations and constraints between tasks

T1 before T2
T2 before T3
T3 before T4, T5
T4 ∥ T5
T6, T7, T8, T9, T10, T8', T11, T12, T13, T14, T15 after T5,
T6 ∥ T7 ∥ T8 ∥ T9 ∥ T10 ∥ T8' ∥ T11 ∥ T12 ∥ T13
T14, T15 after T13
T14 or T5
T2 before T16
T16 before T17
T6, T7, T8, T9, T10, T8', T11, T12, T13, T14, T15 before T17
T17 before T18
T19, T20, T21, T20', T22, T23, T24 after T18
T19 ∥ T20 ∥ T21 ∥ T20' ∥ T22 ∥ T23 ∥ T24
T19, T20, T21, T20, T22, T23, T24 before T25

2.2.1 Principle of process discovery via α-algorithm

The log file includes different scenarios also called cases. In our context, we propose a log file in tabular form and with the following structure: *(ScenarioId, Task, Performer, Receiver(s), Timestamps)*. *Performer* is the organization that performed the tasks while *Receiver* is the possible receiver of the task if the task is a communication. Table 4 illustrates the structure of a scenario contained in a log file.

The algorithm is based on the relation of succession between tasks that it infers three other relationships (see Table 5). The relationship of Direct Succession between tasks is more restrictive than the task before seen previously in Sect. 2.1.1 because it indicates a relation of succession without intermediate.

We now detail the different steps of α-algorithm. Let W be a workflow log on T (a set of tasks). $\alpha(W)$ is constructed according to the Algorithm 1. The first instruction builds

set of transitions from the tasks appearing in the log file W. The instructions 2 and 3 calculate T_I and T_O, respectively. T_I designates set of tasks starting a case (scenario). T_O designates a set of tasks ending a case. The instruction 4 calculates the set X_W of pairs of tasks (A, B) whose elements are in causal relationships. The tasks within A have a relationship of choice between them and it is the same within B. The instruction 5 calculates a minimum subset Y_W of X_W. The instruction 6 calculates the places P_W that connect pairs of set of transitions of Y_W. The instruction 7 calculates the arcs and finally instruction 8 returns the expected result (P_W, T_W, F_W).

Algorithm 1 α-Algorithm to create Petri Nets according to [5]

Input: W (*Log File*)
Output: *PetriNet* (P_W, T_W, F_W)
1: $T_W = \{t \in T \mid \exists_{\sigma \in W} \, t \in \sigma\}$,
2: $T_I = \{t \in T \mid \exists_{\sigma \in W} \, t = first(\sigma)\}$,
3: $T_O = \{t \in T \mid \exists_{\sigma \in W} \, t = last(\sigma)\}$,
4: $X_W = \{(A, B) \mid A \subseteq T_W \wedge B \subseteq T_W \wedge \forall_{a \in A} \forall_{b \in B} \, a \rightarrow_W b \wedge \forall_{a_1, a_2 \in A} \, a_1 \#_W a_2 \wedge \forall_{b_1, b_2 \in B} \, b_1 \#_W b_2\}$,
5: $Y_W = \{(A, B) \in X \mid \forall_{(A', B') \in X} \, A \subseteq A' \wedge B \subseteq B' \Rightarrow (A, B) = (A', B')\}$,
6: $P_W = \{p_{(A, B)} \mid (A, B) \in Y_W\} \cup \{i_W, o_W\}$,
7: $F_W = \{(a, p_{(A, B)}) \mid (A, B) \in Y_W \wedge a \in A\} \cup \{(p_{(A, B)}, b) \mid (A, B) \in Y_W \wedge b \in B\} \cup \{(i_W, t) \mid t \in T_I\} \cup \{(t, o_W) \mid t \in T_O\}$, and
8: $\alpha(W) = (P_W, T_W, F_W)$.

Table 4 The structure of Scenario 1 (26 events) contained in an event log

Sid	Task	Performer	Timestamps
1	T1	Inst. of Geo.	2016-02-25 16:04:20
1	T2	Inst. of Geo.	2016-02-25 17:04:20
1	T3	Local Admin.	2016-02-25 18:04:20
1	T5	Local Admin.	2016-02-25 19:04:20
1	T4	Local Admin.	2016-02-25 20:04:20
1	T11	Police	2016-02-25 21:04:20
1	T8	Military	2016-02-25 22:04:20
1	T10	Military	2016-02-25 23:04:20
1	T9	Military	2016-02-26 00:04:20
1	T13	Health and Red Cross	2016-02-26 01:04:20
1	T7	Communication Unit	2016-02-26 02:04:20
1	T14	Health and Red Cross	2016-02-26 03:04:20
1	T12	Police	2016-02-26 04:04:20
1	T8'	Police	2016-02-26 05:04:20
1	T6	Local Civil D. F.	2016-02-26 06:04:20
1	T16	Inst. of Geo.	2016-02-26 07:04:20
1	T17	Local Admin.	2016-02-26 08:04:20
1	T18	Local Admin.	2016-02-26 09:04:20
1	T22	Police	2016-02-26 10:04:20
1	T20	Military	2016-02-26 11:04:20
1	T19	Communication Unit	2016-02-26 12:04:20
1	T24	Health and Red Cross	2016-02-26 13:04:20
1	T20'	Police	2016-02-26 14:04:20
1	T23	Health and Red Cross	2016-02-26 15:04:20
1	T21	Military	2016-02-26 16:04:20
1	T25	Local Admin.	2016-02-26 17:04:20

Table 5 Relations between tasks in the α-algorithm

Direct succession	$x > y$ iff for some case x is directly followed by y
Direct causality	$x \rightarrow y$ iff $x > y$ and not $y > x$
Parallel	$x \parallel y$ iff $x > y$ and $y > x$
Choice	$x \neq y$ iff not $x > y$ and not $y > x$

2.2.2 Application to Ho Chi Minh plan scenarios

We retain the following six scenarios to consider the crisis response plan of Ho Chi Minh City:

1. Scenario 1 (26 events): T1. T2. T3. T5. T4. T11. T8. T10. T9. T13. T7. T14. T12. T8. T6. T16. T17. T18. T22. T20. T19. T24. T20. T23. T21. T25.
2. Scenario 2 (26 events): T1. T2. T3. T4. T5. T9. T6. T7. T11. T8. T8. T12. T13. T14. T10. T16. T17. T18. T20. T23. T22. T21. T19. T20. T24. T25.

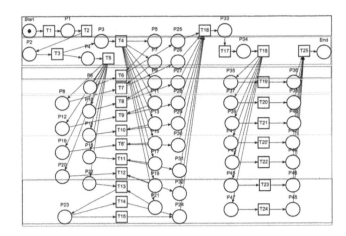

Fig. 4 Petri Net representation of Ho Chi Minh City tsunami response plan

3. Scenario 3 (26 events): T1. T2. T3. T4. T5. T8. T8. T13. T14. T10. T6. T12. T11. T9. T7. T16. T17. T18. T20. T22. T21. T19. T24. T20. T23. T25.
4. Scenario 4 (26 events): T1. T2. T3. T5. T4. T8. T7. T9. T6. T11. T12. T13. T10. T14. T8'. T16. T17. T18. T21. T20. T23. T24. T20. T19. T22. T25.
5. Scenario 5 (26 events): T1. T2. T3. T4. T5. T7. T6. T12. T10. T8. T8'. T9. T13. T14. T11. T16. T17. T18. T20. T23. T19. T21. T24. T20. T22. T25.
6. Scenario 6 (26 events): T1. T2. T3. T5. T4. T7. T8. T13. T11. T12. T8. T6. T15. T10. T9. T16. T17. T18. T20. T21. T24. T19. T20. T22. T23. T25.

When applying α-algorithm with above scenarios, we discover a Petri Net of Fig. 4 that we have redrawn to underline the different organizations involved in our tsunami response plan.

In a reverse manner, from this Petri Net, we can generate all possible scenarios and then use as input cases (of an event log file) to verify the conformance of process. The technique to build a process corresponding to an event log is called Process Mining [5].

2.3 BPMN representation of a plan for stakeholder validation

BPMN is a standard notation, proposed by the Object Management Group (OMG), for modelling business processes. We consider here a core subset of BPMN elements as shown in Fig. 5.

BPMN representation of plan is useful for validation by stakeholders since it integrates an organizational perspective not present in conventional Petri Nets. It is not only easy to read but also available to simulate and analyze the results. In our context, there are two ways to obtain a BPMN representation:

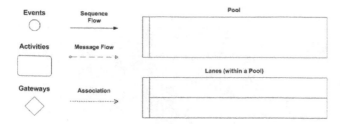

Fig. 5 Core subset of BPMN elements

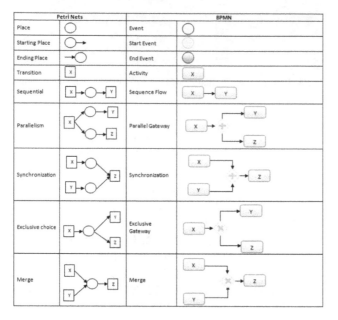

Fig. 6 Mapping Petri Net concepts onto BPMN concepts

1. By mapping the Petri Net discovered from the scenarios onto a BPMN diagram and complete it by organizational elements.
2. The other possible way is to analyze the text and/or the scenarios and draw it directly.

We present in Fig. 6 the relations between the concepts of Petri Nets and BPMN (*sequential, parallelism, synchronization, exclusive choice*, or *merge*).

Using this table, the concepts of Petri Net can be transformed easily into BPMN ones. We need the Petri Net formalism to verify formal theoretical properties (reachability of particular states, termination, liveness, etc.) and perform simulations. We also implemented the mapping from Petri Net to BPMN using ATL[1] technology on top of two meta-models. In fact, the source model of the mapping (cf. our Petri Net in Fig. 4) is expressed under a PNML[2] file containing two separate pages (i.e processes).

_____
[1] ATL Transformation Language.

[2] Petri Net Markup Language.

As the result of mapping, Fig. 7 shows the BPMN model representing HCMC's tsunami response plan. This model obviously eases accountability and awareness. The BPMN model describes some adaptations to put also temporal constraints.

Eight stakeholders can be identified from our Petri Net with reference to the identification of high-level objects from text (cf. 2.1), depicted by two pools (corresponding to two pages of the PNML file) and six lanes with their flow of tasks and mutual interactions.

Some parallel structures between tasks are detected from our Petri Net according to mapping table in Fig. 6, e.g. [T3, T4, T5] corresponding to [X, Y, Z] respectively, [T4, T6, T7], [T5, T6, T7], [T4, T7, T8], [T5, T7, T8], etc. We notice that the Military, Police and Health and Red Cross organizations are supposed to perform their tasks in parallel. In this case, each organization should be distributed over the parallel tasks according to a given policy (proportional distribution, distribution according to the importance given to each task, …).

In addition, an exclusive choice structure is detected from our Petri Net (cf. Fig. 4) regarding to the relationships of T13, T14 and T15. The Health and Red Cross organization has to choose to carry out only one task among two possible ones.

We can identify, in the process model, eight participants represented by rectangular boxes, called Swimlane Objects (aka: Swimlanes). Besides, to visualize coordination process, we use the activity notation (like *T1*: Detect tsunami risk), represented by a rounded-corner rectangle. These activities are connected by the Connectors such as Sequence Flow and Message Flow, and the Flow Objects like Start Event, Intermediate Event, End Event. Moreover, the control structures help to coordinate the different activities, such as parallelism (diamond including "+") or alternatives (diamond with "×").

When the same task is done by two different actors, it is duplicated instead of creating an abstract actor including both actors. In our BPMN diagram (cf. Fig. 7), for example, we express the task Evacuate people realized by two actors (Military and Police) by two tasks *T8* and *T8'*, respectively. Indeed each actor has its own view of tasks, links with partners or situation of extra-works. Moreover, three tasks *T8, T9* and *T10* are performed in parallel by Military and they require probably more resources and high responsibility. Our BPMN model is, therefore, considered as a shared artefact that could be used for negotiation of resources or improve coordination for similar tasks done by different organizations.

3 Mapping from process models to organization models

The coordination among stakeholders, in general, can be represented by several formats such as text, process diagram,

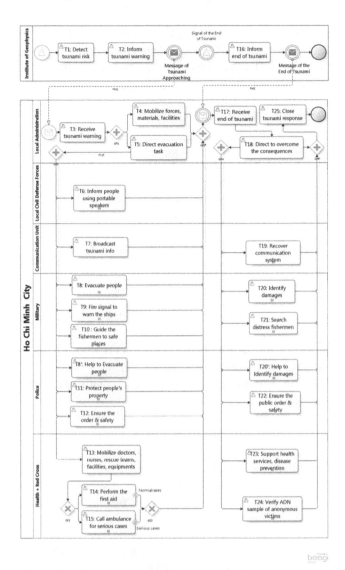

Fig. 7 BPMN representation for tsunami response plan

Table 6 Advantages of some representations of a coordination plan

Models	Views and advantages
Petri Net	A directed bipartite graph based on tokens supporting formal semantics and analysis and possibility of macro-simulation
BPMN	An understandable and aggregate representation of stakeholders' behavior and possibility of analysis and process simulation
Role graph	Focusing on dependency between the roles and enables analysis robustness, flexibility and efficiency of organization structure [2]
BDI-Agent Model	An typical ACMAS representation and possible micro-simulation [10]
AGR	A OCMAS representation and possible macro and micro-simulation

conventional graph, etc. Each of them expresses some aspects of the coordination plan but they differ from one another in terms of abstraction level, precision and expressive power. Combining various representations helps us to have an overall view of the crisis management. The advantages of each representation is given in Table 6.

3.1 Deriving Role graph

The Role graph aims at analyzing the properties of the organization involved in crisis plan, notably its robustness, flexibility and efficiency as done in [2]. The process model thus can be used to build a Role graph corresponding to our tsunami respond plan. This type of representation describes the roles and the relationships between them. Following the typology introduced by Grossi et al. [13], we can distinguish three types of relations: power which corresponds to task delegation; coordination which represents flow of information among actors; control relation between actors: actor A controls actor B if A monitors agent B activities. Regarding the mapping rules, the roles correspond to the name of lanes (or pools without lane) in a process. For the relationships between roles, we met a difficult problem. Because the lanes' relationships are not defined clearly in a BPMN diagram. Hence, we propose three patterns to detect three types of relation by analyzing the semantics of BPMN *Connectors* (Sequence Flow, Message Flow) as follows:

- Power relation: if we detect that a pool/lane A has only one-direction message/sequence flows to another pool/lane B, we could assume that there is a power relation from A to B. For example, as depicted in Fig. 8, the lane *A* connects with lane *B* by two sequences flows and there is no flow in the opposite direction. Thus, we could conclude that the role *A* has a power relation with the role *B*.
- Coordination relation: if we identify a pool/lane A has bidirectional message/sequence flows to another pool/lane B, we could assume that there is a coordination relation between A and B, as illustrated in Fig. 9.
- Control relation: if we detect that a pool/lane A has bidirectional message/sequence flows for all tasks of another pool/lane B, we could assume that A controls B, as illustrated in Fig. 10.

We provide here in this paper only one approach to derive the Role graph based on BPMN patterns. In addition, Artefact elements could be used to describe directly (by text) the

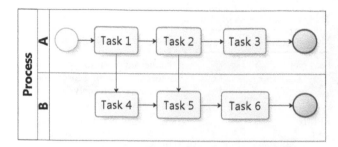

Fig. 8 Pattern of Power relation between two actors

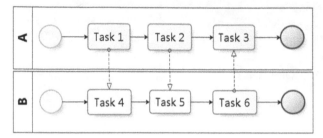

Fig. 9 Pattern of Coordination relation between two actors

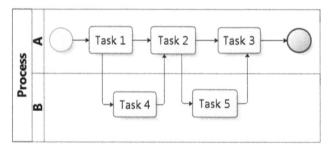

Fig. 10 Pattern of Control relation between two actors

Power, Coordination or Control relations. However, it cannot assure that when designing a process model, the users will supply this relation information.

Based on three proposed patterns, we analyze our BPMN diagram to build its corresponding Role graph. Seven roles are detected: IG for the pool Institute of Geophysics, LA for the lane Local Administration, LCDF for the lane Local Civil Defence Forces, CU for the lane Communication Unit, M for the lane Military, P for the lane Police and HR for the lane Health and Red Cross. Moreover, the pool Institute of Geophysics sends two message flows to the lane Local Administration and there is no flow in opposite direction (Fig. 11). Therefore, we create a Power Relation from Institute of Geophysics to Local Administration.

The lane Local Administration has bidirectional sequence flows for all tasks of lane Local Civil Defence Forces (Fig. 12), Communication Unit, Military, Police and Health and Red Cross. Therefore, we create Control Relations from Local Administration to Local Civil Defence Forces, Communication Unit, Military, Police and Health and Red Cross.

As the result, the derived Role graph based on three above patterns is depicted in Fig. 13, each circle corresponds to a

role. The role IG has Power relation with the role LA. While the role LA has five Control relations with the roles P, M, HR, CU, LCDF. We detect no Coordination relation from our BPMN diagram.

3.2 Deriving BDI-agent

This transformation is based on the work in [10] with some extensions. A BDI-Agent is defined as a tuple $\Delta = (id, P, G, I, B)$. Deriving BDI-Agent from a process model contains nine steps, corresponding to nine rules presented in [10], with the aid of additional information.

1. Step 1: Each pool is considered as an agent (Δ)
2. Step 2: The plan (P) for agent is initiated
3. Step 3: The input list of process ($P.In$) is completed with start events
4. Step 4: The output list of process ($P.Out$) is completed with end events
5. Step 5: The embedded sub-process activities are transferred to another plans of agent (P')
6. Step 6: The independent sub-process activities are mapped to goals of agents (G)
7. Step 7: The elements with *Send* and *Receive* messages are appended to plan's script ($P.Script$)
8. Step 8: The data flows (additional information of pools) are mapped to the belief of agents (B)
9. Step 9: The control flows (gateways) are considered to orchestrate the structure of agents' plan with AND, OR, XOR structure

Table 7 shows the result of mapping from Business Process to BDI-Agent model containing nine steps and additional data. Finally, two BDI-type agents are detected with their attributes (Plan, Belief).

3.3 Deriving AGR model

An organization centred multi-agent system (OCMAS) view, as proposed by Ferber et al. [11], eases macro-simulation regarding the organization and also micro-simulation if agent behaviors are specified. In [11], the authors have introduced a meta-model Agent/Group/Role, called AGR where: "(1) an Agent is an active communicating entity which plays several roles within several groups; (2) a Group is defined as atomic sets of agent aggregation, each agent is part of one or more groups; (3) a Role is an abstract representation of agent function, service or identification within a group and role has some attributes such as constraints (obligations, requirements, skills), benefits (abilities, authorization, profits) or responsibilities". Based on the proposition of Ferber et al., we define $AGR = (A, G, R)$, as follows:

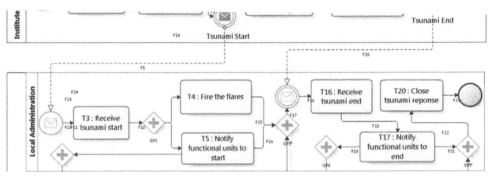

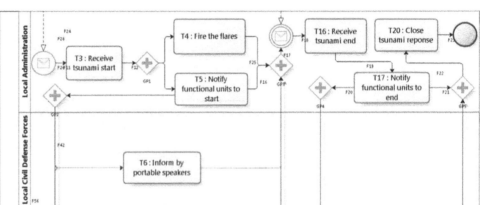

Fig. 12 Relation between the lane Local administration and lane Local civil defence forces

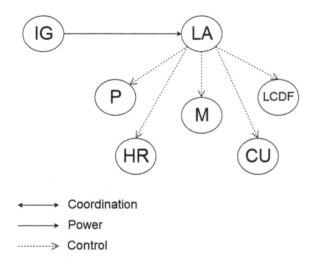

Coordination

Power

Control

Fig. 13 Role graph corresponding to our BPMN diagram

- *A* is a collection of agent. Each agent is tuple $(NameA, T, Rs, Gs)$ where $NameA$ is its identifier; T is its type (reactive or intentional agents); Rs is the list of roles this agent can play; Gs is the list of groups to which this agent may belong.
- *G* is a collection of groups. Each group is couple $(NameG, Rs)$ where $NameG$ is its identifier; Rs is the list of roles involved in this group.

- *R* is set of roles where a role is tuple $(NameR, C, B, D, Pc, I)$ where $NameR$ is its identifier; C is the list of constraints (obligations, requirements, skills); B is the list of benefits (abilities, authorization, profits); D is the list of duties or responsibilities; Pc is the pattern of communication or interaction; I is the list of useful information.

To complete the process-agent mapping, we also define some notations, as follows: $x.send(y, m)$ means agent x sends message m to agent y; $x.Start$ means agent x initiates his state and/or work; $x.Do(act)$ means agent x performs the activity act; $x.Wait(time)$ means agent x has to wait for a time; $x.End$ means agent x terminates his work.

We consider a lane or a pool without lane as a role. A group constitutes a context of interaction for agents. Hence, we consider two cases: (1) each pool with more than one lane becomes a group; (2) for each message flow between two pools A and B, we create also a new group where the role A and B can be played. Regarding agents, they are not given by the BPMN diagram but by some additional information (comments) giving the number of occurrences of each roles. Thus, we just have to create as much agent by role as indicated in the additional document.

Our mapping from process model to AGR model consists five steps, as follows.

Table 7 Mapping from business process to BDI-agent for tsunami response plan

	BPMN	BDI-Agent
Step 1	$O^P(1)$	$\Delta(1) = (O^P(1).name,$ $P\{\}, G\{\}, I\{\}, B\{\})$
	$O^P(2)$	$\Delta(2) = (O^P(2).name,$ $P\{\}, G\{\}, I\{\}, B\{\})$
Step 2	$Pr(1) = O^P(1).process$	$\Delta(1).P =$ $(Pr(1).id, In\{\}, Out\{\}, Script\{\})$
	$Pr(2) = O^P(2).process$	$\Delta(2).P =$ $(Pr(2).id, In\{\}, Out\{\}, Script\{\}$
Step 3	Start event $\Downarrow P.In$	$\Delta(1).P.In+ =$ $(O_S^E(1).name, O_S^E(1).type)$
		$\Delta(2).P.In+ =$ $(O_S^E(2).name, O_S^E(2).type)$
Step 4	End event $\Downarrow P.Out$	$\Delta(1).P.Out+ =$ $(O_E^E(1).name, O_E^E(1).type)$
		$\Delta(2).P.Out+ =$ $(O_E^E(2).name, O_E^E(2).type)$
Step 5	Embedded activity $O_{Sub}^A \rightarrow$ $P.Script\ invoke$	X
Step 6	Independent activity $O_{Sub}^A \rightarrow$ $P.Script\ addGoal$	X
Step 7	O_{At}^A send message $\rightarrow P.Script$ $send$	
	$O_{I,M}^E(1)$	$M(1) = ($"msg_1''", $O^P(1),$ $O^L(1), [msg\_reg1])$
		$\Delta(1).P.Script \leftarrow \{send(M(1)\}$
	$O_{I,M}^E(2)$	$M(2) = ($"msg_2''", $O^P(1),$ $O^L(1), [msg\_reg2])$
		$\Delta(1).P.Script \leftarrow \{send(M(2)\}$
	$O_{S,M}^E(1)$	$\Delta(2).P.Script \leftarrow \{receive(M(1)\}$
	$O_{I,M}^E(3)$	$\Delta(2).P.Script \leftarrow \{receive(M(2)\}$
Step 8	O properties $\rightarrow B$	
Data flow	$O^P(1)$ properties	$\Delta(1).B \leftarrow \{O^P(1).reg, O^P(1).ans\}$
	$O^P(2)$ properties	$\Delta(2).B \leftarrow \{O^P(2).reg, O^P(2).ans\}$
Step 9		
Control flow		

Element	Properties	Assignment
$O^P(1)$	reg: String, ans: String	
$O_{S,M}^E(1)$	msg_reg: String	
$O_{S,M}^E(2)$	msg_reg: String	
$O^P(2)$	reg: String, ans: String	
$O_{S,M}^E(1)$	msg_ans: String	
$O_{S,M}^E(3)$	msg_ans: String	

1. In step 1, we identify the roles and groups extracted from BPMN diagram. Let us illustrate this step through our tsunami response case study. We have the first pool $O^P(1)$ where $O^P(1).name =$ "*Institute of Geo-* *physics*" and it has no lane; therefore, we consider it as a role $R(1)$. On the contrary, for the second pool $O^P(2)$ where $O^P(2).name =$ "*Ho Chi Minh City*", it has six lanes: $O^L(1)$ ($O^L(1).name =$ "*Local Adminis-*

tration"), $O^L(2)$ ($O^L(2).name = $ "Local Civil Defence Forces "), $O^L(3)$ ($O^L(3).name = $ " Communication Unit "), $O^L(4)$ ($O^L(4).name = $ " Military "), $O^L(5)$ ($O^L(5).name = $ " Police ") and $O^L(6)$ ($O^L(6).name = $ " Health & Red Cross "). Thus, we transfer them, respectively, to six roles $R(2)$, $R(3)$, $R(4)$, $R(5)$, $R(6)$ and $R(7)$. All these six roles belong to group $G(1)$.

2. In step 2, we obtain the information extracted from the Artefact elements to identify roles' properties.

3. In step 3, by analyzing additional data, we identify the agents' attributes such as their type, the number of agents playing a role, the number of agents belonging to a group, etc.

4. In step 4, we identify the communication or interaction protocols between groups and create new possible groups by analyzing message flows. In our case study, we create a new group $G(2)$ based on the message flows between two roles $R(1)$ and $R(2)$.

5. Finally, in step 5, we identify the roles' activities by following sequence flows.

As the result, we have two groups and seven roles with their attributes and interactions, as shown in Table 8 (see Appendix). $R(2)$ is the only role which belongs to two groups.

4 Related works

In [11], authors highlight the software engineering benefits of differentiating agent aspect (the Agent-Centred Multi-Agent System or ACMAS) from social aspect (the Organization-Centred Multi-Agent System or OCMAS). They presented the essential drawbacks which cannot be solved with ACMAS. Instead of using ACMAS, Ferber et al. attempt to view complex system under the eye of organizational structure. They propose the Agent/Group/Role meta-model (AGR) as a means to combine efficiently these two aspects in a uniform framework. In our work, we use this meta-model as the destination of the process-agent mapping.

In [10], Endern et al. described the mapping from BPMN to agents using an agent-centred approach (ACMAS). The agents are represented according to the Believe-Desire-Intention (BDI) type, which is in our opinion not fully compliant with BPMN model where the notion of goal and intention are not given. Authors consider that sub-processes determine goals which in our point of view is a strong assumption. They also do not count on the lane concept during the mapping. In our approach, we do not use an ACMAS approach since we believe that an organizational view (OCMAS) [11] is more compliant with BPMN.

In [6,7], the authors presented a model to text transformation (M2T), from BPMN model to a specific agent-oriented language (JADE). This work is too much specific so that we cannot extend it to other languages. On the contrary, we follow a model to model approach (M2M). Thus, the destination model (AGR) can be implemented by any agent-based language.

In [8,9], Onggo introduced a BPMN pattern used to represent agent-based models. He developed specific BPMN diagrams to describe activities of agents according to an ACMAS approach. In our work, we can use an arbitrary BPMN diagram and map it to the corresponding agent model, based on an OCMAS approach.

In [12], the authors described the mapping from BPMN models to Alvis language to formally verify these models. However, the transformation which focuses on the activities forgets the organizational structure.

Concerning the organization assessment, Grossi et al. in [13] proposed a set of equations to evaluate organizational structure based on the Role graph with three dimensions: power, coordination and control. Comparing the results with standard values, we can determine the robustness, flexibility and efficiency of our organization. All these metrics can be performed in our Graph Role as we have demonstrated it in [2].

In [14], the author presented a metric to measure control-flow complexity of a workflow or a process. He also suggested other metrics such as Activity Complexity, Data-Flow Complexity, and Resource Complexity. These metrics, combined with the equations of Role graph [2,13], can help us determine the quality of a coordination plan according to two points of view: process and organization.

5 Conclusion

In this paper, we have introduced an approach to map from process models (Petri Net, BPMN) to organization models (Role graph, ACMAS, OCMAS). Combining several views of the same plan enables the authorities to benefit from the advantages of each representation. This work is the first step towards a visualization and assessment platform for Crisis Management. In a future research, we will continue on developing the assessment part of the different models, illustrated in this paper, using a set of static and dynamic metrics.

Appendix: Mapping table

See Table 8.

Table 8 Mapping process model to AGR model for tsunami response plan

	BPMN	AGR	Applied to HCMC plan
Step 1: Identify roles and groups	$O^P(1)$ has no lane	$R(1) = (O^P(1).name, C\{\}, B\{\}, D\{\}, Pc\{\}, I\{\})$	Institute of geophysics
	$O^P(2)$ has 6 lanes	$R(2) = (O^L(1).name, C\{\}, B\{\}, D\{\}, Pc\{\}, I\{\})$	Local administration
		$R(3) = (O^L(2).name, C\{\}, B\{\}, D\{\}, Pc\{\}, I\{\})$	Local civil defence forces
		$R(4) = (O^L(3).name, C\{\}, B\{\}, D\{\}, Pc\{\}, I\{\})$	Communication unit
		$R(5) = (O^L(4).name, C\{\}, B\{\}, D\{\}, Pc\{\}, I\{\})$	Military
		$R(6) = (O^L(5).name, C\{\}, B\{\}, D\{\}, Pc\{\}, I\{\})$	Police
		$R(7) = (O^L(6).name, C\{\}, B\{\}, D\{\}, Pc\{\}, I\{\})$	Health and Red Cross
		$G(1) = (O^P(2).name, \{R(2), R(3), R(4), R(5), R(6), R(7)\})$	Ho Chi Minh City
Step 2: Identify Roles' Properties by examining artefacts			
Step 3: Identify agents by reading additional data		$A(i) = (Name, Type, Rs(i), Gs(i))$	
		$Rs(i) = \{R_k : Nb_k, R_{k+1} : Nb_{k+1}, ...\}$	
		$Gs(i) = \{G_j, G_{j+1}, ...\}$	
Step 4: Identify communication between groups and create new group based on message flow	$F^M(1)$	$R(1).Pc \leftarrow \{send(R(2), F^M(1).msg)\}$	Message: *Tsunami Start*
		$R(2).Pc \leftarrow \{receive(R(1), F^M(1).msg)\}$	
	$F^M(2)$	$R(1).Pc \leftarrow \{send(R(2), F^M(2).msg)\}$	Message: *Tsunami End*
		$R(2).Pc \leftarrow \{receive(R(1), F^M(2).msg)\}$	
		$G(2) = (F^M(1, 2).msg, \{R(1), R(2)\})$	
Step 5: Identify Roles' activities based on sequence flow	$F^S(1), F^S(2)$	$R(1).D \leftarrow \{Start, Do(O^A_{At}(1))\}, \{Do(O^A_{At}(2))\},$	*T1: Detect Tsunami risk*
	$F^S(4), F^S(5)$	$R(1).D \leftarrow \{Wait(O^E_{I,T}(1))\}, \{Do(O^A_{At}(3))\}$	*T2: Inform Tsunami start* Timer event
	$F^S(6), F^S(8)$	$R(1).D \leftarrow \{Do(O^A_{At}(4))\}, \{End\}$	*T14: Detect Tsunami end*
	...	...	*T15: Inform Tsunami end* End event

References

1. Le, N.N.T., Hanachi, C., Stinckwich, S., Vinh, H.T.: Representing, simulating and analysing Ho Chi Minh City tsunami plan by means of process models. In: ISCRAM Vietnam (Information Systems for Crisis Response and Management) (2013)
2. Le, N.N.T., Hanachi, C., Stinckwich, S., Vinh, H.T.: Combining process simulation and agent organizational structure evaluation in order to analyze disaster response plans. In: 9th International KES Conference on Agents and Multi-Agent Systems—Technologies and Applications (2015)
3. Bénaben, F., Hanachi, C., Lauras, M., Couget, P., Chapurlat, V.: A metamodel and its ontology to guide crisis characterization and its collaborative management. In: Proceedings of the 5th International Conference ISCRAM (2008)
4. Viorica Epure, E., Martin-Rodilla, P., Hug, C., Deneckere, R., Salinesi, C.: Automatic process model discovery from textual methodologies. In: Research Challenges in Information Science (RCIS), IEEE 9th International Conference (2015)
5. Van der Aalst, W.M.P.: Process mining: discovery, conformance and enhancement of business processes. In: Springer Publishing Company Incorporated, ISBN 978-3-642-19345-3 (2011)
6. Küster, T., Lützenberger, M., Heßler, A., Hirsch, B.: Integrating process modelling into multi-agent system engineering. In: Multiagent and Grid Systems, vol. 8, no. 1, pp. 105–124. IOS Press, Amsterdam (2012)
7. Küster, T., Heßler, A., Albayrak, S.: Towards process-oriented modelling and creation of multi-agent systems. In: Engineering Multi-Agent Systems, pp. 163–180. Springer, New York (2014)
8. Onggo, B.S.S.: BPMN pattern for agent-based simulation model representation. In: Winter Simulation Conference (WSC), pp. 1–10. IEEE (2012)
9. Onggo, B.S.S.: Agent-based simulation model representation using BPMN. In: Formal Languages for Computer Simulation: Transdisciplinary Models and Applications, pp. 378–399 (2013)
10. Endert, H., Küster, T., Hirsch, B., Albayrak, S.: Mapping BPMN to agents: an analysis. In: Agents, Web-Services, and Ontologies Integrated Methodologies, pp. 43–58 (2007)

11. Ferber, J., Gutknecht, O., Michel, F.: From agents to organizations: an organizational view of multi-agent systems. In: Agent-Oriented Software Engineering IV: 4th International Workshop, AOSE 2003, Melbourne, Australia, pp. 214–230. Springer, Berlin, Heidelberg (2004)

12. Szpyrka, M., Nalepa, G. J., Ligęza, A., Kluza, K.: Proposal of formal verification of selected BPMN models with Alvis modeling language. In: Intelligent Distributed Computing V: Proceedings of the 5th International Symposium on Intelligent Distributed Computing - IDC 2011, Delft, the Netherlands, pp. 249–255. Springer, Berlin, Heidelberg (2012)

13. Grossi, D., Dignum, F., Dignum, V., Dastani, M., Royakkers, L.: Structural aspects of the evaluation of agent organizations. In: Coordination, Organizations, Institutions, and Norms in Agent Systems II, pp. 3–18. Springer-Verlag, New york (2007)

14. Cardoso, J.: Business process control-flow complexity: metric, evaluation, and validation. In: International Journal of Web Services Research (IJWSR), vol. 5, no. 2, pp. 49–76. IGI Global, USA (2008)

## 3

A bitwise-based indexing and heuristic-driven on-the-fly approach for Web service composition and verification

Khai T. Huynh[1] · Tho T. Quan[1] · Thang H. Bui[1]

Abstract During the last decade, software engineering community has witnessed the emerging of SOA architecture, where Web services play a crucial role. It prompts the concept of Web Service Composition (WSC). Even though interesting, this issue posed some remarkable challenges, one of which is constraint handling. To be more precise, one needs to ensure that the composite Web service fulfills, at the same time, many constraints, including functional constraints, Quality of Service (QoS), and the execution order of the component services, or temporal relations. Those constraints are of different natures, thus finding an efficient verification on all kinds of constraints during the composition process is by no means a trivial task. Backed by a solid foundation of temporal logic, model checking (MC) is a suitable approach to handle this issue. However, MC-based approach suffers from the infamous problem of state-space explosion, making it limited when applied to real-life situations. The work in this paper addresses the problem by proposing various approaches for handling the state-space exploration, including (i) an introduction of an LTS-based model known as LTS4WS, which can avoid generating full schema of Web service composition and allow on-the-fly verification on the state space; (ii) heuristics strategies to find the best potential composition, and (iii) a bitwise-based indexing mechanism for fast location of suitable Web services. All of those approaches are unified in a single tool, known as WSCOVER. As a result, a significant improvement of performance has been made, especially as compared with the other existing works in the same field.

Keywords Web service composition · On-the-fly Web service composition and verification · Web service composition tool · Bitwise-based Web service indexing · Heuristic-driven Web service composition

1 Introduction

1.1 Web service composition and verification

Nowadays, Web Service Composition (WSC) has been raised as an important issue of Service-Oriented Architecture (SOA) [1]. WSC is the process of creating the complexly structured composite Web services from component Web services [2], which has been one of the challenging problems in recent years, when the number of provided component Web services increases and the composition requirements from users become more complex. When composing Web services, in addition to the requirements on functional properties, also known as hard constraints, the requirements on Quality of Service (QoS) properties, also known as soft constraints, are also a very important factor determining the outcome of the composition. There are many QoS properties of Web services, such as response time, execution cost, availability, or reputation, etc. In some circumstances, many services that satisfy hard constraints cannot be used in a composition, because of the dissatisfactions of soft constraints.

Let us consider the following example. Suppose that a user is organizing his trip using the Web services presented in Table 1. By providing information on travel place (*Sightseeing*) and the traveling dates (*Dates*), the user

✉ Khai T. Huynh
htkhai@cse.hcmut.edu.vn

Tho T. Quan
qttho@cse.hcmut.edu.vn

Thang H. Bui
thang@cse.hcmut.edu.vn

[1] Faculty of Computer Science and Engineering, Ho Chi Minh City University of Technology, Ho Chi Minh City, Vietnam

Table 1 Travel Booking Web service repository

#	Service name	Input(s)	Output(s)	respTime
1	HotelReserveService (HR)	Dates, Hotel	HotelReservation	5
2	CityHotelService (CH)	City	Hotel	3
3	HotelCityService (HC)	Hotel	City	3
4	HotelPriceInfoService (HP)	Hotel	Price	10
5	SightseeingCityService (SC)	Sightseeing	City	2
6	SightseeingCityHotelService (SCH)	Sightseeing	City, Hotel	16
7	CitySightseeingService (CS)	City	Sightseeing	4
8	ActivityBeachService (ABS)	Activity	Beach	5
9	AreaWeatherService (AWS)	Area	Weather	5
10	CityWeatherService (CWS)	City	Weather	5

Table 2 Requirements for travel booking Web service

Constraint		Value
Hard constraint:	Input:	*Dates, Sightseeing*
	Output:	*Price, Hotel Reservation*
Soft constraint:		*respTime* ≤ 30
Temporal relation:		$\Box(\neg Hotel Reservation \ \mathrm{U} \ Price)$

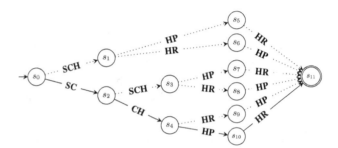

Fig. 1 Full composition schema for travel booking problem

wants to find hotel booking price (*Price*) and the hotel reservation information (*Hotel Reservation*) of the hotels near the *Sightseeing*. Obviously, as observed in Table 1, there is no individual Web service that can completely fulfill the requirement from the user. Thus, one needs to find a composition of the available Web services. Beside the requirements on the above functional constraints (hard constraints), the user can also specify soft constraints, such as "The total response time of the composite Web service should not exceed 30 s". In addition, the user may also want a certain order of service execution, or temporal relation. For instance, we may also need to obtain the information about *Price* before proceeding on *Hotel Reservation*. All of requirements discussed are summarized in Table 2.

Typically, a WSC problem is a Satisfiability (SAT) problem, such that the composition of Web services is considered as a process that creates new logic formula which can satisfy the target formula, known as goal. Verifying the satisfaction of composition with the constraints becomes a theoretical verification problem. Since the hard constraint is typically represented by a traditional form of logic, often as First-Order Logic [3], the verification of whether a WSC satisfies hard constraint or not can adopt a traditional approach, such as SAT solver, in the classic AI planning approach [4].

However, the formal verification of soft constraint becomes more difficult, because the soft constraint conditions may be mathematical expressions representing QoS properties. These functions can be of the non-linear form, which causes serious difficulties for the current provers.

Due to such characteristics, research on the verification of composite Web services often focuses on hard constraint. Recently, an approach that can verify combination of both hard and soft constraints is introduced in [5]. In this approach, first of all, all compositions which satisfy the hard constraint are created, forming a full composition schema. For example, Fig.1 illustrates a full composition schema for the travel booking problem. Subsequently, model checking can be used to verify whether the compositions satisfy the soft constraint or not. As a result, only compositions satisfying soft constraints, for instance, denoted by solid line in Fig.1, are retained. Furthermore, concerning the temporal property described in Table 2, only the composition of $\{s_0 \rightarrow s_2 \rightarrow s_4 \rightarrow s_{10} \rightarrow s_{11}\}$ should be kept. To our knowledge, this is the sole work claimed to verify hard and soft constraints at the same time. Unfortunately, this approach must be extremely expensive for the creation of full schema, which is a classic NP-hard problem. Intuitively, one of the ways that can handle this is to build the schema in an on-the-fly manner to find a satisfied composition without building a full schema in advance. However, unfortunately, in this approach, the full composition schema is used as the model to be verified, and hence, it has to be constructed beforehand.

1.2 Web service indexing

When the number of Web services in repository increases, the cost of composition problem also increases significantly.

There have been many given suggestions to resolve this problem, such as clustering [6,7], or indexing [8,9]. In the clustering approach, we have to address a variety of problems, such as how to compute the similarity between services, how many clusters should be generated, or which clustering algorithm should be chosen, etc.

Alternatively, indexing is considered as a simple and effective approach to reduce the composition time. In literature, there are many ways to index, such as using the hashtable [8] or using the weighted vector [9]. However, in these approaches, the construction of index structure and the application of the processing functions are in high complexity. In general, Web service indexing is a preprocessing step of the Web service composition process. Once an index structure is available, the composition process can quickly retrieve the needed Web services. However, the indexing process is definitely computationally expensive, and it also requires additional space to store the index table. Therefore, we need an effective and low-cost method to build the index table, which should be updated easily when the stored data are modified.

Contributions In this paper, we introduce an extension of our previous work [10], which proposes a novel and effective Web service composition approach. It bases on the model checking approach, but does not require prior full schema of compositions. Instead, the composition will be generated according to the path condition on the state space when the model is verified. Thus, if we use an on-the-fly model checker, such as PAT [11], the composition and verification will be processed in an on-the-fly manner, as well. As a result, we can find a solution that simultaneously satisfies the hard and soft constraints represented by a temporal logic[1] formula, without the need of creating a full composition schema. In addition, this approach makes room for some performance improvement when the outcome of a composition step can be used to optimize the candidate selection for the next step. This optimization process can be implemented by some heuristic rules.

The contribution of the work on [10] is as follows.

- We propose an approach to represent the Web services by the *Labelled Transition System* (LTS), known as *LTS4WS*, to serve for the application of model checking for Web service composition.
- We use the LTS4WS model to verify the hard and soft constraints on WSC. This model checking approach allows us to verify temporal relation on the constraints as well.
- We apply some heuristic based on the characteristics of Web service when performing model checking, so verification performance is improved visibly.

---

[1] Currently, we only support Linear Temporal Logic (LTL).

To extend this work, we propose a bitwise-based indexing technique to organize the Web services in the repository to support the Web service retrieval process more accurately and efficiently. For the motivating example above, our approach just needs to traverse 18 states in the case of using on-the-fly tactic, and is further reduced to 10 states when heuristics are applied (as compared with 108 states needed to be visited to make the full schema in PORSCE II [4]).

The contributions of our extension can be summarized as follows.

- We proposed an approach which combines indexing and model checking for composition and verification of Web services. Compared with [10], this work is enhanced with indexing technique to enjoy a significant improvement of performance.
- We presented a bitwise-based approach to present Web services and indexing technique. This representation allows us to use the bitwise operators in processing and further enjoy more improvement on performance.
- The experiments are performed on multiple real data sets and the results show the effectiveness of this approach compared with [10] and other approaches.

Regarding the novelty of the work presented in this paper, we want to note that using model checking to solve the Web service composition or Web service verification has already been reported in [5,10,12–14]. Likewise, Web service indexing for faster composition is also not a new idea, see [8,9,15]. However, this paper is the first work proposing the combination of these two techniques.

Outline The rest of the paper is organized as follows. Section 2 presents a model for the Web service composition problem. In Sect. 3, we present heuristics to improve the Web service composition performance. We propose a bitwise-based Web service indexing approach in Sect. 4, together with a case study. Then, in Sect. 5, we present our experimentations from a repository of real Web services. In Sect. 6, we present the related works. The conclusion and future work are discussed in Sect. 7.

2 LTS4WS—the model for Web service composition

In this paper, we formalize the composition task as a state-based searching problem. Each state corresponds to a composition of multiple Web services, from which new state can be generated by extending the current composition with another Web service, bringing a new composition. That is, we regard the set of all possible Web services as a model, whose states are feasible combinations of them. Meanwhile, user requirements are regarded as properties, which can be verified over the model using the model checking techniques, in an on-the-fly manner. To carry out this study, our model is developed based on the following definitions.

Definition 1 (Web Service) A *web service* $\mathcal{W}$ is a six-tuple $\mathcal{W} = (\mathcal{N}, \mathcal{I}, \mathcal{O}, \mathcal{P}, \mathcal{E}, \mathcal{Q})$, where

- $\mathcal{N}$ is a string representing the unique name of $\mathcal{W}$.
- $\mathcal{I} = \{t_1^i, t_2^i, \ldots, t_n^i\}$ is a set of input functional properties. We denote $\widetilde{t_j^i}$ as an *input logical term* representing the current informative status of the property t_j^i. $\widetilde{t_j^i} = true$ means that the information of t_j^i is currently available and vice versa.
- $\mathcal{O} = \{t_1^o, t_2^o, \ldots, t_m^o\}$ is a set of output functional properties. We denote $\widetilde{t_k^o}$ as an *output logical term* representing the current informative status of the property t_k^o. Likewise, $\widetilde{t_k^o} = true$ means that the information of t_k^o is currently available and vice versa.
- $\mathcal{P}$ is a logic expression representing the *pre-condition* of $\mathcal{W}$ that must hold before $\mathcal{W}$ is invoked. It is simply a *conjunctive normal form* of all input logical terms, as $\mathcal{P} = \widetilde{t_1^i} \wedge \widetilde{t_2^i} \wedge \ldots \wedge \widetilde{t_n^i} = \bigwedge_j^n \widetilde{t_j^i}$.
- $\mathcal{E}$ is a set of assignment expressions describing the *effect* after $\mathcal{W}$ is invoked. $\mathcal{E}$ has the form of $\{\forall k = 1..m : \widetilde{t_k^o} \overset{\Delta}{=} true\}$, where $\overset{\Delta}{=}$ is the assignment operator. Because $\widetilde{t_k^o}$ is a logical term, we can simply represent it as $\{\forall k = 1 \ldots m : \widetilde{t_k^o}\}$ or $\{\widetilde{t_1^o}; \ldots; \widetilde{t_m^o}; \}$.
- $\mathcal{Q}$ is a set of QoS properties, each of which is a pair of $\langle name : value \rangle$, where *name* is the name of the property and *value* is a numerical amount which evaluates the value returned by $\mathcal{W}$ w.r.t this property.

Example 1 Let us consider the first Web service in Table 1, which provides the hotel reservation information (*Hotel-Reservation*) of a specific hotel (*Hotel*) and the reservation dates (*Dates*). The response time (*respTime*) of this service is of 5 s. This Web service is described by Definition 1 as follows.

$$\mathcal{W} = (\mathcal{N} = HR,$$
$$\mathcal{I} = \{Hotel, Dates\},$$
$$\mathcal{O} = \{HotelReservation\},$$
$$\mathcal{P} = \widetilde{Hotel} \wedge \widetilde{Dates},$$
$$\mathcal{E} = \{\widetilde{HotelReservation}\},$$
$$\mathcal{Q} = \{respTime : 5\})$$

The logic expression $\widetilde{Hotel} \wedge \widetilde{Dates}$ is the pre-condition that must hold before the Web service is invoked. It means that to invoke the service HR (*HotelReserveService*), we must have the information of *Hotel* and *Dates* to reserve this hotel. The effect of this Web service invocation is that we have

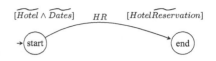

Fig. 2 Visual representation of an LTS

the reservation information of this hotel (*HotelReservation*), i.e., $\widetilde{HotelReservation} = true$. It needs five units of time (*respTime*: 5) in execution.

Definition 2 *(Labelled Transition System)* A *Labelled Transition System* (LTS) is a five-tuple $\mathcal{L} = (V, S, s_0, L, \delta)$, where

- V is a set of variables,
- S is a set of states,
- $s_0 \in S$ is the initial state,
- L is a set of *action labels*,
- $\delta : S \times L \rightarrow S$ is a transition relation, where $(s, a, s') \in \delta$ is denoted as $(s \times a \rightarrow s')$. A transition may also have a *pre-condition* (or the *guard*), a logical expression built over V, which must always hold before the transition is fired. In addition, a transition may also have an *effect*, a set of expressions built over V, which expresses the effect after firing the transition. A LTS that supports those kinds of transitions is called *guarded LTS*, whose transition is represented as:

$$[guard]transition[effect]$$

Example 2 Given a simple LTS containing two states $\{start, end\}$, $start$ is the initial state, as shown in Fig. 2, and a set of variables V consist of $\widetilde{Hotel}$, $\widetilde{Dates}$, and $\widetilde{HotelReservation}$. This LTS describes that in the initial state, if we fire the transition (or invoke the service) HR (*HotelReserveService*), the system will switch to state *end*. The LTS is visually described in Fig. 2 and represented as $System = (V, S, s_0, L, \delta)$, where

- $V = \{\widetilde{Hotel}, \widetilde{Dates}, \widetilde{HotelReservation}\}$,
- $S = \{start, end\}$,
- $s_0 = start$,
- $L = \{HR\}$,
- $\delta = \{[\widetilde{Hotel} \wedge \widetilde{Dates}]start \times HR \rightarrow end$ $[\widetilde{HotelReservation}]\}$

In Fig. 2, we describe the representation of Web service HR (*HotelReservation*) as a transition in an LTS system, where the pre-condition and effect of the Web service are also used as the guard and effect of the transition. In general, all of Web services can be represented as this transition with appropriate guards and effects.

Definition 3 (LTS for Web Services)Let $WS = \{\mathcal{W}_1, \mathcal{W}_2, \ldots, \mathcal{W}_n\}$ be a set of Web services, where $\mathcal{W}_i = (\mathcal{N}_i, \mathcal{I}_i, \mathcal{O}_i, \mathcal{P}_i, \mathcal{E}_i, \mathcal{Q}_i)$ as defined in Definition 1. A *LTS for Web Services* (LTS4WS) of WS is a guarded LTS $\mathcal{L}^{WS} = (V, \{s_0\}, s_0, L, \delta)$, where

- $V = (\bigcup_i^n \mathcal{I}_i) \bigcup (\bigcup_i^n \mathcal{O}_i)$.
- $\{s_0\}$ is a set of states, which has only one state s_0,
- s_0 is the initial state,
- $L = \{\mathcal{N}_1, \mathcal{N}_2, \ldots, \mathcal{N}_n\}$,
- δ is a transition relation of the form $[\mathcal{P}_i]s_0 \times \mathcal{N}_i \to s_0[\mathcal{E}_i]$.

Example 3 The LTS4WS model of the ten Web services in Table 1 is defined as follows.

- The set of variables: $V = \{\widetilde{Dates},\ \widetilde{Hotel},$
  $\widetilde{HotelReservation},\ \widetilde{City},\ \widetilde{Price},\ \widetilde{Sightseeing},$
  $\widetilde{Activity},\ \widetilde{Beach},\ \widetilde{Area},\ \widetilde{Weather}\}$
- The set of states: $\{s_0\}$
- The initial state: s_0
- The set of label actions is the acronym of the name of web services: $L = \{HR, CH, HC, HP, SC, SCH, CS, ABS, AWS, CWS\}$
- The transition relations: $\delta = \{$ $[\widetilde{Hotel} \wedge \widetilde{Dates}]\ s_0 \times$
  $HR \to s_0\ [\widetilde{HotelReservation}],$
  $[\widetilde{City}]\ s_0 \times CH \to s_0\ [\widetilde{Hotel}],$
  $[\widetilde{Hotel}]\ s_0 \times HC \to s_0\ [\widetilde{City}],$
  $[\widetilde{Hotel}]\ s_0 \times HP \to s_0\ [\widetilde{Price}],$
  $[\widetilde{Sightseeing}]\ s_0 \times SC \to s_0\ [\widetilde{City}],$
  $[\widetilde{Sightseeing}]\ s_0 \times SCH \to s_0\ [\widetilde{City}; \widetilde{Hotel}],$
  $[\widetilde{City}]\ s_0 \times CS \to s_0\ [\widetilde{Sightseeing}],$
  $[\widetilde{Activity}]\ s_0 \times ABS \to s_0\ [\widetilde{Beach}],$
  $[\widetilde{Area} \wedge \widetilde{Dates}]\ s_0 \times AWS \to s_0\ [\widetilde{Weather}],$
  $[\widetilde{City} \wedge \widetilde{Dates}]\ s_0 \times CWS \to s_0\ [\widetilde{Weather}]\}$

This LTS4WS model is represented visually in Fig. 5, where $\mathcal{P}_X$ and $\mathcal{E}_X$ are the pre-condition and effect of Web service X, respectively.

In Fig. 3, we describe an LTS4WS model for a Web service repository with ten Web services. As defined in Definition 3, this is an LTS which has only one state, from and to which all of transitions corresponding to the Web services come and go. This simplicity of this LTS renders an important advantage when performing composition and verification as we do not need to generate the full schema in advance like the previous work [5].

A model checker will search over the state space generated from this LTS for a state meeting the requirement specified by hard and soft constraints. For example, the searching problem given in the motivating example can be represented as an LTL formula of $(\widetilde{Dates} \wedge \widetilde{Sightseeing} \to$

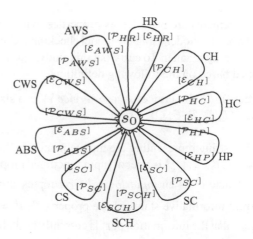

Fig. 3 Example of the LTS4WS model

$\widetilde{Price} \wedge \widetilde{HotelReservation}) \wedge (respTime \leq 30)$. Figure 4 shows a situation, where the goal is found without searching the whole space. Note that we can always prune the paths that violate soft constraints, but virtually, we cannot justify whether a path that will eventually satisfy a hard constraint or not. However, we can choose to explore the path that is most potential. If this path happens to reach the desired goal, other branches are not needed to be considered, as shown in Fig. 4. In the following section, we introduce the heuristic-based approach for doing so.

Listing 1 describes the structure of LTS4WS model in the format of the XML language. Under this structure, the declaration of variables and constants is presented in *Declaration* section; *Process* contains the main contents of the model. In particular, *States* contains the states of the model, which has only one state s_0 as discussed; *Transitions* contains the transitions of the model. In this section, *Event* contains the names of transitions; *Guard* contains the expressions describing the guards of transitions; and Effect contains the expressions describing the effects of transitions.

Listing 1 *LTS4WS model is represented in XML-style*

```
<Declaration>
<!--variables, constants declaration-->
</Declaration>
<ProcessName="System">
  <States>
    <State Name="s0" Init="True"/>
  </States>
  <Transitions>
    <Transition From="s0" To="s0"
      <Event>WebService_Name</Event>
      <Guard>Guarded_Expression</Guard>
      <Effect>Effect_Expression</Effect>
    </Transition>
    <!-- Other transitions -->
  </Transitions>
</Process>
</LTS4WS>
```

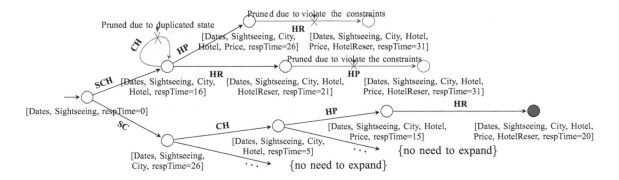

Fig. 4 State-space exploration

Fig. 5 Example illustrates the calculation of the value of G, $H1$, $H2$, and F

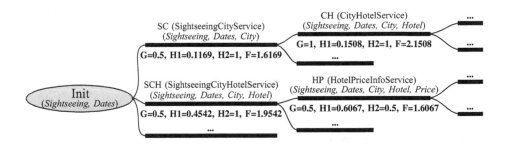

3 Heuristics-based approaches for web service composition

In our research, to perform the process of Web service composition and verification, we use the model checker PAT [11]. As well as other general model checkers, PAT has main functionality of verifying a temporal expression on a model. When the verification fails, a counter example is returned. It is not guaranteed to be an optimal path (the shortest path for instance). This is a general drawback of the model checkers. Another downside of model checkers is the state-space explosion problem. These two disadvantages originate from the causes that PAT (and other model checkers) typically adopts an exhaustive search algorithm, such as breadth first search or depth first search. Therefore, to apply PAT to our research and overcome its weaknesses, this study proposes using the heuristic search method (inspired from the well-known $A*$ algorithm) to improve the search process.

Heuristic function—F(n)

To apply heuristic search, we define the heuristic function $F(n)$ as the following formula:

$$F(n) = \alpha G(n) + \beta H(n), \tag{1}$$

where

- $G(n)$ is the real cost from state $init$ to state n,
- α, β are the corresponding weights of $H(n)$ and $G(n)$.

- $H(n)$ is the estimated cost (heuristic) from n to $goal$, as

$$H(n) = \beta_1 H1(n) + \beta_2 H2(n), \tag{2}$$

where

- $H1(n)$ is the estimated cost based on the QoS properties,
- $H2(n)$ is the estimated cost based on the functional properties,
- β_1, β_2 are the corresponding weights of $H1(n)$ and $H2(n)$.

The value of α, β, β_1, and β_2 can be empirically determined and adjusted by users. By default, all of those parameters have the same influence value of 1.

The real cost function—G(n)

$$G(n) = \frac{i}{l}, \tag{3}$$

where

- i is the number of composition step from $init$ to n.
- l is the number of functional properties that composite Web service must be satisfied.

We assume that each functional property needs one Web service. With l properties, the smaller i, the smaller $G(n)$ value.

Example 4 Supposed that we have a set of Web services as in Table 1 and the requirements as in Table 2. In this case, the number of functional properties is $l = 2$. In the composition process, the values of G are computed as described in Fig. 5. For example, at a state immediately, after the $Init$ state, we have $i = 1$ and $G = 1/2$.

Estimated cost function based on QoS properties—H1(n)

The QoS properties are divided into two categories, positive group and negative group [16]. The higher value in negative property indicates the lower quality whilst the higher one in positive property reflects higher quality and vice versa. In addition, each QoS property has a different calculation unit, such as second (s) for response time, % for availability, etc. Therefore, we also normalize the value sets of the QoS properties before processing. With two different kinds of QoS properties, we then have the different normalized functions, respectively.

Let Q be a QoS property and q the value of Q. Then, the normalized value (q_{nrm}) is calculated as the following formula:

- If Q is a negative property, then

$$q_{nrm} = \begin{cases} \frac{q - q_{min}}{q_{max} - q_{min}} & \text{if } q_{max} - q_{min} \neq 0 \\ 1 & \text{if } q_{max} - q_{min} = 0. \end{cases} \qquad (4)$$

- If Q is a positive property, then

$$q_{nrm} = \begin{cases} \frac{q_{max} - q}{q_{max} - q_{min}} & \text{if } q_{max} - q_{min} \neq 0 \\ 1 & \text{if, } q_{max} - q_{min} = 0. \end{cases} \qquad (5)$$

Here q_{max} and q_{min} is the upper bound and lower bound of q, respectively.

After obtaining the normalized value for each property, we calculate the overall average value ($H1(n)$) for all QoS properties of Web services. The formula for calculating $H1(n)$ is as follows:

$$H1(n) = \sum w_i * q_{nrm_i} \qquad (6)$$

where

- w_i is the weight of property ith, which can be changed by user. By default, all QoS properties have $w_i = 1$.
- q_{nrm_i} is a normalized value of property ith at state n.

Example 5 Concerning the previous example, we now consider a Web service with a QoS property of response time. The response time has value in range from 1 ($q_{min} = 1$) to 60 s ($q_{max} = 60$) and the weight (w_1) of 1. The values of QoS property of Web services are given in Table 1.

With the given QoS property, the value of $H1$ of each state is calculated as follows:

- The initial state (init): $H1 = 0$
- The state after invoking the SC service (*SightseeingCityService*) (state SC in Fig. 5):
  - The response time: $q_{nrm_1} = \frac{2-1}{60-1} = 0.0169$
  - $H1 = \sum w_i * q_{nrm_i} = 0.0169$

Similarly, we will calculate the value of $H1$ for every state, as shown in Fig. 5.

The estimated cost function based on functional properties—H2(n)

For each state in the state space, we have a set of variables so-called environment variables, describing the considered properties. For the functional properties, the corresponding variables will have values of 0 or 1, which implies whether the corresponding property has sufficient information or not.

$H2(n)$ function aims to look ahead, evaluate, and select the state which has the most functional properties satisfying the goal state. $H2(n)$ is calculated by the following formula:

$$H_2(n) = \frac{\text{diff}(\text{funcvar}(goal), \text{funcvar}(n))}{l} \qquad (7)$$

where

- $\text{funcvar}(x)$ is a set of functional properties which we will have (whose value is 1) at the state x.
- $\text{diff}(A, B)$ is a function which counts the number of functional properties appear in A, but does not appear in B. Thus, $\text{diff}(\text{funcvar}(goal), \text{funcvar}(n))$ is the number of functional properties required by users that have not yet achieved at state n. When $\text{diff}(\text{funcvar}(goal), \text{funcvar}(n)) = 0$, in aspect of functionality, state n satisfies the user requirements.

Example 6 Supposed that we have a set of Web services as in Table 1 and the requirements as in Table 2. The set of functional properties of state $goal$ is $\text{funcvar}(goal) = \{Price, Hotel Reservation\}$, $l = 2$. The value of $H1$ of each state is calculated as follows:

- The initial state (init):
  - $\text{funcvar}(init) = \{Sightseeing, Dates\}$
  - $H2(init) = \frac{\text{diff}(\text{funcvar}(goal), \text{funcvar}(init))}{l} = \frac{2}{2} = 1$
- The state after invoking the HP service (*HotelPriceInfoService*) (state HP in Fig. 5):
  - $\text{funcvar}(HP) = \{Sightseeing, Dates, City, Hotel, Price\}$
  - $H2(HP) = \frac{\text{diff}(\text{funcvar}(goal), \text{funcvar}(HP))}{l} = \frac{1}{2} = 0.5$.

After calculating all values $G, H1, H2$, we will calculate the value of the heuristic cost function F by formula (1). Fig. 5 describes a general example of the values of

G, $H1$, $H2$, and F calculated in the process of composition, with the α, β, β_1, and β_2 are equal to 1 and the value of the QoS properties are given in Table 1. Based on these values, at each processing step, composition process will select the state, whose value of cost F is the lowest, to perform further processing.

4 Bitwise-based Web service indexing

In the previous sections, we have presented an approach of representing a repository of Web services as an LTS model, based on which a WSC request will be considered a state-space search problem. We have also discussed using heuristics to reach the search goal on the state space potentially faster. Hence, each composition step corresponds to a subgoal of the search problem.

Obviously, when looking for the candidates of the next composition step, one should only consider the Web services that are relevant to the current subgoal and discard the rest. However, it is not easy to quickly identify the relevant Web services at a current state. In this section, we address this problem by presenting a bitwise-based indexing technique to index the Web service repository. Based on the index information, one can easily locate the Web services relevant to some desired properties.

The idea of this technique is summarized as follows. Each Web service in the repository is represented as a pair of bitwise-based vectors, consisting an input vector and an output vector. In these vectors, each element is a bit representing a property, or feature. If the value of a bit is 0, the corresponding feature is not covered by the Web service and vice versa. The user requirements and subgoals are represented as a pair of bitwise-based vectors in similar manner.

4.1 Index table construction and manipulation

In the index table, each index item is a vector representing one feature. Web services are indexed using bitwise and ($\bar{\wedge}$) operator between its input vector and the vector of each index item. Thus, we can quickly select Web services relevant to the feature represented by the index item. The selection of index items relevant to the user requirements/subgoals is also done in the same way. As a result, we can find Web services relevant to user requirement/subgoals within almost constant complexity. The details of these steps are represented as follows.

4.1.1 The ordered feature set of Web service repository

Given a repository of n Web services with k distinct functional properties (k distinct features), an ordered feature set ($\mathcal{S}$) of the Web service repository is an ordered set with k elements for k sorted features.[2]

Example 7 The Web service repository given in Table 1 can be represented by an ordered set with 12 sorted features as follows. $\mathcal{S} = \{Activity, Adventure, Area, Beach, City, Dates, Hotel, HotelReservation, Price, RuralArea, Sightseeing,$ and $Weather\}$.

4.1.2 Bitwise-based vectors of a Web service and user functional requirements

Definition 4 *(Bitwise-based vector of feature set)* Let $\mathcal{S}$ be a set of properties, or *features*, and $\trianglelefteq$, an order relation on $\mathcal{S}$. We denote $\trianglelefteq(V, i)$ as the ith element of $\mathcal{S}$ when sorted by $\trianglelefteq$. The bitwise-based vector of a subset s of $\mathcal{S}$, denoted as $V_{\mathcal{S}}^s$, is given as follows:

$$V_{\mathcal{S}}^s[i] = \begin{cases} 1 & \text{if } \trianglelefteq (V, i) \in s; \\ 0 & \text{otherwise.} \end{cases} \tag{8}$$

Example 8 For the ordered feature set $\mathcal{S}$ given in Example 7 and subset of features $s = \{Dates, Hotel\}$, we have the bitwise-based vector of s on $\mathcal{S}$ as follows:

$$V_{\mathcal{S}}^s = 000001100000. \tag{9}$$

For each Web service, we have two kinds of features (functional properties), which are inputs and outputs. Therefore, we construct the corresponding input and output bitwise-base vectors as follows.

Definition 5 (Bitwise-based vector of Web service) The bitwise-based vectors of a Web service is a pair $\langle V_i, V_o \rangle$, where V_i and V_o are the bitwise-based vectors of the input features and output features, respectively. V_i and V_o are defined as presented in Definition 4.

Example 9 The bitwise-based input and output vectors of all Web services in Table 1 are in Table 3.

Similarly, the user requirement is also represented as two bitwise-based vectors. They are so-called the bitwise-based supplied vector and the bitwise-based goal vector.

Example 10 The user requirement in the Table 2 can be represented as the bitwise-based vectors as in Table 4.

4.1.3 Bitwise-based indexing for Web service repository

After vectorizing Web services in the repository, we construct the indexing table based on the input vectors of Web services.

---

2 We can apply any sorting criterion here. However, for convenience, the features are sorted by the alphabetical order unless indicated otherwise.

Table 3 Bitwise-based input and output vectors of Web services in Table 1

#	Web service	Bitwise-based input vector	Bitwise-based output vector
1	HotelReserveService (HR)	000001100000	000000010000
2	CityHotelService (CH)	000010000000	000000100000
3	HotelCityService (HC)	000000100000	000010000000
4	HotelPriceInfoService (HP)	000000100000	000000001000
5	SightseeingCityService (SC)	000000000010	000010000000
6	SightseeingCityHotelService (SCH)	000000000010	000010100000
7	CitySightseeingService (CS)	000010000000	000000000010
8	AdventureRuralAreaService (ARA)	010000000000	000000000100
9	ActivityBeachService (ABS)	100000000000	000100000000
10	AreaWeatherService (AWS)	001000000000	000000000001

Table 4 Bitwise-based vector of user requirement

User requirement	Bitwise-based supplied vector	Bitwise-based goal vector
Input: *Dates, Sightseeing* Output: *Price, HotelReservation*	000001000010	000000011000

The indexing table is a two-column table. The first column contains unit vectors, each of which represents a feature in the ordered feature set. To represent the ith feature, the ith bit of the corresponding unit vector is set as 1, whereas other bits of the vector are kept as 0. In the same row of the index table, the second column stores the Web services relevant to the feature represented by the unit vector at the first column.

The process of construction of the index table is presented in Algorithm 1.

Algorithm 1 Index table construction
***
Input: A Web service repository with n Web services
Output: The index table

Step 1. Build the ordered feature set S

1: Extract features from Web services and build the ordered feature set S

Step 2. Build the initial index table – T

2: **for** i from 0 to $S.size() - 1$ **do**
3:      Build the unit vector v_i of which bit i^{th} is 1
4:      $T[i][0] \leftarrow v_i$

Step 3. Update the index table

5: **for** each Web service w in the repository **do**
6:      Build the input vector $v_{w_{in}}$ and output vector $v_{w_{out}}$ of w
7:      **for** i from 0 to $T.size() - 1$ **do**
8:          $v_i \leftarrow T[i][0]$
9:          **if** $v_i \barwedge v_{w_{in}} \neq 0$ **then**   // $\barwedge$ *is the bitwise AND operator*
10:             $T[i][1].add(w)$
11: return T

Example 11 The index table of the Web service repository in Table 1, built by Algorithm 1, is in Table 5.

Table 5 Indexing table of Web service repository

Index item	List of Web services
100000000000	(100000000000,000100000000) (ABS)
010000000000	(010000000000,000000000100) (ARA)
001000000000	(001000000000,000000000001) (AWS)
000100000000	
000010000000	(000010000000,000000100000) (CH),
	(000010000000,000000000010) (CS)
000001000000	(000001100000,000000010000) (HR)
000000100000	(000001100000,000000010000) (HR),
	(000000100000,000010000000) (HC),
	(000000100000,000000001000) (HP)
000000010000	
000000001000	
000000000100	
000000000010	(000000000010,000010000000) (SC),
	(000000000010,000010100000) (SCH)
000000000001	

4.1.4 Choosing indexing items and choosing Web services

As discussed earlier in this text, at each composition, the Web services that are matched with indexing items corresponding with the current subgoal (i.e., they are relevant to the subgoal features) will be chosen as the candidates for the next step. The matching mechanism is implemented as follows.

Definition 6 *(Bitwise-based matching)* Let V be the bitwise-based input vector of the current subgoal, and V_k be the bitwise-based vector representing the kth index item. The kth item is a *matched index item* iff:

$$V \bar{\wedge} V_k = V_k \tag{10}$$

where $\bar{\wedge}$ is the bitwise AND operator.

Example 12 Taking the user requirement in Table 2 as the initial current subgoal, the inputs at the first composition step are *Sightseeing, Dates* with the corresponding input vector 000001000010. The chosen index items are 000001000000 (corresponding to the value of sixth bit being 1) and 000000000010 (corresponding to the value of eleventh bit being 1). Therefore, the chosen Web services are *HR, SC, SCH*. In this case, the model checker will verify and choose *SC* and *SCH* to expand (Fig. 4). The Web service *HR* is rejected, as it requires the input of *Dates* that we do not have at that point.

After selecting the Web services to put into the composition process at each composition step, the composition process will execute normally and the heuristic function will choose the best Web service to compose first, as previously discussed. The output of this web service is added the current input of the next subgoal. In that case, a Composite Bitwise-based Vector is generated as follows.

Definition 7 *(Composite bitwise-based vector)* Let V be the bitwise-based vector of the input of the current subgoal, WS_k be the chosen Web service to compose, $V_{k_{out}}$ be the bitwise-based vectors of the output of WS_k. The bitwise-based vector V_c of the resulted composite Web service is calculated as follows:

$$V_c = V \underline{\vee} V_{k_{out}} \tag{11}$$

where $\underline{\vee}$ is the bitwise OR operator.

Example 13 Assumed that the input of current subgoal is *Sightseeing, Dates*, corresponding to vector $V = 000001000010$. Supposed that the Web service *SightseeingCityService* is selected with $V_{k_{in}} = 000000000010$ and $V_{k_{out}} = 000010000000$. The bitwise-based vector of the composite Web service (V_c) is calculated as follows:

$$V_c = V \underline{\vee} V_{k_{out}} = 000001000010 \underline{\vee} 000010000000$$
$$= 000011000010. \tag{12}$$

4.1.5 Reducing the number of chosen Web services

In the approach of selecting Web services, as presented in Sect. 4.1.4, after each composition step, the number of

obtained features, i.e., the 1-valued bits on the bitwise-based vector of the current composite Web service, obviously increases. Therefore, the number of selected index item and selected Web services considered as candidates for each step also increases. After several steps, the number of chosen index items will be enormous and almost all of Web services will be selected. This unfavorably increases the complexity of the composition process. Therefore, we need to consider reducing the number of selected Web services at each composition step reasonably.

To reduce the number of selected Web services, we consider the following remarks.

Eliminating the redundant Web services

The redundant Web service is the Web service of which the bitwise-based output vector is contained in bitwise-based vector of the current input. The contained relationship between two bitwise-based vectors is defined as in Definition 8.

Definition 8 *(The bitwise-based contained relationship)* Let V and $V_{k_{out}}$ are two bitwise-based vectors. V contains $V_{k_{out}}$ or $V_{k_{out}}$ is contained in V iff

$$V \bar{\wedge} V_{k_{out}} = V_{k_{out}} \tag{13}$$

where $\bar{\wedge}$ is the bitwise AND operator.

Example 14 Suppose that at a specific composition step, we have obtained information of the features of *Sightseeing, Dates, City*, corresponding to the bitwise-based vector of the current input $V = 000011000010$. The index items which satisfy vector V are 000010000000, 000001000000, and 000000000010, and the satisfied Web services which will be used in the composition process are HR, SC, SCH, CH, and CS (see details in Table 5). Let us consider the Web service CS (*CitySightseeingService*), which takes in the *City* and returns the *Sightseeing*, corresponding to the bitwise-based out vector is $V_{k_{out}} = 000000000010$. Since $V_{k_{out}}$ and V satisfy the bitwise-based contained relationship as follows:

$$V \bar{\wedge} V_{k_{out}} = 000011000010 \bar{\wedge} 000000000010$$
$$= 000000000010 = V_{k_{out}} \tag{14}$$

the Web service CS is a redundant Web service and will not be selected to put into the considered set.

4.1.6 The satisfied composite Web service

The composition process stops when the obtained features satisfy the initial user requirement. It means that the bitwise-based vector of current input (V) contains the bitwise-based vector of user goal (V_g), or

$$V \bar{\wedge} V_g = V_g \qquad (15)$$

Current input features	Current input vector (V)	Chosen index	Chosen web services		
			WS	Bitwise-based input vector	Bitwise-based output vector
Sightseeing, Dates, City	000011000010	000001000000	HR	000001100000	000000010000
		000000000010	SCH	000000000010	000010100000
		000010000000	CH	000010000000	000000100000

4.2 Case study

In this case study, we consider the set of Web services listed in Table 1. Then, the corresponding bitwise-based indexing table is represented as in Table 5. For the user requirement presented in Table 2, the composition process is performed with the following steps.

Step 1

Current input features	Current input vector (V)	Chosen index	Chosen web services		
			WS	Bitwise-based input vector	Bitwise-based output vector
Sightseeing, Dates	000001000010	000001000000	HR	000001100000	000000010000
		000000000010	SC	000000000010	000010000000
			SCH	000000000010	000010100000

Supposed that in the composition process, the heuristic function evaluates that the Web service SC is the most suitable Web service to be invoked. After invoking Web service CS, the bitwise-based vector of current input $V = V \veebar V_{CS_{out}} = 000001000010 \veebar 000010000000 =$

000011000010. This vector does not contain the vector of user goal $(V \bar{\wedge} V_g \neq V_g)$. Therefore, the composition process will be continued.

Step 2

At this step, we have three chosen index items with five Web services (HR, SC, SCH, CH, CS). However, the Web services SC and CS are eliminated, as they are redundant.

As in above table, we have three Web services used in composition $(HR, SCH, \text{and } CH)$. The heuristic function chooses the Web service CH to compose in next step. After invoking this Web service, the bitwise-based vector of current input $V = V \veebar V_{CH_{out}} = 000011000010 \veebar 000000100000 = 000011100010$. This vector does not contain the vector of user goal $(V \bar{\wedge} V_g \neq V_g)$. The composition process will be continued.

Step 3

At this step, we have four chosen index items with seven Web services $(HR, SC, SCH, CH, CS, HC, HP)$, as in the table below.

Current input features	Current input vector (V)	Chosen index	Chosen web services		
			WS	Bitwise-based input vector	Bitwise-based output vector
Sightseeing, Dates, City, Hotel	000011100010	000001000000	HR	000001100000	000000010000
		000000000010			
		000010000000			
		000000100000	HP	000000100000	000000001000

According to above table, many Web services will be filtered out. In particular, $SC, CH, SCH, CS,$ and HC are thrown away, because they are the redundant Web service; HR in the sixth row is removed, because it is duplicated. Therefore, we have only two remained Web services of HR and HP. The heuristic function will choose the Web service HP to compose, and the current input vector is updated

Table 6 Experiment data sets

Data set	No. of Web services	Description
Travel Booking (TB)	20	Including web services providing information to serve the travel booking
Medical Services (MS)	50	Services support to look up hospital, treatment, medicine, etc.
Education Services (EDS)	100	Services related to education, such as scholarship, courses, degrees, etc.
Economy Services (ECS)	200	Including services provided information on goods, restaurant, food, etc.
Global	1000	1000 random services from OWL-S-TC [17]

as $V = V \veebar V_{H P_{\text{out}}} = 000011100010 \veebar 000000001000 = 000011101010$. This vector does not contain the vector of user goal ($V \barwedge V_g \neq V_g$). The composition process will be continued in Step 4.

Step 4

At this step, with the input vector of $V = 000011101010$, we have one more index item, corresponding to the vector 000000001000. However, this index item does not contain any Web service. Therefore, there is only one service HR to compose, as depicted in the following table.

five sub-data sets, whose numbers of web services are varied 20 to 1000 services, as shown in Table 6.

We conduct experiment scenarios based on four different approaches, named full schema verification, on-the-fly composition and verification, heuristic-driven on-the-fly composition and verification, and combined bitwise-based indexing with heuristic-driven on-the-fly composition and verification. The first one is the typical approach adopted by [5]. The last three approaches are our proposed ones, with and without using heuristics, and combined heuristic with bitwise-based

Current input features	Current input vector (V)	Chosen index	Chosen web services		
			WS	Bitwise-based input vector	Bitwise-based output vector
Sightseeing, Dates, City	000011100010	000001000000 000000000010 000010000000 000000100000 000000001000	HR _There is no web service_	000001100000	000000010000

After invoking the Web service HR, the up-to-date bitwise-based vector V is 000011111010 (for obtained features of *Sightseeing, Dates, City, Hotel, Price* and *Hotel-Reservation*). This vector contains the vector of user goal ($V \barwedge V_g = 000011111010 \barwedge 000000011000 = 000000011000 = V_g$). Therefore, the composition process stops.

In summary, we have the composite Web service which consists of four Web services as $SC \bullet CH \bullet HP \bullet HR$.

5 Experimentations

In this section, we present the experimental results of our approach, which was built as the tool known as WSCOVER[3]. The tool WSCOVER is experimented on the real data sets obtained from the project OWL-S-TC [17]. OWL-S-TC provides over 1000 Web services classified into different domains, described by OWL-S [18]. In this data set, we select

indexing. The experiment is performed on a PC with core i5-5200 processor (4 x 2.7 GHz), 8.0 GB RAM, running on the 64-bit Windows 7 operating system. The experimental results are evaluated in three aspects: the number of expanded states, the number of visited states, and the execution time, and analyzed statistically, as depicted in Table 7 and Fig. 6.

The experimental results confirm our hypothesis that the indexing helps in reducing the number of expanded states (see Fig. 6a) significantly.

Note that the heuristic algorithm in the WSCOVER tool always chooses the best way, i.e., the way that is evaluated most potential to reach to goal, to travel in the state space. Our heuristic approach showed it efficiency when there is almost no back-tracking step taken when the model checker explores the state space (i.e., the states suggested by the heuristic algorithm are, in fact, the states in the right path to the goal). Thus, the third and the fourth approaches, empowered by this heuristic strategy, enjoy a far less numbers of visited states, as compared with those in the first and the second approaches (Fig. 6b).

---

[3] This tool and its guidelines and also all experimental data sets can be downloaded from http://cse.hcmut.edu.vn/~save/project/wscover/start.

Table 7 Experimentation results

Data sets	Approaches	Expanded states	Visited states	Execution time (s)
TB (20)	Full schema verification	1100	56	0.250
	On-the-fly composition and verification	825	56	0.210
	Heuristic-driven on-the-fly composition and verification	316	35	0.155
	Combined bitwise-based indexing with heuristic-driven on-the-fly composition and verification	316	35	0.155
MS (50)	Full schema verification	16,720	210	2.597
	On-the-fly composition and verification	12,331	210	2.022
	Heuristic-driven on-the-fly composition and verification	2143	119	1.538
	Combined bitwise-based indexing with heuristic-driven on-the-fly composition and verification	316	35	0.155
EDS (100)	Full schema verification	27,400	275	5.570
	On-the-fly composition and verification	20,824	275	4.579
	Heuristic-driven on-the-fly composition and verification	3021	151	3.294
	Combined bitwise-based indexing with heuristic-driven on-the-fly composition and verification	316	35	0.155
ECS (200)	Full schema verification	102,800	515	28.198
	On-the-fly composition and verification	76,586	515	23.030
	Heuristic-driven on-the-fly composition and verification	8324	287	18.273
	Combined bitwise-based indexing with heuristic-driven on-the-fly composition and verification	316	35	0.155
Global (1000)	Full schema verification	Out-of-memory	Out-of-memory	Out-of-memory
	On-the-fly composition and verification	Out-of-memory	Out-of-memory	Out-of-memory
	Heuristic-driven on-the-fly composition and verification	91,457	1429	597.228
	Combined bitwise-based indexing with heuristic-driven on-the-fly composition and verification	316	35	0.155

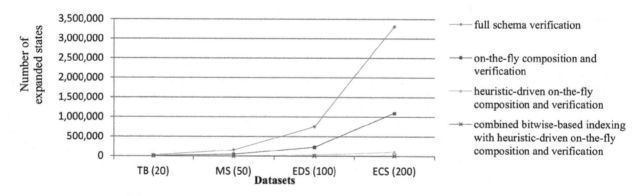

(a) Visual comparison between approaches according to the number of expanded states

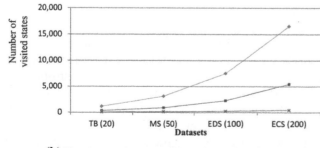

(b) Visual comparison according to the number of visited states

(c) Visual comparison according to execution time

Fig. 6 Visual representation of the experimental results

As expected result, where the execution time mostly depends on the number of expanded states and visited states, all of our proposed methods are faster than the original one in existing work and our new proposed bitwise-based indexing approach achieves the fastest execution time (Fig. 6c).

6 Related works

6.1 Web service composition and verification

Research community has a lot of work related to WSC problem, which can be classified into three groups as follows.

6.1.1 Composition based on hard constraints

WSC only involves the functional properties (*hard constraints*) which is the classic problem of SOA, which are mostly based on the theory of planning of the artificial intelligence field (AI Planning), such as [4] and [19]. Some recent studies are based on abstract models, such as Petri net or Colored Petri Net [12–14] to compose and verify Web services. PORSCE II [4] is a framework implementing the WSC-based on the requirements on input and output of the services. Similarly, OWL-S-XPlan [19] also uses Web services expressed by OWL-S to transform the problem from WSC domain to planning domain and uses the planner named XPlan, constructed by author. The studies [12–14] give the automatic WSC techniques based on Petri net (or Colored Petri net).

6.1.2 Composition based on hard and soft constraints

WSC method which combines functional properties (hard constraints) and QoS properties (soft constraints) has been proposed in [16]. In [16], the authors have proposed applying genetic algorithm (GA) to solve the problem with each possible composition encoded as a gene, to calculate value for specific kinds of QoS properties. However, this study only provides us a mechanism to choose the best (possible) composition from a set of composition ways (full composition schema) rather than composes from the component Web services. Besides, the application of genetic algorithms has increased the complexity of the problem and thus very difficult to apply in practice.

A different approach proposes the automated recovery when a WSC falls into the failure state (a Web service could not be accessed or unsatisfied the user requirement) [20]. With this approach, we have to have a full composition schema described in BPEL [21] language, which is transformed into a Labelled Transition System (LTS), monitored by a *monitor automata*. When an error arises (a state that cannot be reached, corresponding to a Web service cannot be accessed), the system will start calculating to choose the recovery plan using the genetic algorithm. The difference

between [20] and [16] is that the size of gene in [20] is unfixed, which depends on the number of back-tracking steps from the error state.

6.1.3 Web service verification

As discussed, most of current researches of Web service verification only verify separately hard or soft constraints of the services. WS-Engineer [22] is typical work for the Web service verification based on the functional properties. A recent study carried out to verify combined functional and non-functional requirements of WSC is introduced as VeriWS [5], which takes in a full composition schema expressed in BPEL and uses the model checker to verify.

6.2 Web service indexing

The number of web services is increasing rapidly. That makes the Web service composition approaches become more complex and face many difficulties. Therefore, the Web service indexing was suggested to support Web service accessing more efficient. This issue has received the attention of many researchers.

Aiello et al. [8] index the Web service repository based on the services descriptions represented by the WSDL language. This approach uses the hash table to implement the index. The index structure consists of two tables, Partname Index and Service Index. Partname Index uses a hashtable to maintain the mapping from each partname into two lists of service names, namely, in list and out list. The Service Index utilizes a hashtable that maps a service name into detail information of the correspondent service. The information is request partnames, and response partnames. The study in [8] was implemented as the VitaLab system which performs the indexing of a large collection of WSDL service description following a semantic description of operations (given as a tree of "is-a" relations) and, given a request for a service, composes the available services to satisfy the request.

Zhou et al. [15] proposed the way by which inverted indexing can be used for fast discovery of Web services. The indexing mechanisms can be either inverted indexing or latent semantic indexing. Here, inverted index can be used as a measure to check OWL-S description contain the given term. Each keyword is connected to a list of document ids, in which keyword occurs.

Czyszczo and Aleksander in [9] proposed the solution for the problem of Web service retrieval by presenting a new approach to indexing of both SOAP and RESTful Web services. This approach uses index structure called parametric index that allows users to retrieve ranked results in accordance with specific parameters. The parameters refer to service's integral components and are covered in presented formal definition of a Web service. Second, the services are

Table 8 Comparison on some of Web service composition and verification tools

Tool	Composition	Verification	Hard const.	Soft const.	Temporal	Input
OWL-S-XPlan	X		X			OWL-S
PORSCE II	X		X			OWL-S
WS-Engineer		X	X			BPEL
AgFlow		X		X		Statechart
VeriWS		X	X	X	X	BPEL
WSCOVER	X	X	X	X	X	OWL-S

modelled in vector space that allows the evaluation of their mutual relevance and enables obtaining ranked search results. To reduce the index size and to decrease the search time, the approach in [9] uses the method of conceptual indexing which groups relevant service components into concepts.

6.3 Evaluation and comparison of our approach with other studies

Table 8 presents the functional comparison our tool with others previously discussed. As observed, WSCOVER can perform both composition and verification at the same time and on-the-fly. Our tool composes and verifies a composite Web service on all kinds of constraints, hard and soft constraint, and also the temporal relations between component Web services.

To support model checking for composition and verification of Web services against a pre-defined goal in an effective manner, our work suggested representing a repository of Web services as a mathematical model, based on Labelled Transition System (LTS), known as LTS for Web Services (LTS4WS). Some other works, like the VeriWS tool [5], also propose using LTS models for enabling the formal verification of a WSC composition. However, our work distinguishes to this work as follows:

- In [5], the LTS model is rebuilt when we consider new composition goal, even though the repository remains the same. In contrast, our LTS4WS model can be applied for several various goals without being rebuilt.
- The work in [5] only verifies the composite Web service, it does not perform the composition phase. Meanwhile, our approach combines composition and verification at the same time.
- We apply the heuristic search to model checking engine based on the characteristics of Web service, so the verification performance is improved significantly.
- We also apply the bitwise-based indexing technique to index the Web service repository. This approach helps us to retrieve the Web services further faster and more reasonably. To the best of our knowledge, it is the first

work that combines formal verification with indexing techniques in the area of Web services processing.

7 Conclusion and future work

The tool WSCOVER, developed in this research, has offered several useful functions that the other similar works do not support, including the capability of composing and verifying Web services, in an on-the-fly manner; and extending the model checker by applying the heuristics specifying the Web service nature. In addition, also through this paper, we have some contributions about the formal representation of Web service; the bitwise-based Web service indexing method to index the Web service repository using the bitwise operators. This helps the building of the index table as well as the retrieval of Web services more efficient.

As a result, WSCOVER can locate a composition solution faster and more optimally. However, in the future, this effort also needs to be compared with some other techniques, such as the clustering approaches to learn more about the pros and cons of our approach. In addition, in this work, we have not yet considered the semantic aspect of the features of Web services. We are going to develop a mechanism to calculate the similarity between two sets of features when they do not match completely.

Acknowledgements This research is funded by Vietnam National University HoChiMinh City under Grant Number C2015-20-10.

References

1. Yin, R.: Study of composing web service based on soa, In: Proceedings of the 2nd International Conference on Green Communications and Networks 2012 (GCN 2012), vol. 2, pp. 209–214. Springer (2013)
2. Rostami, N. H., Kheirkhah, E., Jalali, M.: Web services composition methods and techniques: a review. Int J Comput Sci Eng Inf Technol 3(6), 15–29 (2013)

3. Fitting, M.: First-order logic. In: First-order logic and automated theorem proving, pp. 97–125. Springer, US (1990)

4. Hatzi, O., Vrakas, D., Bassiliades, N., Anagnostopoulos, D., Vlahavas, I.: The porsce ii framework: using ai planning for automated semantic web service composition. Knowl Eng Rev **28**(02), 137–156 (2013)

5. Chen, M., Tan, T. H., Sun, J., Liu, Y., Dong, J. S.: Veriws: a tool for verification of combined functional and non-functional requirements of web service composition. In: Proceedings of the 36th International Conference on Software Engineering. ACM, pp. 564–567 (2014)

6. Kumara, B.T., Paik, I., Chen, W., Ryu, K.H.: Web service clustering using a hybrid term-similarity measure with ontology learning. Int J Web Serv Res (IJWSR) **11**(2), 24–45 (2014)

7. Du, Y.Y., Zhang, Y.J., Zhang, X.L.: A semantic approach of service clustering and web service discovery. Inf Technol J **12**(5), 967–974 (2013)

8. Aiello, M., Platzer, C., Rosenberg, F., Tran, H., Vasko, M., Dustdar, S.: Web service indexing for efficient retrieval and composition. In: E-Commerce Technology, 2006. The 8th IEEE International Conference on and Enterprise Computing, E-Commerce, and E-Services, The 3rd IEEE International Conference on. IEEE, pp. 63–63 (2006)

9. Czyszczoń, A., Zgrzywa, A.: Indexing method for effective web service retrieval. Int J Intell Inf Database Syst **8**(3), 189–208 (2014)

10. Huynh, K. T., Quan, T. T., Bui, T. H.: Fast and formalized: Heuristics-based on-the-fly web service composition and verification. In: Information and Computer Science (NICS), 2015 2nd National Foundation for Science and Technology Development Conference on. IEEE, pp. 174–179 (2015)

11. Liu, Y., Sun, J., Dong, J. S.: Developing model checkers using PAT. In: International symposium on automated technology for verification and Analysis, pp. 371–377. Springer, Berlin, Heidelberg (2010)

12. Fan, G., Yu, H., Chen, L., Liu, D.: Petri net based techniques for constructing reliable service composition. J Syst Softw **86**(4), 1089–1106 (2013)

13. Maung, Y.W.M., Hein, A.A.: Colored petri-nets (cpn) based model for web services composition. IJCCER **2**, 169–172 (2014)

14. Tian, B., Gu, Y.: Formal modeling and verification for web service composition. J Softw **8**(11), 2733–2737 (2013)

15. Zhou, B., Huang, T., Liu, J., Shen, M.: Using inverted indexing to semantic web service discovery search model. In: Wireless Communications, Networking and Mobile Computing, 2009. WiCom'09. 5th International Conference on. IEEE, pp. 1–4 (2009)

16. AllamehAmiri, M., Derhami, V., Ghasemzadeh, M.: Qos-based web service composition based on genetic algorithm. J AI Data Min **1**(2), 63–73 (2013)

17. Klusch, M.: Owls-tc: Owl-s service retrieval test collection, version 2.1. http://projects.semwebcentral.org/projects/owls-tc/

18. Burstein, M., Hobbs, J., Lassila, O., Mcdermott, D., Mcilraith, S., Narayanan, S., Paolucci, M., Parsia, B., Payne, T., Sirin, E., et al.: Owl-s: Semantic markup for web services. W3C Member Submission (2004)

19. Klusch, M., Gerber, A., Schmidt, M.: Semantic web service composition planning with owls-xplan. In: Proceedings of the AAAI Fall Symposium on Semantic Web and Agents. AAAI Press, USA (2005)

20. Tan, T. H., Chen, M., André, É., Sun, J., Liu, Y., et al.: Automated runtime recovery for qos-based service composition. In: Proceedings of the 23rd international conference on World wide web. International World Wide Web Conferences Steering Committee, pp. 563–574 (2014)

21. Jordan, D., Evdemon, J., Alves et al.: Web services business process execution language version 2.0. OASIS Stand **11**, 10 (2007)

22. Foster, H., Uchitel, S., Magee, J., Kramer, J.: Wsengineer: A model-based approach to engineering web service compositions and choreography. In: Test and analysis of web services, pp. 87–103. Springer, Berlin, Heidelberg (2007)

4

Enhancing the sentence similarity measure by semantic and syntactico-semantic knowledge

Wafa Wali[1] · Bilel Gargouri[1] · Abdelmajid Ben Hamadou[2]

Abstract The measure of sentence similarity is useful in various research fields, such as artificial intelligence, knowledge management, and information retrieval. Several methods have been proposed to measure the sentence similarity based on syntactic and/or semantic knowledge. Most proposals are evaluated on English sentences where the accuracy can decrease when these proposals are applied to other languages. Moreover, the results of these methods are unsatisfactory, as much relevant semantic knowledge, such as semantic class, thematic role and syntactico-semantic knowledge like the semantic predicates, are not taken into account. We must acknowledge that this kind of knowledge is rare in most of the lexical resources. Recently, the International Organization for Standardization (ISO) has published the Lexical Markup Framework (LMF) ISO-24613 norm for the development of lexical resources. This norm provides, for each meaning of a lexical entry, all the semantic and syntactico-semantic knowledge in a fine structure. Profiting from the availability of LMF-standardized dictionaries, we propose, in this paper, a generic method that enhances the measure of sentence similarity by applying semantic and syntactico-semantic knowledge. An experiment was carried out on Arabic, as this language is processed within our research team and an LMF-standardized Arabic dictionary is at hand where the semantic and the syntactico-semantic knowledge are accessible and well structured. Moreover, the experiments yielded better results, showing a high correlation with human ratings.

Keywords Sentence similarity · Lexical semantic knowledge · Syntactico-semantic knowledge · LMF-ISO 24613 · Standardized dictionaries

1 Introduction

The issue of measuring similarity between sentences is crucial in some research fields, such as knowledge management, information retrieval and artificial intelligence. Computing sentence similarity is not a trivial task due to the variability of natural language expressions. In the last few years, sentence similarity measure has been increasingly in demand from a variety of applications and numerous achievements which have been carried out recently in this area and classified into three categories: statistical-based methods, semantic-based methods and hybrid methods. Initially, researchers started with statistical-based methods such as [2] and [14]. These methods compute the sentence similarity by calculating the co-occurring words in a string sequence. However, these methods may not fit to sentences as they may be very similar while co-occurring words are infrequent. To overcome this drawback, other authors proposed the semantic-based methods, such as [12] and [14]. These approaches used the semantic nets, like the WordNet, the vector space model and the statistical corpus to compute the semantic similarity between words using different known measures, such as Leacock and Chodorow [11], Wu and Palmer [22] and Jiang and Conrath [8]. Nevertheless, these semantic-based methods are limited to computing the sentence similarity based only on semantic similarity between words, whereas the syntactic

✉ Wafa Wali
wafa.wali@fsegs.rnu.tn

Bilel Gargouri
bilel.gargouri@fsegs.rnu.tn

Abdelmajid Ben Hamadou
abdelmajid.benhamadou@isimsf.rnu.tn

1 MIR@CL Laboratory FSEGS, Sfax, Tunisia

2 MIR@CL Laboratory ISIMS, Sfax, Tunisia

information and other semantic knowledge, such as semantic class and thematic roles, are missing. To address this weakness, other researchers proposed hybrid methods to compute sentence similarity taking into account both semantic and syntactic knowledge, such as [6,13] and [19]. However, these hybrid methods may have some disadvantages, such that the semantic measurement is isolated from the syntactic measurement in which the semantic similarity is calculated based on word semantic similarity, while string matching, word order and word co-occurring are counted to compute the syntactic similarity. Moreover, the results of these proposals are far away from the aims of a human expert and are evaluated on English databases where accuracy can decrease if they are applied to other languages. Furthermore, some knowledge is not considered in measuring sentence similarities, such as the semantic class, the thematic role and the relationship between syntactic and semantic levels through the semantic predicates. Indeed, when two sentences have the same syntactic structure (subject verb object) but the semantic classes of these objects are dissimilar (i.e., the first is human and the second is vegetal), the pair of these sentences is syntactically similar according to these hybrid methods, whereas in reality both sentences are totally different according to an expert. The semantic class and the thematic role for each argument of a sentence provide knowledge about the relationships between words and perform a role in conveying the meaning of sentences. Besides, the syntactico-semantic knowledge supplied a mechanism for the interaction between the syntactic processor, the discourse model and the real-world knowledge. Furthermore, the semantic predicates favor the creation of coherence in the local discourse structure. Thus, incorporating the semantic and syntactico-semantic knowledge in computation sentence similarity improves the quality of the sentence similarity measure. Unfortunately, there is a lack of linguistic resources that provide such relevant knowledge. Few years ago, the technical committee ISO TC37/SC4 of the International Organization for Standardization (ISO) published the Lexical Markup Framework (LMF) ISO-24613 norm [3]. This norm promotes the construction of large lexical resources in a fine and modular structure. In particular, it provides for each meaning of a lexical entry, the whole semantic and syntactico-semantic knowledge. In this paper, we propose profiting from the available knowledge in LMF standardized dictionaries, notably the semantic and syntactico-semantic knowledge, to enhance the measure of sentence similarity. Our proposal consists of a hybrid method that can be applied to all natural languages. The proposed method is an extension of the existing ones. It measures the semantic similarity via the synonymy relations between words in sentences. Besides, the syntactico-semantic similarity is measured based on the common semantic arguments that are associated with semantic predicates in terms of the thematic role and the semantic class. An experiment was car-

ried out on Arabic, because this language is dealt with within our research team and the existence of an LMF standardized Arabic dictionary in which semantic and syntactico-semantic knowledge can be accessed and well structured. Due to the lack of Arabic suitable benchmarks for the evaluation of sentence similarity, we assess the outcome of our proposal using 690 pairs of Arabic sentences extracted from various definitions and examples of Arabic dictionaries of human use, such as Alwasit, AlMuhit, Lissan Al Arab and Tj-Al-Arous. The results demonstrate that our proposal presents a good performance that approximates to human intuitions.

This paper is organized as follows. First, we present an overview of the existing methods of similarity measures. Section 3 presents the main features of the LMF standard. Our proposed method is described in Sect. 4. Section 5 reports on the experiments and the obtained results. The final section presents the conclusion and recommendations for future works.

2 State of the art

2.1 Overview on the sentences similarity methods

There is extensive literature on measuring the similarity between sentences, which can be grouped into three categories: syntactic-based methods, semantic-based methods, and hybrid methods. In this section, we report only hybrid methods to explore their advantages and limitations.

Li et al. [13] defined a sentence similarity measure as a linear combination of semantic vector similarity and word order similarity. Their proposed method dynamically forms a joint word set only by using all the distinct words in the pairs of sentences. For each sentence, a raw semantic vector is derived with the assistance of the WordNet lexical database [15]. Moreover, a word order vector is formed for each sentence. Since each word in a sentence contributes differently to the meaning of the whole sentence, the significance of a word is weighted by using information content derived from a corpus. By combining the raw semantic vector with information content from the corpus, a semantic vector is obtained for each of the two sentences. Semantic similarity is computed based on the two semantic vectors. An order of similarity is calculated using the two order vectors. Finally, the sentence similarity is derived by combining semantic similarity and order similarity. The relative contribution of semantic and syntactic measures is controlled by an alpha coefficient. It has been empirically proved that a sentence similarity measure performs better when the semantic measure is weighted more than the syntactic one.

Islam and Inkpen [6] determined the similarity between two sentences from semantic and syntactic information (in terms of common word order) that they contain. Indeed, the string similarity is computed using a normalized and modified version of the longest common subsequence (LCS) string matching algorithm. The authors used the longest common subsequence (LCS) measure with some normalization and small modifications for their string similarity measure. They used three different modified versions of LCS. Finally, the sentence similarity is derived by combining the string similarity, the semantic similarity and the common word order. This measure has several inadequacies, particularly, the time complexity of the string matching.

Lee et al. [12] introduced an algorithm to compute the similarity between sentences using semantic and syntactic relationships derived from natural languages. The algorithm proposed a semantic model using the word similarity based on the WordNet and the grammatical rules taking advantage of the Stanford parser.

In addition, [19] proposed the method for computing sentence semantic similarity by exploiting a set of its characteristics, namely features-based measure of sentences semantic similarity (FM3S). The proposed method aggregates in a non-linear function between three components: the noun-based semantic similarity, including compound nouns, the verb-based semantic similarity using the tense information, and the common word order similarity. It measures the semantic similarity between concepts that play the same syntactic role. Concerning the word-based semantic similarity, an information content-based measure is used to estimate the semantic similarity degree between words by exploiting the WordNet is-a taxonomy. The proposed method yielded competitive results compared to the previously proposed measures with regard to Li's benchmark [13], showing a high correlation with human ratings.

However, the hybrid methods presented previously are evaluated on the English databases where accuracy can decrease if these methods are applied to other languages. Besides, in these methods, some semantic knowledge, such as semantic class, thematic role and semantic predicates, are not taken into account in measuring sentence similarity.

In the following section, we will detail the proposed sentence similarity method that takes into account semantic and syntactic–semantic knowledge extracted from LMF-standardized dictionaries [3].

2.2 LMF-ISO 24613 standard

LMF [3] was developed by the technical committee TC 37/SC of the ISO. It was conceived as a generic platform for the specification of lexical structures at any level of linguistic description covering monolingual and multilingual lexicons. The specification of LMF follows the Unified Mod-

eling Language (UML)[1] modeling principles defined by the Object Management Group (OMG).[2] It is composed of core meta-model and lexical extensions. The modeling principles allow a lexical database designer to combine any component of the LMF meta-model with data categories to create an appropriate model. These data categories function as UML attribute–value pairs in the diagrams. The core model covers the backbone of a lexical entry. It specifies the basic concepts of vocabulary, word, form and sense. The LMF core model is a hierarchical structure consisting of several components. The lexical entry is one of the components that represents the basic resource in the lexicon.

Figure 1 shows the principle classes of LMF standardized dictionaries and their appropriate attributes. It focalizes on the lexical entry and its related meaning knowledge and associated syntactical knowledge. We can show in this figure that a lexical entry might contain many meanings (or sense). Each meaning is explained by definitions, examples, a subject field and has some relations (i.e., synonymy, antonymy). Each meaning has other specific semantic knowledge such as the semantic class. Each meaning is attached to the possible syntactic behaviours and semantic predicates. Moreover, several researchers elaborated the LMF dictionaries for many languages. Elmadar[3] is an Arabic lexical resource that conforms to the LMF standard ISO-24613. The model of this dictionary [10] covers all lexical levels: morphological, syntactic, semantic and syntactico-semantic. This dictionary contains about 37,000 lexical entries, among which 10,800 are verbs and 3800 roots.

3 The proposed method

In this section, we are proposing a hybrid method to measure sentence similarity. It consists of an extension of previous methods by considering the most relevant semantic knowledge and the syntactico-semantic knowledge, taking advantage of the LMF standardized dictionaries [21]. The proposed method is composed of three phases, as indicated in Fig. 2, such as preprocessing, similarity score attribution and supervised learning.

3.1 Preprocessing

Most of the content-based detection methods include a preprocessing phase in which stop words are removed and words are reduced to their root forms. In our context, we will not remove the stop words because they can be bearer data.

---

[1] https://www.labri.fr/perso/guibert/DocumentsEnseignement/UML.pdf.

[2] www.omg.org.

[3] http://elmadar.miracl-apps.com/.

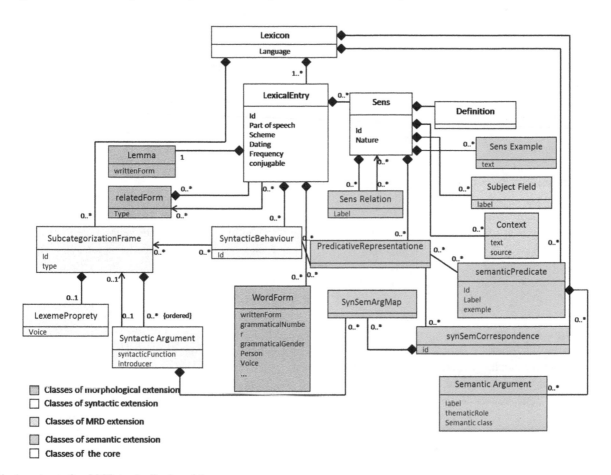

Fig. 1 An extract of an LMF standardized model

Fig. 2 The proposed phases for measuring the similarity between sentences

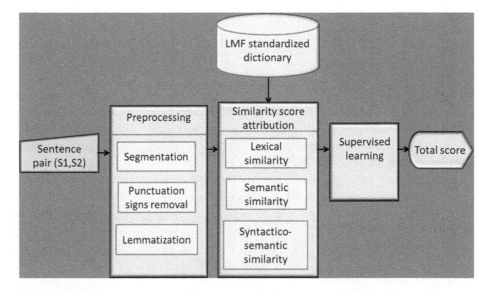

For example, in the sentences S1: "the boy goes to school" and S2: "the boy does not go to school", if we remove the word "not" as a stop word, both sentences become similar, whereas they have contradictory meanings. Besides, we will not reduce the word to its root form, but to its stem form. Indeed, the meaning of the word can be different from that of its root, like in Arabic the word "كتيب -booklet" does not have the same meaning as its root "كتب -write".

The following steps are performed to transform a sentence into a structured and formatted representation, which will be more convenient for the similarity computation process.

- Tokenization: input sentences are broken up into tokens (words).
- Punctuation sign removal: punctuation signs are used in any text. They are considered as unimportant information between sentences. They are removed to get more significant results.
- Lemmatization: morphological variants are reduced to their stem form.

3.2 Similarity scores attribution

We measure three similarity scores as lexical, semantic and syntactico-semantic based on the content of the LMF standardized dictionaries [3].

The score of lexical similarity is computed based on the lexical unit constituting the sentences to extract the lexically similar words.

The lexical similarity score is based on the number of common terms between the sentences. To calculate the score SL(S1,S2), we used Jaccard coefficient [7] that is a fairly quite useful and easy standard to automate the measurement. Thus, the following formula describes how to compute the lexical similarity between sentences.

$$SL(S1,\ S2) = \frac{MC}{MS1 + MS2 - MC},\qquad(1)$$

where:

MC is the number of common words between the sentences S1 and S2,
MS1 is the number of words contained in sentence S1 and
MS2 is the number of words contained in sentence S2.

The score of the semantic similarity is computed by the use of LMF standardized dictionaries [3]. The procedure to compute the semantic similarity consists, firstly, in forming a joint word set using only the distinct stems in the pair of sentences. For each sentence, a raw semantic vector is derived and enriched using the LMF standardized dictionary

[3]. Indeed, each sentence is readily represented by the use of the joint word set as follows: The vector derived from the joint word set is denoted T. Each entry of the semantic vector corresponds to a stem in the joint word set, so the dimension equals the number of stems in the joint word set. The value of an entry of the lexical semantic vector, Ti ($i = 1, 2, m$), is determined by the semantic similarity of the word corresponding to a word in the sentence. Given that Wi is the word of the joint word set,

Case 1: if Wi appears in the sentence, then Ti is set to 1.
Case 2: if Wi is not contained in the sentence, then a semantic similarity score is computed between Wi and each word in the sentence using the synonymy relations of LMF standardized dictionary (extracted from Sense Relation class). Thus, the most similar word to Wi in sentence is the one with the highest similarity score θ, then Ti is set to θ.

The process of semantic similarity detection is presented in Fig. 3.

In fact, the LMF normalized dictionary model defines many types of semantic relationships (e.g., synonymy, antonymy, etc.) between the meanings of two or several lexical entries by means of the Sense Relation class. Given two words W1 and W2, we need to find the semantic similarity Sim(W1,W2). We can do this by analyzing the synonymy relations between the senses of words as follows: words are linked by a semantic relationship in the LMF standardized dictionary and with relation pointers to other synsets. One direct method for word similarity calculation is to find the synonymy set of each word so as to detect the common synonyms between the two words. For example, the common synonyms between the words "stable" and "constant" are "steady" and "firm", as the synonyms of "stable" are steady, constant, enduring, firm, stabile, while the synonyms of "constant" are steady, abiding, firm, perpetual, hourly.

Once the two sets of synonyms for each word are collected, we calculate the degree of similarity between them using the Jaccard coefficient [7]:

Fig. 3 Semantic similarity computation diagram

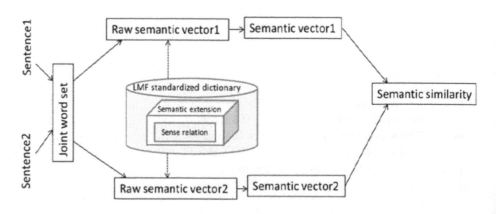

$$\text{Sim}(W1, W2) = \frac{MC}{MW1} + MW2 - MC, \qquad (2)$$

where:

MC is the number of common words between the two synonym sets,

MW1 is the number of words contained in the w1 synonym set and

MW2 is the number of words contained in the w2 synonym set. From the generated semantic vectors, as described above, we compute the semantic similarity score, which we call SM(S1, S2), between them, using the Cosine similarity [18].

$$\text{SM}(S1, S2) = \frac{V1.V2}{||V1||.||V2||}, \qquad (3)$$

where:

V1 is the semantic vector of sentence S1 and

V2 is the semantic vector of sentence S2. Semantic knowledge and especially semantic arguments, which aim at characterizing the meanings of lexical units in sentences, have attracted considerable interest in both linguistic and computational linguistic domains. Such semantic arguments can be defined as a semantic linguistic property that can be used as a valuable means of comprehending the specific meaning of a sentence. Moreover, the semantic argument is characterized by the semantic class and the thematic role that provides information about the relationships between words and provides a mechanism of interaction among the syntactic processors. The thematic role refers to a semantic relationship between a predicate and its arguments. For example, the thematic role, "the broom-handle" is different in a sentence

S1: "He banged the broom-handle on the ceiling", and S2: "He banged the ceiling with the broom-handle", because it presents an object in S1 and an instrument in S2. Likewise, the semantic argument "the ceiling" plays the role of a location in S1 and an object in S2.

In our method, these bits of knowledge are extracted from the semantic argument class of LMF normalized dictionary that are associated with a semantic predicate and linked to an appropriate syntactic behaviour.

To calculate the syntactico-semantic similarity, we have first proceeded to extract the proprieties of the semantic arguments of each sentence from LMF dictionary [3]. Therefore, we have used, on the one hand, a syntactic parser to determine the syntactic behaviour of the sentences, and on the other hand, with the help of an expert, the semantic predicates are determined. Then, in the LMF-standardized dictionary, we have looked for the meanings of the lexical entry (verb of the sentence), the predicative representation that combines the syntactic behaviour and the semantic predicate predefined in the first step. Once the predicative representation is found, we extract the semantic arguments. The pairs of the semantic arguments are considered similar if they have the same attributes like the thematic role and the semantic class. The process that describes the determining of semantic class and the thematic role of each sentence argument is presented in Fig. 4.

Afterward, we calculate the degree of syntactico-semantic similarity between the two sentences, S1 and S2, from the common semantic arguments between the pair of sentences, which we call SSM(S1,S2), using the Jaccard coefficient [7]:

$$\text{SSM}(S1, S2) = \frac{ASC}{ASS1 + ASS2 - ASC}, \qquad (4)$$

Fig. 4 Determination diagram semantic argument properties

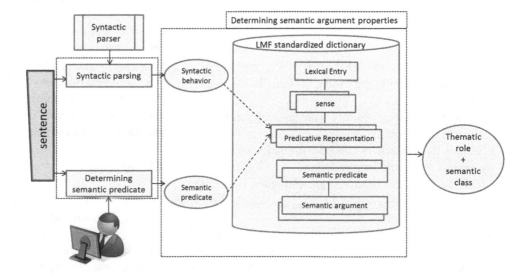

where:

ASC is the number of common semantic arguments between the two sentences,

ASS1 is the number of semantic arguments contained in sentence S1 and

ASS2 is the number of semantic arguments contained in sentence S2.

3.3 Supervised learning

We propose using supervised learning to define the appropriate coefficients of the similarity scores described below [20]. In this context, the aim is to apply, in the first time a hyperplane equation (decision boundary, such as similar or not similar) on sentences S1 and S2, and deduct a total score similarity "Sim (S1,S2)" in the second time. The total score similarity "Sim (S1,S2)" aggregates the lexical, semantic and syntactico-semantic scores. The process of determining the suitable coefficients includes two phases: the first is the training phase that aims at getting a hyperplane equation via the learning algorithm, such as supervised vector machine (SVM). The second is the test phase that validates the generated equation (hyperplane equation) by the cross-validation method. In the training phase, we first prepare the extraction vectors "V" where each vector describes a pair of sentences "S1" and "S2". Generally, any vector "Vi" is described by the collection of lexical (SL), semantic (SM) and syntactico-semantic similarity (SSM) scores. Each vector "Vi" is completed by a Boolean criterion, namely D. This criterion class is determined by an expert who decides whether the pair of sentences is similar or not. However, the repetition of a number of identical vectors and other contradiction is possible. The extraction vector "Vi" is defined as follows:

Vi (SL, SM, SSM, Di),

where:

Vi is the vector extracting the pair of sentences,

SL is the lexical similarity score between the elements of a pair of sentences,

SM is the semantic similarity score between the elements of a pair of sentences,

SSM is the syntactico-semantic similarity between the elements of a pair of sentences and

Di is the Boolean criterion representing the class of the similar or dissimilar vector Vi .

Then, the SVM learning algorithm is applied to the generated extraction vectors to have an optimal hyperplane that separates two classes (similar and not similar). Indeed, the use of

the standard SVM learning algorithms was limited to a group of researchers as these algorithms were long and difficult to implement.

Platt [17] developed a learning algorithm called SMO, "sequential minimal optimization" that can quickly solve the problem of quadratic optimization (QP). This algorithm is usually faster and easier to implement and requires a reduced memory space [9]. The classification equation defined by SMO function is presented as follows:

$$\mathrm{Sim}(S1, S2) = \alpha * SL + \beta * SM + \gamma * SSM + C, \qquad (5)$$

where

α is the weight attributed to lexical similarity,

β is the weight attributed to semantic similarity,

γ is the weight attributed to syntactico-semantic similarity and

C is constant.

The test phase consists in validating the classification equation generated in the training phase by the cross-validation method. Indeed, this cross-validation method is a model validation technique of assessing how the results of a statistical analysis generalize to an independent data set.

After the computing process of the sentence similarity score, the similarity class is detected as follows:

If Sim (S1, S2)$\geq$ threshold, then the sentences are similar. If Sim (S1, S2) < threshold, then the sentences are not similar.

4 Experiments and results

Experiments use on the one hand the LMF standardized Arabic dictionary [10] as a resource to exploit [10] the synonymy of words and properties of semantic arguments (semantic class and thematic role)and, on the other hand, the Stanford Parser [4], the MADAMIRA tool [16] to reduce words to their stem or lemma by removing the suffix, the prefix. After that, they match the remaining word with verbal or noun patterns and the Weka software package [5] to find out the optimal parameters in the learning phase.

4.1 The databases

There are currently no suitable Arabic benchmark data sets (or even standard text sets) for the evaluation of sentence (or a very short text) similarity methods. Building such a data set is not a trivial task due to subjectivity in the interpretation of a language, which is in part due to the lack of deeper contextual information. To evaluate our similarity measure, a preliminary data set of sentence pairs is constructed with human similarity scores provided by five participants. Indeed, each participant is asked to rate the sentences on the scale 0.0–4.0 according to the similarity of the meaning.

These sentences consist of dictionary definitions and examples of words. Then, a further data set of sentences is produced from the Arabic dictionaries for human use such as Lissan Al-Arab, Al-Wassit, Al-Muhit and Tj Al-Arous. Our selection is composed of 690 pairs of sentences as indicated in Table 1.

Table 1 Data sets used in the evaluation of sentence similarity measure

Dataset	#Pairs
Lissan Al-Arab	480
Al-Wassit	266
Al-Muhit	178
Tj Al-Arous	456

4.2 An experiment with human similarities of Arabic sentence pairs

The participants were asked to complete the rating similarity of the sentence pairs on the scale from 0.0 (minimum similarity) to 4.0 (maximum similarity). A rubric containing linguistic anchors was provided for the five major scale points 0.0 (the sentences are unrelated in meaning), 1.0 (the sentences are vaguely similar in meaning), 2.0 (the sentences are very much alike in meaning.), 3.0 (the sentences are strongly related in meaning) and 4.0 (the sentences are identical in meaning). The values are taken from a study by Charles [1], which yielded psychometric properties analogous to an interval scale. The use of the linguistic anchors reconciles these wise conflicting requirements. Each of the 690 sentence pairs was assigned a sentence similarity score calculated as the mean of the judgements made by the experts. Table 2 presents a comparison of our similarity measure with the all human

Table 2 Arabic sentence data set results

Arabic sentence	English translation	Human similarity (mean)	Our proposed method
كتب الله النجاة للمريض	God decreed the patient's survival	0.7	0.75
كتب الله الشفاء للمريض	God decreed the patient's healing		
خط المتسول الطعام	The beggar took the food	0.6	0.75
خط المتسول في الطعام	The beggar took in the food		
أحس بالوجع	I feel pain	0.5	0.5
أحس بألم في بطني	I have an ache in my belly		
حلاء فلانا درهما	He gave a person the money	0.7	0.75
حلاءه درهما	He gave the money to him		
كتب له الأرض	He wrote him the ground	0.3	0.25
كتب له رسالة	He wrote him a letter		
أغمط المطر	The rain continues	0.4	0.25
أغمطت السماء بالمطر	The sky continues with the rain		
شجرة رفيقة	Shelving tree	1	1
شجر رفيف	Shelving trees		
حقنته المرضة إبرة	The nurse gave an injection	0.45	0.5
حقنت المرضة المريض بلئبرة	The nurse gave the patient an injection		
أبعده الله	God kept him away	0	0
لا أبعده الله	God did not keep him away		
أمحن أعداءه	He weakened his enemies	0.3	0.5
أمحن في عدوه	He weakened his enemies with wounds		

similarity scores provided as the score mean for each pair and scaled into the range [0,1].

Furthermore, the weight to lexical similarity "SL(S1,S2)" is 0.2, the weight to semantic similarity "SM(S1,S2)" is 0.35 and the weight to syntactico-semantic similarity "SSM(S1,S2)" is 0.45 in the total similarity score between sentences "Sim (S1,S2)". Two sentences are considered similar if the total similarity score "Sim (S1,S2)" is superior to 0.85.

4.3 Results and discussion

To evaluate our sentence similarity measure, we used the correlation coefficient to link the scores computed by a measure to the judgements provided by humans in the database. The Pearson correlation coefficient r can be used as a metric evaluation. It indicates how well the results of a measure are similar to human judgements, where a value 0 means no correlation and 1 means perfect correlation. Pearson r is computed as follows:

$$r = \frac{n\left(\sum x_i y_i\right) - \left(\sum x_i\right)\left(\sum y_i\right)}{\sqrt{n\left(\sum x_i^2\right)\left(\sum x_i\right)^2}\sqrt{n\left(\sum y_i^2\right)\left(\sum y_i\right)^2}}, \quad (6)$$

where x_i refers to the ith element in the list of human judgements, y_i refers to the corresponding ith element in the list of sentence similarity computed by our proposed measure and n is the number of sentence pairs.

Our sentence similarity measure achieved a reasonably good Pearson correlation coefficient of 0.92, with the human ratings significant at the 0.01 level. In Table 3, we present the results that have calculated the correlation coefficient r for the judgements for each participant against the rest of the group and then kept the means.

The evaluation of our proposal is achieved following the cross-validation method and using the Weka tool. To realize this, we divided the training corpus into two distinct parts, one for learning (80 %) and one for testing (20 %). The results are given in Table 4.

The obtained results are encouraging and represent a good start to implement automatic learning in measuring sentence similarity in Arabic. We noticed that the analysis of short sentences ($\leq$10 words) presents the highest measures of recall and precision. As the sentence gets longer, there will be a more complex computation, which reduces the system performance. We believe that these results can be improved. In fact, we think that we can improve the learning stage by adding other features besides the semantic argument and synonymy senses. As an example of additional features, we can incorporate other types of relations, such as hyponymy. We will explore the effects of the integration of phrase functions in the learning phase. During the implementation of

Table 3 Similarity correlations

	Correlation r
Our proposed measure	0.92
Mean of all participants	0.938
Worst participant	0.73
Best participant	0.947

Table 4 Evaluation results

Precision (%)	Recall (%)	F-score (%)
88.12	83.24	85.61

our system, we noticed that the bigger the number of sentences, the higher are the recall and precision. Therefore, we believe that the enrichment of our database of Arabic sentences can significantly enhance the results. In addition, the performance of our system depends on the lemmatizer system, syntactical parser, synonyms and semantic predicates retrieved from the Arabic LMF dictionary [10]. According to a comparative evaluation study of Arabic language stemmers and syntactical parsers, MADAMIRA [16] and the Stanford parser [4] achieved the highest accuracy. Consequently, we do not expect to increase the performance of our proposed measure using other lemmatizers or syntactical parsers.

5 Conclusion

Sentence similarity measures are an old and valuable area for various applications. However, they have not considered some relevant semantic knowledge, such as, the thematic role, the semantic class and syntactico-semantic knowledge like the semantic predicate in computing the sentence similarity. In this paper, we proposed a method to extend the previous methods by enhancing the similarity measure between sentences with the semantic and syntactico-semantic knowledge profiting from the LMF standardized dictionaries. In fact, a standardized LMF dictionary is a finely structured source, rich in lexical, semantic and syntactic knowledge. Our method consists of three stages. It starts with preprocessing the sentence pairs; then it proceeds by attribution the following similarity scores lexical, semantic and syntactico-semantic, and finally ends with computation total score using supervised learning. Besides, the proposed method is proven to be reliable despite the illustrations carried out on the Arabic language, the choice of which is explained by three main motives. The first one is the great deficiency of works on the Arabic language measuring sentence similarity; the second is the processing within our research team of the Arabic language; and the third an LMF standardized Arabic dictionary is at hand where the syntactico-semantic component is available and well structured. Additionally, we evaluate our proposal on 690 pairs of sentences taken from various definitions and examples of Arabic dictionaries. In fact, we reached a good correlation $r = 0.92$ for the formed Arabic data set close to human judgements. As perspectives of our work, we aim to extend our sentence similarity measure in enriching the Arabic dataset by including other kinds of semantic relations, such as hyponymy. Finally, we propose to apply our method to other languages.

References

1. Charles, W.G.: Contextual correlates of meaning. Appl. Psycholinguist. **21**, 505–524 (2000)
2. Chatterjee, N. A.: Statistical approach for similarity measurement between sentences for EBMT. In: Proceedings STRANS-2001, IT Kanpur, pp. 122–1318 (2001)
3. Francopoulo, G.: LMF Lexical Markup Framework. ISBN: 978-1-84821-430-9. Wiley, New York, 288 pages (2013)
4. Green, S., Manning, C.D: Better arabic parsing: baselines, evaluations, and analysis. In: Proceedings of the 23rd International Conference on Computational Linguistics, Association for Computational Linguistics, pp. 394–402 (2010)
5. Hall, M., Frank, E., Holmes, G., Pfahringer, B., Reutemann, P., Witten, I.H.: The WEKA data mining software: an update. ACM SIGKDD Explorations Newsletter **11**(1), 10–18 (2009)
6. Islam, A., Inkpen, D.: Semantic text similarity using corpus-based word similarity and string similarity. ACM Trans Knowl Discov Data TKDD **2**(2), 10 (2008)
7. Jaccard, P.: Etude comparative de la distribution florale dans une portion des Alpes et du Jura. Impr, Corbaz (1901)
8. Jiang, J.J., Conrath, D.W.: Semantic similarity based on corpus statistics and lexical taxonomy. cmp-lg (1997)
9. Keerthi, S.S., Shevade, S.K., Bhattacharyya, C., Murthy, K.R.K.: Improvements to Platt's SMO algorithm for SVM classifier design. Neural Comput. **13**(3), 637–649 (2001)
10. Khemakhem, A., Gargouri, B., Hamadou, A.B., Francopoulo, G.: ISO standard modeling of a large arabic dictionary. Natural Language Engineering, pp. 1–31 (2016). doi: 10.1017/S1351324915000224
11. Leaock, C., Chodorow, M., Miller G.: Combining local context andwordnet similarity forword sense identification. In: Fellbaum, C. (ed.) WordNet. An Electronic Lexical Database, pp. 265–283. MIT Press, Cambridge (1998)
12. Lee, C.M., Chang, J.W., Hsieh, T.C., Chen, H.H., Chen, C.H.: Similarity measure based on semantic patterns. Adv. Inf. Sci. Serv. Sci. AISS **4**(18), 10 (2012)
13. Li, Y., Mclean, D., Bandar, Z.A., O'Shea, J.D., Crockett, K.: Sentence similarity based on semantic nets and corpus statistics. IEEE Trans Knowl Data Eng **18**(8), 1138–1150 (2006)
14. Mandreoli, F., Martoglia, R., Tiberio, P.: A syntactic approach for searching similarities within sentences. In: Proceedings of the Eleventh International Conference on Information and Knowledge Management, CIKM '02, ACM, New York, pp. 635–637. (2002)
15. Miller, G.A., Beckwith, R., Fellbaum, C., Gross, D., Miller, K.J.: Introduction to wordnet: an on-line lexical database. Int. J. Lexicogr. **3**(4), 235–244 (1990)
16. Pasha, A., Al-Badrashiny, M., Diab, M.T., El Kholy, A., Eskander, R., Habash, N., Pooleery, M., Rambow, O., Roth, R.: Madamira: a fast, comprehensive tool for morphological analysis and disambiguation of Arabic. LREC **14**, 1094–1101 (2014)
17. Platt, J.C.: 12 fast training of support vector machines using sequential minimal optimization. Adv. Kernel Methods, pp. 185–208 (1999)
18. Salton, G.: Automatic information organization and retrieval. McGraw Hill, New York (1968)
19. Taieb, M.A.H., Aouicha, M.B., Bourouis, Y.: Fm3s: features-based measure of sentences semantic similarity. In: Hybrid Artificial Intelligent Systems, pp. 515–529. Springer, Heidelberg (2015)
20. Wali, W., Gargouri, B., et al. Supervised learning to measure the semantic similarity between Arabic sentences. In: Computational Collective Intelligence, pp. 158–167. Springer, Heidelberg (2015)
21. Wali, W., Gargouri, B., Hamadou, A.B.: Using standardized lexical semantic knowledge to measure similarity. In: Knowledge Science, Engineering and Management, pp. 93–104. Springer, Heidelberg (2014)
22. Wu, Z., Palmer, M.: Verbs semantics and lexical selection. In: Proceedings of the 32nd annual meeting on Association for Computational Linguistics, pp. 133–138. Association for Computational Linguistics (1994)

## 5

An HVS-inspired video deinterlacer based on visual saliency

Umang Aggarwal[1] · Maria Trocan[1] · Francois-Xavier Coudoux[2]

Abstract Video deinterlacing is a technique wherein the interlaced video format is converted into progressive scan format for nowadays display devices. In this paper, a spatial saliency-guided motion-compensated deinterlacing method is proposed which accounts for the properties of the Human Visual System (HVS): our algorithm classifies the field according to its texture and viewer's region of interest and adapts the motion estimation and compensation, as well as the saliency-guided interpolation to ensure high-quality frame reconstruction. Two different saliency models, namely the graph-based visual saliency (GBVS) model and the spectral residual visual saliency (SRVS) model, have been studied and compared in terms of visual quality performances as well as computational complexity. The experimental results on a great variety of video test sequences show significant improvement of reconstructed video quality with the GBVS-based proposed method compared to classical motion-compensated and adaptive deinterlacing techniques, with up to 4.5 dB gains in terms of PSNR. Simulations also show that the SRVS-based deinterlacing process can result to significant reductions of complexity (up to 25 times a decrease of the computation time compared with the GBVS-based method) at the expense of a PSNR decrease.

Keywords Deinterlacing · Visual saliency · Human visual system (HVS) · Video quality

✉ Maria Trocan
maria.trocan@isep.fr

Francois-Xavier Coudoux
francois-xavier.coudoux@univ-valenciennes.fr

[1] Institut Superieur d'Electronique de Paris, 28 Rue Notre Dame des Champs, Paris, France

[2] IEMN (UMR CNRS 8520) Department OAE, Valenciennes University, 59313 Valenciennes Cedex 9, France

1 Introduction

The process of deinterlacing involves converting a stream of interlaced frames within a video sequence to progressive frames [1], to ensure their playback on nowadays progressive devices. Such video processing has been widely studied in the recent literature [2–8], as the interlaced video format is still preferred for the acquisition systems when high-fidelity motion accuracy is needed. Deinterlacing requires the display device to buffer one or more fields and recombine them to a full progressive frame. There are various methods to deinterlace a video and each method produces its own artifacts, due to the temporal lack of information and the dynamics of the video sequence.

Spatial deinterlacers [2,4,7,9] use the information from the current field to interpolate the missing field lines. The most common types of spatial deinterlacing methods are line averaging and directional spatial interpolation. Edge-based line averaging is done by interpolation along the edge direction, by comparing the gradients of various directions. The interpolation accuracy of edge-based line averaging is increased by an efficient estimation of the directional spatial correlations of neighboring pixels. Usually, the spatial deinterlacing methods have low computational power.

However, one disadvantage of spatial deinterlacing is that this class of methods is not optimal due to the fact that motion activity is not considered in interpolation; moreover, these kind of algorithms fail to remove the flickering artifacts.

Motion adaptive methods, such the ones proposed in [5,6,8], use consecutive fields to analyze the characteristics of motion in order to choose the appropriate interpolation scheme. In such deinterlacers, dynamic areas are interpolated spatially and the static segments are interpolated temporally. The best class of deinterlacers is given by the motion-compensated ones [3,10]. In these schemes, the motion trajectory is estimated and the interpolation of the missing fields is done along the motion flow. However, motion-compensated deinterlacers need massive computational resources. To reduce their complexity, block-based motion estimation is used at the expense of blocking artifacts and some unreliable motion information [11], which severely degrades the visual quality of the reconstructed video sequences.

A single-field interpolation algorithm based on blockwise autoregression that considers mutual influence between the missing high-resolution pixels and the given interlaced, low-resolution pixels in a slip window is introduced in [4]. A method to use different interpolation techniques based on classification of each missing pixel into two categories according to different local region gradient features is discussed in [5]. Further, a statistical-based approach which uses Bayes theory to model the residual of the images as Gaussian and Laplacian distribution can be used to estimate the missing pixels in [6]. To improve the accuracy of motion vectors for video deinterlacing by selectively using optical flow results, for assisting the block-based motion estimation is proposed in [12], at a high computational cost. The computational load of block-based compensation can be reduced using predictive area search algorithms, which estimate the motion vectors (MV) of the current block using the MVs of previous blocks [13]. Neural networks and fuzzy logic can also be used as deinterlacing solutions. A way to exploit fuzzy reasoning to reinforce contours for improving an edge-adaptive deinterlacing algorithm without an excessive increase in computational complexity is discussed in [14]. Another approach for fuzzy logic deinterlacing is to use a fuzzy-bilateral filtering method which considers the range and domain filters based on a fuzzy metric [2,8].

In this paper, in order to reduce the blocking artifacts hence improving the Quality of Experience (QoE) of human viewers, we propose to use the block-based motion estimation on smooth areas, while on highly textured areas optical flow based pixel velocity is used [15] because this method is free of blocking effect. For improving the frame reconstruction quality, visual saliency-guided interpolation of the estimated temporal field is used. The use of visual saliency [16] as trigger for the spatio-temporal interpolator has two advantages: for non-salient regions, no motion estimation is performed, the areas being spatially interpolated, hence highly reducing the proposed deinterlacer complexity.

The second advantage is the corollary of the first one: the computing resources, translated mainly into the motion estimation process, can be used entirely on the region-of-interest area.

In the sequel, the paper is organized as follows: Sect. 2 first introduces the notion of visual saliency and present some existing saliency models. In particular, a focus is made on the graph-based visual saliency (GBVS) model that outperforms the reference model, as well as the spectral residual visual saliency (SRVS) model. Then, Sect. 3 describes the proposed saliency spatio-temporal video deinterlacing method. Some experimental results obtained with the proposed method for different video sequences are presented in Sect. 4. A comparison between deinterlacing processes using different saliency models is also proposed. Simulation results are presented and discussed. Finally, conclusions are drawn in Sect. 5.

2 Visual saliency

Visual saliency is defined in [17] as *the distinct subjective perceptual quality which makes some items in the world stand out from their neighbors and immediately grab our attention*. The visual saliency process allows a human observer to specifically focus her/his attention on one or more visual stimuli into a scene depending on some semantic features like orientation, motion or color.

It constitutes one of the most important properties of the human visual system (HVS) with numerous applications in digital imaging applications including content-aware video coding, segmentation or image resizing [18,19]. To model human visual attention, several visual saliency models have been recently proposed in the literature [20–22]. Generally, these models allow computing a so-called visual saliency map as a topographically arranged map that represents visually salient parts, also called regions of interest (ROI), of a visual scene. Among the different existing saliency models, the one proposed by Itti et al. [17,23] is the most popular.

The Itti algorithm exploits three low-level semantic features of an image: color, orientation and intensity. These features are extracted from the image to establish feature maps. Finally, the saliency map is computed from these feature maps after normalization and pooling.

In [16], the authors propose a Graph-Based Visual Saliency (GBVS) model which improves the model developed by Itti et al. The GBVS model relies on a fully connected graph between feature maps at multiple spatial scales. It is shown that the GBVS model outperforms the Itti model in predicting human visual attention while viewing natural images. However, the computational complexity of the GBVS model constitutes a significant drawback for deinterlacing implementation purposes. Hence, other low-complex saliency models have been considered to replace the GBVS one.

Among these, we retain the so-called spectral residual visual saliency (SRVS) model described in [10,15]. Figure 1 represents the flowchart of the spectral residual saliency model's computation. The model relies on spectral residual saliency detection. Spectral residual saliency detection is an approach developed in computer vision to simulate the behavior of pre-attentive visual search. Different from

Fig. 1 Flowchart diagram of
the spectral saliency model

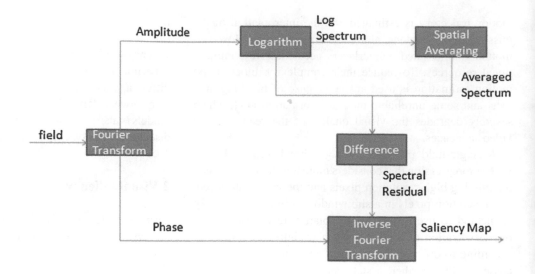

traditional image statistical models, it analyzes the log spectrum of each image of the video sequence and estimates the corresponding spectral residual. Then, the spectral residual is transformed to the spatial domain to obtain the saliency map. This method explores the properties of the background areas, rather than the target objects. The procedure can be detailed as follows.

Given the luminance component (Y) of a field, the amplitude spectrum noted $A(f)$ and the phase spectrum noted $P(f)$ are first evaluated as the real and the imaginary part of the two-dimensional Fourier transform of the luminance component, respectively:

$$A(f) = \sqrt{\text{Re}[F(Y)]^2 + \text{Im}[F(Y)]^2} \tag{1}$$

$$P(f) = \tan^{-1} \frac{\text{Im}\,[F(Y)]}{\text{Re}\,[F(Y)]} \tag{2}$$

where F represents the Fourier transform. The log spectrum $L(f)$ is then obtained by:

$$L(f) = \log[A(f)] \tag{3}$$

The average spectrum can be approximated by convoluting the log spectrum with a matrix $h_n(f)$:

$$A_s(f) = h_n(f) * L(f) \tag{4}$$

where $h_n(f)$ is a $n x n$ unit matrix with all entries equal to $1/n^2$.

Finally, the spectral residual $R(f)$ consists in the statistical singularities specific to the input image and is obtained, for each frame of a video sequence, as the difference between the log spectrum and the averaged spectrum, respectively:

$$R(f) = L(f) - A_s(f) \tag{5}$$

Spectral residual is then converted to the saliency map $S(x)$ using inverse two-dimensional Fourier transform. The resulting saliency map contains primarily the non-trivial part of the visual scene. The value at each point in a saliency map is squared to indicate the estimation error. For better visual effects, the saliency map is traditionally smoothed with a Gaussian filter $g(x)$ with typical variance of 8:

$$S(x) = g(x) * F^{-1}\left[\exp(P(f) + R(f))^2\right]. \tag{6}$$

3 Saliency-based deinterlacing

The flowchart of the proposed algorithm is depicted in Fig. 2. As the field interpolation model depends on the saliency map, the first step of our algorithm is given by the computation of the spatial saliency of the current field to the deinterlaced. To compute the so-called saliency map, the two models described in the Sect. 2 have been considered: the GBVS model proposed in [16], and the spectral saliency model. The obtained saliency map denoted in the followings by S (i.e., depicted in Fig. 3 in the case of the GBVS model) and consisting of gray values $S(i, j) \in \{0 \dots 255\}$ will trigger, along with the texture type, the interpolation used for the current field. Equally, a Canny edge detector is applied on the current field and the edges mask C is obtained.

Further, the current field is partitioned into blocks of fixed size B^2, each block being categorized depending on its belonging to the salient region, as follows: the block b_n of size B^2 is said to be salient/important, i.e.:

$$S_{b_n} = \Sigma_{i=1}^{B} \Sigma_{j=1}^{B} s_n(i, j)/B^2 \tag{7}$$

if the mean S_{b_n} of the entire collocated block s_n within the saliency map S is higher than a given threshold T_s; otherwise, the block is classified as smooth.

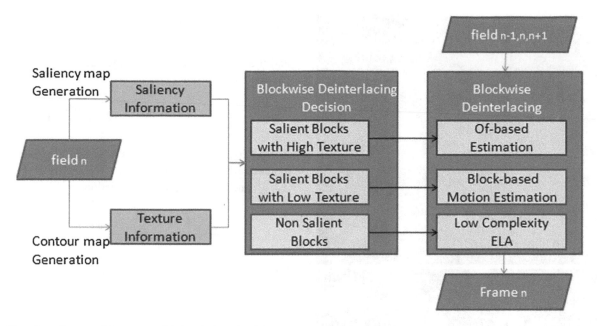

Fig. 2 Flowchart diagram of the proposed deinterlacing algorithm

Also, for each block b_n belonging to the current field f_n, its number of edges is derived as in Eq. (8), by counting the amount of pixels on contours in the collocated block c_n in the mask field C, obtained with the Canny filter:

$$CE_{b_n} = \Sigma_{i=1}^{B} \Sigma_{j=1}^{B} c_n(i, j) \qquad (8)$$

where, CE_{b_n} is the number of identified edges in block b_n. The block b_n is classified as highly textured if CE_{b_n} is significant with respect to the blocksize B^2, i.e.:

$$CE_{b_n} > T_b \qquad (9)$$

(T_b is a threshold depending on B^2), or smooth, if Eq. (9) does not hold.

If the block b_n belongs to a salient region and its number of contours is significant (as in Eq. 9), optical flow-based motion estimation is implemented; otherwise, we use block-based estimation.

If the block b_n is determined as not belonging to a salient region, simple spatial 5-tap edge-line averaging techniques (Fig. 4) are used to obtain the deinterlaced block $\hat{b}_n(i, j)$, i.e.:

$$\hat{b}_n(i, j) = \frac{b_n(i - 1, j + x_0) + b_n(i + 1, j - x_0)}{2}, \qquad (10)$$

where the exact value of x_0 is given by the minimization:

$$|b_n(i - 1, j + x_0) - b_n(i + 1, j - x_0)|$$
$$= \min_{x_0 \in \{-2, -1, 0, 1, 2\}} |b_n(i - 1, j + x_0) - b_n(i + 1, j - x_0)|. \qquad (11)$$

For the salient blocks, the motion vectors (MV) are obtained on the backward and forward directions for the current field, and applying either OF-based estimation proposed by Liu in [5], or simple block-based ME.

We assume that the motion trajectory is linear; so, the obtained forward motion vectors (MVs) are split into backward (MVB) and forward (MVF) motion vector fields for the current field f_n. As a block in f_n could have zero or more than one MVs passing through, the corresponding MV_n for the block $b_n \in f_n$ is obtained by the minimization of the Euclidean distance between b_n's center, $(y_{n,0}, x_{n,0})$, and the passing vectors MVs. In our minimization, we consider only the MVs obtained for the blocks in the neighborhood of the collocated block b_{n-1} in the left field f_{n-1} (thus, a total of nine MVs, obtained for b_{n-1} and the blocks adjacent to $b_{n-1} \in f_{n-1}$, as these MVs are supposed to be the most correlated to the one in the current block, e.g., belonging to the same motion object).

If the motion vector MV corresponding to the collocated block $b_{n-1} \in f_{n-1}$ lies on the line:

$$\frac{y - y_{n-1,0}}{MV_y} = \frac{x - x_{n-1,0}}{MV_x} \qquad (12)$$

where $(y_{n-1,0}, x_{n-1,0})$ is the center of b_{n-1}; and MV_x, respectively, MV_y, measures the displacement along the x, respectively, y axis; the distances from the center $(y_{n,0}, x_{n,0})$ of the current block b_n to the MVs lines are obtained as:

Fig. 3 Saliency map obtained for (**a**) 10th frame of "Foreman" sequence, (**b**) 21st frame of "Salesman" sequence

$$D_{k \in \{1,\ldots,9\}} = \frac{\left| MV_{k,x} y_{n,0} - MV_{k,y} x_{n,0} + MV_{k,y} x_{n-1,k} - MV_{k,x} y_{n-1,k} \right|}{\sqrt{MV_{k,x}^2 + MV_{k,y}^2}}.$$

$$(13)$$

MV^n is the closest motion vector to the current block b_n, if its corresponding distance to the center of b_n, $(y_{n,0}, x_{n,0})$, is minimal, i.e., $D_n = min(D_{k \in \{1,\ldots,9\}})$. Hence, MV^n is generated for each block, containing the motion estimation in the x and y directions for every pixel.

The forward and backward MVs for each block are obtained as:

$$MV_B^n = \frac{-MV^n}{2}, \quad MV_F^n = \frac{MV^n}{2}. \tag{14}$$

The backward prediction of b_n, denoted by $\mathcal{F}_{MV_B}^n$, is obtained as:

$$\mathcal{F}_{MV_B}^n(i, j) = b_{n-1}\left(i + MV_{By}^n, j + MV_{Bx}^n\right), \tag{15}$$

and the forward prediction of the current block, $\mathcal{F}_{MV_F}^n$, is obtained as:

$$\mathcal{F}_{MV_F}^n(i, j) = b_{n+1}\left(i + MV_{Fy}^n, j + MV_{Fx}^n\right), \tag{16}$$

The motion-compensated block $\hat{b}^n$ to be further used for the deinterlacing of b_n is obtained as average of the backward, $\mathcal{F}_{MV_B}^n$, and forward, $\mathcal{F}_{MV_F}^n$, predictions:

$$\hat{b}^n(i, j) = \frac{\mathcal{F}_{MV_B}^n(i, j) + \mathcal{F}_{MV_B}^n(i, j)}{2}. \tag{17}$$

Finally, the deinterlaced block is found in a saliency-based motion-compensated manner, as:

$$\hat{b}_n(i, j) = \frac{b_n(i - 1, j + x_0) + b_n(i + 1, j - x_0) + s_n(i, j)\hat{b}^n(i, j)}{s_n(i, j) + 2},$$

$$(18)$$

s_n being the corresponding saliency value within the saliency map S, acting as a weight for the motion-compensated interpolation, and x_0 is obtained by the edge line minimization in (11).

4 Experimental results

To objectively and comprehensively present the performance of the proposed deinterlacing approach, our method has been tested on several CIF-352 × 288 ("Foreman", "Hall", "Mobile", "Stefan" and "News") and QCIF-176 × 144 ("Carphone" and "Salesman") video sequences. These well-known test sequences have been chosen for their different texture content and motion dynamics. Such spatio-temporal characteristics can be explicited by computing the relative spatial information (SI) and temporal information (TI) found in these video contents, as described in [24]. Figure 5 shows the relative amount of spatial and temporal information for the selected test scenes. We can note that they span a large portion of the SI–TI plane, as desired. Moreover, the two (SI,TI) pairs located in the top right part of the diagram correspond to the "Mobile" and "Stefan" CIF sequences which are known to contain very high spatio-temporal activity.

The selected video sequences were originally in progressive format. To generate interlaced content, the even lines of the even frames and the odd lines of the odd frames were removed, as shown in Fig. 6. This way, objective quality measurements could be done, using the original sequences—progressive frames—as references.

Fig. 4 5-Tap Edge Line
Average (ELA): the five
interpolation directions are
represented with different
dashed lines. *Gray nodes*
correspond to original pixels
from the *upper* and *lower lines*
(*solid lines*); the *black node* is
the interpolated pixel

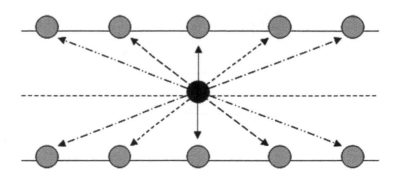

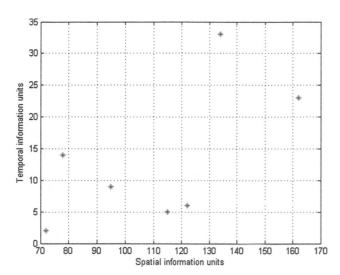

Fig. 5 Spatial–temporal information diagram for the test video scene
set

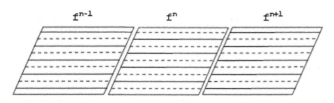

Fig. 6 Progressive to interlaced format frame conversion, by removing
the *dashed lines*

In our experimental framework, the GBVS model is first
considered. We have used 8×8 ($B = 8$) pixel blocks for
a 16×16 ($S = 16$) search motion estimation window, for
the salient blocks b_n having a small $CE_{b_n} < T_b$ number of
contours. The parameter T_s for saliency detector was set up
to 20, and the edge threshold T_b to 32 (e.g., at least half of
the block pixels are situated on contours).

The tests were run on 50 frames for each sequence.
The deinterlacing performance of our method is presented
in terms of peak signal-to-noise ratio (PSNR) computed
on the luminance component. The efficiency of our proposed method—denoted in the followings by SGAD—is
compared in Table 1 to Vertical Average (VA), Edge Line
Average (ELA), Temporal Field Average (TFA), Adap-

tive Motion Estimation (AME) and Motion-Compensated
Deinterlacing (MCD), which are the most common implementations in deinterlacing systems. Moreover, the proposed
algorithm is compared to the work in [27], denoted by
EPMC, [28] denoted by SMCD and the methods proposed in [29] (high-fidelity motion estimation based deinterlacer), [30] (adaptive motion-compensated interpolator
with overlapped motion estimation) and [31] (hybrid low-
complexity motion-compensated-based deinterlacer), which
are all motion-compensation-based algorithms with different complexity degrees. (these latter results are reported
as in the corresponding references, NC denoting the non-
communicated ones). In the present case, the GBVS model
is considered.

For visually showing the results of the proposed method,
two deinterlaced frames are illustrated in Fig. 7.

As it can be seen in the presented results, our proposed
method using the GBVS model has an average PSNR gain
of $\approx$ 4.5 dBs with respect to a wild range of deinterlacers.
Our framework has been implemented in Matlab (8.0.0.783
(R2012b)) and the tests have been realized on a quad-
core Intel-PC@4 GHz. Due to the independent block-based
processing, the proposed deinterlacing approach is prone to
distributed/parallel implementation, thus highly reducing the
computation time obtained with a sequential implementation. Moreover, as the proposed algorithm adapts the motion
estimation in function of region's saliency, due to our used
threshold T_s for motion computation, only $\approx$ 1/3 of field
regions is motion processed (as it can be seen in Fig. 3).
The parameterization allows, thus, to drastically decrease
the complexity attached to motion-compensated schemes, by
preserving its advantages where the user attention is focused.

However, it is known that the GBVS model requires a
lot of computational resources to be computed. Such computational complexity can be a severe issue particularly for
real-time applications. For lower complexity, we propose in
what follows to replace the GBVS model by the SRVS one
to compute the saliency values. Because optical flow is also
complex to implement, only block-based MC is used in the
low-complex approach; the implementation of the algorithm
is left unchanged. The performances of the low-complex

Table 1 Y-PSNR results (in dB)

	Foreman	Hall	Mobile	Stefan	News	Carphone	Salesman
VA	32.15	28.26	25.38	27.30	34.64	32.17	31.52
ELA	33.14	30.74	23.47	26.04	32.19	32.33	30.51
TFA	34.08	37.47	27.96	26.83	41.06	37.39	45.22
AME	33.19	27.27	20.95	23.84	27.36	29.63	28.24
MCD	35.42	34.23	25.26	27.32	35.49	33.55	33.16
EPMC (S1)	37.09	39.27	31.54	30.02	41.63	37.53	45.61
EPMC (S2)	37.18	39.08	30.56	30.11	39.44	37.55	42.28
[29]	33.77	NC	27.66	28.79	NC	NC	NC
[30]	NC	NC	NC	24.59	NC	NC	NC
[31]	33.93	38.79	24.67	26.88	NC	NC	NC
SMCD (S1)	37.52	39.71	30.41	31.77	41.85	37.59	45.95
SMCD (S2)	37.63	39.86	30.58	31.82	42.00	37.74	45.09
SGAD	39.07	43.86	37.54	34.23	44.35	40.33	50.70

Fig. 7 Deinterlacing result for the **a** 10th frame of "Foreman" sequence, **b** 21th frame of "Salesman" sequence

SGAD algorithm using the SRVS model are evaluated by comparing the PSNR and computation time values with the GBVS-based method for the video data set. Table 2 summarizes the results that include the average PSNR value, the average number of blocks on which the ELA algorithm is used (noted N_e), the average number of blocks on which block-based MC is used (noted N_m), and the average total computation time noted CT (saliency's estimation then adaptive block processing).

First, we can note that the average PSNR values are reduced compared to the ones obtained with the GBVS-based method. The quality loss is due to the artifacts introduced by the block-based MC process, as opposed to optical flow mostly, but also due to the saliency model performance: the GBVS model has the best results, but unfortunately at the expense of processing time (it takes about 1 min to extract the saliency map). Nevertheless, we verify that the low-complex algorithm offers performances which are mostly similar to conventional deinterlacing techniques in terms of video quality. Concerning the total processing time, it varies between 4.49 and 20.1 s. This time must be set against that required for the GBVS-based version which varies approximately from 100 s for QCIF video contents to 350–400 s for CIF ones. Such time penalty for the initial version of our algorithm is mainly due to the optical flow computation, especially if highly textured salient regions are represent in the initial scene. Hence, the modified version of the SGAD algorithm can be adapted for real-time deinterlacing while maintaining a satisfactory video quality though slightly reduced. On the contrary, the GBVS version should be better suited for storage for which deinterlacing time is not an issue; so,

Table 2 performances of the modified low-complex SGAD algorithm

	Foreman	Hall	Mobile	Stefan	News	Carphone	Salesman
PSNR (dB)	37.32	36.99	29.49	30.78	41.65	37.81	41.48
N_e (%)	73	8	1	6	9	9	9
N_m (%)	27	92	99	94	91	91	91
CT (s)	6.57	19.68	20.10	19.90	19.16	4.49	4.76

it is mainly designed for adapting the content from interlaced cameras to progressive display devices. To conclude, it should be noted that further gains should be expected for the proposed SGAD method because the code is still not optimized.

5 Conclusion

In this paper, a spatial saliency-guided motion-compensated method for video deinterlacing is proposed. Our approach is an efficient deinterlacing tool, being able to adapt the interpolation method depending both on region of interest and its texture content. Experiments show that the proposed algorithm generates high-quality results, having more than 4.5 dBs PSNR gain, in average, compared to other deinterlacing approaches. Furthermore, the proposed method acknowledges the possibility of improving image quality and simultaneously reducing execution time, based on the saliency map. Finally, we have presented two models: the first one for storage applications (in this case, deinterlacing time is not a critical issue, so it is mainly designed for high-quality conversion from interlaced cameras to progressive display devices), and the other one with less but still acceptable video quality performances, which can be adapted for real-time deinterlacers.

References

1. Haan, G.D., Bellers, E.B.: Deinterlacing: an overview. Proc. IEEE **86**(9), 1839–1857 (1998)
2. Jeon, G., Anisetti, M., Wang, L., Damiani, E.: Locally estimated heterogeneity property and its fuzzy filter application for deinterlacing. Inf. Sci. **354**, 112–130 (2016)
3. Yang, W.-J., Chung, K.-L., Huang, Y.-H., Lin, L.-C.: Quality-efficient syntax element-based deinterlacing method for H.264-coded video sequences with various resolutions. J. Vis. Commun. Image R **25**, 466–477 (2014)
4. Wang, J., Jeon, G., Jeong, J.: A block-wise autoregression-based deinterlacing algorithm. J. Disp. Technol. **10**(5), 414–419 (2014)
5. Zhang, H., Rong, M.: Deinterlacing algorithm using gradient-guided interpolation and weighted average of directional estimation. IET Image Process. **9**(6), 450–460 (2015)
6. Wang, J., Jeon, G., Jeong, J.: A hybrid algorithm using maximum a posteriori for interlaced to progressive scanning format conversion. J. Disp. Technol. **11**(2), 183–192 (2015)
7. Abboud, F., Chouzenoux, E., Pesquet, J.-C., Chenot, J.-H., Laborelli, L.: A dual block coordinate proximal algorithm with application to deconvolution of interlaced video sequences. In: IEEE International Conference on Image Processing, pp. 4917–4921 (2015)
8. Jeon, G., Kang, S., Lee, J.-K.: A robust fuzzy-bilateral filtering method and its application to video deinterlacing. J. Real-Time Image Proc. **11**(1), 223–233 (2016)
9. Atkins, C.B.: Optical image scaling using pixel classification. In: International Conference on Image Processing (2001)
10. Liu, C.: Beyond pixels: exploring new representations and applications for motion analysis. Doctoral Thesis, MIT (2009)
11. Trocan, M., Mikovicova, B., Zhanguzin, D.: An adaptive motion compensated approach for video deinterlacing. Multimed. Tools Appl. **61**(3), 819–837 (2011)
12. Wang, C., Huang, R., Miao, W., Zhao, J., He, J.: Video deinterlacing method based-on optical flow. In: IEEE International Conference on Wireless Communications and Signal Processing (WCSP) (2012)
13. Abdoli, B.: A dynamic predictive search algorithm for fast block-based motion estimation. Theses and Dissertations, Digital Library Ryerson Canada (2012)
14. Brox, P., Baturone, I., Sanchez-Solano, S., Gutierrez-Rios, J.: Edge-adaptive spatial video deinterlacing algorithms based on fuzzy logic. IEEE Trans. Consum. Electr. **60**(3), 375–383 (2014)
15. Horn, B.K.P., Schunck, B.G.: Determining optical flow. Artif. Intell. **17**, 185203 (1981)
16. Harel, J., Koch, C., Pietro, P.: Graph-Based Visual Saliency. In: Advances in Neural Information Processing Systems (2006)
17. Itti, L., Koch, C., Niebur, E.: A model of saliency-based visual attention for rapid scene analysis. IEEE Trans. PAMI **20**(11), 1254–1259 (1998)
18. Itti, L.: Automatic foveation for video compression using a neurobiological model of visual attention. IEEE Trans. Image Process. **13**(10), 1304–1318 (2004)
19. Hou, X., Zhang, L.: Saliency detection: a spectral residual approach. IEEE Conf. Comput. Vis. Pattern Recogn. **1**, 1–8 (2007)
20. Schauerte, B., Stiefelhagen, R.: Quaternion-based spectral saliency detection for eye fixation prediction. Eur. Conf. Comput. Vis. (ECCV) **7573**, 116–129 (2012)
21. Rahtu, E., Kannala, J., et al.: Segmenting salient objects from images and videos. In: Proceedings of European Conference on Computer Vision (ECCV2010), pp. 321–332 (2010)
22. Zhang, L., Tong, M., et al.: SUN: a Bayesian framework for saliency using natural statistics. J. Vis. **9**(7), 1–20 (2008)

23. Lu, S., Lim, J.-H.: Saliency modeling from image histograms. In: European Conference on Computer Vision (ECCV), pp. 321–332. Florence (2012)

24. Recommendation ITU-T P. 910: Subjective video quality assessment methods for multimedia applications, pp. 14–17 (2008)

25. Seo, H.-J., Milanfar, P.: Static and space-time visual saliency detection by self-resemblance. J. Vis. 9(12), 1–12 (2009)

26. Itti, L., Koch, C.: Computational modeling of visual attention. Nat. Rev. Neurosci. 2(3), 194–203 (2001)

27. Zhanguzin, D., Trocan, M., Mikovicova, B.: An edge-preserving motion-compensated approach for video deinterlacing. IEEE/IET/BCS3rd International Workshop on Future Multimedia Networking (2010)

28. Trocan, M., Mikovicova, B.: Smooth motion compensated video deinterlacing. In: Image and Signal Processing and Analysis (ISPA), 7th International Symposium (2011)

29. Chen, Y., Tai, S.: True motion- compensated deinterlacing algorithm. IEEE Trans. Circ. Syst. Video Technol 19, 1489–1498 (2009)

30. Wang, S.-B., Chang, T.-S.: Adaptive deinterlacing with robust overlapped block motion compensation. IEEE Trans. Circ. Syst. Video Technol. 18(10), 1437–1440 (2008)

31. Lee, G., Wang, M., Li, H., et al.: A motion-adaptive deinterlacer via hybrid motion detection and edge-pattern recognition. J Image Video Proc 2008:741290 (2008). doi:10.1155/2008/741290

## 6

Authority estimation within social networks using regression analysis

Kristína Machová[1] · Jaroslav Štefaník[1]

Abstract This paper focuses on methods of machine learning, particularly on regression analysis to solve a problem of authority identification within social networks. Within this paper, linear, polynomial, and non-linear regression types were considered. The aim was to find an approximation of dependency of the authority value on variables representing parameters of the structure and particularly the content of selected web discussions. The approximation function can be used at first for computation of the authority value of a given discussant, at second, for discrimination of an authoritative discussant from non-authoritative contributors to the web discussion. This information is important for web users, who search for truthful and reliable information in the process of decision making about important things. The web users would like to be influenced by some credible professionals. The various regression methods were tested, particularly linear, polynomial, and non-linear regression models. The best solution was implemented in the Application for the Machine Authority Identification.

Keywords Authority identification · Social networks · Web mining · Linear regression · Non-linear regression · Web forums

✉ Kristína Machová
kristina.machova@tuke.sk
http://people.tuke.sk/kristina.machova/

Jaroslav Štefaník
jaroslav.stefanik@student.tuke.sk

[1] Department of Cybernetics and Artificial Intelligence, Technical University, Letná 9, 04200 Košice, Slovakia

1 Introduction

We live in the information era. A volume of information, which is discovered each day, is too large and too time-consuming to be processed by a human. Everybody from us needs sometimes an access to the relevant supporting information for our decision-making. To know the relevance of information we have found, we need information about sources of the obtained information and their credibility. In other words, it is important to know the sources, which are authoritative ones. A web forum discussion can be a repository of various kinds of useful information: facts, opinions, ideas, attitudes, and so on. However, useful information is mixed with non-useful or misleading information. Every web user can join the web discussion, but many of them have not sufficient experiences or theoretical knowledge about the discussed themes. The web discussion often contains an opinion spam and an information trash. Therefore, it is the matter of principal to search for authoritative discussants to let them influence our important decisions. And just the searching for an authority and its machine identification among all discussants of web forum is our challenge.

To achieve our main goal—machine authority identification, we had to do the following three steps:

1. To find such variables—parameters of the structure and content of the web discussion, which are the most related to the authoritative contributing.
2. To define a dependency of the variable "authority" of a web discussion on the independent variables selected in the first step. We tried to find an approximation of this dependency using the linear and non-linear regression [1] based on the method of the ordinary least squares (OLSs) [2].

3. To use this approximation function for the discrimination of the authoritative from non-authoritative contributors to the web discussion.

Before starting the machine authority identification, we had to solve a number of technical problems. The first one was the automatic extraction of the conversation content and structure from the web page with the web discussion. The second one was to extract the values of selected independent variables from previously obtained information about the discussion. Another problem was how to obtain the values of dependent variable "authority" for regression function training. We decided for two alternative ways— to obtain values of "authority" from human "expert" and to extract them directly from the web discussion as so-called "wisdom of a crowd."

Finally, all learned results were tested using widely used measures of the efficiency—the precision and the recall. The best solution was implemented within the Application for the Machine Authority Identification (AMAI).

2 Authority and web discussion

2.1 Web discussion group

Our attention was on an authority of a web discussion forum. The discussion group was developed in the society Usenet from the beginning of 80th years of twentieth century [3]. Two computer specialists Jim Ellis and Truscott have come with a new idea to create a system of rules for the contributions creation. Nowadays, WWW society becomes the main organization, which supports and spreads various platforms for Internet discussion groups using various settings up of different web servers. The internet discussion is represented by a web page, where users insert their contributions (opinions and reactions). Within this paper, the web users joining a web discussion will be called the contributors or discussants. They add their opinions, ideas, and attitudes to the web discussion, and in this way, they create the so-called "conversational content." The authority identification represents the mining of this conversational content and its internal structure. There are different types of Internet discussion forums according to their scope [4]:

- *Discussion connected to a web article* In this case, the discussion is only an additional function to the content of the article to enable feedback. The subject of such discussion can be the text of the article or the concerning theme or product.
- *Guestbook* A place on a web site dedicated to reactions on the given web project, for example, a personal web page or a web page relevant to some theme.

- *Discussion forum* A part of a more extensive discussion project. It enables to establish new discussion pages and to sectionalize them into groups according to themes. It is a place, where users can leave the contributions. These contributions (e.g., news) are often longer than one line as they are within chatrooms. They are temporarily archived. An approval of new contributions by moderator of the discussion can be desired before the contributions became visible for all users.
- *Questions and answers* Some public institutions offer the public answering of question, suggestions or complaints on special web pages. In this case, a pronouncement of a responsible representative of the institution is expected.

There are many other social web platforms, where the conversational content is cumulated, for example, chats, Internet Relay Chat, blog and micro-blog platforms, and so on. However, the paper focuses on the web discussions dedicated to some given theme.

2.2 Authority identification in general

The concept "authority" comes from the Latin word "augere." It denotes a person, whose opinions, attitudes or decisions are respected by other members of the group and whose decisions and advices are expected by other members of the group. The authority is derived from the relations between people (web users), positions, and hierarchies [5]. There are many kinds of authorities. For example, according to prestige, authority can be:

- *Formal (functional) authority* It represents a measure of influence of some person following from his formal position regardless of personal properties. It is leadership of the person, who is mandated to make decisions. It is obviously the result of a position, title or function of some person within an organization (an arbiter, teacher, politician, and so on). A leader could require submission, although this person is not honest or brave or predictable or able of a quick decision-making.
- *Informal (natural) authority* It is based on human and personal properties and professional assumptions of a person. It is the result of a personal profile, capability, adequate self-confidence, and social activities. Such person has natural, spontaneous influence on others, because of his/her persuasiveness and good experiences with his/her advices and decisions. The people, who let an authority to lead them, enforce the weight of this authority.

An important characteristic of the authority is using of no pressure and no force. The process of obtaining an authority is demanding and time-consuming; nevertheless, more difficult thing is to maintaining it. The formal authority can be at the same time the informal one. The formal authority can sometimes change his status to informal and vice versa.

2.3 Authority of a web discussion

The virtual web authority has different characteristics as the authority in real life. It is related to the structure of the web, which is based on hyperlinks among web pages. The Google has discovered very complicated relations among web pages and references. Well-known tool for the web page authority calculation is PageRank [6]. Other known approaches to the web page authority calculating are hyperlink-induced topic search (HITS) algorithm [7] and stochastic approach for link-structure analysis (SALSA) [8]. These approaches are also based on an input and output hyperlinks of the evaluated web page. There are also tools of the respected portal "Seomoz," for example, MozTrust(Moz's global link trust score) [9] and Open Site Explorer [10]. All these tools cannot be easily used for calculating of an authority of the web discussion forum. There is also interesting work [11] concerned on a qualitative analysis of discussion forum. However, this work has not the aim to estimate the value of Authority of web discussant.

The authority identification from web discussion forums is a similar problem as web page authority calculation, because authority identification from web discussion is concentrated on web page, the discussion runs on. On the other hand, it is also a different problem, because no input or output references between this page and other pages are considered. Only references inside this page between various discussants are considered. These references are represented by reactions on contributions. All mentioned methods (PageRank, HITS, SALSA, MozTrust, and Open Site Explorer) calculate authority of each web page separately. One page leads to one measure of authority. Within the authority mining from the web conversation, not only one but all contributions of the given discussant are evaluated. All information about all contributions related to one discussant has to be concentrated and used for the authority estimation. Nevertheless, we can inspire ourselves by these techniques and take into account the number of references as reactions on an actual contribution.

In our previous work [12], we have taken into account mentioned number of reactions on all contributions of evaluated discussant, but also the number of all contributions of this discussant, the number of reaction of the discussant on the bottom level of the conversation tree (Fig. 4), the polarity matching between opinion of the discussant and opinion of all discussion, the positions of contributions in the conversation tree and the length of his/her contributions. Some of these variables have appeared to be not so important for the precise estimation of the authority. Another problem of

this approach was in way of the estimation function generation. For these reasons, we decided to modify the set of variables—arguments of the conversational structure and to use the regression methods for training the authority estimation function.

3 Used methods

We tried to solve the problem of the authority estimation within the web discussion forum using a machine learning method based on regression analysis. Within scientific works, there is often quantitative evaluation of two or more variables (for example, x and y) and a function relation f among these variables has to be determined. There is a mutual statistical correlation z between these variables, as can be modeled by:

$$y = f(x), \quad z = \varphi(y, x). \tag{1}$$

The regression analysis can be:

- A simple regression, which is represented in (1),
- A multiple regression—we are searching for a relation of one dependent variable (y) on a set of independent variables ($x_1, x_2, \ldots x_n$)—see Eq. (2). These independent variables are called "regressors" or "predictors":

$$y = f(x_1, x_2, \ldots, x_n). \tag{2}$$

Within the regression analysis, it is very important to realize, which one of variables is dependent and which are independent. The goal of the regression analysis is to describe the relation between a dependent variable (y) and independent variables ($x_1, x_2, \ldots x_n$) by a suitable mathematical model, for example by linear or non-linear function. The result will be a regression curve, which should optimally match the empirical polygon [13].

3.1 Linear and non-linear regression

A regression function can be considered as a linear function in the case, when it is a linear function of the unknown parameters. Some examples of linear regression functions are as follows:

- $y = b_0 + b_1 x$ (basic linear regression)
- $y = b_0 + b_1 x + b_2 x^2$ (quadratic regression)
- $y = b_0 + b_1 x + \cdots + b_r x^r$ (polynomial regression)

All these equations represent linear regression, because any unknown constants are not in the exponent. They are linear from the point of view of the regression analysis. Within

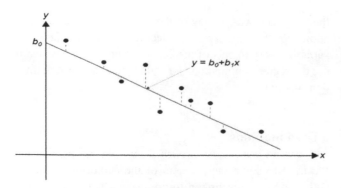

Fig. 1 Linear regression in two-dimensional space [14]

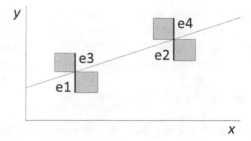

Fig. 2 The sum of square errors within OLS method in two-dimensional space [14]

the problem of the authority estimation, we have used the basic linear and polynomial regressions. The basic linear regression for two-dimensional space is shown in Fig. 1.

The goal is to find such values of constants $b_0, b_1, \ldots,$ b_n in the formula (3) (in two-dimensional space b_0 and b_1 of the linear line, see Fig. 1) to achieve the optimal matching between the linear line and the point graph, which consists of m points (observations). These constants can be dedicated from the point estimation using the ordinary least squares (OLS) method [2]:

$$y_i = b_0 + b_1 x_{i1} + \cdots + b_n x_{in} + \varepsilon_i. \tag{3}$$

Sometimes, it is not possible to find a satisfactory precise linear relation. In this case, the relation can be modeled by some non-linear function, the most frequently exponential function ($y = be^{cx}$) or logarithmic function ($y = b_0 + b_1 \ell n x$) [1]. Within the problem of the authority estimation, we have used the non-linear modification of the polynomial function in the form $y = b_0 + b_1 x^{c_1} + \cdots + b_n x^{c_n}$. In this function, not only constants b_i but also exponents c_i represent the searched constants. It is a more general form of the polynomial function with parameters in its exponents, where exponents need not to be integer values.

3.2 Ordinary least squares method

This OLS method belongs to mathematical and statistical methods. Through it, it is possible to solve the tasks of both types of regressions, linear and non-linear. In general, the method minimizes the sum of square errors (see Fig. 2). The sum arises when the differences between theoretical and empirical values exist. The theoretical values are calculated using the regression function, and the empirical values are obtained by a measurement or by an observation [2].

At first, values of parameters $\hat{a}_0$ (b_0 in Sect. 3.1) and $\hat{a}_1$ (b_1 in Sect. 3.1) in two-dimensional space are found. These values represent a point estimations of parameters. For these parameters, a residual sum of squares SSE (sum of square errors) is calculated according to (4). This sum is shown by

gray squares in Fig. 2. The basic principle of the OLS method is the minimization of this sum:

$$SSE\left(\hat{a}_0, \hat{a}_1\right) = \sum_{i=1}^{n} e_i^2 = \sum_{i=1}^{n} \left(y_i - \hat{y}_i\right)^2 = \sum_{i=1}^{n} \left(y_i - \hat{a}_0 \hat{a}_1 x_i\right)^2. \tag{4}$$

After all necessary operations, the parameters $\hat{a}_0, \hat{a}_1$ are calculated according to the following:

$$\hat{a}_1 = \frac{n \cdot \sum_{i=1}^{n} x_i \cdot y_i - \sum_{i=1}^{n} x_i \cdot \sum_{i=1}^{n} y_i}{n \cdot \sum_{i=1}^{n} x_i^2 - \left(\sum_{i=1}^{n} x_i\right)^2}, \tag{5}$$

$$\hat{a}_0 = \frac{\sum_{i=1}^{n} y_i - \hat{a}_1 \cdot \sum_{i=1}^{n} x_i}{n} = \bar{y} - \hat{a}_1 \cdot \bar{x}. \tag{6}$$

3.3 Specification of the variables of a discussion structure

We have selected 120 discussants from the portal "http://www.sme.sk". Consequently, the following variables for each discussant were extracted from all his contributions:

- *AE* Average evaluation of the contribution.
- *K* Value of the karma of the user, which is the contribution author.
- *NCH* Number of characters within his/her contributions.
- *AL* Average layer in the conversation tree (see Fig. 4).
- *ANR* Average number of reactions on his/her contributions.
- *NC* Number of contributions of given discussant.

These variables were used to form the training set (is shown in Fig. 3) for selected regression method.

Average evaluation of the contribution (AE) is represented by the ratio of the sum of all reactions [agree (+) and disagree (−)] on the contributions of given discussant to the number of all his contributions. This average evaluation is available on the web discussion page. The range of the *AE* is the number from 0 to 80.

Nickname	AE	K	NCH	AL	ANR	NC
Peter 2	60	108	26,0	0	1	1
V12	80	182	220,0	2	0,5	2
fero	80	171	548,5	3	2,5	2
sandokan555	80	162	57,5	4	0,5	2
Peter_5	50	99	112,5	6	0	2
darkman	80	167	117,0	3	0	1
Jesse Pickman	40	74	210,5	1,5	1,5	2
mm	60	108	22,0	1	1	1

Fig. 3 Each *line* of the training set represents one discussant and contains the values of variables *AE, K, NCH, AL, ANR, and NC*

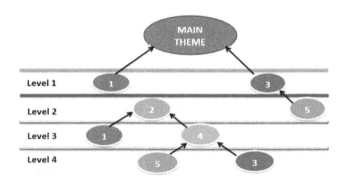

Fig. 4 The conversation tree has four levels, the main theme is in the root and reactions are situated on levels 1–4, and all reactions of the same discussant have the same tint of the *gray* color

Value of *karma* (*K*) of the discussant is also available on the discussion web page. The karma is a number from 0 to 200, which represents activity of the discussant from last 3 months (within the portal "http://www.sme.sk").

Number of characters (*NCH*) represents the average length of discussant contributions. It penalized authors with too short and so less informative contributions. We assume that an authoritative contributor does not insert extremely short contributions.

Average layer (AL) in the conversation tree (see Fig. 4) is the average number of all layers, which the contributions of the discussant are situated in. The conversation tree is a graphical representation of the web discussion. The *AL* represents the information, when the discussant joined the discussion, from the beginning or at the end.

Average number of reactions (ANR) on the all contributions of the given discussant is the number of reactions per one his contribution.

Number of contributions (NC) is simply the whole number of contributions of the given discussant. The parameter NC penalizes authors, which join a discussion rarely.

Table 1 Average deviation of four versions of authority estimation function

Version	Average deviation
L-EXPERT	17.3489
L-CROWD	3.2998
PL-EXPERT	24.0123
PL-CROWD	8.7912
NL-EXPERT	18.1131
NL-CROWD	6.5618

All these parameters, taking separately, indicate rather chatty contributors than authoritative ones. However, taking them together as one entity, the emergency phenomenon arises. This phenomenon can indicate the authoritative contributors.

It may happen that a good contribution of already well known authority finishes the discussion on the Web. It is truth that in such a case, there is no reaction on this contribution. It does not disturb the measure of the authority, because of high probability that there were more previous contributions of this contributor with many reactions within the given discussion. These reactions can balance the lack of reactions on the finishing contribution.

All these variables were considered to be independent variables. The dependent variable of the regression function *Y* was dedicated from:

1. Evaluation of each discussant by "human expert";
2. Evaluation of each discussant by other discussants and it represents "wisdoms of the crowd."

4 Implementation and testing

The authority value A≡Y was estimated by a linear and nonlinear function of selected variables (AE, K, NCH, AL, ANR, and NC). The six regression functions for authority estimation were generated in the process of machine learning:

1. Linear function learned from the "human expert" (L-EXPERT) is represented by:

$$A = 0.4383\text{AE} + 0.0746K + 0.0281\text{NCH} - 2.1932\text{AL} - 3.4386\text{ANR} + 8.0102\text{NC} \qquad (7)$$

2. Linear function learned from the "wisdoms of the crowd" (L-CROWD) is represented by:

$$A = 0.4385\text{AE} + 0.325K + 0.002\text{NCH} - 0.2928\text{AL} - 0.0853\text{ANR} + 1.0728\text{NC} \qquad (8)$$

Table 2 Values of precision and recall of six versions of regression functions were obtained in the three-time cross validation

Test	Version	Precision		Recall	
		Expert	Crowd	Expert	Crowd
Cross val. 12_3	Linear regression	0.78	0.99	0.69	0.99
	Polynomial regression	0.77	0.84	0.65	0.97
	Non-linear regression	0.72	0.99	0.66	0.88
Cross val. 13_2	Linear regression	0.65	0.98	0.65	0.93
	Polynomial regression	0.63	0.77	0.60	0.91
	Non-linear regression	0.67	0.97	0.67	0.86
Cross val. 23_1	Linear regression	0.68	0.97	0.67	0.67
	Polynomial regression	0.62	0.72	0.58	0.95
	Non-linear regression	0.69	0.97	0.69	0.67
Average	Linear regression	0.70	0.98	0.67	0.80
	Polynomial regression	0.67	0.78	0.61	0.94
	Non-linear regression	0.67	0.97	0.67	0.80

3. Polynomial function learned from the "human expert" (PL-EXPERT) is represented by:

$$A = 0.0001\text{AE}^3 - 0.0004K^2 + 0.0303\text{NCH} - 1.5539\text{AL} \\ - 2.0557\text{ANR} + 12.1589\text{NC} \tag{9}$$

4. Polynomial function learned from the "wisdoms of the crowd" (PL-CROWD) is represented by:

$$A = 0.0001\text{AE}^3 - 0.0009K^2 + 0.0043\text{NCH} + 0.7473\text{AL} \\ + 1.9875\text{ANR} + 6.7507\text{NC} \tag{10}$$

5. Non-linear function learned from the "human expert" (NL-EXPERT) is represented by:

$$A = 0.0382\text{AE}^{1,7192} - 0.3295K^{0,959} + 0.4470\text{NCH}^{0,681} \\ + 0.1825\text{AL}^{0,0001} - 0.6269\text{ANR}^{3,2394} + 20.2509\text{NC}^{0,2977} \tag{11}$$

6. Non-linear function learned from the "wisdoms of the crowd" (NL-CROWD) is represented by:

$$A = 0.0185\text{AE}^{1,8135} + 141.5704K^{-78,39} + 0.0018\text{NCH}^{1,0457} \\ - 0.0011\text{AL}^{3,7717} - 0.5562\text{ANR}^{0,0001} + 37.6642\text{NC}^{0,0038} \tag{12}$$

All these functions were created using standard MATLAB functions: "regress" in the case of linear and "lsqnonlin" in the case of non-linear relations. No auxiliary regularization method was used, because the input data matrix was regular. The input data can hardly be considered as noise data obtained, for example, from a device. These used input data map the structure of the given web discussion using defined variables. In the case of non-linear regression, also exponential parameters were elicited from the training data using the function "lsqnonlin." It solves non-linear least-squares (non-linear data-fitting) problems and uses numerical optimization method "Trust-Region-Reflective Least Squares Algorithm."

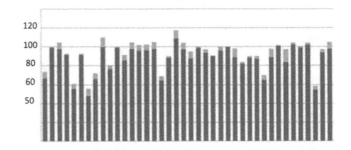

Fig. 5 The illustration of estimated values of authority of some particular contributors (*dark gray* color column for each contributor) and deviations (*light gray* color) for some of tested discussants for the best version L-CROWD. The authority value can be from 0 to 120 (it is the range of *Y* values)

The default settings were used, and only the number of iterations was extended.

All the versions of the regression function for authority estimation (from (7) to (12)) were tested. The concise results of these tests are shown in Tables 1 and 2.

At first, the average deviations were calculated. According to the results in Table 1, the better functions were obtained by learning from the "crowd" than by learning from the "expert". The deviations for some of tested discussants for the best version L-CROWD are shown in Fig. 5.

At second, these six versions of regression function were tested using obvious measures of a machine learning efficiency: precision and recall. The regression problem, when the value of *A* (authority) attribute should be estimated from the interval $\langle 0, 100 \rangle$ using formulas (7)–(12), was adopted to classification problem in the following way. A threshold *T* has been stated experimentally (*T* = 70) and discussants were classified into categories: "authority" and "non-authority". The discussants were classified to the class "authority" when their value of *A* was equal to or greater than

T and they were classified to the class "non-authority" when their value of A was smaller than T. The precision π and recall ρ were calculated according to the following equations:

$$\pi_j = \frac{\text{TP}_j}{\text{TP}_j + \text{FP}_j}, \tag{13}$$

$$\rho_j = \frac{\text{TP}_j}{\text{TP}_j + \text{FN}_j}, \tag{14}$$

where TP is the number of true positives [the method classifies these examples as positive (authority) and they are truly positive according to the expert's (crowd's) opinion]. FP is the number of false positives [the method classifies these examples as positive (authority), but they are not positive according to the expert's or crowd's opinion]. FN is the number of false negatives [the method classifies the examples as negative (non-authority), but they are positive according to the expert's (crowd's) opinion].

Some key and the most important achieved results of tests are presented in Table 2.

The linear regression learned from the "crowd," with the best test results, was implemented in the Application for the Machine Authority Identification (AMAI). This application provides the list of all discussants with the actual value of their authority. The AMAI also displays the value of the authority of the discussant, which was selected by a user. This value is from the interval $\langle 0, 100 \rangle$. The application provides not only the binary decision whether the discussant is or is not the authority, but also it provides a precise numeric value of its authority.

5 Conclusions

The design of solving the problem of the authority identification from conversational content using the linear and non-linear regression was presented. The measure of the authority A was estimated as dependency on variables (AE, K, NCH, AL, ANR, and NC)—parameters of the structure and content of given web discussions. Another parameter which could be relevant is the vocabulary of the discussant—the literary language with scientific concepts can determine the level of the discussant and thus indicate the authority of the writer. In addition, the type of emoticons used in the discussion could be helpful. On the contrary, the dirty language may reflect a low level of the discussant. This language can be identified using some prepared special dictionary of dirty words. We would like to involve these parameters in the future.

The six generated estimation functions were tested. According to the values of average deviations (see Table 1), the best solution is the linear function learned from crowd (L-

CROWD). The second one is the non-linear function learned for crowd (NL-CROWD). Linear and non-linear functions learned from a single human evaluator—expert—seem to be worse. The same conclusions can be deduced from the resulting average values of precision and recall in Table 2. It is surprising that the linear model is better than the higher order model. It can be caused by a character of input data—parameters of the web discussion. Together with an increasing of values of these parameters, also the value of authority increases. Therefore, linear model is sufficient for the authority estimation.

It can be hardly said who is the expert on the authority identification. In addition, an opinion of a psychologist may be also subjective. On the other hand, combined opinion of many discussants can be objective.

There are other existing authority identification methods, as Klout, TwentyFeet, My Web Carrer [14], and our previous work [12]. All these methods use formulas for authority estimation, but these formulas were generated more experimentally without considering a theoretically based way. For this reason, we tried to generate the relation between the authority and the structure of web discussion using the classic mathematical approach based on the linear and non-linear regressions. For the future, we plan to elicit the constants of linear and non-linear equations using evolutionary algorithms [15,16] to calculate not only constant values but the form of a non-linear regression function as well.

The presented approach can be used also in weighted opinion analysis of some discussions on social networks. Within the classic opinion analysis, the whole discussion is recognized to be positive (or negative) when there are more positive (or negative) contributions within it and each contribution has the same weight within determination of the summarized opinion. The weighted opinion analysis could multiply the measure of positivity of a given contribution with the weight represented by the estimated authority value of the contributor, who is the author of the given contribution. Thus, the opinions of authoritative contributors would have greater influence on the summarized opinion. We would like to apply the weighted opinion analysis in a domain of recognizing personality aberration from written text [17]. The designed approach and its implementation can be used to solve the problem of the decreasing of a web user cognitive load [18].

Acknowledgements The work presented in this paper was supported by the Slovak Grant Agency of the Ministry of Education and Academy of Science of the Slovak Republic under VEGA Grant No. 1/0493/16.

References

1. Pazman, A., Lacko V.: Lectures from Regression Models (in Slovak), vol. 132. University of Comenius Bratislava, Bratislava, Slovakia (2012). ISBN: 978-80-223-3070-1
2. Pohlman, J.T., Leitner, D.W.: A comparison of ordinary least squares and logic regression. Ohio J. Sci. **103**(5), 118–125 (2003)
3. What is Usenet?. http://www.usenet.org. (2016). Accessed 15 Sept 2016
4. Machová, K., Penzéš, T.: Extraction of web discussion texts for opinion analysis. In: IEEE 10th jubilee international symposium on applied machine intelligence and informatics, SAMI 2012, Herl'any, 26–28 January 2012, pp. 31–35. Óbuda University, Budapest, Hungary (2012) **(ISBN 978-1-4577-0195-5)**
5. Chavalkova, K.: Authority of ateacher (in Czech). Philosophic-faculty of the University of Pardubice, Pardubice, Czech republic (2011)
6. Fiala, D.: Time-aware PageRunk for bibliographic networks. J. Infometrics **6**(3), 370–388 (2012)
7. Li, L., Shang, Y., Zhang, W.: Improvement of HITS-based algorithms on web documents. In: 11th International Conference on the WWW, pp. 527–535. ACM, Hawaii, USA (2002)
8. Lempel, R., Moran, S.: The stochastic approach for link structure analysis (SALSA) and the TKC effect. Comput. Netw. Int. J. Comput. Telecommun. Netw. **33**(1–6), 387–401 (2000)
9. Hallur, A.: MozRunk and MozTrust: everything you should know. http://www.gobloggingtips.com/mozrank-and-moztrust/ (2016). Accessed 15 Sept 2016
10. Fishkin, R.: Open site explorer news link building opportunity section (2016). http://moz.com/blog/open-site-explorers-new-link-building-opportunities-section. Accessed 20 April 2016
11. Azevedo, B.F.T., Behar, P.A., Reategui, E.B.: Qualitative analysis of discussion forums. Int. J. Comput. Inf. Syst. Ind. Manag. Appl. **3**, 671–678 (2011). ISSN: 2150-7988
12. Machová, K., Sendek, M.: Authoritative authors mining within web discussion forums. In: 9th International Conference on Systems, pp. 154–159. International Academy, Research and Industry Association, Nice, France (2014)
13. Introduction to regress analysis (in Czech) (2016). http://www.statsoft.cz/file1/PDF/newsletter/2014_26_03_StatSoft_Uvod_do_regresni_analyzy.pdf. Accessed 20 April 2016
14. Štefaník, J.: Approximation of the relation of an authority on the parameters of the structure of web discussion(in Slovak). Technical University of Košice, Košice, Slovakia (2015)
15. Mach, M.: Evolution algorithms—problems solving (in Slovak). FEI Technical University, Košice, p. 135 (2013). ISBN: 978-80-553-1445-7
16. Ćádrik, T., Mach, M.: Evolution classifier systems (in Slovak). Electrical Engineering and Informatics IV. In: Proc. of the FEI Technical University of Košice, Košice, pp. 168–172 (2013). ISBN: 978-80-553-1440-2
17. Šaloun, P., Ondrejka, A., Malčík, M.: Personality disorders identification in written texts. In: International Conference on Advanced Engineering Theory and Applications, Ho Chi Minh City, Lecture Notes in Electrical Engineering, vol. 371, no. 1, pp. 143–154. Springer, New Yok (2016). ISBN: 978-331927245-0, ISSN: 1876-1100
18. Machová, K., Klimko, I.: Classification and clustering methods in the decreasing of the internet cognitive load. Acta Elektrotech. et Inf. vol. 6, no.2, pp. 52–56. FEI TU Košice (2006). ISSN: 1335-8243

## 7

A scalable distributed architecture for client and server-side software agents

Mirjana Ivanović[1] · Milan Vidaković[2] · Zoran Budimac[1] · Dejan Mitrović[1]

Abstract This paper describes recent developments of the Siebog agent middleware regarding performance. This middleware supports both server-side and client-side agents. Server side agents exist as EJB session beans on the JavaEE application server, while client-side agents exist as JavaScript Worker objects in the browser. Siebog employs enterprise technologies on the server side to provide automatic agent load-balancing and fault-tolerance. On the client side this distributed architecture relies on HTML5 and related standards to support smooth running on a wide variety of hardware and software platforms. Such architecture supports rather easy, reliable and efficient communication, interaction, and coexistence between numerous agents. With the automatic clustering and state persistence, Siebog can support thousands of server-side agents, as well as thousands of external devices hosting tens of client-side agents. Performed and presented experiments showed promising results for real life applications of our architecture.

Keywords Agent middleware · Clustering · Load-balancing · Fault-tolerance · HTML5

✉ Mirjana Ivanović
mira@dmi.uns.ac.rs

Milan Vidaković
minja@uns.ac.rs

Zoran Budimac
zjb@dmi.uns.ac.rs

Dejan Mitrović
mitrovic.dejan@gmail.com

[1] Department of Mathematics and Informatics, Faculty of Sciences, University of Novi Sad, Novi Sad, Serbia

[2] Faculty of Technical Sciences, University of Novi Sad, Novi Sad, Serbia

1 Introduction

During the last decade, there has been an obvious paradigm shift in software development. The web has evolved into an environment capable of providing functionalities not so long ago available only in desktop applications. One of the main reasons for the increasing popularity of web-only applications is their cross-platform nature, which allows the end-users to access their favorite applications in a wide variety of ways and devices. As the overall result, the server-based generation of web content is becoming less and less relevant, having browser-based code (namely JavaScript) to interact with the user and perform just like the desktop applications used to work.

Computer clusters are unavoidable nowadays and they play an important role in modern web and enterprise applications and in development of complex software applications. They provide high-availability of deployed applications [1]. This feature provides continuous, uninterrupted delivery of services, regardless of hardware and software failures, or numbers of incoming requests. The high-availability is achieved through the so-called horizontal scaling, which is the process of adding more nodes to the cluster as the demands for processing power increase.

Siebog is our multiagent middleware designed and implemented to provide support for intelligent software agents in clustered environments [2]. It efficiently combines the HTML5 and related web standards on the client side [3,4], and the Enterprise edition of Java (Java EE) on the server side [2,5,6], in an effort to bridge the gap between the agent technology and useful industry applications.

By utilizing the standards and technologies readily-available in Java EE, Siebog offers "native" support for computer clusters on the server. The purpose of this paper is to provide results of clustering of agents on the server side, and to discuss how this support is extended to the client side of Siebog as well. The goal is to provide the support for clusters that consist of arbitrary client devices, such as personal computers, smartphones, and tablets.

The motivation for this approach is straightforward. There can be an order of magnitude more external client devices than there can be server-side computers. Siebog could be used to distribute agents among connected clients and to support applications that require launching large populations of agents. Since the state-of-the-art smartphones have more processing power that many laptop or desktop machines, they represent a significant computational resource.

This approach, however, does pose some technical challenges. Client-side clusters are highly dynamic, in the sense that clients are able to join and leave at any time. To deal with this situation, we added a highly-scalable infrastructure for agent state persistence which allows the agents to "rise above" the interruptions and to operate regardless of their physical locations.

The rest of the paper is organized as follows. Section 2 discusses the overall motivation behind this paper, and presents relevant related work. Section 3 presents our approach for server-side clustering, while Sect. 4 shows how the support for dynamic and heterogeneous client-side clusters was incorporated into the Siebog. The experimental evaluation of proposed architecture and overall performance of the evaluation are presented in Sects. 5 and 6 (server-side and client-side, respectively). The final conclusions and future research directions are given in Sect. 7.

2 Background

With the rise of popularity of multi-agent systems, a large number of different software tools, systems, platforms and environments that allow development and deployment of multi-agent systems and their applications in different domains have been designed and implemented. Most of them rely on proprietary solutions, while only a handful of them use some industrial-ready solution integrated in the system. As a consequence, most of the multi-agent systems do not offer clustering, or has it implemented on a very poor level. On the other hand, the Siebog agent middleware uses as much JavaEE technology as possible for most of its subsystems. For example, it uses Java Messaging System (JMS) to exchange messages, Java Naming and Directory Interface (JNDI) for agent lookup, Enterprize Java Beans (EJB) for agent implementation, etc. This enables Siebog to use tested and proven solutions implemented into the JavaEE application servers, having clustering, load-balancing, and safe-failover working out of box. Significant functionality and challenge of our architecture is that agents deployed in the Siebog can operate on clusters, being able to sur-

vive node failures and being able to serve numerous clients [2,4].

On the client side, we have web applications playing an increasingly important role in the contemporary computing. They offer a number of advantages over traditional desktop application, such as the lack of need for installation, configuration, or upgrade. The importance of web applications is emphasized by the continuously increasing sales of mobile devices and the ability of web applications to run as native applications on these devices [7].

To maintain its relevance in this new era, the agent technology not only needs to move to the web, but it needs to do so in accordance to the modern standards and the end-users' expectations. Agent-based applications need to seamlessly be integrated into web and enterprise applications to reach the end-users more easily, and to stay relevant in this new state of affairs.

Current research in the agent technology area is very dynamic and promising, there exists a large number of both open-source and commercial agent middlewares [8,9]. However, almost none of these systems have fully exploited the advantages of web environments. Some efforts aimed at extending existing systems with web support have been made, but usually in an inefficient manner. For example, in many Java-based middlewares, such as JADE [10] or JaCa-Web [11], the extensions are based on Java applets. But, Java applets require a browser plug-in to run, which is unavailable on some platforms (e.g. iOS and Smart TVs). With some desktop-based browsers also starting to disable Java support, the applicability of Java-based web solutions becomes limited to a narrower set of hardware and software platforms.

One of the prominent and promising ways of migrating and intensively using agent technology in the web is to use the expanding HTML5 and related set of standards [12]. HTML5 covers various aspects of web and enterprise applications, from audio and video playbacks, to offline application support, to more advanced features, such as multi-threaded execution and push-based communication. In addition, since web browser vendors keep investing significant resources into improving the overall performance of their respective JavaScript virtual machines, the HTML5 is expected to become "a mainstream enterprise application development environment" in near future [13]. One of the important elements in our approach, comparing to other existing approaches, is the usage of essential HTML5 concepts for client-side agents that enables them to "spread" over wide range of client browsers.

2.1 Related work

As outlined in [9], a large number of multi-agent middlewares has been developed over the years. However it appears that not all of those systems are still being actively developed and/or used today. Most of them have been developed for academic and scientific purposes within specific projects and their development and use finishes after completion of the projects. As the first step in making agent development more popular and practically applicable is to allow agents' frameworks and architectures to be opened and freely available to wide range of agent communities. It offers other research groups possibility to actively use them and also further improve and update them. For this reason the full source code of our system is freely available [2].

Agent Developing Framework [14] enables the user to build an interoperable, flexible, and scalable application. Agent Developing Framework uses Java EE technologies such as JNDI, JMS and JMX. Communication is done synchronously or asynchronously through JMS (Java Message Service). Although this framework uses the same technology as the Siebog, ADF is no longer maintained. Currently downloadable version is from the year 2005 and practically is not any more adjusted to the modern trends and technologies of development multi-agent systems.

Voyager [15] is middleware software designed for distributed application development, and it does provide the option of developing applications using multi-agent programming, although that is not its main purpose. Latest version available is Voyager 8.0. It's a simple yet powerful technology for creating mobile agents in Java. It represented an improvement over other existing platforms (Concordia, Aglets, Odyssey, etc.) which only allowed developers to create agents and launch them into a network to fulfill its mission. But none of the mentioned platforms and middleware allowed sending messages to a moving agent, which made it difficult to communicate with an agent once it has been launched and also for agents to communicate with other agents. Voyager seamlessly integrated fundamental distributed computing with agent technology. Voyager provides flexible life spans for agents, by supporting a variety of life span methods. In spite the fact that this framework supports scalability and fault-tolerance as our middleware, its main drawback comparing to our system is that it is a commercial product.

JADE [10] is a MAS written in Java and strongly adherent to the FIPA [16] standard and provides a wide range of functionalities to agent developers, either as built-in features, or through its extensive ecosystem of plug-ins. The system itself can be executed as a set of containers on top of a computer network. Fault-tolerance is achieved through both container and agent state replication processes.

In [17] authors have established through experiments a correlation between the number of computers and the latency, as well as between the number of computers and throughput. They have used JADE in an online auction system for their experiments.

In [18] authors have established a set of benchmarks which are used to measure performance of the JADE. We were inspired by this paper as well as by [19] when we measured performance of the Siebog middleware.

Siebog, the system we have been developing for several years uses JMS for message exchange, while JADE has its own system. The main difference between these two systems, however, lies in the fact that, when creating clusters, JADE agents have to be manually divided between cluster nodes, while in Siebog it is done automatically. So another important characteristic of Siebog system is that in it an agent is defined at the level of the computer cluster, and not at an individual node.

Two systems are applicable to different scenarios. We argue that, due to its clustering features, Siebog represents a better solution for applications that need to launch large populations of agents (e.g. [20]), and/or need to provide high-level of fault-tolerance. For example, JADE consumes a single thread per agent and has a predefined number of message processing threads. In Siebog, these numbers are increased or decreased automatically, depending on the current load. For other use-cases, using JADE might represent a better approach, since it consumes less resources and its usage is a bit simpler.

Along with the more recent trends, there have been several proposals of using mobile agents within the so-called Internet of Things (IoT) concept [13], in smart objects [21,22] and in smart cities [23]. The role of Siebog in these practical applications is possible and feasible and would be in providing a standards-compliant, platform-independent, and efficient [4] multiagent middleware. In addition, with the work presented in this paper, we intend to bring the more traditional agent applications to the web. As it is discussed later, Siebog is suitable and reliable for distributed systems with large populations of agents. A concrete example of its possible practical application would be in the area of swarm intelligence, as it is presented [23].

As we discussed previously in [3,4], many traditional (i.e. desktop- or server-based) multiagent middlewares have exposed their functionalities to the web through Java applets. This approach does provide many important benefits, such as the immediate availability of complex reasoning agents in web browsers [11]. However, with the lack of Java support in many popular modern platforms, this approach is no longer sufficient.

To the best of our knowledge, currently there exists only one additional HTML5-based multiagent middleware [24, 25]. The middleware is focused on using (primarily) mobile agents to support the IoT requirements while our primary attention is to develop system that could be widely used in different areas and environments. On the technical viewpoint, the client side of their system, in comparison to our approach, does not utilize the full range of HTML5 and related standards (such as Web Workers [12]). In approach presented in [24,25] it is also not clear how multiple agents could be started within the same host, and how would they interact with each other without the server. The authors show how the most advanced variant of moving code, mobile agents, can be used for operating and managing Internet-connected systems composed of gadgets, sensors and actuators. They pointed out that the use of mobile agents brings several benefits but practical use is not presented clearly. One of them is that mobile agents help to reduce the network load, overcome network latency, and encapsulate protocols. The need for moving agents is even more significant if the applications and other factors of the overall experience should follow the user to new contexts. When multiple agents are used to provide the user with services, some mechanisms to manage the agents are needed. In the context of Internet-of-Things such management should reflect the physical spaces and other relevant contexts. The backend in their approach is conveniently based on Node.js, which simplifies certain development aspects (such as mobility), but lacks several advanced features found in Siebog, namely automated agent load-balancing and fault-tolerance.

To summarize above discussion we can pointed out that Siebog is a web-based, enterprise-scale multiagent middleware. Its uniqueness is that it combines the enterprise technologies on the server with HTML5 and related standards on the client. Such combination together with scaling possibilities represent the main contribution, advantages and differences of our approach comparing to above presented systems and approaches. As well usage of well-proven industrial solution for the JavaEE application server provides server-side agents with the possibility of operating in clusters with features like load-balancing and safe-failover working out of box. Additionally the usage of essential HTML5 concepts supports client-side agents to "spread" over enormous number of client browsers, with the number of instances.

3 Clustering server-side Siebog agents

In this section we will briefly cover Siebog implementation of clustered agent middleware. The goal of Siebog is to provide an infrastructure for reliable executing agents in web environments, but in accordance to the modern standards. It is built on our previous two systems, XJAF [6] and Radigost [4], in a way that it not only combines their individual functionalities, but it also adds new features on both server and client side. On the server side Siebog offers:

- **Scalability**: Agents are automatically distributed across the cluster to reduce to computational load of individual nodes. This makes Siebog suitable for applications that need to launch large populations of agents in a computer cluster.

- **Fault-tolerance**: The state of each server-side component, including agents themselves, is copied to other nodes making the whole system resilient to hardware and software failures.

Siebog heavily depends on the JavaEE application server features such as clustering, load-balancing and safe-failover. Currently, the Siebog is deployed on the JBoss application server called Wildfly [26]. The framework is organized as a set of loosely-coupled components called managers, as shown in Fig. 1. Each manager is dedicated to handling a distinct part of the overall functionality. A manager is represented and used only by its interface, and even multiple implementations of the same interface can be active simultaneously. AgentManager keeps record of available and used agents. MessageManager delivers messages to agents, while ConnectionManager keeps track of other Siebog instances. This design approach offers the highest level of flexibility, and allows third-party re-implementations of individual components.

The organization of the Siebog cluster is shown in Fig. 2. A single node within the cluster is described as master, while the others (zero or more) are described as slaves. Within a node, the JBoss host controller is used to manage the Siebog instance [26]. In addition, the master node can be used to remotely control the entire cluster, through the JBoss domain controller [26]. This is the only difference between the master and the slaves; all nodes in a cluster have the same execution priority, can directly communicate to each other, etc.

The preferred approach of inter-node communication and information sharing is given through the Infinispan cache system [3]. Infinispan cache is one of the core clustering technologies used by JBoss. It is a distributed, concurrent and highly-efficient key/value data structure. Infinispan cache represents the backbone of the state replication and failover process described later, but it can also store arbitrary user data. Whenever it runs a new agent, for example, the agent manager stores all the necessary information in the Infinispancache (e.g. agentIdentifier -> beanInstance). This information can later be retrieved by the message manager to deliver a message to the agent. Since the cache is distributed across the cluster, the managers themselves can be hosted on any node. In fact, for maximum performance, they are implemented as clustered stateless beans by default.

The cluster has two main functionalities: state replication and failover&load-balancing. State replication and failover are applicable to stateful beans only. Whenever a stateful bean's internal state is changed, the replication process copies it across other nodes in the cluster. In case the bean's node becomes unavailable, the failover process fully restores the bean object on one of the remaining nodes. From the client's

Fig. 1 Architecture of the
Siebog agent middleware

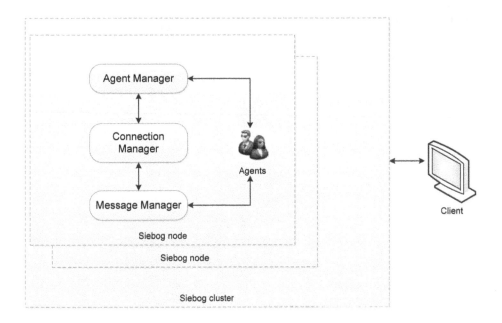

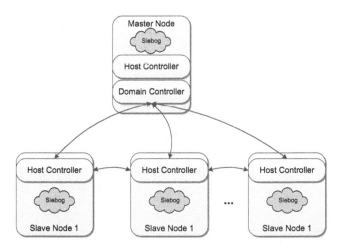

Fig. 2 Siebog operates in a symmetric cluster; each node is connected
to other node

4 Clustering client-side agents

As we already mentioned in previous section Siebog provides
an infrastructure for executing agents in web environments,
adding new features on both server and client side.

The client-side component of Siebog has the following set
of unique characteristics:

- It is platform-independent, supporting a range of hardware and software platforms. To agent developers, this
  provides the write once, run anywhere approach. The
  end-users, on the other hand, can utilize the benefits of
  the agent technology in the most convenient manner.
- It requires no prior installation or configuration steps.
- Its client-side runtime performance is comparable to that
  of a classical, desktop multiagent platform

In this section we will describe how Siebog is extended to
support automatic clustering and load-balancing of its client-
side agents [27]. More concretely, we discuss how a possibly
large set of heterogeneous client-side devices can be observed
as a coherent cluster. The cluster can then be used to execute
resource-demanding and computationally-expensive tasks,
such as launching large populations of agents.

The support for the client-side clustering is shown graphi-
cally in Fig. 3. On the server side, Siebog introduces one more
manager, for the client-side agent management: WebClient
Manager, which acts as an intermediary for server-to-client
(i.e. push) messaging, and also handles state persistence for
client-side agents.

Client-side agents are executed inside web browsers [2–
4] or possibly in dedicated JavaScript runtimes of external
devices. Inside a device, agents rely on the Siebog client

point of view, the entire process is executed transparently:
all subsequent method invocation will end-up in the newly
created object.

Load-balancing is used to automatically distribute agents
across different nodes in the cluster, and to speed up the overall runtime performance of Siebog. It works with both stateful
and stateless beans, although the behavior is slightly different. When the client creates a new stateful bean instance, the
server places it in one of the available nodes, and all subsequent invocations of the bean's methods end-up there. In case
of stateless beans, the load-balancing works on a per-method
basis. At any time, there can be many instances of the same
stateless bean running in parallel across the cluster. Once the
client invokes a method of the bean, one of the instances is
selected to serve the request.

Fig. 3 Client-side clustering support in the Siebog middleware

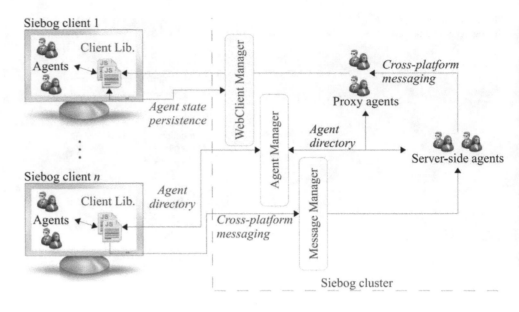

Fig. 4 Transparent communication of client-side agents across different devices

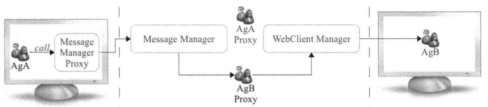

library for execution support and for communicating with the server. For example, the client library offers proxy implementations of server-side components. To send a message to the server-side agent, the client-side agent simply invokes the proxy implementation of the MessageManager. Underneath, the proxy then turns this invocation into a corresponding AJAX call to the server.

Another important feature of Siebog is that its server can (if configured) hold a proxy representation of each client-side agent. This representation simply forwards all incoming messages to the corresponding client-side counterpart (and through the WebClient Manager). This feature opens-up the possibility for transparent agent communication across different devices.

An illustrative example is shown in Fig. 4. Suppose that there exist two agents, AgA and AgB, hosted by two different devices, Device A and Device B, respectively. When the AgA decides to send a message to AgB, the message will be delivered in the following way:

- AgA makes the appropriate call to the MessageManager Proxy.
- This call is transformed into an AJAX call to the server-side MessageManager.
- The MessageManager delivers the message to the AgB proxy.

- Since this is a proxy representation, it forwards the message to the WebClient Manager.
- The WebClient Manager, which is aware of all external clients, finally pushes the message to the target agent.

Due to limitations imposed by certain web browsers [4], each client device can run up to a few dozens of agents. But, there can be large number of physical devices that are active simultaneously. The main idea here is to exploit this possibility to distribute portions of a large population of agents. This is conceptually similar to, for example, the famous SETI@home scientific experiment. As an important advantage, the Siebog does not require any software installation: all the end-user needs to do is to visit the corresponding web page. The main issue here is how to efficiently support these large numbers of external devices, and to deal with their inherently dynamic availability.

4.1 Managing heterogeneous and dynamic clusters

A central component in a computer cluster is a load-balancer with the task of distributing the work across available machines. In the context of Siebog, the load-balancer continuously accepts tasks that need to be solved. For example, it can accept large maps for the Traveling Salesman Problem and then partition each map [28] and send it (along with the corresponding set of ants) to a subset of available devices.

In the majority of existing non agent-based distributed architectures, the load-balancer selects the target device randomly. In this way, the workload is distributed "for free" and, in the longer run, equally among all available devices. However, the clusters that consist of Siebog clients are heterogeneous, in the sense that they can include devices with very different processing capabilities. Therefore, the load-balancing process is a bit more complex.

When it comes to load-balancing in heterogeneous systems, the agent-oriented research has proposed some rather complex approaches (e.g. [29–31]). In case of Siebog, however, we decided to follow the industry norms of keeping things as simple as possible. Once a device joins the cluster for the first time, a performance benchmark is executed. The results of this benchmark are used to assign a number of compute units (CUs) to the device. Now, during the load-balancing phase, the target device is selected with the probability that corresponds to its number of CUs.

From the end-user's point of view, joining the Siebog cluster is fairly simple: he/she only needs to visit the appropriate web page that hosts the worker agents. Unfortunately, it is also very easy to leave the cluster; once the end-user closes the web browser or switches of the device, the hosted agents are lost. For meaningful practical applications, however, the agents need to be able to run regardless of these interruptions.

To support possibly large numbers of agents, Siebog needs a scalable datastore, one capable of serving multitudes of requests per second. The datastore should also be fault-tolerant—capable of surviving server crashes. More formally, these requirements can be described as principles of the so-called Dynamo systems [32]. Currently, there exist several concrete Dynamo realizations. After a careful evaluation of these solutions, we determined that the open-source Apache Cassandra datastore fulfills the needs of the Siebog client-side clusters. The client-side Siebog library has been extended to allow the agents the interact with the datastore directly, and over the WebSocket protocol [3,4].

The integrated Siebog architecture enables transparent inter-agent communication and action coordination, regardless of the types and physical locations of agents. A client-side agent can send a message to a server-side agent via the appropriate stub call. However, if the target agent is actually a stub representation of a different client-side agent, the message may end up in a different web page or on a different device. This opens up a range of possible practical applications; for example, in case of smart environments agents hosted in physically distributed smart objects can seamlessly exchange information and coordinate their actions.

The performance evaluation of the new architecture we proposed in this paper is discussed in the following two sections.

5 Performance evaluation of server-side agents

In addition to the advanced programming features described earlier, an important factor for the wider acceptance of Siebog is its runtime performance. Therefore, a case-study has been developed to assess this aspect of our system [33]. The case-study includes a pair of agents, named Sender and Receiver. The first agent issues a request to the second, which then performs a computationally expensive task, and replies with the result. The message round-trip time (RTT) is used as a measure; it expresses the time since the Sender issues the request and until it receives the reply. This relatively simple, but effective performance study is inspired by those described in paper [4,18,19,34]. More complex use-cases, e.g. implementation of an ant colony optimization algorithm for the Traveling salesman problem [20], can be found at our recent paper [2] in which the description of Siebog is given together with link to homepage of our system. There reader can find detailed manual and precise directions how to use Siebog [2].

Experimental setup was as follows:

- Hardware: Intel Dual-Core CPU at 3 GHz, with 2 GB of RAM. The CPU is capable of executing four threads simultaneously;
- 32-bit version of Ubuntu 14.04LTS;
- OpenJDK 7 for JADE, and OpenJDK 8 for Siebog; the maximum heap size for each Siebog node/JADE container was set to 512 MB;
- JBoss Wildfly 9.0;
- The Receiver agent used a brute-force algorithm for finding all prime numbers up to a certain limit;
- Each of the two messages exchanged between a Sender and the Receiver included a string of 65 K random characters.

The utilized Wildfly server has a specific feature. When one EJB (directly or indirectly) invokes a method of another EJB, the target will be executed on the same node as the source EJB. This is an optimization feature, applied to reduce expensive network communication: if two agents exchange a lot of messages, then they should reside in the same node. Although this default behavior can (and, in case of multi-agent systems, often should) be changed, it was left as-is for this case-study. This means that the Sender and its corresponding Receiver are always executed on the same node.

A set of analogous JADE agents was implemented and used as a reference point. By default, during the load-balancing process JBoss selects an available cluster node randomly. To achieve a similar distribution of agents in both Siebog and JADE implementations, and obtain more relevant results, we've setup the JBoss server to use a round robin node selector. The final organization of the case-study and the distribution of agents in both implementations are shown in Fig. 5.

Two evaluation scenarios were executed. First, we measured how many agents each of the frameworks can execute per machine and how the average RTT changes as the number of agents increases. The results of this experiment are shown in Fig. 6. For lower numbers of agents, JADE offers better runtime performance. This is expected, since there is an overhead associated with remote EJB invocations. However, as the number of agents increases, Siebog scales better. Moreover, in our setup, once the number of pairs is set to 2048 (i.e. 4096 agents), JADE starts discarding messages and eventually crashes with the out-of-memory error. On the other hand, our system Siebog is perfectly capable of executing this many agents (and more), due to built-in optimization features described earlier.

The second scenario was designed to measure the scaling factor of Siebog as more and more nodes are added to the cluster. The number of agent pairs was fixed to 2048 (i.e.

4096 agents), and the prime limit on the Receiver's end was set to 60,000. Four rounds of experiment were conducted: using 1, 2, 4 and 8 nodes, each having the same hardware and software configuration. In this evaluation, it was observed that, as the number of nodes doubles, the execution speed of Siebog increases approximately 3.5 times, which is an excellent outcome (the ideal would be 4 times).

These achieved and presented experimental results are very encouraging for the performances of our framework, and work in favor of the intended usage of it. They confirm the effectiveness of the inherent load-balancing capability. Along with other clustering features offered by the modern enterprise application server, Siebog represents an excellent framework for applications that require and support larger populations of agents.

6 Performance evaluation of client-side agents

The newly proposed architecture of Siebog needs to be able to serve large numbers of running agents, which are concurrently, and at high frequencies, storing and retrieving their respective internal states. To evaluate this feature, we used the open-source Yahoo! Cloud Serving Benchmark (YCSB) [35] tool. YCSB is designed for load-testing of (primarily) NoSQL databases, and can be configured through a range of parameters, including the desired number of operations per second (throughput), the number of concurrent threads, maximum execution time, etc.

The experiments were performed using two machines, each with 8 virtual CPUs and 28 GB of RAM, running 64-bit version of Ubuntu 14.04 LTS. One machine was hosting the Apache Cassandra datastore and the Siebog server (deployed on the Wildfly 9.0 application server), while the other one was used to launch YCSB-simulated external devices. Each external device was represented by a separate WebSocket

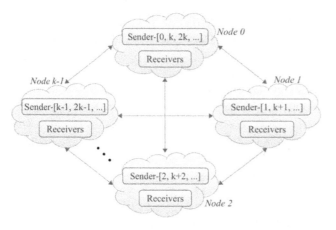

Fig. 5 Organization of the case-study and the round robin-based distribution of Sender–Receiver pairs in both the Siebog and the JADE implementation

Fig. 6 Correlations between the number of agents and the average RTTs in Siebog and JADE implementations of the Sender–Receiver experiment (prime limit = 20,000)

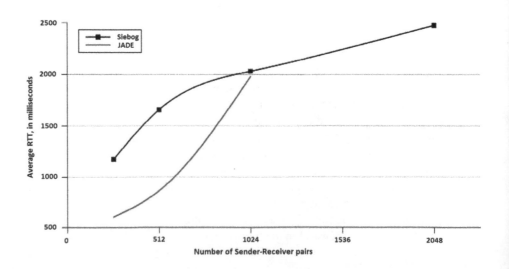

that the server needed to maintain. We have used different server machines for the client-side test, since we only had these two virtual machines. For the server-side clustering (described in the Sect. 5), we have had entire computer lab, so we were able to increase the number of computers in the cluster.

In a realistic use-case, there will be many more writes to the store than reads. That is, the internal state of an agent will usually be read only once: when the web page is loaded and the agent is started. On the other hand, the state can be stored multiple times during the agent's execution, e.g. after each processed message or after each computational sub-step. Therefore, the YCSB workload was set up as write-heavy, so that 90 % of all operations are writes.

The goal of the experiment was to determine the maximum number of external devices as well as client-side agents that our system can support. For this goal, several test-cases were executed. With each successive test-case, the total number of connected devices was increased. Then we would try to find the maximum throughput (i.e. the number of operations per second) that the Siebog server can support. A test-case was executed for one hour, and the maximum throughput value that was stable during this period was taken as the end-result.

We started with 100 external devices, increased the number for each test case, and finally reached the limit of approximately 16,000 devices. This number actually represents the maximum number of open connections that the operating system could support. Nonetheless, being able to support 16,000 external devices using a single-node Siebog cluster is an excellent result, given the fact that the cluster can easily be extended with more nodes as the demands

grow. The results of this test-case are shown in Fig. 7. More concretely, the figure shows average read and write latencies during the one hour period, calculated at one minute intervals. The latencies are very low (expressed in microseconds), due to the WebSocket protocol's support for asynchronous I/O.

For each test-case, through trial-and-error, we determined that the value of approximately 6000 operations per second is the maximum throughput that remained stable during the one hour period. Our systems is capable of serving much larger numbers than this (i.e. up to 100,000 operations per second), but only in "short bursts," after which the backend datastore needed some time to manage all the write operations.

Although the 6000 operations per second might not seem as a large number at first, it is worth noting that an agent is not supposed to store its internal state at every second. So even if agents store their respective states at every 10 s, we reach the conclusion that our Siebog multiagent middleware can manage 60,000 agents distributed across 16,000 devices, using only one server side node.

7 Conclusions and future work

Siebog is a web-based, enterprise-scale multiagent middleware. It combines the enterprise technologies on the server with HTML5 and related standards on the client to support multiagent solutions whose functionalities meet the expectations of modern software systems. This combination of server-side and client-side technologies is the unique up to now and represents the main contribution of this paper, since it is (to the best of our knowledge) the only agent middleware which scales well on both server and client sides. With the usage of well-proven industrial solution for the JavaEE application server, we have managed to provide server-side agents with the possibility of operating in clusters with features like load-balancing and safe-failover working out of box. On the other hand, the usage of HTML5 concepts like WebWorkers and WebSockets gave the opportunity for client-side agents to "spread" over enormous number of client browsers, with the number of instances greatly surpassing the number of server-side instances. In this paper, we have, therefore, presented how Siebog was updated to support dynamic clusters of heterogeneous client-side devices, as well as to support server-side agents in a clustered environment.

The two new components of our system are the load-balancer, which is in charge of distributing agents across the connected devices, and a highly-scalable backend datastore used for persisting the internal states of client-side agents. Evaluation tests proved that the Siebog can scale up in a clustered environment and that it can handle increased load on the server-side. Server-side agents are deployed as EJB beans, so they are multiplied on the server in case of stateless

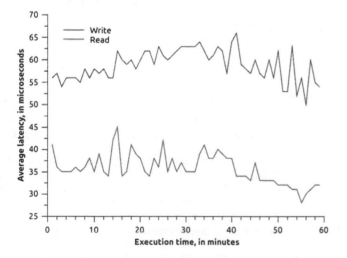

Fig. 7 Average read and write latencies of the test-case simulating 16,000 external devices and 6000 operations per second, during the one hour period. The latencies are calculated at one minute intervals

beans. In case of stateful beans, they can be reconstructed on other nodes, in situation of failure of the node they reside in. On the client side, the cluster is actually replaced with multiple browsers, having multiple JavaScript-based agents, who are capable of saving their state to the server, in case user closes the browser. Client-side agents can exchange messages between them, but they also can exchange messages with client-side agents on other browsers, as well as with server-side browsers.

For any meaningful application of Siebog, its client-side agents need to become "detached" from their host environments (e.g. web pages). As shown in the paper, thanks to the use of Dynamo architecture and the WebSocket protocol, on just one server node the state persistence system in Siebog can support thousands of external devices hosting tens of thousands of client-side agents, which is an excellent result.

Future developments of Siebog will be focused on an even tighter integration of client-side and server-side agents. Also, the system will be extended with an interoperability module, allowing it to interact with third-party multiagent solutions. Although Siebog already supports BDI agents on the server, the work is underway to develop a unique architecture for intelligent agents.

References

1. Michael, M., Moreira, J.E., Shiloach, D., Wisniewski, R.W.: Scale-up x scale-out: a case study using Nutch/Lucene. In: IEEE International Parallel and Distributed Processing Symposium, pp. 1–8 (2007)
2. Mitrović, D., Ivanović, M., Vidaković Budimac, Z.: The Siebog multiagent middleware. Knowl.-Based Syst. **103**, 56–59 (2016)
3. Mitrović, D., Ivanović, M., Bădică, C.: Delivering the multiagent technology to end-users through the web. In: Proceedings of the 4th International Conference on Web Intelligence, Mining and Semantics (WIMS), pp. 54:1–54:6 (2014)
4. Mitrović, D., Ivanović, M., Budimac, Z., Radigost Vidaković, M.: Interoperable web-based multi-agent platform. J Syst Softw **90**, 167–178 (2014)
5. Mitrović, D., Ivanović, M., Vidaković, M., Budimac, Z.: The Siebog multiagent middleware. Knowl.-Based Syst. **103**, 56–59 (2016)
6. Vidaković, M., Ivanović, M., Mitrović, D., Budimac, Z.: Extensible java EE-based agent framework—past, present, future. In: Ganzha, M., Jain, L.C. (eds.) Multiagent Systems and Applications, Intelligent Systems Reference Library, vol. 45, pp. 55–88. Springer, Berlin (2013)
7. Xanthopoulos, S., Xinogalos, S.: A comparative analysis of cross-platform development approaches for mobile applications. In: Proceedings of the 6th Balkan Conference in Informatics (BCI), pp 213–220. ACM, New York (2013)
8. Bordini, R.H., Braubach, L., Dastani, M., El, A., Seghrouchni, F., Gomez-sanz, J.J., Leite, J., Pokahr, A., Ricci, A.: A survey of programming languages and platforms for multi-agent systems. Informatica **30**, 33–44 (2006)
9. Bădică, C., Budimac, Z., Burkhard, H.D., Ivanović, M.: Software agents: languages, tools, platforms. Comput Sci Inf Syst ComSIS **8**(2), 255–298 (2011)
10. Bellifemine, F., Caire, G., Greenwood, D.: Developing multi-agent systems with JADE. Wiley, New York (2007)
11. Minotti, M., Santi, A., Ricci, A.: Developing web client applications with JaCaWeb. In: Omicini, A., Viroli, M. (eds.) Proceedings of the 11th WOA 2010 workshop, Dagli Oggetti Agli Agenti, Rimini, Italy, September 5–7, 2010. CEUR Workshop Proceedings, vol. 621. CEUR-WS.org (2010)
12. HTML5: a vocabulary and associated APIs for HTML and XHTML (2014). http://www.w3.org/TR/html5/. Accessed 29 April 2016
13. Gartner identifies the top 10 strategic technology trends for 2014 (2013). http://www.gartner.com/newsroom/id/2603623. Accessed 29 April 2016
14. Agent Developing Framework Homepage. http://adf.sourceforge.net/index.html. Accessed 29 April 2016
15. Voyager Homepage. http://www.recursionsw.com/voyager-intro/. Accessed 29 April 2016
16. FIPA Homepage. http://www.fipa.org. Accessed 29 April 2016
17. Badica, C., Ilie, S., Muscar, A., Badica, A., Sandu, L., Sbora, R., Ganzha, M., Paprzycki, M.: Distributed agent-based online auction system. Comput Inf **33**(3), 518–552 (2014)
18. Such, J.M., Alberola, J.M., Mulet, L., Espinosa, A., Garcia-Fornes, A., Botti, V.: Large-scale multiagent platform benchmarks. In: Proceedings of the MultiAgent Logics, Languages, and Organisations—Federated Workshops, Languages, Methodologies and Development Tools for Multi-agent Systems (LADS), pp. 192–204 (2007)
19. Jurasovic, K., Jezic, G., Kusek, M.: A performance analysis of multi-agent systems. Int Trans Syst Sci Appl **1**(4), 335–342 (2006)
20. Ilie, S., Bădică, A., Bădică, C.: Distributed agent-based ant colony optimization for solving traveling salesman problem on a partitioned map. In: Proceedings of the International Conference on Web Intelligence, Mining and Semantics. pp. 23:1–23:9. WIMS '11, ACM, New York (2011)
21. Aiello, F., Fortino, G., Gravina, R., Guerrieri, A.: A java-based agent platform for programming wireless sensor networks. Comput J **54**(3), 439–454 (2011)
22. Fortino, G., Guerrieri, A., Russo, W.: Agent-oriented smart objects development. In: 16th International Conference on Computer Supported Cooperative Work in Design (CSCWD), pp. 907–912 (2012)
23. Verma, P., Gupta, M., Bhattacharya, T., Das, P.K.: Improving services using mobile agents-based IoT in a smart city. In: International Conference on Contemporary Computing and Informatics (IC3I), pp. 107–111 (2014)
24. Jarvenpaa, L., Lintinen, M., Mattila, A.L., Mikkonen, T., Systa, K., Voutilainen, J.P.: Mobile agents for the internet of things. In: 17th International Conference on System Theory, Control and Computing (ICSTCC), pp. 763–767 (2013)
25. Systa, K., Mikkonen, T., Jarvenpaa, L.: Html5 agents: mobile agents for the web. In: Krempels, K.H., Stocker, A. (eds.) Web Information Systems and Technologies, Lecture Notes in Business Information Processing, vol. 189, pp. 53–67. Springer, Berlin (2014)
26. WildFly Homepage. http://wildfly.org/. Accessed 29 April 2016
27. Mitrović, D., Ivanović, M., Vidaković, M., Budimac, Z.: A scalable distributed architecture for web-based software agents. In: 7'th International Conference on Computational Collective Intelligence (ICCCI), pp. 67–76 (2015)
28. Ilie, S., Bădică, C.: Multi-agent approach to distributed ant colony optimization. Sci. Comput. Program. **78**(6), 762–774 (2013)
29. Cao, J., Spooner, D.P., Jarvis, S.A., Nudd, G.R.: Grid load balancing using intelligent agents. Future Gener. Comput. Syst. **21**(1), 135–149 (2005)

30. Nehra, N., Patel, R.: Towards dynamic load balancing in hetero-geneous cluster using mobile agent. Int. Conf. Comput. Intell. Multimed. Appl. **1**, 15–21 (2007)
31. Zhang, Z., Zhang, X.: A load balancing mechanism based on ant colony and complex network theory in open cloud computing feder-ation. In: 2nd International Conference on Industrial Mechatronics and Automation (ICIMA), vol. 2, pp 240–243 (2010)
32. DeCandia, G., Hastorun, D., Jampani, M., Kakulapati, G., Lak-shman, A., Pilchin, A., Sivasubramanian, S., Vosshall, P., Vogels, W.: Dynamo: Amazon's highly available key-value store. In: Pro-ceedings of Twenty-first ACM SIGOPS Symposium on Operating Systems Principles, pp. 205–220. SOSP '07 (2007)
33. Mitrović, D., Ivanović, M., Vidaković, M., Budimac, Z.: Exten-sible Java EE-based agent framework in clustered environments. In: Mueller, J., Weyrich, M., Bazzan, A.L.C. (eds.) 12th German Conference on Multiagent System Technologies. Lecture Notes in Computer Science, vol. 8732, pp. 202–215. Springer, Berlin (2014)
34. Pérez-Carro, P., Grimaldo, F., Lozano, M., Orduña, J.M.: Charac-terization of the Jason multi-agent platform on multicore proces-sors. Sci Program **22**(1), 21–35 (2014)
35. Cooper, B.F., Silberstein, A., Tam, E., Ramakrishnan, R., Sears, R.: Benchmarking cloud serving systems with YCSB. In: Proceedings of the 1st ACM Symposium on Cloud Computing (SoCC), pp. 143–154. ACM, New York (2010)

## 8

Extracting user behavior-related words and phrases using temporal patterns of sequential pattern evaluation indices

Hidenao Abe[1] 🅾

Abstract The growth of social media sites, such as Twitter, which can provide a visual record of the daily interests and concerns of people in the form of their tweets and tweeting behaviors, has led to an increasing demand among enterprise users, to be able to identify those users who are interested in the services and products that these enterprises offer. However, accurately determining whether people who receive information, such as tweets, from enterprise users have a genuine interest in it can be difficult. In this study, a method for extracting feature words and phrases from the past users' tweets using temporal patterns of sequential pattern evaluation indices and phrase importance evaluation indices is developed. In this method, a variety of the followers interests are first analyzed using the feature words and phrases retweeted by the followers. Next, the temporal patterns of each evaluation index that are created based on the usage frequencies of feature words and phrases obtained from the historical followers' tweeting behaviors are extracted. An experimental result has shown that this method successfully extracted the sets of words and phrases based on the followers' tweeting behaviors as the temporal patterns for each evaluation index and the following retailer's account. These sets of words and phrases lead to understand the variety of the followers' interests with more clues.

Keywords Temporal text mining · Sequential pattern evaluation index · User behavior prediction

1 Introduction

The recent growth of social media sites, such as Twitter, provides a media-based visual records of the talk and behavior of people, simply called users in this paper, which reflect their interests and concerns. Consequently, users, such as corporations and politicians, have begun looking for more efficient ways to communicate ideas with a large number of other users who have similar interests or concerns to theirs. As a result, many approaches have been developed to distinguish users having similar interests, using network analysis methods or/and text mining-based analysis methods [1].

However, because accurate identification of future user behavior without considering the user's speech and behavior history is difficult, there is a severe need to develop other methods that more accurately describe user's interests as feature words for predicting a targeted behavior such as retweeting. To this end, some studies attempted to predict users' information diffusions using frequencies of appearances of words and phrases, users' actions count, and other features related to the users' behavior in the past tweets of the users [2–4]. In [3], the method needs the emotional categories of the words that were constructed using an expensive tool. This prediction method cannot work with the Linguistic Inquiry and Word Count (LIWC) dictionary. On the other hand, in [4], they introduced the time-dependent features that obtained from the history of tweeting actions and not the usage history of the words. Regarding these previous studies, the problem of connecting the users' behavior with the content of the users' tweets seems unsolved.

Considering the above-mentioned issue, this study focuses on the temporal behaviors of the Twitter service known as "retweeting," in which users disseminate information by resending a previous tweet, and develops a method for extracting feature words and phrases that can predict retweet-

✉ Hidenao Abe
hidenao@shonan.bunkyo.ac.jp

[1] Department of Information Systems, Bunkyo University, 1100 Namegaya, Chigasaki, Kanagawa 2538550, Japan

ing behavior using the content of the users' tweeting history. To tackle the problem of absence of the words in a prepared dictionary, we use the values of pattern evaluation indices that assume words and phrases as patterns. The use of values of the pattern evaluation indices separates the surface form of the words and phrases from their statistical nature. In addition, we should also solve the problem of preparing the categories of the words and phrases for characterizing users' tweeting behaviors. As for grouping words and phrases, we can use the temporal values of the pattern evaluation indices. By clustering the temporal values as the temporal patterns, the words and the phrases are categorized based on their statistical nature. On a set of temporal clusters, the centroids of the clusters represent the temporal patterns of anonymized words and phrases that are represented by averaged temporal values and their ranges on each timestamp of the established pattern evaluation index.

In this paper, the proposed method first extracts the differences between groups of feature words and phrases contained in retweeted text and groups of feature words contained in the tweeting history of users believed to be interested in information from particular Twitter account holders, who are known as followers. Then, the temporal patterns of the words and phrases evaluation indices, calculated using the usage frequencies of feature words and phrases contained in the followers' past tweets, are obtained. These results are used to discuss the development of the method for constructing a model that predicts information-retweeting behavior using the temporal patterns of evaluation indices in the tweeting history instead of using the feature words and phrases appearances directly.

Although the original idea of this study and a part of the experimental results are described in our previous work [5], the purpose of this paper is to describe availability and efficiency of this method more methodologically, and to explain the availability and efficiency of the approach using additional results of the experiment. Adding to the experimental results, we also introduce a temporal trend analysis for utilizing the obtained temporal patterns as the features for constructing information-retweeting predictive models.

This paper is organized as follows. Section 2 describes the proposed method. Section 3 presents evaluation index group definitions used for feature word selection. In Sect. 4, the feature words and phrases extraction is performed to three well-known online retailers' Twitter accounts that had a substantial number of followers in Japan. The method extracts feature word groups contained in retweeted text and in the tweet histories of retweeting followers. It also generates temporal patterns of the indices that are used for choosing keywords and feature sequential patterns. For evaluating the stability of the proposed method, the method is applied to another set of tweets from the different period in Sect. 5. Finally, a conclusion is offered in Sect. 6.

2 Extraction of difference of retweeting users using temporal patterns in tweeting history

In this method, we assume that users' targeted retweeting behavior is affected not only by the content of received tweets but also their history of tweets. To construct a model for predicting such targeted tweeting behavior of followers, we should set up more proper features for considering the history of their tweets, which are obtained from their past tweeted content and actions.

In the text analysis, feature word extraction from a text corpus is a well-known method for obtaining the features from text in previously posted content. Then, a huge number of the feature words and phrases are often selected by the conventional methods, which are dependent on one particular evaluation index. However, it is very difficult to develop universal evaluation index on various context. In various situation, there is no trivial answer for evaluating usefulness of the feature words. In addition, feature word groups that are obtained using feature word extraction do not indicate when the information was obtained or their temporal trends. Therefore, we focus on patterns of change over time (temporal patterns), and developed for constructing a model that predicts the appearance of phrases using the temporal patterns of the evaluation indices of multiple phrases [6].

From the point of view that more various features can enable more explicit descriptions of hidden dependent variable relationships, it is not trivial that conventional features based on the appearance of feature sequential patterns may or may not be better predictors than temporal patterns [7]. Therefore, an improved method should use both the appearance of feature words and the phrases' temporal patterns, which were obtained from the user tweet history, as features to more accurately characterize the content history. Moreover, this method could also identify behaviors by similarly linking temporal patterns of the tweet counts and intervals.

The whole process of this method is described as the followings:

1. Finding features of users who are interested in an account.

    (a) Finding words and phrases used in the main concerned tweets by extracting as feature them from retweeted tweets of the account.

2. Extracting feature words and phrases in the past users' tweets as temporal patterns of the evaluation indices.

    (b) Extracting candidates of users' feature words and phrases.

    (c) Calculating evaluation index values of the candidates in the temporal corpus of the users' tweets.

    (d) Constructing temporal patterns of each evaluation index.

(e) Extracting sets of words and phrases included in each temporal pattern.

(f) Constructing the features for predictive models based on the temporal pattern of evaluation indices.

3. Finding concrete understandings of the difference of the interested users as predictive models.

In this paper, we implemented above step 1 and 2 using the tools for extracting the feature words and phrases. First, an automatic meaningful words and phrases extraction method obtained the candidates of the feature words and phrases. Then, the method calculates some sequential pattern evaluation indices and importance evaluation indices of words and phrases on the temporal corpus of the followers for obtaining temporal patterns of each evaluation index. After obtaining the temporal clusters, to utilize the clusters as the features for predictive model construction, we should know the meanings of the temporal patterns. For this issue, we calculate a temporal correlation between the overall averaged values on every time-point and each temporal pattern as the variance ratio (F-statistics) of the differences. According to the F-statistics, we determine whether we should use the levels of an index averaged value or the shapes of the index for each period using the F test. The variance ration is calculated as the following:

$$F\left(X, A\right) = \frac{\sum \left(\Delta x - \overline{\Delta x}\right)^2}{\sum \left(\Delta a - \overline{\Delta a}\right)^2},$$

where a centroid values of each temporal cluster consists of $X = \{x_1, \ldots, x_n\}$, and the overall average of the evaluation index data set consists of $A = \{a_1, \ldots, a_n\}$ within a period with n time-points. Δx denotes the differential between x_t and x_{t+1}, $1 \le t \le n - 1$. Δa denotes the differential of the overall averages. $\overline{\Delta x}$ and $\overline{\Delta a}$ denote the average of the differentials of each temporal pattern and the differentials of the overall temporal values of the evaluation index, respectively. The F-statistics is test with the F-distribution under $n - 1$ degree of freedom.

As for step 3, some actual extraction results show that this method can find the different set of words and phrases as the features of the interests of the followers.

3 Evaluation indices based on appearance frequency of words and sequential patterns

In the text, words and phrases[1] are represented by a series of one or more words. Given two words w_a and w_b in a sequential relationship, the order relation $a < b$ is always

true, and a term term$_i$ that is formed from these two words is expressed as term$_i = \langle w_a, w_b \rangle$. Because of this phrase property, all sentences can be considered sequential data, having an ordered sequential relationship, and terms can be considered to be subsequences. With considering the common ordered relations of items in each data of the data set, both of a natural language processing-based phrase importance indices and sequential pattern evaluation indices can be used to evaluate phrases. The definitions of these indices are shown in Table 1.

3.1 Importance evaluation indices for words and phrases

Multiple importance evaluation indices have been developed for natural language processing and text mining to measure the importance of words and phrases for extracting features. The primary standard that these indices use is the appearance frequency of the word or phrases. Two appearance measurement references are commonly used for term appearance frequency: the term frequency (TF), which counts the number of times a term is repeated in one or more documents, and the document frequency (DF), which counts the number of documents in which the term appears.

Table 1 shows the typical evaluation indices for a term consisting of L words ($L \ge 1$), i.e., term$_i = \langle w_1, \ldots, w_L \rangle$. The term frequency and inverse document frequency (TFIDF) method is most commonly used to evaluate the importance of the words and phrases for keyword extraction. It considers both the TF and DF and uses the ratio between the entire target document $|D|$ and the DF as a weight. A simple ratio that compares every pair of appearance frequency measurement standards can be used to index measuring properties based on appearance frequency.

3.2 Phrase evaluation indices using sequential pattern evaluation indices

Sequential pattern evaluation indices are indices that quantify multiple properties of sequential patterns using the appearance frequency freq(α, D) of partial sequence α in sequential data set $D = \{s_i\}$, containing sequential data $s_i = \langle i_1, \ldots, i_m \rangle$, which are strings of items $i \in I$ that belong to item set I. Similar to the method used to determine keyword evaluation indices, two appearance frequency standards are typically used to count the appearance frequency of partial sequence $a = \langle i_1, \ldots, i_j \rangle (j \le m)$ in sequential data set D.

Applying the TF frequency standard, which considers repetitions in each document, and the DF frequency standard, which does not consider repetitions, a confidence-based index is defined using an evaluation index group for the non-

---

[1]   Hereafter, words and phrases are called 'term.' Each term consists of one or more words.

Table 1 Importance evaluation indices and sequential pattern indices for each appearance frequency measurement standard for a term from [5]

	Frequency measurement standard	
	Document frequency $DF = |D_{\in term_i}|$	Term frequency $TF = \sum_j freq(term_i, d_j)$
Support	$DF/|D|$	$TF/\sum TF_{term_i}$
Odds	$DF/(|D| - DF)$	$TF/(\sum TF_{term_i} - TF)$
Self-information	$(DF/|D|) \log_2 (DF/|D|)$	$TF/(\sum TF_{term_i}) \log_2 TF/(\sum TF_{term_i})$
Jaccard coefficient	$\frac{DF}{DF(w_1 \cup ... \cup w_L)}$	$\frac{TF}{TF(w_1 \cup ... \cup w_L)}$
TFIDF	$TF * \log(|D|/DF)$	
Head confidence (H-Conf)	$\frac{DF}{DF(w_1, D)}$	$\frac{TF}{TF(w_1, D)}$
Max confidence (MaxConf)	$\max \left(\frac{DF}{DF(w_x, D)} \right)$	$\max \left(\frac{TF}{TF(w_x, D)} \right)$
All confidence (AllConf)	$\frac{DF}{\max(DF(w_x, D))}$	$\frac{TF}{\max(TF(w_x, D))}$
Sequential all confidence (SeqAllConf)	$\frac{DF}{\max(DF(\beta \subseteq term_i, D))}$	$\frac{TF}{\max(TF(\beta \subseteq term_i, D))}$

sequential item set [8] and an evaluation index group that considers the items in a sequential pattern [9]. We consider a sequence α to be the term $term_i$ and each item to be word w_x, where $1 \leq x \leq L$, within $term_i$.

As also shown in Table 1, when the sequential relationships between the items of a phrase's sequential pattern are considered, more than eight indices can be defined for the various confidences, which are the combined ratio of the appearance frequency of α and the appearance frequency of β, a subsequence of α.

4 Tweeting behavior analysis of online retail twitter accounts and their followers

This section examines user-sent texts (tweets), which contain 140 characters or less, obtained from a Twitter application programming interface (API) [10]. By gathering tweets both from some prominent account holders and from their followers tweets over the time, the relationships between the users' interests and concerns are analyzed as the features of resent tweets (retweets) that originate from the well-known Twitter accounts and of tweets sent by the retweeting users during a previous time period. To provide a broader analysis of general user interests, we define retweeting as the action of tweeting a feature word contained in a retweeted tweet.

The analysis procedure is as follows.

1. The feature words contained in tweets that were retweeted by some followers from a well-known Twitter account during a given period are extracted.
2. The followers that retweeted tweets including the feature words in (1) are listed.
3. The tweets sent by the followers in (2) during a time period prior to that of (1) are gathered.

4. The feature words contained in the tweets gathered in (3) and the temporal patterns of evaluation index groups based on their appearance frequencies are extracted.

The goal of this study is to develop a method for constructing a model that predicts information-based retweeting behavior using the temporal patterns of the tweeting history. Thus, the following analysis was performed as an application of this method using the procedure described above.

To obtain candidate phrases, or characteristic phrases, from the gathered text, an automatic terminology extraction method, used in natural language processing, is applied to each document set. In addition, to extract the phrases serving as feature word candidates, we used the FLR score-based automatic terminology extraction method developed by Nakagawa [11], which is defined as follows:

$$FLR(CN) = F(CN) \times \left\{ \prod_{i=1}^{L} (FL(N_i)+1)(FR(N_i)+1) \right\}^{\frac{1}{2L}},$$

where $F(CN)$ denotes the frequency of the candidate (composed) noun CN. Each CN consists of one or more nouns N_i. $FL(N_i)$ denotes the counts of the different nouns on the left-hand side in each bigram of N_i. Similar to the FL function, $FR(N_i)$ denotes the counts of the different nouns on the right-hand side in the bigrams of N_i. The basic idea of the FLR score comes from the HITS algorithm [12], which measures the degree of the hubness of each node in a linked network structure. The calculated values for each CN are the geometric average of the differences in each sequenced noun, which corresponds to each node in the continued network structure. This indicates meaningfulness on the statistical linguistic property of each CN.

The nouns N_i used in the FLR score calculation were identified from morphological analysis results using MeCab [13]

Table 2 Number of retweeted tweets and number of FLR score-based candidate phrases in tweets sent from three major retail Twitter accounts between January 15 and 20, 2015 from [5]

Retailer	$|D|$	FLR score-based candidate phrases
7 Net shopping	76	369
Amazon.co.jp	193	857
Rakuten Ichiba	127	540

and the IPA[2] dictionary (mecab-ipadic-2.7.0-20070801) distributed with MeCab. Applying the FLR score calculation results, the candidate words and phrases were selected from phrases having FLR(CN, D) > 1.0 in the experiments mentioned below.

4.1 Extraction of feature words contained in retweeted text

Our test extracted feature words from sets of retweeted text (retweets) that were sent from the official Twitter accounts of 7 Net Shopping (7_netshopping), Amazon.co.jp (AmazonJP), and Rakuten Ichiba (RakutenJP).

The covered tweets were sent from these Twitter accounts between January 15 and 20, 2015. Table 2 shows the number of retweeted tweets and the number of FLR score-based feature word candidate phrases in the retweeted tweets.

Table 3 shows the top ten phrases for the Twitter accounts based on their TFIDF values, along with the support and the head confidence (H-Conf) measures for these phrases. The support and the head confidence were calculated using a standard for counting frequencies based on document frequency (DF).

The results in Table 3 provide characteristic phrase groups for the tweets that the followers retweeted. These feature word groups are phrases contained in the tweets sent by the Twitter accounts and can be considered to align with some of the followers' interests.

However, these feature words and phrases do not reflect the followers' interests directly, because the followers do not tweet these terms in their tweets. The issue is to capture more implicit interests and concerns of the followers from their behavioral history. Therefore, to obtain term groups that corresponded to groups of follower interests, the historic tweet content of followers who retweeted the tweets containing the original phrases must be examined. This will result in changes in the usage frequency of feature words and phrases.

4.2 Feature words and temporal patterns of text retweeted by users

Twitter accounts can attract followers, who will receive all the information sent from the account. Tweets sent from followers contain various phrases, which are determined by their interests and most likely reflect those interests. Thus, this method hypothesized that when users retweeted tweets sent from the three well-known Twitter accounts, these retweets would contain feature words that relate to their previously sent tweets.

This section describes our process for testing this hypothesis by examining the content of tweets sent from the followers of our three well-known online retail Twitter accounts before the retweets were sent. To obtain the temporal patterns of the evaluation indices, we extracted feature words and the patterns of temporal change from these previous tweets. For followers who retweeted tweets sent from the three well-known Twitter accounts between January 15 and 20, 2015, we gathered the tweets sent between January 1 and 20, 2015 by the followers[3] of each of the well-known accounts. Then, the tweets gathered between January 1 and 14 are used to obtain the following temporal patterns of each evaluation index on each well-known retailer followers' tweet. For all of the terms, the 18 evaluation indices values were calcluated in each timestamped data set. Then, the values of each term consists of each data of the term.

Table 4 shows the number of gathered tweets between January 1 and 14, 2015[4] of the followers who sent tweets containing one of the phrases listed in Table 3 between January 15 and 20, 2015 for each account.

After applying the FLR scores to extract feature terms from these user tweets, the candidate terms were extracted, as shown in Table 5. For each top 1000 terms with the FLR score, the importance evaluation indices and sequential pattern evaluation indices are calculated in each daily set of documents. Then, for each evaluation index, the values for each timepoint, every daily set, of each term was converted into one temporal data. Therefore, the data set of one particular evaluation index for temporal pattern extraction contains up to 1000 instances with the values on each timepoint in this experiment.

Subsequently, a clustering method was then applied to the converted temporal data sets to obtain the temporal patterns of each index. The instances in this data set consist of the index values in each timepoint that represent the followers' activities before retweeting the tweets from the well-known

---

[2] This IPA dictionary is a Japanese morpheme dictionary made by the project run by the Information-Technology Promoting Agency in Japan.

[3] Due to restrictions in the Twitter API, these users were the users who met the criteria from the randomly acquired 5000 users.

[4] Considering more realistic situation, the gathered tweets are not re-retrieved in the prior period after listing the followers who tweeted the tweets containing the feature words and phrases listed in Table 3.

Table 3 Top ten phrases for Twitter accounts based on TFIDF values and the support and the head confidence levels for these phrases (document frequency standard) from [5]

	7 Net Shopping			Amazon.co.jp			Rakuten Ichiba		
Terms	TFIDF	Support(DF)	H-Conf(DF)	Term	TFIDF	Support(DF)	H-Conf(DF)	Term	TFIDF	Support(DF)	H-Conf(DF)
限定 (Limited)	41.39	0.26	1.00	タイム セール (Time Sales)	73.57	0.22	1.00	楽天 ポイント ("Rakuten" Points)	84.18	0.23	0.58
セブン(Seven)	33.47	0.29	1.00	OFF	63.38	0.20	1.00	楽天 ("Rakuten")	74.57	0.39	1.00
特典 (Special-gift)	32.95	0.22	1.00	人気(Popular)	53.11	0.14	1.00	応募 (Application)	51.21	0.26	1.00
予約 (Reservation)	32.53	0.43	1.00	PC	52.78	0.06	1.00	フォロワー (Follower)	51.21	0.26	1.00
予約 受付 (Reservation Accepting)	31.95	0.37	0.85	限定(Limited)	52.14	0.10	1.00	♪	46.70	0.38	1.00
月 (Month)	30.02	0.17	1.00	受付 (Accepting)	52.12	0.12	1.00	フォロー 解除 (Unfollow)	44.47	0.26	1.00
発売(For-sale)	29.21	0.20	1.00	チェック (Check-it)	51.10	0.13	1.00	当選 確率 (Winning Probability)	44.47	0.26	1.00
アカチャンホンポ ("Akachan-honpo")	27.06	0.14	1.00	予約 受付 (Reservation Accepting)	50.03	0.12	0.89	完了 (Finished)	44.47	0.26	1.00
セブン ネット ("Seven Net")	26.96	0.22	0.77	% OFF	48.80	0.11	0.75	下 (Under)	44.31	0.23	1.00
DVD	26.49	0.21	1.00	最大 (Maximum)	45.34	0.10	1.00	RT	43.29	0.24	1.00

Table 4 Number of tweets between January 1 and 14 sent by the retweeting followers

	Following account		
	7 Net shopping	Amazon.co.jp	Rakuten Ichiba
1 st Januray	19,577	130	0
2nd January	20,906	55	15
3rd January	21,571	37	67
4th January	22,103	2,303	27
5th January	22,773	10,899	0
6th January	25,776	18,012	0
7th January	24,636	19,734	109
8th January	23,771	24,189	96
9th January	25,467	22,746	16
10th January	26,956	23,358	13
11th January	27,542	24,815	100
12th January	27,902	25,817	107
13th January	36,810	33,992	5073
14th January	35,835	30,273	22,651
Total	361,625	236,360	28,274

Table 5 Number of candidate feature words and phrases based on the FLR score in the entire data set of tweets counted in Table 4 for each well-known account from [5]

Retailer	|D|	FLR score-based candidate phrases
7 Net shopping	361,625	271,234
Amazon.co.jp	236,360	211,730
Rakuten Ichiba	28,274	40,080

account. As for the clustering method, a simple k-means implementation in Weka [14] was applied to the data sets in this analysis. The value of k was set up 10, which is the upper limit for obtaining clusters, since null clusters were allowed in this execution. For calculating the similarity between pairs of instances, the Euclidean distance with normalization on each variable was employed.

Table 6 shows the numbers of temporal clusters obtained and their sum of squared errors (s.s.e) values within the clusters on each data set from the five evaluation indices. The s.s.e is calculated using the following definition.

$$\text{s.s.e}(D_{\text{index}}) = \sum_{k} \sum_{i} \sum_{j} (v_{ij} - c_{kj})^2,$$

where c_{kj} is the jth time stamped value of the centroid of the temporal cluster k, and v_{ij} is the value of each evaluation index.

As shown in Table 6, TFIDF and support achieved smaller s.s.e values. This means the clusters obtained by these indices are cohering to the centroids of the clusters. In general, the s.s.e value increases when the number of clusters becomes smaller. Therefore, the clusters for MaxConf (DF) of 7 Net Shopping achieved greater cohesion as the temporal clustering.

4.3 Results for the temporal patterns with the evaluation indices from the different viewpoints

Figures 1 and 2 show the temporal patterns of the indices of 7 Net Shopping and Amazon.co.jp followers who retweeted

Table 6 Description of the clusters obtained for each evaluation index on each account data set from [5]

	Following account					
	7 Net shopping		Amazon.co.jp		Rakuten Ichiba	
	# Clusters	s.s.e	# Clusters	s.s.e	# Clusters	s.s.e
TFIDF	10	4.07	10	9.95	10	15.62
Support (DF)	10	3.62	10	5.02	10	6.38
Support (TF)	10	1.34	10	6.77	10	9.14
MaxConf (DF)	6	105.31	7	126.30	7	17.87
MaxConf (TF)	7	115.95	7	148.77	7	20.50

Fig. 1 Temporal patterns of TFIDF (**a**) and MaxConf (DF) (**b**) in 7 Net Shopping's retweeting followers' tweets from [5]

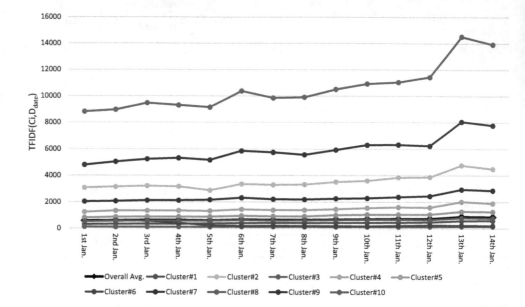

(**a**) Temporal Cluster Centroids from the TFIDF Dataset

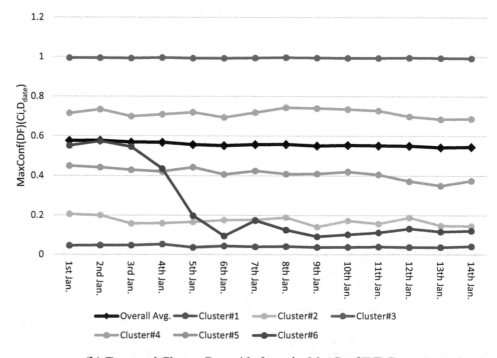

(**b**) Temporal Cluster Centroids from the MaxConf(DF) Dataset

Fig. 2 Temporal patterns of TFIDF (**a**) and MaxConf (DF) (**b**) in AmazonJP's retweeting followers' tweets

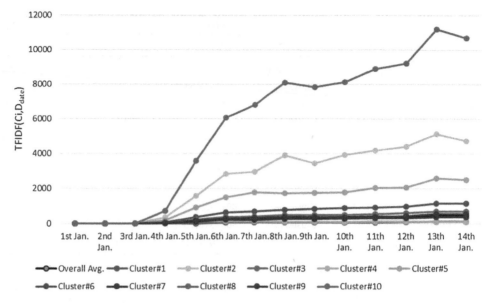

(**a**) Temporal Cluster Centroids from the TFIDF Dataset

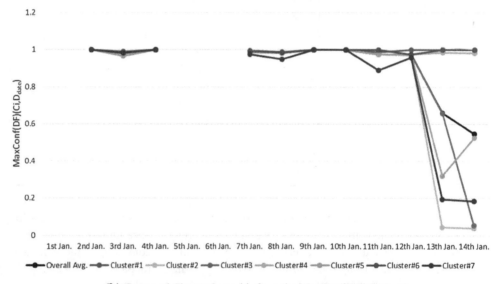

(**b**) Temporal Cluster Centroids from the MaxConf(DF) Dataset

their tweets between January 15 and 20, respectively. Since the clusters are obtained using the Euclidean distance, the lines, the centroids of each cluster, are calculated as the averages of each cluster.

Most of the patterns represents the differences of the averages of each evaluation index based on their temporal values in Fig. 1. As shown in Fig. 1a, the temporal patterns represent the levels of the averaged values of the member of each cluster. This means that the averaged value of this evaluation index is suitable for describing the features using TFIDF. However, as shown in Fig. 1b, Cluster#6 of MaxConf (DF) shows significant difference from the other patterns. This indicates that the use of both of the averaged value and the

membership value to each cluster is suitable for MaxConf (DF) index.

To determine whether we should use the average of the obtained temporal clusters' centroid or the shape (membership) of them, the variance ratio between the differentials of the overall average and the differentials of each temporal cluster centroid is statistically tested. Table 7 shows the variance ratio of the differentials between the overall average and each temporal cluster and their F test results.

On the other hand, the temporal patterns made for tweeted terms of retweeting followers of Amazon.co.jp, as shown in Fig. 2, show the different patterns, compared with that of 7 Net Shopping. Since there are smaller numbers of tweets in

Table 7 Variance ratios of the differentials and F test results (**$p < 0.05$) of the TFIDF and MaxConf (DF) temporal clusters of 7 Net Shopping

	TFIDF			MaxConf (DF)		
	Variance	Var. ratio	F test	Variance	Var. ratio	F test
Overall avg.	2575.72			2.63E−05		
Cluster#1	827.51	0.32		3.44E−05	1.31	
Cluster#2	96, 603.54	37.51	**	6.64E−04	25.30	**
Cluster#3	96.24	0.04		3.23E−06	0.12	
Cluster#4	17, 849.92	6.93	**	3.91E−04	14.90	**
Cluster#5	4471.01	1.74		3.94E−04	14.99	**
Cluster#6	5417.91	2.10		6.39E−03	243.27	**
Cluster#7	21, 785.78	8.46	**			
Cluster#8	891, 739.52	346.21	**			
Cluster#9	305, 310.90	118.53	**			
Cluster#10	2074.96	0.81				

Table 8 Variance ratios of the differentials and F test results (**$p < 0.05$) of the TFIDF and MaxConf (DF) temporal clusters of AmazonJP

	TFIDF			MaxConK (DF)		
	Variance	Var. ratio	F test	Variance	Var. ratio	F test
Overall avg.	2016.04			0.12		
Cluster#1	416.88	0.21		0.10	1.00	
Cluster#2	295,954.64	146.80	**	0.20	2.06	
Cluster#3	290.38	0.14		0.16	1.63	
Cluster#4	2046.45	1.02		0.10	1.00	
Cluster#5	75,021.05	37.21	**	0.16	1.61	
Cluster#6	9735.64	4.83		0.10	1.00	
Cluster#7	1600.72	0.79		0.17	1.75	
Cluster#8	3813.31	1.89				
Cluster#9	2550.98	1.27				
Cluster#10	1,117,910.31	554.51	**			

the begining of the period, the values of these two evaluation indices are influenced by the size of these data sets. However, the centroids of TFIDF temporal patterns show that the levels of the average values through the period are more inportant than the trend of the index or the movement of the index. As shown in Fig. 2b, MaxConf shows the different tempral patterns that are both the levels of their averages and the other usage of the terms, because the index reflects combinations of words included in each term.

As the same as Table 7, Table 8 shows the F test results of the differentials between the overall averaged sequence and the other temporal cluster centroid sequences. Based on the result in Table 8, the features constructed for the AmazonJP retweeting followers' tweets can be distinguished whether we should use the levels of averages of TFIDF and the membership to Cluster #2, #5, and #10 of TFIDF.

Based on these results, analysts can understand that the followers who are interested in the targeted account have not only different usages of words and phrases, but also they make some similar patterns by focusing on their temporal changes of their usages as reflected by the evaluation indices.

Subsequently, according to the F test results of the variance ratio of the differentials, we can construct the features consisting of the average values of the period and the temporal pattern memberships for predicting followers' retweeting behavior.

Detailed results of the obtained temporal patterns

To consider more detailed differences of the contents of the extracted temporal patterns, the followings are the details of the results shown in Figs. 1 and 2. Those contained words and phrases included in the temporal patterns as the temporal clusters have calculated their similarity to the cluster centroid in each cluster using Euclidean distance.

Figure 3 shows that the top ten similar words and phrases included in Cluster#6 of Fig. 1b. By examining the temporal values of these words and phrases, most of these phrases appeared after January 5 for promoting new popular games on smartphones such as Android terminals. The pattern obtained using MaxConf (DF), that is Max Confidence based on Document Frequency, and its contents describe the changing of

Fig. 3 Representative words and phrases of Cluster#6 of MaxConf (DF) in 7 Net Shopping retweeting followers' tweets from [5]

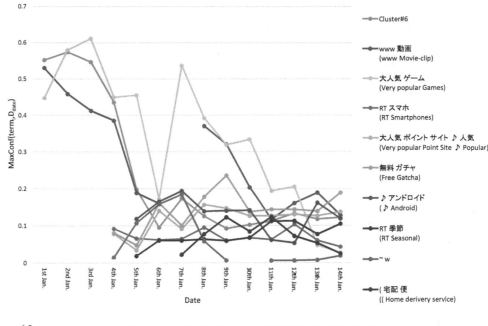

Fig. 4 Representative words and phrases of Cluster#5 of MaxConf (DF) in Amazon.co.jp retweeting followers' tweets

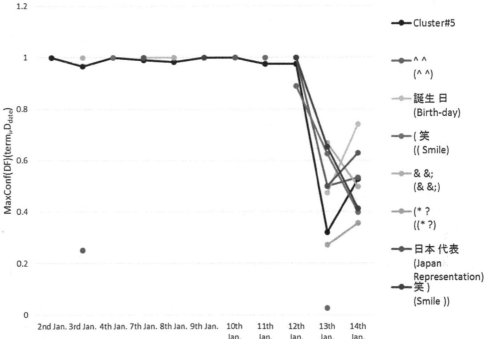

the promotion targets of the retweeting followers. They seem interested in smartphones and games on the smartphones. At the same time, they also tried to advertise their affiliated services such as online points and in-game coins.

Figure 4 also shows the top ten similar words and phrases on the Euclidean distance to the cluster centroid of Cluster#5 in Fig. 2b. These words and phrases are related to some face marks and emoticons in Japanese that are frequently used for make their tweets more friendly. In contrast to the words and phrases shown in Fig. 3, the interested followers to Amazon.co.jp often use less advertising expreessions

in their tweets. In addition, they use more different combinations including these phrases in the last few days before retweeting the tweets of Amazon.co.jp or tweeting with containing the feature terms of Amazon.co.jp's tweets.

These results demonstrate that we can capture different aspects of the historical behaviors of the users by obtaining the temporal clusters of the different types of evaluation indices. These patterns will reveal about the followers' concerns from the viewpoint of the enterprise users more concretely, because the temporal patterns contain concrete feature words and phrases of the followers. This will help analysts for promoting their sales items to adequate followers by selecting the temporal patterns and the term groups included in the selected temporal pattern. By targeting the follower's action to promotions of false rumors, it will be able to detect demagogues more quickly based on the values of the evaluation indices of the temporal pattern, which are not needed any preliminary appearance of particular word or phrase itself.

In addition to the above-mentioned effect, these behaviors also include mechanical accounts (called "bots") as well as human accounts. Among the viral marketing and social media mining field, it is one of the important issue to distinguish such mechanical bots as spam. Therefore, the different behaviors reflected by the temporal patterns and their including words and phrases will also help in distinguishing the spam accounts.

5 Evaluating stability of the proposed retweeting user analysis method based on the evaluation index behavior as the temporal pattern

To evaluate our proposed user behavior analysis method, we applied this method to the sets of retweeted tweets and followers' tweets from the different period. In this experiment, we use the three retailers retweeted tweets and the followers' tweets in 2016.

5.1 Extracting feature words and phrases of retweeted tweets in 2016

As the same as the feature words and phrases extraction in Sect. 4.1, we gathered the retrweeted tweets of the three retailers from February 17 to 23, 2016. Table 9 shows the numbers of retweeted tweets and the extracted composed nouns using the automatic term extraction method based on the FLR score [11].

For the candidate words and phrases in Table 7, the 19 evaluation indices defined in Table 1 are calculated. Table 10 shows the top ten words and phrases, which are sorted by the TFIDF index.

As shown in Table 10, the retweeted words and phrases are not so different in the 7 Net Shopping and Amazon.co.jp.

Table 9 Number of retweeted tweets and number of FLR score-based candidate phrases in tweets sent from three major retail Twitter accounts between February 17 to 23, 2016

Retailer	|D|	FLR score-based candidate phrases
7 Net shopping	113	336
Amazon.co.jp	499	1492
Rakuten Ichiba	81	162

In addition, the retailer's tweets and its retweeted tweets are changed by that of Rakuten Ichiba. Although the rank of the feature words and phrases is effected by their appearances, the meaning of the rank is not effected.

5.2 Feature words and temporal patterns of text retweeted by users in 2016

As for the temporal set of tweets, we gathered the followers' tweets who were retweeted the tweets from the three retailer accounts. As the same as the setting in Sect. 4.2, the tweets from the followers were picked up from the former period of the retweeting actions. The period for observing the followers' behavior was from February 1 to 16, 2016. The numbers of gathered followers' tweets in this period are shown in Table 11.

From the entire set of follower's tweets for each retailer's account, we extracted the candidate words and phrases for extracting feature words and phrases as the temporal patterns. Table 12 shows the number of entire follows' tweets on the 2016 period and the extracted candidate words and phrases based on the FLR score using $FLR(term_i) > 1.0$.

After calculating the evaluation indices, the data sets for temporal clustering on each evaluation index are constructed. Then, we selected top 1000 words and phrases based on FLR score for each data set. This process is for selecting more meaningful words and phrases based on the statistical score.

By applying the k-means clustering algorithm to these data sets, the results are obtained, as shown in Table 13. For constructing clusters, the value of k was set up 10, which is the upper limit for obtaining clusters, since null clusters were allowed in this execution. For calculating the similarity between pairs of instances, the Euclidean distance with normalization on each variable was employed.

The values of the sum of squared errors (s.s.e.) show larger gap between the Support indices and the maximum confidence (MaxConf) indices, as shown in Table 13. This indicates that the clusters using MaxConf have more variance in each cluster. Although the s.s.e. values of the support are smaller than the values of TFIDF, the raw values of TFIDF are some thousands times bigger than the raw values of the Support.

Results for the temporal patterns with the evaluation indices on the 2016 data set

Figure 5 shows the temporal patterns of the indices of 7 Net Shopping followers who retweeted 7 Net's tweets between February 17 and 23 in 2016. Since the raw values of TFIDF are bigger than the values of support, we show the result of TFIDF as Fig. 5.

The lines in Fig. 5 show the centroids of each cluster, which are calculated as the averages of members included in

Table 10 Top ten retweeted words and phrases based on TFIDF values and the support and the head confidence levels for these phrases (document frequency standard) on 2016

	7 Net Shopping			Amazon.co.jp			Rakuten Ichiba		
Terms	TFIDF	Support(DF)	H-Conf(DF)	Term	TFIDF	Support(DF)	H-Conf(DF)	Term	TFIDF	Support(DF)	H-Conf(DF)
セブン(Seven)	32.13	0.32	1.00	RT	100.49	0.18	1.00	アプリ(Application)	84.18	0.23	0.58
企業(Enterprise)	27.40	0.05	1.00	セール(For-Sale)	97.73	0.13	1.00	楽天 市場("Rakuten" "Ichiba")	74.57	0.39	1.00
特典(Special-gift)	27.07	0.22	1.00	%	92.49	0.13	1.00	お客様(Customers)	51.21	0.26	1.00
DVD	25.57	0.22	1.00	#	91.74	0.11	1.00	楽天 市場 アプリ("Rakuten" "Ichiba" Application)	51.21	0.26	1.00
限定(Limited)	25.27	0.33	1.00	OFF	90.53	0.12	1.00	県(Prefecture)	46.70	0.38	1.00
発売(For-sale)	23.80	0.29	1.00	% OFF	86.17	0.11	0.86	Ver	44.47	0.26	1.00
予約 受付(Reservation Accepting)	23.72	0.43	0.82	タイム セール(Time Sales)	80.05	0.09	0.97	メルマガ(Mail-Magazine)	44.47	0.26	1.00
月(Month)	20.94	0.17	1.00	チェック(Check-it)	70.35	0.09	1.00	利用(Use-of)	44.47	0.26	1.00
セブン ネット("Seven Net")	20.52	0.21	0.65	春(Spring)	68.71	0.06	1.00	県民(Residents)	44.31	0.23	1.00
付き(With a S/T)	19.90	0.19	1.00	登場(First-Appearance)	66.93	0.08	1.00	問い合わせ(Contact)	43.29	0.24	1.00

Table 11 Number of tweets between February 1 and 16, 2016 sent by the retweeting followers

	Following account		
	7 Net shopping	Amazon.co.jp	Rakuten Ichiba
1st February	1205	1504	926
2nd February	1302	1760	924
3rd February	1520	1851	1005
4th February	1376	1771	1229
5th February	1643	2115	1250
6th February	2098	2374	1379
7th February	2223	2787	1683
8th February	2255	2987	1811
9th February	2369	3731	2192
10th February	2923	4081	2165
11th February	3419	4848	3309
12th February	4588	5978	4500
13th February	6247	7527	5186
14th February	9376	9729	6729
15th February	11,403	10,808	7190
16th February	13,799	16,882	11,006
Total	67,746	80,733	52,484

Table 12 Number of candidate feature words and phrases based on the FLR score in the entire data set of tweets counted in Table 9 for each well-known account

Retailer	$|D|$	FLR score-based candidate phrases
7 Net shopping	67,746	98,283
Amazon.co.jp	80,733	113,923
Rakuten Ichiba	52,484	85,204

each cluster is more informative than using the levels of the index values.

As shown in this result, the proposed temporal pattern extraction method using the sequential pattern evaluation indices from the different viewpoints obtains both of the features with/without temporal trends and the groups of the words and phrases at the same time, according to the temporal values of each evaluation index property.

6 Conclusion

In this paper, we examined the Twitter behavior known as retweeting, which refers to the dissemination of information that occurs when users resend tweets. We examined the differences between the feature word groups that are contained in retweeted text and the feature word groups contained in the tweet history of the followers. We assume that these users have an interest in the information sent from specific Twitter accounts. In our assessment of three well-known retailers' Twitter accounts, the method discovered the significant terms

each cluster. Most of these centroids as the temporal pattterns show almost same trends compared to the overall average.

On the other hand, the temporal patterns of the cluster centroids show different trends excepting Cluster #3, #4, #9, and #10 based on th F test for the differentials of the sequences, as shown in Table 14. This indicates that the membership to

Table 13 Description of the clusters obtained for each evaluation index on each account data set in 2016 February

	Following account					
	7 Net shopping		Amazon.co.jp		Rakuten Ichiba	
	# Clusters	s.s.e	# Clusters	s.s.e	# Clusters	s.s.e
TFIDF	10	11.90	10	9.59	10	13.39
Support (DF)	10	0.64	10	0.52	10	0.68
Support (TF)	10	4.04	10	0.35	10	1.40
MaxConf (DF)	9	434.92	9	415.64	7	430.52
MaxConf (TF)	9	383.46	9	369.96	7	380.99

Fig. 5 Temporal patterns of TFIDF in 7 Net Shopping's retweeting followers' tweets between February 1 and 16, 2016

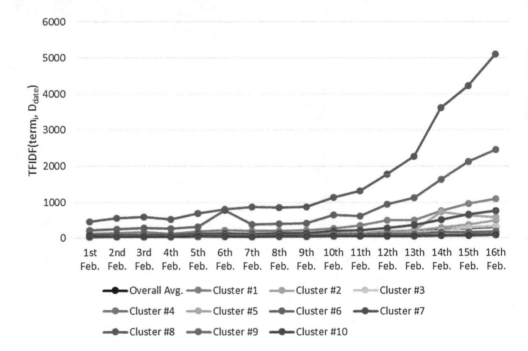

Table 14 Variance ratios of the differentials and F test results (**$p < 0.05$) of the TFIDF temporal clusters of 7 Net Shopping in 2016 February data set

	TFIDF		
	Variance	Var. ratio	F test
Overall Avg.	451.96		
Cluster#1	8684.86	19.22	**
Cluster#2	1710.86	3.79	**
Cluster#3	617.08	1.37	
Cluster#4	56.85	0.13	
Cluster#5	20,509.42	45.38	**
Cluster#6	64,502.22	142.72	**
Cluster#7	3397.68	7.52	**
Cluster#8	161,977.50	358.39	**
Cluster#9	161.18	0.36	
Cluster#10	66.64	0.15	

their tweeted words and phrases. By testing the trends of the temporal patterns, the results indicate whether the temporal patterns mean the characteristic trends or the levels of the evaluation index value.

Our future goal is to use this study for constructing a predictive model using the presence or absence of these temporal patterns as an explanatory variable for retweeting behavior. In addition to the patterns of phrase usage frequency changes, we will also acquire the temporal patterns of behavior changes, such as tweeting intervals, for the purpose of developing a method of constructing a predictive model that can be combined with the conventional feature word-based characterization.

Acknowledgements This work was supported by JSPS KAKENHI Grant Numbers 24500175 and 26240036.

that the terms contained in retweets differed from those of the users' previous tweets. We further conclude that the obtained temporal patterns enable to describe the followers' characteristics not only as their tweeting behaviors but also as

References

1. Goonetilleke, O., Sellis, T., Zhang, X., Sathe, S.: Twitter analytics: a big data management perspective. SIGKDD Explor. Newsl. **16**(1), 11–20 (2014)
2. Guille, A., Hacid, H., Favre, C., Zighed, D.A.: Information diffusion in online social networks: a survey. SIGMOD Rec. **42**(2), 17–28 (2013)
3. Mahmud, J., Chen, J., Nichols, J.: Why are you more engaged? Predicting Social Engagement from Word Use, The Computer Research Repository (CoRR) (2014). arXiv:1402.6690
4. Bo, J., Sha, Y., Wang, L.: A multi-view retweeting behaviors prediction in social networks, Web Technologies and Applications, pp. 756–767. Springer International Publishing, New York (2015)
5. Abe, H.: Analyzing user behaviors based on temporal patterns of sequential pattern evaluation indices on twitter. Trends and Applications in Knowledge Discovery and Data Mining, pp. 177–188. Springer International Publishing, New York (2015)
6. Abe, H.: Analysis for finding innovative concepts based on temporal patterns of terms in documents, theory and applications for advanced text mining. In: Sakurai, S. (ed.), pp. 37–50 (2012)
7. Abe, H., Tsumoto, S.: Mining classification rules for detecting medication order changes by using characteristic CPOE subsequences, foundations of intelligent systems. In: Proceedings of ISMIS 2011, LNCS 6804, pp. 80–89 (2011)
8. Wu, T., Chen, Y., Han, J.: Association mining in large databases: a re-examination of its measures. In: Proceedings of the 11th European Conference on Principles and Practice of Knowledge Discovery in Databases, pp. 621–628 (2007)
9. Lin C. X, Ji, M., Danilevsky, M., Han, J.: Efficient mining of correlated sequential patterns based on null hypothesis. In: Proceedings of the 2012 international workshop on Web-scale knowledge representation, retrieval and reasoning (Web-KR '12), pp. 17–24 (2012)
10. Twitter Web API 1.1. http://dev.twitter.com/docs/api/1.1
11. Nakagawa, H.: Automatic term recognition based on statistics of compound nouns. Terminology **6**(2), 195–210 (2000)
12. Kleinberg, M.J.: Authoritative Sources in a Hyperlinked Environment. J. ACM **46**(5), 604–632 (1999)
13. MeCab: Yet Another Part-of-Speech and Morphological Analyzer. http://taku910.github.io/mecab/
14. Witten, I.H., Frank, E.: Data Mining: PracticalMachine Learning Tools and Techniques with Java Implementations. Morgan Kaufmann, USA (2000)

## 9

Source separation employing beamforming and SRP-PHAT localization in three-speaker room environments

Hai Quang Hong Dam[1] · Sven Nordholm[2]

Abstract This paper presents a new blind speech separation algorithm using beamforming technique that is capable of extracting each individual speech signal from a mixture of three speech sources in a room. The speech separation algorithm utilizes the steered response power phase transform for obtaining a localization estimate for each individual speech source in the frequency domain. Based on those estimates each desired speech signal is extracted from the speech mixture using an optimal beamforming technique. To solve the permutation problem, a permutation alignment algorithm based on the mutual output correlation is employed to group the output signals into the correct sources from each frequency bin. Evaluations using real speech recordings in a room environment show that the proposed blind speech separation algorithm offers high interference suppression level whilst maintaining low distortion level for each desired signal.

Keywords Blind speech separation · SRP-PHAT · Beamformer

1 Introduction

Over the last 10–15 years research in machine interfaces for voice pick-up in reverberant and noisy environments has been very actively conducted using multi-channel systems

like microphone arrays [1–4]. Multi-channel techniques have been useful in many applications such as hearing aids, hands-free communication, robotics, audio and video conference systems, and speech recognition [1,2,5,6]. One of the most popular techniques applied to multi-microphone systems is the optimal beamforming technique [1]. Optimal beamformers are formulated to exploit spatial information of desired and undesired signals in such a way that the desired one is extracted and undesired signals are suppressed [1,2]. Many methods have been proposed for determining the location of the desired source such as predefined well-determined array geometry combined with source localization [7,8], a calibration method using training samples of pre-recording desired and undesired sources [9,10]. Based on this information, optimal beamformers are designed using the spatial information to suppress the contribution of all undesired signals while reserving the contribution of the desired signal [1,11,12]. Specifically, the optimal beamformer weights are calculated using knowledge about the location of the target signal and array geometry. It is also possible to obtain estimates of speech and noise correlation matrices. These estimates are then used to form the optimal beamformer weights; for this method to be efficient a priori knowledge about the statistical characteristics of the noise is necessary. When the background noise is stationary over the measurement period either a voice activity detector (VAD) [2] estimate or a relative transfer function (RTF) estimate can be found [13]. Either of these estimates can be used to form optimal beamformers [2]. This leads us to a more general case where the spatial knowledge is not known a priori and the observed mixture signals are the only available information to be used for speech separation and noise suppression. In this case, blind source separation (BSS) techniques can be deployed for separating the different sound sources. Many blind source separation techniques using microphone array have been proposed for speech sep-

✉ Hai Quang Hong Dam
damhai@uit.edu.vn

Sven Nordholm
S.Nordholm@curtin.edu.au

[1] University of Information Technology, Ho Chi Minh City, Vietnam

[2] Curtin University of Technology, Perth, Australia

aration in both time domain and frequency domain. Some prominent BSS techniques for speech separation are independent component analysis (ICA), maximum likelihood, second-order gradient, and kurtosis maximization [14–18]. Most of the BSS techniques are based on either statistical independence or non-stationarity of the different input sources in the observed signal.

Speech separation in cocktail party or multiple-speaker environment is one of the significant problems in speech enhancement research. It occurs when the observed signals are obtained from several speakers in different spatial locations. Here, the spatial separation of speech sources is very important for speech separation due to the fact that all speech signals have the same spectral characteristic. We can categorize two different cases:

1. When the sources' spatial information is available, many separation techniques such as steering beamforming, optimum beamforming, and post-filtering have been proposed [3,4,6,10,19]. In [19], we introduced a post-filtering method which is implemented after an optimum beamformer to extract the desired speech source from a mixture of signals in multiple speakers environments. However, the source spatial information in those studies was obtained using a calibration method.

2. When the sources' spatial information is not available then blind separation techniques in a multiple-speaker environment need to be employed. For this scenario, a number of different BSS techniques have been proposed for the case of two speech sources in both time domain and time–frequency domain [4,18,20–22]. When the number of speech sources is more than two, the blind signal separation is more of a complicated and computational intense problem [23–25]. For this case, popular blind separation techniques are conducted to extract the desired source signal by finding a separating vector that maximizes the deterministic character (such as non-Gaussianity in ICA technique) of the extracted source signals [4,24,26,27].

In this paper, a blind signal separation method is proposed which estimates the source spatial information without having prior knowledge about the spatial location of speech sources in three-speaker environments. Once the source spatial information is estimated, it is used to design optimum beamformers for extracting speech sources from the observed signal. As such, the source spatial information estimation is performed in the frequency domain without having prior knowledge about the spatial location of the speech sources. Here, a spatial localization technique employing steered response power phase transform (SRP-PHAT) is proposed for estimating each source's spatial information based on the observed signal. The SRP-PHAT localization employs cross-

correlation and phase transform weighting of the received signals from all microphone pairs in the array [28]. From the SRP-PHAT estimates, the proposed spatial localization technique calculates the spatial information of three speech sources from the observed signal. Based on the spatial information of the three speech sources, an optimum beamformer is proposed for extraction of each individual speech source from the observed signal. A permutation alignment is used for grouping each extracted signal into the correct source output before transforming them into the time domain. The performance of the proposed algorithm shows that the proposed algorithm offers a good interference suppression level while maintaining low speech distortion.

The paper is organized as follows: Sect. 2 outlines the problem formulation and details the signal model. In Sect. 3, the spatial localization method is derived and discussed in detail. Section 4 provides the details and derivation of the optimum beamforming technique. Section 5 discusses the method used for permutation alignment. In Sect. 6, the experimental results are presented and discussed. Finally, Sect. 7 summarizes the paper.

2 Problem formulation

Consider a linear microphone array, according to Fig. 1, consisting of L microphones and observed mixture signals $\mathbf{x}(n)$. The observed signals are a speech mixture from three speakers sitting in front of the microphones. The observed sampled signal $\mathbf{x}(n)$ at one time instant is an $L \times 1$ vector, which can be expressed as

$$\mathbf{x}(n) = \mathbf{s}_1(n) + \mathbf{s}_2(n) + \mathbf{s}_3(n) \tag{1}$$

where $\mathbf{s}_1(n)$, $\mathbf{s}_2(n)$ and $\mathbf{s}_3(n)$ are the received signals from each respective speech source. In the short-term time–

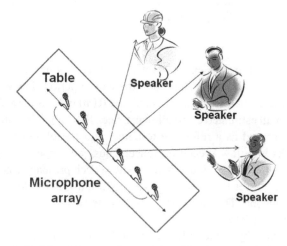

Fig. 1 Position of three speakers and the microphone array in the three-speaker environment

frequency (STFT) domain, the observed signal can be written as

$$\mathbf{x}(\omega, k) = \mathbf{s}_1(\omega, k) + \mathbf{s}_2(\omega, k) + \mathbf{s}_3(\omega, k) \tag{2}$$

where $\mathbf{x}(\omega, k)$, $\mathbf{s}_1(\omega, k)$, $\mathbf{s}_2(\omega, k)$ and $\mathbf{s}_3(\omega, k)$ are the contribution from the observed signal, the first, the second and the third speech sources, respectively. The objective is to separate each individual source signal from the observed signal. As such, one speech source is treated as the desired source while the others become undesired in a round robin fashion. In this case, the VAD cannot be employed to detect the desired source active or inactive periods because all sources can be active at the same time. Thus, a spatial localization technique needs to be employed. In this case, SRP-PHAT is utilized to estimate the spatial information for each speech source based only on the statistics of the observed signal.

3 Spatial localization technique employing SRP-PHAT

For the SRP-PHAT processing, we divide the sequence of observed signal into Q blocks, each consisting of N samples with the index $[(q-1)N + 1, qN]$, $1 \leq q \leq Q$. The estimated correlation matrix $\mathbf{R}(\omega, q)$ of the observed signal in the qth block can be obtained as

$$\mathbf{R}(\omega, q) = \frac{1}{N} \sum_{k=(q-1)N+1}^{qN} \mathbf{x}(\omega, k)\mathbf{x}^H(\omega, k). \tag{3}$$

Denote by $\mathbf{R}(\omega)$ the estimated correlation matrix of the observed signal. This matrix can be obtained based on $\mathbf{R}(\omega, q)$ as

$$\mathbf{R}(\omega) = \frac{1}{QN} \sum_{k=1}^{QN} \mathbf{x}(\omega, k)\mathbf{x}^H(\omega, k) = \frac{1}{Q} \sum_{q=1}^{Q} \mathbf{R}(\omega, q). \tag{4}$$

Clearly, during the conversation either speech sources can be active or non-active. Therefore, there exist periods in which all speech sources are inactive. Since, $\mathbf{R}(\omega)$ in (4) is the average of all estimated correlation matrices $\mathbf{R}(\omega, q)$, this matrix can be used as a reference to detect non-speech blocks or blocks with low speech presence. Thus, we propose to use a threshold $\varepsilon R(\ell, \ell, \omega)$ to detect the speech presence where ε is a pre-set threshold, $0 < \varepsilon < 1$, and ℓ is a reference microphone. The value $R(\ell, \ell, \omega)$ is the (ℓ, ℓ)th element of the matrix $\mathbf{R}(\omega)$.

Denote by $\mathcal{S}$ the index set of all blocks with at least one active speech source. Based on the proposed threshold, this set can be obtained as

$$\mathcal{S} = \{q, \, 1 \leq q \leq Q : R(\ell, \ell, \omega, q) > \varepsilon R(\ell, \ell, \omega)\} \tag{5}$$

where $R(\ell, \ell, \omega, q)$ is the (ℓ, ℓ)th element of the matrix $\mathbf{R}(\omega, q)$. Note that $\mathcal{S}$ is not an empty set since $R(\ell, \ell, \omega)$ is the average of $R(\ell, \ell, \omega, q)$, see (4). For each $q \in \mathcal{S}$, denote by $\bar{\mathbf{R}}_x(\omega, q)$ the normalized correlation matrix of the qth block

$$\bar{\mathbf{R}}(\omega, q) = \frac{\mathbf{R}(\omega, q)}{R(\ell, \ell, \omega, q)}. \tag{6}$$

By assuming that the speech signals of three speakers are statistically independent, the matrix $\mathbf{R}(\omega, q)$ can be decomposed as

$$\mathbf{R}(\omega, q) = \mathbf{R}_1(\omega, q) + \mathbf{R}_2(\omega, q) + \mathbf{R}_3(\omega, q) \tag{7}$$

where $\mathbf{R}_1(\omega, q)$, $\mathbf{R}_2(\omega, q)$ and $\mathbf{R}_3(\omega, q)$ are the correlation matrices for the first, the second and the third speech signals, respectively. We have

$$\mathbf{R}(\omega, q) = p_1(\omega, q)\bar{\mathbf{R}}_1(\omega) + p_2(\omega, q)\bar{\mathbf{R}}_2(\omega) + p_3(\omega, q)\bar{\mathbf{R}}_3(\omega) \tag{8}$$

where $p_1(\omega, q)$, $p_2(\omega, q)$, $p_3(\omega, q)$ and $\bar{\mathbf{R}}_1(\omega)$, $\bar{\mathbf{R}}_2(\omega)$, $\bar{\mathbf{R}}_3(\omega)$ are, respectively, the PSD and the normalized spatial correlation matrices of the first, the second and the third speech signals with (ℓ, ℓ)th elements are 1. Based on the idea of DOA estimation of acoustic signals using Near-field model [29], the spatial correlation matrices of speakers' speech signals are available. Since the (ℓ, ℓ)th elements of the normalized spatial correlation matrices $\bar{\mathbf{R}}_1(\omega)$, $\bar{\mathbf{R}}_2(\omega)$ and $\bar{\mathbf{R}}_3(\omega)$ are one, it follows from (8) that (6) can be rewritten as

$$\begin{aligned} \bar{\mathbf{R}}(\omega, q) &= \frac{p_1(\omega, q)}{p_1(\omega, q) + p_2(\omega, q) + p_3(\omega, q)}\bar{\mathbf{R}}_1(\omega) \\ &+ \frac{p_2(\omega, q)}{p_1(\omega, q) + p_2(\omega, q) + p_3(\omega, q)}\bar{\mathbf{R}}_2(\omega) \\ &+ \frac{p_3(\omega, q)}{p_1(\omega, q) + p_2(\omega, q) + p_3(\omega, q)}\bar{\mathbf{R}}_3(\omega). \end{aligned} \tag{9}$$

Eq. (9) can then be expressed as

$$\bar{\mathbf{R}}(\omega, q) = \gamma_1(\omega, q)\bar{\mathbf{R}}_1(\omega) + \gamma_2(\omega, q)\bar{\mathbf{R}}_2(\omega) + \gamma_3(\omega, q)\bar{\mathbf{R}}_3(\omega) \tag{10}$$

where the values $\gamma_1(\omega, q)$, $\gamma_2(\omega, q)$ and $\gamma_3(\omega, q)$ represent, respectively, the proportions of the matrices $\bar{\mathbf{R}}_1(\omega)$, $\bar{\mathbf{R}}_2(\omega)$ and $\bar{\mathbf{R}}_3(\omega)$ in the normalized correlation matrix $\bar{\mathbf{R}}(\omega, q)$, i.e.,

$$\gamma_1(\omega, q) = \frac{p_1(\omega, q)}{p_1(\omega, q) + p_2(\omega, q) + p_3(\omega, q)} \tag{11}$$

and

$$\gamma_2(\omega, q) = \frac{p_2(\omega, q)}{p_1(\omega, q) + p_2(\omega, q) + p_3(\omega, q)}. \quad (12)$$

and

$$\gamma_3(\omega, q) = \frac{p_3(\omega, q)}{p_1(\omega, q) + p_2(\omega, q) + p_3(\omega, q)}. \quad (13)$$

Since $p_1(\omega, q) \geq 0$, $p_2(\omega, q) \geq 0$ and $p_3(\omega, q) \geq 0$ we have

$$\gamma_1(\omega, q) \geq 0, \ \gamma_2(\omega, q) \geq 0, \ \gamma_3(\omega, q) \geq 0 \quad (14)$$

and

$$\gamma_1(\omega, q) + \gamma_2(\omega, q) + \gamma_3(\omega, q) - 1. \quad (15)$$

Since $\mathbf{R}(\omega)$ in (4) is the correlation matrix of the observed signal it follows

$$\bar{\mathbf{R}}(\omega) = \gamma_1(\omega)\bar{\mathbf{R}}_1(\omega) + \gamma_2(\omega)\bar{\mathbf{R}}_2(\omega) + \gamma_3(\omega)\bar{\mathbf{R}}_3(\omega) \quad (16)$$

where $\bar{\mathbf{R}}(\omega)$ is the normalized correlation matrix of the observed signal. The values $\gamma_1(\omega)$, $\gamma_2(\omega)$ and $\gamma_3(\omega)$ represent, respectively, the proportions of the matrices $\bar{\mathbf{R}}_1(\omega)$, $\bar{\mathbf{R}}_2(\omega)$ and $\bar{\mathbf{R}}_3(\omega)$ in the matrix $\bar{\mathbf{R}}(\omega)$, also

$$\gamma_1(\omega) \geq 0, \ \gamma_2(\omega) \geq 0, \ \gamma_3(\omega) \geq 0 \quad (17)$$

and

$$\gamma_1(\omega) + \gamma_2(\omega) + \gamma_3(\omega) = 1. \quad (18)$$

In the sequel, a spatial localization technique employing SRP-PHAT is proposed. Here, the (m, m)th element of $\mathbf{R}(\omega, q)$ is the cross-correlation of mth and nth microphone observed signals in the qth block. As such, the SRP-PHAT in block q can be estimated as follows

$$\Psi(\bar{\mathbf{R}}(\omega, q)) = \sum_{m=1}^{L} \sum_{n=m+1}^{L} \bar{R}(m, n, \omega, q) \quad (19)$$

where $\bar{R}(m, n, \omega, q)$ is the (m, n) element of the normalized correlation matrix $\bar{\mathbf{R}}(\omega, q)$. From (19) and (10), we have the following

$$\Psi(\bar{\mathbf{R}}(\omega, q)) = \gamma_1(\omega, q)\Psi(\bar{\mathbf{R}}_1(\omega)) $$
$$+ \gamma_2(\omega, q)\Psi(\bar{\mathbf{R}}_2(\omega)) + \gamma_3(\omega, q)\Psi(\bar{\mathbf{R}}_3(\omega)). \quad (20)$$

Clearly, the Eq. (20) shows the contribution balance of three speech sources in block q. As such, during the conversation,

each speech sources can be active and non-active so the correlation matrices of blocks, in which only one speech source is active, are useful for speech spatial estimation. In the block of only one active source, the contribution of this source should be 1 and all contributions of other sources should be 0. In the complex plane, based on (14) (15) (20), the point of $\Psi(\bar{\mathbf{R}}(\omega, q))$ is located inside a triangle, with vertices given by these points $\Psi(\bar{\mathbf{R}}_1(\omega))$, $\Psi(\bar{\mathbf{R}}_2(\omega))$ and $\Psi(\bar{\mathbf{R}}_3(\omega))$. In addition, based on (14), the point of $\Psi(\bar{\mathbf{R}}(\omega))$ is located inside this triangle too, see Fig. 2a. As such, normalized spatial correlation matrices $\bar{\mathbf{R}}_1(\omega)$, $\bar{\mathbf{R}}_2(\omega)$ and $\bar{\mathbf{R}}_3(\omega)$ can be estimated by detecting triangle vertices of blocks' SRP-PHAT of observed signal, see Fig. 2b. Hence, a spatial detection of speech sources is proposed that employs an algorithm for finding triangle vertices, i.e., the blocks of only one source active.

The block of only first source active is detected as block q_1 as follows:

$$q_1 = \arg \max_q |\Psi(\bar{\mathbf{R}}(\omega, q)) - \Psi(\bar{\mathbf{R}}(\omega))| \quad (21)$$

here $| \cdot |$ is the absolute operation. The block of only second source active is detected as block q_2 as follows:

$$q_2 = \arg \max_q |\Psi(\bar{\mathbf{R}}(\omega, q)) - \Psi(\bar{R}(\omega, q_1))|. \quad (22)$$

The block of only third source active is detected as block q_3 as follows:

$$q_3 = \arg \max_q \{|\Psi(\bar{\mathbf{R}}(\omega, q)) - \Psi(\bar{R}(\omega, q_1))|$$
$$+ |\Psi(\bar{\mathbf{R}}(\omega, q)) - \Psi(\bar{R}(\omega, q_2))|\}. \quad (23)$$

Here, the correlation matrix of the observed signal in the block of only one active source contains only spatial characteristic of the active source. As such, the normalized spatial correlation matrix for the active source can be estimated as normalized correlation matrix in the block of only this source active. To reduce the correlation mismatch, we propose to estimate the normalized spatial correlation matrices for the speech sources by taking the average of the estimated normalized correlation matrices corresponding to I blocks which SRP-PHAT are nearest to estimated triangle vertices.

The average is employed to reduce the estimation error which can occur due to a limited number of samples in each block. Then, $\mathcal{S}_1$, $\mathcal{S}_2$, and $\mathcal{S}_3$ are proposed to be subsets of S and each subset has I block's indexes of blocks which SRP-PHAT are nearest to SRP-PHAT of blocks q_1, q_2, and q_3, respectively. In practice, the value I can be chosen smaller than 5 % of the number of elements in $\mathcal{S}$. The normalized spatial correlation matrix $\hat{\bar{\mathbf{R}}}_1(\omega)$ for the first source can be estimated as follows:

Fig. 2 **a** The triangle with SRP-PHAT vertices in the complex plane; **b** SRP-PHAT values of the observed signal for frequency of 2100 Hz from the simulation in Sect. 6

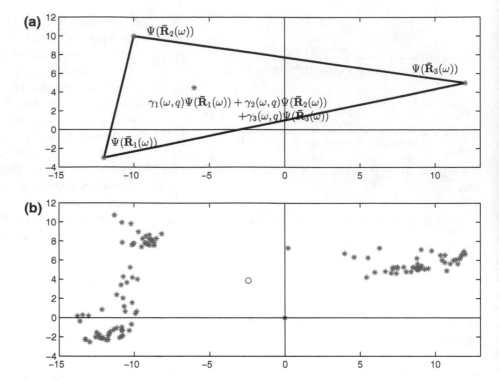

$$\hat{\bar{\mathbf{R}}}_1(\omega) = \frac{1}{I} \sum_{i \subseteq \mathcal{S}_1} \bar{\mathbf{R}}(\omega, q_{1,i}). \tag{24}$$

The normalized spatial correlation matrix $\hat{\bar{\mathbf{R}}}_2(\omega)$ for the second source can be estimated as follows:

$$\hat{\bar{\mathbf{R}}}_2(\omega) = \frac{1}{I} \sum_{i \subseteq \mathcal{S}_2} \bar{\mathbf{R}}(\omega, q_{2,i}). \tag{25}$$

The normalized spatial correlation matrix $\hat{\bar{\mathbf{R}}}_3(\omega)$ for the second source can be estimated as follows:

$$\hat{\bar{\mathbf{R}}}_3(\omega) = \frac{1}{I} \sum_{i \subseteq \mathcal{S}_3} \bar{\mathbf{R}}(\omega, q_{3,i}). \tag{26}$$

Due to the small value of I, the proportion of non-desired sources in the matrices $\hat{\bar{\mathbf{R}}}_1(\omega)$, $\hat{\bar{\mathbf{R}}}_2(\omega)$, and $\hat{\bar{\mathbf{R}}}_3(\omega)$ is approximately close to zero and their contribution can be neglected. These matrices are now used to estimate the optimum beamformer in each frequency bin.

4 Optimum beamformer using spatial information

Based on the estimated normalized spatial correlation matrices $\hat{\bar{\mathbf{R}}}_1(\omega)$, $\hat{\bar{\mathbf{R}}}_2(\omega)$, and $\hat{\bar{\mathbf{R}}}_3(\omega)$, an optimum beamformer is proposed for each desired source in the frequency bin ω. For extracting one speech source from the observed signal,

an optimum beamformer is desired to suppress all undesired sources whilst preserving the desired one. Then, the first source is assumed to be the desired source so two other sources are undesired and denote by $\mathbf{w}_1(\omega)$ the filter weight for the first source in the frequency bin ω. The filter weight $\mathbf{w}_1(\omega)$ is designed to minimize two weighted cost functions $\mathbf{w}_1(\omega)^H \hat{\bar{\mathbf{R}}}_2(\omega)\mathbf{w}_1(\omega)$ and $\mathbf{w}_1(\omega)^H \hat{\bar{\mathbf{R}}}_3(\omega)\mathbf{w}_1(\omega)$ while maintaining the source direction as follows:

$$\begin{cases} \min_{\mathbf{w}_1(\omega)} \mathbf{w}_1(\omega)^H \hat{\bar{\mathbf{R}}}_2(\omega)\mathbf{w}_1(\omega) \, , \, \mathbf{w}_1(\omega)^H \hat{\bar{\mathbf{R}}}_3(\omega)\mathbf{w}_1(\omega) \\ \text{subject to } \mathbf{w}(\omega)^H \hat{\bar{\mathbf{d}}}_1(\omega) = 1. \end{cases} \tag{27}$$

where $\hat{\bar{\mathbf{d}}}_1(\omega)$ is the estimated cross-correlation vector between the first source at a ℓth reference microphone. This vector is also the ℓth column of the matrix $\hat{\bar{\mathbf{R}}}_1(\omega)$. Thus, from (27) we propose to minimize the following weighted cost function $\mathbf{w}_1(\omega)^H \left[\hat{\bar{\mathbf{R}}}_2(\omega) + \hat{\bar{\mathbf{R}}}_3(\omega) \right] \mathbf{w}_1(\omega)$ and the filter weight $\mathbf{w}_1(\omega)$ can be obtained by solving the optimization problem

$$\begin{cases} \min \mathbf{w}_1^H(\omega) \left[\hat{\bar{\mathbf{R}}}_2(\omega) + \hat{\bar{\mathbf{R}}}_3(\omega) \right] \mathbf{w}_1(\omega) \\ \text{subject to } \mathbf{w}_1^H \hat{\bar{\mathbf{d}}}_1(\omega) = 1 \end{cases} \tag{28}$$

Similarly, the beamformer weight $\mathbf{w}_2(\omega)$ for the second source can be obtained as the solution to the optimization problem

$$\begin{cases} \min \ \mathbf{w}_2^H(\omega) \left[\hat{\bar{\mathbf{R}}}_1(\omega) + \hat{\bar{\mathbf{R}}}_3(\omega) \right] \mathbf{w}_2(\omega) \\ \text{subject to } \mathbf{w}_2^H \hat{\bar{\mathbf{d}}}_2(\omega) = 1 \end{cases} \quad (29)$$

where $\hat{\bar{\mathbf{d}}}_2(\omega)$ is the ℓth column of the matrix $\hat{\bar{\mathbf{R}}}_2(\omega)$. The beamformer weight $\mathbf{w}_3(\omega)$ for the third source can be obtained as the solution to the optimization problem

$$\begin{cases} \min \ \mathbf{w}_3^H(\omega) \left[\hat{\bar{\mathbf{R}}}_1(\omega) + \hat{\bar{\mathbf{R}}}_2(\omega) \right] \mathbf{w}_3(\omega) \\ \text{subject to } \mathbf{w}_3^H \hat{\bar{\mathbf{d}}}_3(\omega) = 1 \end{cases} \quad (30)$$

where $\hat{\bar{\mathbf{d}}}_3(\omega)$ is the ℓth column of the matrix $\hat{\bar{\mathbf{R}}}_3(\omega)$. The solutions to three optimization problems can be expressed as

$$\mathbf{w}_1(\omega) = \frac{\left[\hat{\bar{\mathbf{R}}}_2(\omega) + \hat{\bar{\mathbf{R}}}_3(\omega) \right]^{-1} \hat{\bar{\mathbf{d}}}_1(\omega)}{\hat{\bar{\mathbf{d}}}_1^H(\omega) \left[\hat{\bar{\mathbf{R}}}_2(\omega) + \hat{\bar{\mathbf{R}}}_3(\omega) \right]^{-1} \hat{\bar{\mathbf{d}}}_1(\omega)} \quad (31)$$

and

$$\mathbf{w}_2(\omega) = \frac{\left[\hat{\bar{\mathbf{R}}}_1(\omega) + \hat{\bar{\mathbf{R}}}_3(\omega) \right]^{-1} \hat{\bar{\mathbf{d}}}_2(\omega)}{\hat{\bar{\mathbf{d}}}_2^H(\omega) \left[\hat{\bar{\mathbf{R}}}_1(\omega) + \hat{\bar{\mathbf{R}}}_3(\omega) \right]^{-1} \hat{\bar{\mathbf{d}}}_2(\omega)} \quad (32)$$

and

$$\mathbf{w}_3(\omega) = \frac{\left[\hat{\bar{\mathbf{R}}}_1(\omega) + \hat{\bar{\mathbf{R}}}_2(\omega) \right]^{-1} \hat{\bar{\mathbf{d}}}_3(\omega)}{\hat{\bar{\mathbf{d}}}_3^H(\omega) \left[\hat{\bar{\mathbf{R}}}_1(\omega) + \hat{\bar{\mathbf{R}}}_2(\omega) \right]^{-1} \hat{\bar{\mathbf{d}}}_3(\omega)} \quad (33)$$

The beamformer outputs for the three sources are calculated as

$$y_1(\omega, k) = \mathbf{w}_1^H(\omega) \mathbf{x}(\omega, k) \quad (34)$$

and

$$y_2(\omega, k) = \mathbf{w}_2^H(\omega) \mathbf{x}(\omega, k). \quad (35)$$

and

$$y_3(\omega, k) = \mathbf{w}_3^H(\omega) \mathbf{x}(\omega, k). \quad (36)$$

The remaining problem is to align the beamformer output in different frequency bins to the same source. In the sequel, the correlation between the beamformer outputs in neighboring frequencies is employed to overcome the permutation problem.

5 Permutation alignment

Since the optimum beamformers are performed in each frequency bin, the permutation alignment is needed before transforming the signals to the time domain. Here, the correlation approach is chosen for the permutation alignment and permutation decision is based on inter-frequency correlation of the output signal amplitudes based on the assumption that the amplitudes of the output signals from the one speech signal are correlated with adjoining frequencies. The permutation alignment can be performed continuously with a reference frequency in the middle of the frequency range. In this case, permutation correlation is performed in two directions, with increasing and decreasing frequency indexes until the end of the frequency range. For two neighboring frequencies ω_m and ω_{m+1}, the following correlations between the ith beamformer output of frequencies ω_m and jth beamformer output of frequencies ω_{m+1} are obtained as follows:

$$\text{cor}_{i,j} = \frac{\mu(|y_i(\omega_m, k) y_j(\omega_{m+1}, k)|) - \mu(|y_i(\omega_m, k)|)\mu(|y_j(\omega_{m+1}, k)|)}{\sigma(|y_i(\omega_m, k)|)\sigma(|y_j(\omega_{m+1}, k)|)} \quad (37)$$

where $\mu(\cdot)$ and $\sigma(\cdot)$ are, respectively, the mean and the standard deviation of $(\cdot)$. Permutation decision Π is made with permutation alignment Π as follows

$$\Pi = \arg \max_{\Pi} \sum_{i,j \in \Pi} \text{cor}_{i,j}, \quad (38)$$

After permutation alignment, three output signals in all frequencies are passed through the synthesis filters for obtaining the output signals with three speech sources in the time domain.

6 Experimental results

For performance evaluations of the proposed blind speech separation algorithm, a simulation is performed in a real room environment using a linear microphone array consisting of 6 microphones. Here, the distance between two adjacent microphones is 6 cm and the positions of three speakers are shown in Fig. 1. The distances between the array and speakers are about 1–1.5 m. The duration of the observed signal is 150 s and the value N was chosen as the number of samples in 0.5 s period while I and ε were chosen as 10 and 0.1, respectively. With the chosen N and I, the evaluation time of each speech source is about 5 s. Based on our experience, the evaluation time 5 s is enough for evaluation of the spatial characteristic of the speech source. We conducted our numerical experiments on HP Laptop with Intel Core i7 and 16GB RAM, using Matlab (R2013b).

Fig. 3 Time domain plots of
the original speech signals and
the observed signal at the fourth
microphone

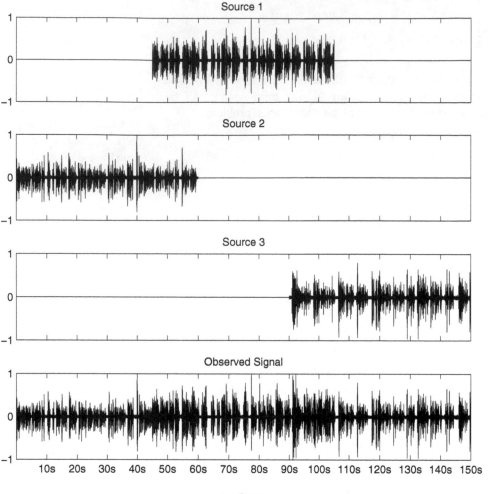

Fig. 4 Time domain plots of
the second-order BSS algorithm
outputs

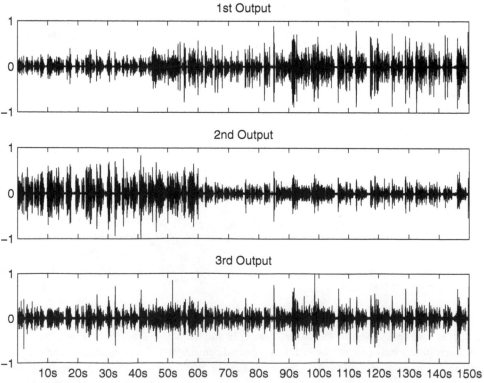

Fig. 5 Time domain plots of the proposed algorithm outputs

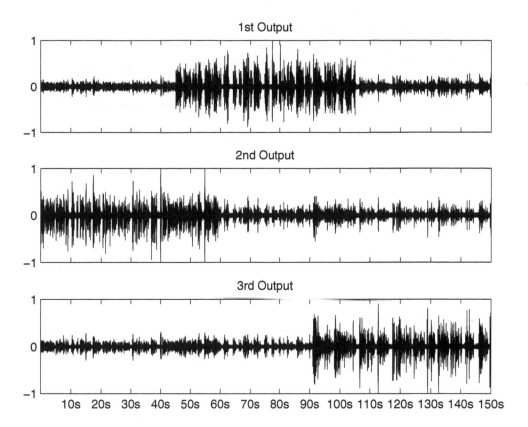

The observed signals are decomposed into sub-bands using an oversampled analysis filter bank. Here, an oversampling factor of two is chosen to reduce the aliasing effects between the adjacent sub-bands [30]. After the decomposition, the implementation of the proposed algorithm is performed in sub-bands. Figure 3 shows time domain plots of three speech signals and the observed signal. The speech signals from three speakers occur at different times and can overlap with each other in the observed signal. The overlapping signals simulate simultaneous conversation.

We have compared a second-order BSS algorithm with the suggested method. In Fig. 4, the results for when the second-order blind signal separation (BSS) algorithm is used for separating the observed signal are given. This second-order BBS algorithm was used in [22] for speech separation in two speaker environment. Figure 4 depicts time domain plots of the three outputs of the second-order BSS algorithm. The three outputs are speech signals extracted for three speakers from the observed signal. Hence, Fig. 4 shows a little differ-

ence between three output signals and the separation did not have a good result.

Figure 5 depicts time domain plots of the three outputs of the proposed separation algorithm when the proposed blind separation algorithm is used for separating the observed signal. The three outputs are speech signals extracted for three speakers from the observed signal. Thus, Fig. 5 shows that the proposed algorithm can separate the three speech signals from the observed mixture. Informal listening tests suggest the good listening quality of signal outputs from the proposed algorithm. From the Table 1, it is clear that the computation time of proposed algorithm is lower than computation time of the second-order BSS algorithm.

To quantify the performance of the second-order BSS algorithm and the proposed algorithm, the interference suppression (IS) and source distortion (SD) measures as presented in [31] are employed. As such, the speech signal from one speaker is viewed as the desired signal and other speech signals are interferences. Table 1 shows the IS and SD levels

Table 1 The interference suppression and the source distortion levels in the outputs of the proposed blind speech separation algorithm

Methods	First output		Second output		Third output		Computation time (s)
	IS (dB)	SD (dB)	IS (dB)	SD (dB)	IS (dB)	SD (dB)	
Second-order BSS algorithm	1.8	−25.1	2.9	−24.3	2.1	−23.4	42
Proposed algorithm	6.8	−29.2	5.7	−26.6	6.3	−26	27

for the three outputs of the second-order BSS algorithm and the proposed algorithm; the proposed algorithm has a better performance. In addition, the proposed blind speech separation algorithm offers a good interference suppression level (5–7 dB) whilst maintaining a low distortion level (−26 to −29 dB) for the desired source.

7 Summary

In this paper, a new blind speech separation algorithm in the frequency domain was developed for the three-speaker environment. Since, the position of the sources are unknown, the SRP-PHAT localization is used for estimating the spatial location of all speakers in each frequency bin. Based on that information, an optimum beamformer is designed for each speech source to extract the desired signal. The permutation alignment is used before transforming the signals to the time domain. Simulation results show that the proposed blind speech separation algorithm offers a good interference suppression level whilst maintaining a low distortion level for the desired source.

Acknowledgements This research is funded by Vietnam National University Ho Chi Minh City (VNU-HCM) under Grant Number C2014-26-01.

References

1. Nordholm, S., Dam, H., Lai, C., Lehmann, E.: Broadband beamforming and optimization. Signal processing: array and statistical signal processing, vol 3, pp. 553–598. Academic Press Library (2014)
2. Doclo, S., Kellermann, W., Makino, S., Nordholm, S.E.: Multichannel signal enhancement algorithms for assisted listening devices: exploiting spatial diversity using multiple microphones. IEEE Signal Process. Mag. **32**(2), 18–30 (2015)
3. Cohen, I., Benesty, J., Gannot, S. (eds.): Speech Processing in Modern Communication: Challenges and Perspectives. Springer, Berlin, Heidelberg (2010). ISBN 978-3642111297
4. Benesty, J., Makino, S., Chen, J.: Speech Enhancement. Springer, Berlin, Heidelberg (2005). ISBN 978-3540240396
5. Bai, M.R., Ih, J.-G., Benesty, J.: Acoustic Array Systems: Theory, Implementation, and Application. Wiley-IEEE Press, Singapore (2013). ISBN 978-0470827239
6. Benesty, J., Chen, J., Huang, Y.: Microphone Array Signal Processing Springer, Berlin, Heidelberg (2008). ISBN 978-3540786115
7. Nordebo, S., Claesson, I., Nordholm, S.: Adaptive beamforming: spatial filter designed blocking matrix. IEEE J. Ocean. Eng. **19**, 583–590 (1994)
8. Nagata, Y., Abe, M.: Two-channel adaptive microphone array with target tracking. Electron. Commun. Jpn. **83**(12), 860–866 (2000)
9. Nakadai, K., Nakamura, K., Ince, G.: Real-time super-resolution sound source localization for robots. In: Proceedings of 2012 IEEE/RSJ International Conference on Intelligent Robots and Systems (IROS 2012), pp. 694–699. IEEE, Vilamoura (2012)
10. Grbić, N., Nordholm, S., Cantoni, A.: Optimal fir subband beamforming for speech enhancement in multipath environments. IEEE Signal Process. Lett. **10**(11), 335–338 (2003)
11. Brandstein, M., Ward, D. (eds.): Microphone Arrays: Signal Processing Techniques and Applications. Springer, Berlin, Heidelberg (2001). ISBN 978-3540419532
12. Fallon, M., Godsill, S.: Acoustic source localization and tracking of a time-varying number of speakers. IEEE Trans. Audio Speech Lang. Process. **20**(4), 1409–1415 (2012)
13. Gannot, S., Burshtein, D., Weinstein, E.: Signal enhancement using beamforming and nonstationarity with applications to speech. IEEE Trans. Signal Process. **49**, 1614–1626 (2001)
14. Low, S.Y., Nordholm, S., Togneri, R.: Convolutive blind signal separation with post-processing. IEEE Trans. Speech Audio Process. **12**(5), 539–548 (2004)
15. Grbić, N., Tao, X.J., Nordholm, S., Claesson, I.: Blind signal separation using overcomplete subband representation. IEEE Trans. Speech Audio Process. **9**(5), 524–533 (2001)
16. Parra, L., Spence, C.: Convolutive blind separation of nonstationary sources. IEEE Trans. Speech Audio Process. **8**(3), 320–327 (2000)
17. Dam, H.H., Nordholm, S., Low, S.Y., Cantoni, A.: Blind signal separation using steepest descent method. IEEE Trans. Signal Process. **55**(8), 4198–4207 (2007)
18. Sawada, H., Araki, S., Makino, S.: Underdetermined convolutive blind source separation via frequency bin-wise clustering and permutation alignment. IEEE Trans. Audio Speech Lang. Process. **19**(3), 516–527 (2011)
19. Dam, H.Q., Nordholm, S., Dam, H.H., Low, S.Y.: Postfiltering using multichannel spectral estimation in multispeaker environments. EURASIP J. Adv. Signal Process ID **860360**, 1–10 (2008)
20. Krishnamoorthy, P., Prasanna, S.R.M.: Two speaker speech separation by lp residual weighting and harmonics enhancement. Int. J. Speech Technol. **13**(3), 117–139 (2010)
21. Dam, H.Q.: Blind multi-channel speech separation using spatial estimation in two-speaker environments. J. Sci. Technol. Spec. Issue Theor. Appl. Comput. Sci. **48**(4), 109–119 (2010)
22. Dam, H.Q., Nordholm, S.: Sound source localization for subband-based two speech separation in room environment. In: 2013 International Conference on Control, Automation and Information Sciences (ICCAIS), pp. 223–227. IEEE, Nha Trang City (2013)
23. Tariqullah, J., Wenwu, W., DeLiang, W.: A multistage approach to blind separation of convolutive speech mixtures. Speech Commun. **53**, 524–539 (2011)
24. Minhas, S.F., Gaydecki, P.: A hybrid algorithm for blind source separation of a convolutive mixture of three speech sources. EURASIP J. Adv. Signal Process. **1**(92), 1–15 (2014)
25. Araki, S., Mukai, R., Makino, S., Nishikawa, T., Saruwatari, H.: The fundamental limitation of frequency domain blind source separation for convolutive mixtures of speech. IEEE Trans. Speech Audio Process. **11**(2), 109–116 (2003)
26. Makino, H.S.S., Lee, T.-W., Sawada, H. (eds.): Blind Speech Separation. Springer, Netherlands (2007). ISBN 978-1402064784
27. Naik, G.R., Wang, W. (eds.): Blind Source Separation: Advances in Theory. Algorithms and Applications. Springer, Berlin, Heidelberg (2014). ISBN 978-3642550157
28. Cobos, M., Marti, A., Lopez, J.J.: A modified srp-phat functional for robust real-time sound source localization with scalable spatial sampling. IEEE Signal Process. Lett. **18**(1), 71–74 (2010)

29. Sawada, H., Mukai, R., Araki, S., Makino, S.: Frequency-domain blind source separation. In: Speech Enhancement. Signals and Communication Technology, pp. 299–327. Springer, Berlin, Heidelberg (2005). ISBN: 978-3540240396

30. Vaidyanathan, P.P.: Multirate Systems and Filter Banks. Prentice Hall, Englewood Cliffs (1993). ISBN 978-0136057185

31. Dam, H.Q., Nordholm, S., Dam, H.H., Low, S.Y.: Adaptive beamformer for hands-free communication system in noisy environments. IEEE Int. Symp. Circuits Syst. 2, 856–859 (2005)

## 10

Using internal evaluation measures to validate the quality of diverse stream clustering algorithms

Marwan Hassani[1] [iD] · Thomas Seidl[2]

Abstract Measuring the quality of a clustering algorithm has shown to be as important as the algorithm itself. It is a crucial part of choosing the clustering algorithm that performs best for an input data. Streaming input data have many features that make them much more challenging than static ones. They are endless, varying and emerging with high speeds. This raised new challenges for the clustering algorithms as well as for their evaluation measures. Up till now, external evaluation measures were exclusively used for validating stream clustering algorithms. While external validation requires a ground truth which is not provided in most applications, particularly in the streaming case, internal clustering validation is efficient and realistic. In this article, we analyze the properties and performances of eleven internal clustering measures. In particular, we apply these measures to carefully synthesized stream scenarios to reveal how they react to clusterings on evolving data streams using both k-means-based and density-based clustering algorithms. A series of experimental results show that different from the case with static data, the *Calinski-Harabasz index* performs the best in coping with common aspects and errors of stream clustering for k-means-based algorithms, while the *revised validity index* performs the best for density-based ones.

Keywords Stream clustering · Internal evaluation measures · Clustering · Validation · MOA

✉ Marwan Hassani
m.hassani@tue.nl

Thomas Seidl
seidl@dbs.ifi.lmu.de

[1] Architecture of Information Systems Group, Eindhoven University of Technology, Eindhoven, The Netherlands

[2] Database Systems Group, LMU Munich, Munich, Germany

1 Introduction

Clustering of data objects is a well-established data mining task that aims at grouping these objects. The grouping is made such that *similar* objects are aggregated together in the same group (or cluster) while *dissimilar* ones are grouped in different clusters. In this context, the definition of similarity, and thus the final clustering is highly dependent on the applied distance function between the data objects. Different to classification, clustering does not use a subset of the data objects with known class labels to learn a classification model. As a completely unsupervised task, clustering calculates the similarity between objects without having any information about their correct distribution (also known as the ground truth). The latter fact motivated the research in the field of clustering validation notably more than the field of classification evaluation. It has been even stated that clustering validation is regarded as important as the clustering itself [32].

There are two types of clustering validation [31]. The *external* validation, which compares the clustering result to a reference result which is considered as the ground truth. If the result is somehow similar to the reference, we regard this final output as a "good" clustering. This validation is straightforward when the similarity between two clusterings has been well-defined, however, it has fundamental caveat that the reference result is not provided in most real applications. Therefore, external evaluation is largely used for synthetic data and mostly for tuning clustering algorithms.

Internal validation is the other type clustering evaluation, where the evaluation of the clustering is compared only with the result itself, i.e., the structure of found clusters and their relations to each other. This is much more realistic and efficient in many real-world scenarios as it does not refer to any assumed references from outside which is not always feasible to obtain. Particularly, with the huge increase of the data size and dimensionality as in recent applications with streaming data outputs, one can hardly claim that a complete knowledge of the ground truth is available or always valid.

Obviously, clustering evaluation is a stand-alone process that is not included within clustering task. It is usually performed after the final clustering output is generated. However, internal evaluation methods have been used in the validation phase within some clustering algorithms like k-means [29], k-medoids [26], EM [8] and k-center [19].

Stream clustering deals with evolving input objects where the distribution, the density and the labels of objects are continuously changing [16]. Whether it is high-dimensional stream clustering [14,24], hierarchical stream clustering [15,23] or sensor data clustering [19–21], evaluating the clustering output using external evaluation measures (like SubCMM [17,18]) requires a ground truth that is very difficult to obtain in the above-mentioned scenarios.

For the previous reasons, we focus in this article on the internal clustering validation and study its usability for drifting streaming data. To fairly discuss the ability of internal measures to validate the quality of different types of stream clustering algorithms. We expand the study to cover both a k-means-based stream clustering algorithm [1] as well as a density-based stream clustering one [6]. This is mainly motivated by the fact that those algorithms are good representatives of the two main different categories of stream clustering algorithms.

The remainder of this article is organized as follows: Sect. 2 examines some popular criteria of deciding whether found clusters are valid, and the general procedure we used in this article to evaluate stream clustering. In Sect. 3, we list eleven different mostly used internal evaluation measures and shortly show how they are actually exploited in clustering evaluation. In Sect. 4, we introduce a set of thorough experiments on different kinds of data streams with different errors to show the behaviors of these internal measures in practice with a k-means-based stream clustering algorithm. In addition, we investigate more concretely how the internal measures react to stream-specific properties of data. To do this, several common error scenarios in stream clusterings are simulated and also evaluated with internal clustering validation. In Sect. 5, the internal evaluation measures are again used to validate a density-based stream clustering. This is done by first extracting a "ground truth" of the clustering quality using external evaluation measures and then checking which of the internal measures has the highest correlation with that ground truth. Finally, in Sect. 6, we summarize the contents of this article.

This article further discusses the initial technical results introduced in [22] and extends them by elaborating the algorithmic description in Sect. 2, enriching the results in Sect. 4 and introducing Sect. 5 completely.

2 Internal clustering validation

In this section, we describe our concept of internal clustering validation and how they are realized for existing internal validation measures. Additionally, we will show an abstract procedure to make use of these measures in streaming environments in practice.

2.1 Validation criteria

Contrary to external validation, internal clustering validation is based only on the intrinsic information of the data. Since we can only refer to the input dataset itself, internal validation needs assumptions about a "good" structure of found clusters which are normally given by reference result in external validation. Two main concepts, the compactness and the separation, are the most popular ones. Most other concepts are actually just combinations of variations of these two [34].

The *Compactness* measures how closely data points are grouped in a cluster. Grouped points in the cluster are supposed to be related to each other, by sharing a common feature which reflects a meaningful pattern in practice. Compactness is normally based on distances between in-cluster points. The very popular way of calculating the compactness is through variance, i.e., average distance to the mean, to estimate how objects are bonded together with its mean as its center. A small variance indicates a high compactness (cf. Fig. 1). Quantitatively, one way of calculating the compactness using the average distance is explained in Eq. 1.

The *Separation* measures how different the found clusters are from each other. Users of clustering algorithms are not interested in similar or vague patterns when clusters are not well-separated (cf. Fig. 2). A distinct cluster that is far from the others corresponds to a unique pattern. Similar to the compactness, the distances between objects are widely used to measure separation, e.g., pairwise distances between cluster centers, or pairwise minimum distances between objects in different clusters. Separation is an inter-cluster criterion in the sense of relation between clusters. An example of how to quantitatively calculate the separation using the average distance is explained in Eq. 2.

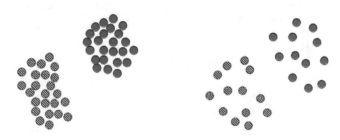

Fig. 1 Clusters on the *left* have better compactness than the ones on the *right*

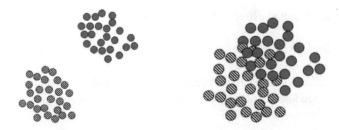

Fig. 2 Clusters on the *left* have better separation than the ones on the *right*

2.2 General procedure

Using a carefully generated synthetic data set, where we know the underlying partitioning and the distribution of the data, we apply the internal validation measures using different parameters of the clustering algorithms. The target is now to observe which of the evaluation measures is reaching its best value when setting the parameters of the selected clustering algorithm to best reflect the distribution of the data set. We collect the values of the internal measures for each batch, and finally average the values of all batches. An abstract procedure of this process is listed in Algorithm 1. The algorithm explains both cases of a k-means-based algorithm and a DBSCAN-based algorithm.

Algorithm 1: InternalValidationProcedure()

Prepare the current stream batch from the dataset
initialize the clustering algorithm (a k-means-based or a DBSCAN-based one);
initialize a set $\mathcal{T}$ of all combinations of meaningful ranges for each parameter;
foreach *parameter setting* $ps \in \mathcal{T}$ **do**

    Run the selected clustering algorithm with the parameter setting ps;
    foreach *batch in the stream* **do**

        Compute the corresponding internal validation index of the clustering output;
    end
    Average the clustering quality of the validation index over all batches from the stream;
end
if *the current algorithm is k-means based* **then**
    Check which index is reaching its best values with the correct number of generated clusters k in the data set;
end
else
    Check which parameter setting $ps_i \in \mathcal{T}$ causes best values of **external** evaluation measures over the current DBSCAN-based algorithm;
    Check which internal index has the highest correlation with the external measures w.r.t. ps_i;
end

---

3 Considered existing internal evaluation measures

In this section, we briefly review the most used eleven internal clustering measures in recent works. One can easily figure out of each measure which design criteria is chosen and how they are realized in mathematical form. We will first introduce important notations used in the formula of these measures: D is the input dataset, n is the number of points in D, g is the center of whole dataset D, P is the number of dimensions of D, NC is the number of clusters, Ci is the i-th cluster, n_i is the number of data points in C_i, c_i is the center of cluster C_i, $\sigma(C_i)$ is the variance vector of C_i, and $d(x, y)$ is the distance between points x and y. For the convenience, we will put an abbreviation for each measure and use it through the rest of this article.

First, some measures are designed to evaluate either only one of compactness or separation. The simplest one is the *Root-mean-square standard deviation (RMSSTD)*:

$$RMSSTD = \left(\frac{\sum_i \sum_{x \in C_i} \|x - c_i\|^2}{P \sum_i (n_i - 1)} \right)^{1/2} \quad (1)$$

This measure is the square root of the pooled sample variance of all the attributes, which measures only the compactness of found clusters [10]. Another measure which considers only the separation between clusters is the *R-squared (RS)* [10]:

$$RS = \frac{\sum_{x \in D} \|x - g\|^2 - \sum_i \sum_{x \in C_i} \|x - c_i\|^2}{\sum_{x \in D} \|x - g\|^2} \quad (2)$$

RS is the complement of the ratio of sum of squared distances between objects in different clusters to the total sum of squares. It is an intuitive and simple formulation of measuring the differences between clusters. Another measure considering only separation is the *Modified Hubert Γ statistic (Γ)* [25]:

$$\Gamma = \frac{2}{n(n-1)} \sum_{i,j \in \{1 \cdots NC\}, i \neq j} \sum_{x \in C_i} \sum_{y \in C_j} d(x, y) \cdot d(c_i, c_j)$$

$$(3)$$

Γ calculates the average weighted pairwise distances between data points belonging to different clusters by multiplying them by the distances between the centers of their clusters.

The following measures are designed to reflect both compactness and separation at the same time. Naturally, considering only one of the two criteria is not enough to evaluate complex clusterings. We will introduce first the *Calinski-Harabasz index (CH)* [5]:

$$CH = \frac{\sum_i d^2(c_i, g)/(NC - 1)}{\sum_i \sum_{x \in C_i} d^2(x, c_i)/(n - NC)} \qquad (4)$$

CH measures the two criteria simultaneously with the help of average between and within cluster sum of squares. The numerator reflects the degree of separation in the way of how much the cluster centers are spread, and the denominator corresponds to compactness, to reflect how close the in-cluster objects are gathered around the cluster center. The following two measures also share this type of formulation, i.e., numerator-separation/denominator-compactness. First, the I index (I) [30]:

$$I = \left(\frac{1}{NC} \frac{\sum_{x \in D} d(x, g)}{\sum_i \sum_{x \in C_i} d(x, c_i)} \max_{i,j} d(c_i, c_j) \right)^P \qquad (5)$$

To measure separation, I adopts the maximum distance between cluster centers. For compactness, the distance from a data point to its cluster center is used like CH. Another famous measure is the *Dunn's indices (D)* [9]:

$$D = \frac{\min_i \min_j \left(\min_{x \in C_i, y \in C_j} d(x, y) \right)}{\max_k \left(\max_{x, y \in C_k} d(x, y) \right)} \qquad (6)$$

D uses the minimum pairwise distance between points in different clusters as the inter-cluster separation and the maximum diameter among all clusters as the intra-cluster compactness. As mentioned above, CH, I, and D follow the form $(Separation)/(Compactness)$, though they use different distances and different weights of the two factors. The optimal cluster number can be achieved by maximizing these three indices.

Another commonly used measure is *Silhouette index (S)* [33]:

$$S = \frac{1}{NC} \sum_i \left(\frac{1}{n_i} \sum_{x \in C_i} \frac{b(x) - a(x)}{max[b(x), a(x)]} \right) \qquad (7)$$

where $a(x) = \frac{1}{n_i - 1} \sum_{y \in C_i, y \neq x} d(x, y)$
and $b(x) = \min_{j \neq i} \left[\frac{1}{n_j} \sum_{y \in C_j} d(x, y) \right]$.

S does not take c_i or g into account and uses pairwise distance between all the objects in a cluster for numerating compactness $(a(x))$. Here, $b(x)$ measures the separation with the average distance of objects to alternative cluster, i.e., second closest cluster. *Davies-Bouldin index (DB)* [7] is an old but still widely used internal validation measure:

$$DB = \frac{1}{NC} \sum_i \max_{j \neq i} \frac{\frac{1}{n_i} \sum_{x \in C_i} d(x, c_i) + \frac{1}{n_j} \sum_{x \in C_j} d(x, c_j)}{d(c_i, c_j)} \qquad (8)$$

DB uses intra-cluster variance and inter-cluster center distance to find the worst partner cluster, i.e., the closest most scattered one for each cluster. Thus, minimizing DB gives us the optimal number of clusters. The *Xie-Beni index (XB)* [35] is defined as:

$$XB = \frac{\sum_i \sum_{x \in C_i} d^2(x, c_i)}{n \cdot \min_{i \neq j} d^2(c_i, c_j)} \qquad (9)$$

Apparently, the smaller the values of XB, the better the clustering quality. Along with DB, XB has a form of $(Compactness)/(Separation)$ which is the opposite of CH, I, and D. Therefore, it reaches the optimum clustering by being minimized. It defines the inter-cluster separation as the minimum square distance between cluster centers, and the intra-cluster compactness as the mean square distance between each data object and its cluster center.

In the following, we present more recent clustering validation measures. The *SD validity index (SD)* [12]:

$$SD = NCmax \cdot Scat(NC) + Dis(NC) \qquad (10)$$

- NCmax is the maximum number of possible clusters
- $Scat(NC) = \frac{1}{NC} \sum_i \frac{\|\sigma(C_i)\|}{\|\sigma(D)\|}$
- $Dis(NC) = \frac{\max_{i,j} d(c_i, c_j)}{\min_{i,j} d(c_i, c_j)} \sum_i \left(\sum_j d(c_i, c_j) \right)^{-1}$

SD is composed of two terms; $Scat(NC)$ stands for the scattering within clusters and $Dis(NC)$ stands for the dispersion between clusters. Like DB and XB, SD measures the compactness with variance of clustered objects and separation with distance between cluster centers, but uses them in a different way. The smaller the value of SD, the better. A revised version of SD is S_Dbw [11]:

$$S\_Dbw = Scat(NC) + Dens\_bw(NC) \qquad (11)$$

- $Dens\_bw(NC) = \frac{1}{NC(NC-1)} \sum_i$
  $\times \left(\sum_{j \neq i} \frac{\sum_{x \in C_i \cup C_j} f(x, u_{ij})}{\max\left(\sum_{x \in C_i} f(x, c_i), \sum_{x \in C_j} f(x, c_j) \right)} \right)$
- $f(x, y) = \begin{cases} 0 & \text{if } d(x, y) > \tau, \\ 1 & \text{otherwise.} \end{cases}$

where u_{ij} is the middle point of c_i and c_j, τ is a threshold to determine the neighbors approximated by the average standard deviation of cluster centers: $\tau = \frac{1}{NC} \sqrt{\sum_{i=1}^{NC} \|\sigma(c_i)\|}$, and $Scat(NC)$ is the same as that of SD. S_Dbw takes the density into account to measure the separation between clusters. It assumes that for each pair of cluster centers, at least one of their densities should be larger than the density of their midpoint to be a "good" clustering. Both SD and S_Dbw indicate the optimal clustering when they are minimized.

4 Internal validation of stream clusterings

In this section, we evaluate the result of stream clustering algorithms with internal validation measures.

4.1 Robustness to conventional clustering aspects

The results on using internal evaluation measures for clustering static data with simple errors in [28] prove that the performance of the internal measures is affected by various aspects of input data, i.e., noise, density of clusters, skewness, and subclusters. Each measure of the discussed 11 evaluation measures reacts differently to those aspects. We perform more complex experiments than the ones in [28], this time on stream clusterings to see how the internal measures behave in real-time continuous data. We run the CluStream [1] clustering algorithm with different parameters, choose the optimal number of clusters according to the evaluation results, and compare it to the true number of clusters. According to [10], *RMSSTD*, *RS* and Γ have the property of monotonicity and their curves will have either an upwards or a downwards tendency towards the optimum when we monotonically increase (or decrease) the number of clusters (or the parameter at hand). The optimal value for each of these measures is at the shift point of their curves which is also known as the "elbow".

Streaming data has usually complex properties that are happening at the same time. The experiments in [28], however, are limited to very simple toy datasets reflecting only one clustering aspect at a time. To make it more realistic, we use a data stream reflecting five conventional clustering aspects at the same time.

4.1.1 Experimental settings

To simulate streaming scenarios, we use *MOA (Massive Online Analysis)* [4] framework. We have chosen *Random-RBFGenerator*, which emits data instances continuously from a set of circular clusters, as the input stream generator (cf. Fig. 3). In this stream, we can specify the size, density, and moving speed of the instance-generating clusters, from which we can simulate the skewness, the different densities, and the subcluster aspect. We set the parameters as follows: number of generating clusters = 5, radius of clusters = 0.11, their dimensionality = 10, varying range of cluster radius = 0.07, varying range of cluster density = 1, cluster speed = 0.01 *per* 200 *points*, noise level = 0.1, noise does not appear inside clusters. The parameters which are not mentioned are not directly related to this experiment and are set to the default values of MOA.

For the clustering algorithm, we have chosen *CluStream* [1] with *k-means* as its macro-clusterer. We vary the parameter k from 2 to 9, where the optimal number of clusters is 5. We set the evaluation frequency to 1000 points and run our

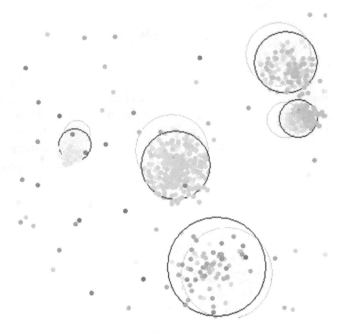

Fig. 3 A screenshot of the Dimensions 1 and 2 of the synthetic data stream used in the experiment. *Colored points* represent the incoming instances, and the *colors* are faded out as the processing time passes. Ground truth cluster boundaries are drawn in *black circle*. *Gray circles* indicate the former state, expressing that the clusters are moving. *Black* (faded out to *gray*) points represent noise points. (color figure online)

stream generator till 30000 points, which gives 30 evaluation results.

4.1.2 Results

Table 1 contains the mean value of 30 evaluation results which we obtained in the whole streaming interval. It shows that *RMSSTD*, *RS*, *CH*, *I*, and *S_Dbw* correctly reach their optimal number of clusters, while the others do not. According to the results in [28], the optimal value of each of *RMSSTD*, *RS*, and Γ is difficult to determine. For this reason, we do not accept their results even if some of them show a good performance.

In the static case in [28], *CH* and *I* were unable to find the right optimal number of clusters. *CH* is shown to be vulnerable to noise, since the noise inclusion (in cases when $k < 5$) makes the found clusters larger and less compact. However, in the streaming case, most clustering algorithms follow the online-offline-phases model. The online phase removes a lot of noise when summarizing the data into microclusters, and the offline phase (k-means in the case of CluStream [1]) deals only with these "cleaned" summaries. Of course, there will be always a chance to get a summary that is completely formed of noise points, but those will have less impact over the final clustering than the static case. Thus, since not all the noise points are integrated into the clusters, the amount of cluster expansion is a bit smaller than the static case.

Table 1 Evaluation results of internal validation on the stream clusterings

k	RMSSTD	RS	Γ	CH	I	D	S	DB	XB	SD	S_Dbw
2	0.0998	0.7992	0.3522	3196	0.4980	0.1921	**0.6535**	**0.5528**	0.1065	**4.5086**	0.2284
3	0.0763	0.8593	0.3724	3619	0.5564	**0.2208**	0.6003	0.5782	0.1561	6.1623	0.1601
4	0.0621	0.9117	0.3834	3860	0.5840	0.0936	0.6143	0.5531	**0.0932**	6.7154	0.1251
5	**0.0538**	**0.9330**	0.3967	**4157**	**0.6134**	0.0669	0.5855	0.5656	0.1143	8.6382	**0.1087**
6	0.0528	0.9355	**0.4007**	3510	0.4945	0.0309	0.5200	0.6360	0.1845	11.1729	0.1319
7	0.0481	0.9464	0.4002	3435	0.4697	0.0042	0.4861	0.6610	0.2580	14.7443	0.1192
8	0.0463	0.9512	0.4007	3095	0.4001	0.0099	0.4617	0.6853	0.2977	16.8715	0.1338
9	0.0430	0.9580	0.4026	3154	0.3943	0.0000	0.4544	0.6913	0.3085	19.5362	0.1355

The best obtained values for each parameter (not necessarily the maximum or the minimum) are in bold. The best values for *RMSSTD*, *RS* and Γ are selected as the first "elbow" in their monotonically increasing or decreasing curves (according to [10])

Therefore, the effect of noise to *CH* is less in the streaming case than the static one.

In the static case, *I* was slightly affected by the different densities of the clusters, and the reasons were not well revealed. Therefore, it is not surprising that *I* performs well as we take average of its evaluation results for the whole streaming interval.

The evaluation of *D* did not result with a very useful output, since it gives unconditional zero values in most evaluation points (before they are averaged as in Table 1). This is because the numerator of Equation (6) could be zero when at least one pair of x and y happens to be equal to each other, i.e., the distance between x and y is zero. This case rises when C_i and C_j are overlapped and the pair (x, y) is elected from the overlapped region. Streaming data has high possibility to have overlapped clusters, and so does the input of this experiment. This drives *D* to produce zero, making it an unstable measure in streaming environments.

Similar to the static data case, *S*, *DB*, *XB*, and *SD* perform bad in the streaming settings. The main reason also lies in the overlapping of clusters. Overlapping clusters are the extreme case of subclusters in the experiments of the static case discussed in [28].

4.2 Sensitivity to common errors of stream clustering

In this section, we perform a more detailed study on the behaviors of internal measures in streaming environments. The previous experiment is more or less a general test on a single data stream, so we use here the internal clustering indices on a series of elaborately designed experiments which well reflects the stream clustering scenarios. *MOA* framework has an interesting tool called *ClusterGenerator*, which can produce a found clustering by manipulating ground truth clusters with a certain error level. It can simulate different kinds of error types and even combine them to construct complicated clustering error scenarios. It is very useful since

we can test the sensitivity of evaluation measures to specific errors [27].

Evaluating a variation of the ground truth seems a bit awkward in the sense of internal validation since it actually refers to the predefined result. However, this kind of experiment is absolutely meaningful, because we can watch reactions of internal measures to some errors of interest. [27] used this tool to show the behavior of internal measures, e.g., *S*, *Sum of Squares (SSQ)*, and *C-index*. Although the error types exploited in [27] are limited, those measures are not of our interest and already proved to be bad in the previous experiments.

4.2.1 Experimental Settings

Due to the drifting nature of streaming data, certain errors are common to appear for stream clustering algorithms. These errors are reflected by a wrong grouping of the drifting objects. The "correct" grouping of the objects is reflected in the original data set, where we assume that the real distribution of the objects (and thus the grouping) is previously known. This already known assignment of the drifting objects to their correct clusters is called *the ground truth*. The closer the output of a clustering algorithm to this ground truth, the better its quality. The above-mentioned errors are the deviations of the output of clustering algorithms from the ground truth. A good validation measure should be able to evaluate the amounts of these errors correctly. In the case of internal validation measures, this should be possible even without accessing the ground truth.

To obtain a controlled amount of this error, a simulation of a stream clustering algorithm is embedded in the MOA framework [4]. This previous explained simulation, called *ClusterGenerator*, allows the user to control the amount of deviations from the ground truth using different parameters. The *ClusterGenerator* has six error types as its parameters, and they effectively reflect common errors of stream clusterings. "Radius increase" and "Radius decrease" change the

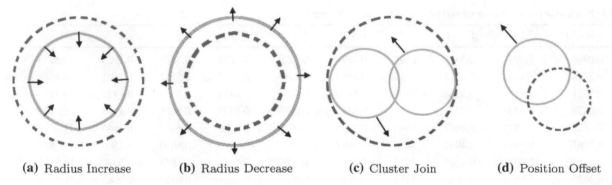

Fig. 4 Common errors of stream clusterings. A *solid circle* represents a true cluster, and a *dashed circle* indicates the corresponding found cluster (error). The cause of the error is the fast evolution of the stream in the direction of the *arrows*.

radius of clusters (Fig. 4a, b), which normally happens in the stream clustering since data points keep fading in and out.

Thus, in Fig. 4a, for instance, the ground truth is represented by the solid line, and the arrows represent the direction of the evolution of the data in the ground truth where the cluster is shrinking. The dashed line represents, however, the output of the simulated clustering algorithm using the *ClusterGenerator* that suffers from the: "Radius Increase" error. The same explanation applies to all other errors depicted in Fig. 4.

"Cluster add" and "Cluster remove" change the number of found clusters, which are caused by grouping noise points or falsely detecting meaningful patterns as a noise cloud. "Cluster join" merges two overlapping clusters as one cluster (Fig. 4c), which is a crucial error in streaming scenarios. Finally, "Position offset" changes the cluster position, and this commonly happens due to the movement of clusters in data streams (Fig. 4d).

We perform the experiments on all the above error types. We increase the level of one error at a time and evaluate its output with CH, I and S_Dbw, which performed well in the previous experiment. For the input stream, we use the same stream settings as in Sect. 4.2.1.

4.2.2 Results

In Fig. 5, the evaluation values are plotted on the y-axis according to the corresponding error level on the x-axis. From Fig. 5a, we can see that CH value decreases as the level of "Radius increase", "Cluster add", "Cluster join", and "Position offset" errors increases. CH correctly and constantly penalizes the four errors, since smaller CH value corresponds to worse clustering. However, it shows completely reversed curves in "Radius decrease" and "Cluster remove" errors. The reason for wrong rewarding of the "Radius decrease" error, is that the reduction of the size of clusters increases their compactness, and thus both CH and I increase. The "Cluster remove" error detection is a gen-

eral problem for all internal measures as they compare their clustering result only to its self. Regardless of the "Radius decrease" and the "Cluster remove" errors, CH has generally the best performance on streaming data compared to the other measures.

We can see in Fig. 5b that using I results in a misinterpretation of the "Radius decrease" and "Cluster remove" error situations. The reason for it is similar to that of CH, since the usage of I results also in adopting the distance between objects within clusters as the intra-cluster compactness and the distance between cluster centers as the inter-cluster separation. In addition, using I wrongly favorites the "Position offset" error instead of penalizing it. If the boundaries of found clusters are moved besides the truth, they often miss the data points, which produces a similar situation to "Radius decrease" which I is vulnerable to.

S_Dbw produces high values when it regards a clustering as a bad result, which is opposite to the previous two measures. In Fig. 5c, we can see that it correctly penalizes the three error types "Radius increase", "Cluster add", and "Cluster join". For "Position offset" error, one can say that the value is somehow increasing but the curve is actually fluctuating too much. It also fails to penalize "Cluster remove" correctly.

From these results, we can determine that among the discussed internal evaluation measures, CH is the best internal evaluation one which can well handle many stream clustering errors. Even though S_Dbw performs very well on the static data (cf. [28]) and on the streaming data in the previous experiments (cf. Sect. 4.2.2), we observed that it has weak capability to capture common errors of stream clustering.

5 Internal evaluation measures of density-based stream clustering algorithms

In this section, we evaluate the performance of internal stream clustering measures using a density-based stream clustering

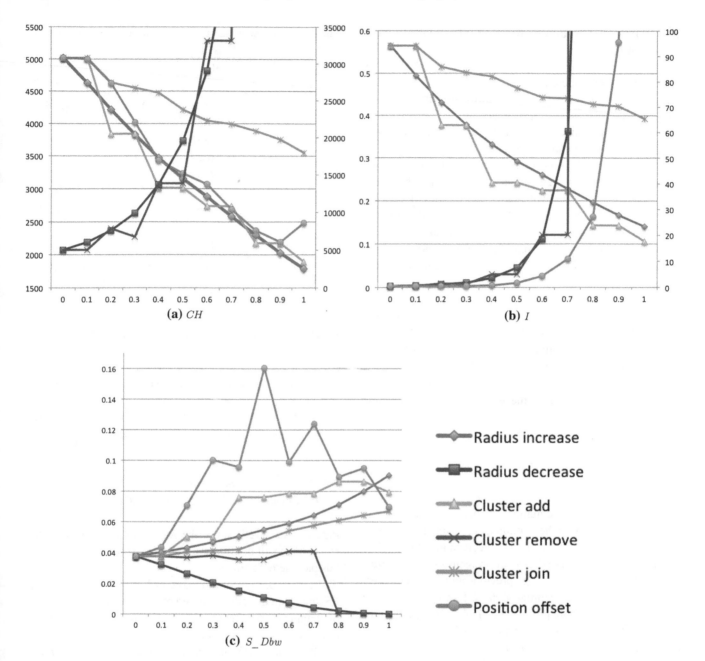

Fig. 5 Experimental results for each error type. Evaluation values (*y*-axis) are plotted according to each error level (*x*-axis). Some error curves are drawn on a secondary axis due to its range: **a** "Radius decrease" and "Cluster remove", **b** "Radius decrease", "Cluster remove", and "Position offset".

algorithm, namely DenStream [6]. We will start by experimenting DenStream using external evaluation measures to get some kind of "ground truth", then we will compare the performance of the internal evaluation measures using how close they are to this ground truth. Similar to the previous section, we use *MOA (Massive Online Analysis)* [4] framework for the evaluation. Again we have used the RandomRBFGenerator to create a 10-dimensional dataset of 30,000 objects forming 5 drifting clusters with different and varying densities and sizes. For DenStream [6] and MOA, we set the parameter settings as follows: the evaluation horizon = 1000, the outlier microcluster controlling threshold: $\beta = 0.15$, the initial number of objects initPoints = 1000, the offline factor of ϵ compared to the online one = 2, the decaying factor $\lambda = 0.25$, and the processing speed of the evaluation = 100. The parameters which are not mentioned are not directly related to this experiment and are set to the defaults of MOA.

5.1 Deriving the ground truth using external evaluation measures

Internal evaluation measures do not benefit from the ground truth information provided in the form of cluster label in our dataset. This was not a problem in the case of the k-means-based algorithm CluStream [1] discussed in Sect. 4.1, since the optimal parameter setting was simply $k = 5$ as we have generated 5 clusters. In the case of the density-based stream clustering algorithm DenStream [6] this is not as straightforward. To obtain some kind of ground truth for a density-based stream clustering algorithm like DenStream, we used the results from some external evaluation measures to derive the parameter settings for the best and the worst clustering results. The following external evaluation measures were used.

The first one is the **F**1 [3] measure which is a widely used external evaluation that harmonizes the precision and the recall of the clustering output.

The other one is the **purity measure** which is widely used [2,6,24] to evaluate the quality of a clustering. Intuitively, the purity can be seen as the pureness of the final clusters compared to the classes of the ground truth. The average purity is defined as follows:

$$\text{purity} = \frac{\sum_{i=1}^{NC} \frac{n_i^d}{n_i}}{NC} \qquad (12)$$

where NC represents the number of clusters, n_i^d denotes the number of objects with the dominant class label in cluster C_i and n_i denotes the number of the objects in the cluster C_i.

The third used external evaluation measure is the **number of clusters** which averages previous numbers of clusters within the H window. Similarly, the $F1$ and the purity are computed over a certain predefined window H from the current time. This is done since the weights of the objects decay over time. Thus, the number of found clusters could be any real value, while $F1$ and purity could be any real value from 0 to 1.

5.1.1 Results

Table 2 contains the mean value of 5 evaluation results which we obtained in the whole streaming interval when considering the external evaluation measures: $F1$, purity and the number of clusters for different settings of the μ and ϵ parameters of DenStream. The bold values of each column represent the best value of the index among the outputs of the used parameter settings. It is the highest value in the case of $F1$ and the purity, and the closest value to 5 in the case of the number of clusters. The worst values in each column are underlined. It can be seen from Table 2 that among the

Table 2 Evaluation results of external validation on the stream clusterings

μ	ϵ	F1	Purity	Number of clusters
2	0.06	**0.6454**	**1.00**	**4.7959**
2	0.12	0.6250	0.9999	4.5918
2	0.18	<u>0.5873</u>	<u>0.9095</u>	<u>4.0204</u>
3	0.06	0.6220	**1.00**	4.6531
3	0.12	0.6139	**1.00**	4.5714
3	0.18	0.5857	0.9169	4.0816
4	0.06	0.6166	**1.00**	4.7143
4	0.12	0.6157	**1.00**	4.6735
4	0.18	0.5741	0.9233	4.1020

The best obtained values for each measure are in bold, the worst ones are underlined

selected 9 parameter settings, $\mu = 2$ and $\epsilon = 0.18$ results in the worst clustering output of DenStream over the current dataset while $\mu = 2$ and $\epsilon = 0.06$ results in the best one. Figure 6 depicts the external evaluation measures values for these settings.

Our task now is to get the internal evaluation measure that shows the highest correlation with this result.

5.2 The results of using internal evaluation measures for density-based stream clustering

Figures 7, 8 and 9 show the mean values of 5 evaluation results using all internal evaluation measures over the previous parameter settings.

These results are summarized in Table 3, where $RMSSTD$, RS and Γ are directly excluded due to the subjective process of defining the first "elbow" in their monotonically increasing or decreasing curves (according to [10]). We obtained these results for the different selected parameter settings, and the final values are summarized from the measurements in the whole streaming interval.

Table 3 shows that all the internal evaluation measures except for SD reach their worst values (underlined values) exactly at the setting ($\mu = 2$ and $\epsilon = 0.18$). This shows that the results of those internal measures are inline with those of the external ones w.r.t. punishing the worst setting.

What is left now is to check which of those measures reaches its best value at the same setting where the external evaluation measures are reaching their best values (i.e., $\mu = 2$ and $\epsilon = 0.06$). It can be seen from Table 3 that none of the internal evaluation measures is reaching the best value (in bold) at that parameter setting.

We have to calculate now which of those internal evaluation measures has the highest (local) correlation between its

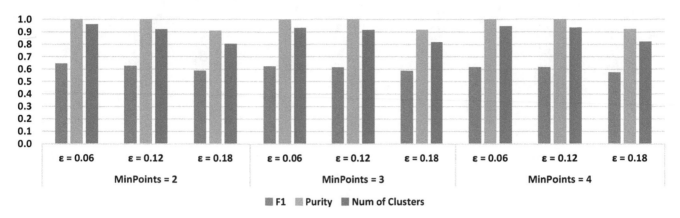

Fig. 6 External evaluation measures on the y-axis using different parameter settings of DenStream on the x-axis.

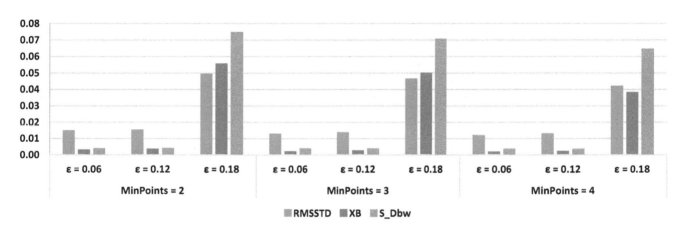

Fig. 7 Performance of the internal evaluation measures: *RMSSTD*, *XB* and *S_Dbw* on the y-axis using different parameter settings of DenStreamon the x-axis.

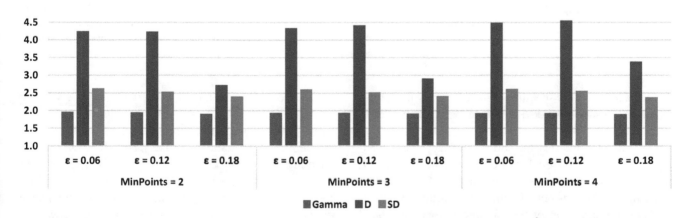

Fig. 8 Performance of the internal evaluation measures: Γ, D and SD on the y-axis using different parameter settings of DenStream on the x-axis.

best value V_{best}^i, and the value calculated at the best ground truth setting ($\mu = 2$ and $\epsilon = 0.06$), we call this value V_{truth}^i.

Let:

$$V_{avg}^i = \frac{\sum_{s=1}^{9} V_s^i}{9} \qquad (13)$$

be the average of the values taken for each internal measure i over the each setting s of the 9 considered parameter settings. Our target is to get out of the 7 winning internal measures in Table 3, the internal evaluation measure i that achieves:

$$min_i \left(\frac{V_{best}^i - V_{truth}^i}{V_{best}^i - V_{avg}^i} \right) \qquad (14)$$

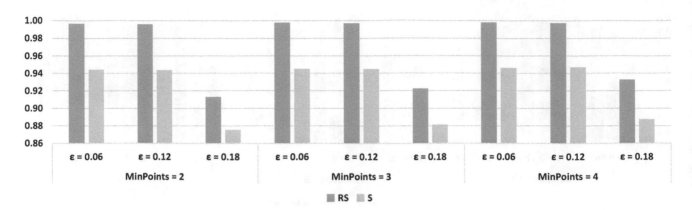

Fig. 9 Performance of the internal evaluation measures: *RS* and *S* on the *y*-axis using different parameter settings of DenStream on the *x*-axis.

Table 3 Evaluation results of internal validation on the stream clusterings

μ	ϵ	CH	I	D	S	DB	XB	SD	S_Dbw
2	0.06	50911	58.711	4.2364	0.9441	0.1240	0.0032	2.6188	0.0041
2	0.12	54495	65.131	4.2261	0.9436	0.1297	0.0037	2.5212	0.0042
2	0.18	<u>34451</u>	<u>37.131</u>	<u>2.7138</u>	<u>0.8753</u>	<u>0.2859</u>	<u>0.0557</u>	2.3928	<u>0.0749</u>
3	0.06	66717	88.312	4.3258	0.9451	0.1038	0.0021	2.5936	0.0040
3	0.12	65504	84.805	4.4055	0.9447	0.1132	0.0027	2.5111	0.0041
3	0.18	40237	45.474	2.8965	0.8812	0.2640	0.0501	2.4014	0.0708
4	0.06	**74205**	**102.57**	4.4786	0.9462	**0.0974**	**0.0019**	<u>2.6039</u>	0.0038
4	0.12	72501	100.93	**4.5413**	**0.9469**	0.1059	0.0023	2.5455	**0.0038**
4	0.18	48553	60.397	3.3772	0.8873	0.2368	0.0382	**2.3713**	0.0648

The best obtained values (not necessarily the maximum or the minimum) are in bold

Table 4 Testing the winning internal measures (i.e., those whose worst value in Table 3 matched the worst ground truth)

Internal measure i	CH	I	D	S	DB	XB	S_Dbw
$\dfrac{V_{best}^i - V_{truth}^i}{V_{best}^i - V_{avg}^i}$	1.30807	1.41513	0.48392	0.11849	0.40945	0.08125	**0.01208**

The test is aiming to find which i of those has the highest correlation between its best value V_{best}^i and its value at the best ground truth setting V_{truth}^i

In other words, we are seeking for the measure whose V_{best}^i has the smallest relative deviation from V_{truth}^i compared to its deviation from the mean.

It should be noted that the simple tendency check mentioned in Eq. 14 is reliable. For a specific measure i, minimizing the fraction mentioned in Eq. 14 implies that the numerator is considerably smaller than the denominator. Thus, the deviation of the measure i from the ground truth V_{truth}^i is considerably smaller than the deviation from its own mean. Thus, we can get some kind of guaranty that this correlation is strong enough. As we are unable to find an internal measure i whose $V_{best}^i = V_{truth}^i$, we perform this approximation to find the one with the closest tendency to make V_{truth}^i its V_{best}^i.

Table 4 shows that *S_Dbw* has the highest correlation between its $V_{best}^{S\_Dbw}$ value and the ground truth $V_{truth}^{S\_Dbw}$ value. This is because it has the smallest $\frac{V_{best} - V_{truth}}{V_{best} - V_{avg}}$ value highlighted in bold.

This means that the among the tested internal evaluation measures, *S_Dbw* has shown the best results when considering the density-based stream clustering algorithm DenStream [6]. Similar to the static data case, *CH, I, D S, DB*, and *SD* perform bad in the streaming settings. This is different to the *k*-means stream clustering case, where *CH* performed the best. On the other hand, *S_Dbw* performed the best which is similar to the static case results reported in [28]. *XB* worked also well.

6 Conclusions and outlook

Evaluating clustering results is very important to the success of clustering tasks. In this article, we discussed the internal clustering validation scheme in both *k*-means and density-based stream clustering scenarios. This is much more efficient and easier to apply in the absence of any previous knowledge about the data than the external validation. We explained fundamental theories of internal validation measures and its examples. In the k-means-based case, we performed a set of clustering validation experiments that well reflect the properties of streaming environment with five common clustering aspects at the same time. These aspects reflect monotonicity, noise, different densities of clusters, skewness and the existence of subclusters in the underlying streaming data. The three winners from the first experimental evaluation were then further evaluated in the second phase of experiments. The sensitivity of each of those three measures was tested w.r.t. six stream clustering errors. Different to the results gained in a recent work on static data, our final experimental results on streaming data showed that *Calinski-Harabasz index (CH)* [5] has, in general, the best performance in k-means-based streaming environments. It is robust to the combination of the five conventional aspects of clustering, and also correctly penalizes the common errors in stream clustering.

In the density-based case, we performed a set of experiments over different parameter settings using the DenStream [6] algorithm. We used external evaluation measures to extract some ground truth. We used the ground truth to define the best, and the worst parameter settings. Then, we tested which of the internal measures has the highest correlation with the ground truth. Our results showed that the *revised validity index*: *S_Dbw* [11] shows the best performance under density-based stream clustering algorithms. This is inline with the results reported over static data in [28]. Additionally, the *Xie-Beni index (XB)* [35] has shown also a good performance.

In the future, we want to test those measures on different categories of advanced stream clustering algorithms like adaptive hierarchical density-based ones (e.g., HAStream [15]) or projected/subspace ones (e.g., PreDeConStream [24] and SubClusTree [14]). Additionally, we want to evaluate the measures when streams of clusters available in subspaces [13] are processed by the above algorithms.

References

1. Aggarwal, C.C., Han, J., Wang, J., Yu, P.S.: A framework for clustering evolving data streams. In: VLDB, pp. 81–92 (2003)
2. Aggarwal, C.C., Han, J., Wang, J., Yu, P.S.: A framework for projected clustering of high dimensional data streams. In: VLDB, pp. 852–863 (2004)
3. Assent, I., Krieger, R., Müller, E., Seidl, T.: INSCY: Indexing subspace clusters with in-process-removal of redundancy. In: Proceedings of the 8th IEEE International Conference on Data Mining, ICDM '08, pp. 719–724. IEEE (2008)
4. Bifet, A., Holmes, G., Pfahringer, B., Kranen, P., Kremer, H., Jansen, T., Seidl, T.: MOA: Massive online analysis, a framework for stream classification and clustering. JMLR **11**, 44–50 (2010)
5. Calinski, T., Harabasz, J.: A dendrite method for cluster analysis. Comm. Stat. **3**(1), 1–27 (1974)
6. Cao, F., Ester, M., Qian, W., Zhou, A.: Density-based clustering over an evolving data stream with noise. In: SIAM SDM, pp. 328–339 (2006)
7. Davies, D., Bouldin, D.: A cluster separation measure. IEEE PAMI **1**(2), 224–227 (1979)
8. Dempster, A.P., Laird, N.M., Rubin, D.B.: Maximum likelihood from incomplete data via the EM algorithm. J. R. Stat. Soc. Ser. B. **39**(1), 1–38 (1977)
9. Dunn, J.: Well separated clusters and optimal fuzzy partitions. J. Cybern. **4**(1), 95–104 (1974)
10. Halkidi, M., Batistakis, Y., Vazirgiannis, M.: On clustering validation techniques. J. Intell. Inf. Syst. **17**(2), 107–145 (2001)
11. Halkidi, M., Vazirgiannis, M.: Clustering validity assessment: Finding the optimal partitioning of a data set. In: IEEE ICDM, pp. 187–194 (2001)
12. Halkidi, M., Vazirgiannis, M., Batistakis, Y.: Quality scheme assessment in the clustering process. In: PKDD, pp. 265–276 (2000)
13. Hassani, M., Kim, Y., Seidl, T.: Subspace MOA: subspace stream clustering evaluation using the MOA framework. In: DASFAA, pp. 446–449 (2013)
14. Hassani, M., Kranen, P., Saini, R., Seidl, T.: Subspace anytime stream clustering. In: SSDBM, p. 37 (2014)
15. Hassani, M., Spaus, P., Seidl, T.: Adaptive multiple-resolution stream clustering. In: MLDM, MLDM'14, pp. 134–148 (2014)
16. Hassani, M.: Efficient clustering of big data streams. PhD thesis, RWTH Aachen University (2015)
17. Hassani, M., Kim, Y., Choi, S., Seidl, T.: Effective evaluation measures for subspace clustering of data streams. In: Trends and Applications in Knowledge Discovery and Data Mining—PAKDD 2013 International Workshops, pp. 342–353 (2013)
18. Hassani, M., Kim, Y., Choi, S., Seidl, T.: Subspace clustering of data streams: new algorithms and effective evaluation measures. J. Intell. Inf. Syst. **45**(3), 319–335 (2015)
19. Hassani, M., Müller, E., Seidl, T.: EDISKCO: Energy Efficient Distributed In-Sensor-Network K-center Clustering with Outliers. In: Proceedings of the 3rd International Workshop on Knowledge Discovery from Sensor Data, SensorKDD '09 @KDD '09, pp. 39–48. ACM (2009)
20. Hassani, M., Müller, E., Spaus, P., Faqolli, A., Palpanas, T., Seidl, T.: Self-organizing energy aware clustering of nodes in sensor networks using relevant attributes. In: Proceedings of the 4th International Workshop on Knowledge Discovery from Sensor Data, SensorKDD '10 @KDD '10, pp.39–48. ACM (2010)
21. Hassani, M., Seidl, T.: Distributed weighted clustering of evolving sensor data streams with noise. J. Dig. Inf. Manag. (JDIM) **10**(6), 410–420 (2012)
22. Hassani, M., Seidl, T.: Internal clustering evaluation of data streams. In: Trends and Applications in Knowledge Discovery and Data Mining—PAKDD 2015 Workshop: QIMIE, 2015. Revised Selected Papers, pp. 198–209 (2015)
23. Hassani, M., Spaus, P., Cuzzocrea, A., Seidl, T.: Adaptive stream clustering using incremental graph maintenance. In: Proceedings of the 4th International Workshop on Big Data, Streams and Heterogeneous Source Mining: Algorithms, Systems, Programming Models and Applications, BigMine 2015 at KDD'15, pp. 49–64 (2015)

24. Hassani, M., Spaus, P., Gaber, M.M., Seidl, T.: Density-based projected clustering of data streams. In: Proceedings of the 6th International Conference on Scalable Uncertainty Management, SUM '12, pp. 311–324 (2012)

25. Hubert, L., Arabie, P.: Comparing partitions. J. Intell. Inf. Syst. 2(1), 193–218 (1985)

26. Kaufman, L., Rousseeuw, P.: Clustering by means of medoids. Statistical Data Analysis Based on the L_1 *Norm*, pp. 405–416 (1987)

27. Kremer, H., Kranen, P., Jansen, T., Seidl, T., Bifet, A., Holmes, G., Pfahringer, B.: An effective evaluation measure for clustering on evolving data streams. In: ACM SIGKDD, pp. 868–876 (2011)

28. Liu, Y., Li, Z., Xiong, H., Gao, X., Wu, J.: Understanding of internal clustering validation measures. In: ICDM, pp. 911–916 (2010)

29. MacQueen, J.B.: Some methods for classification and analysis of multivariate observations. In: Proceedings of 5th Berkeley Symposium on Mathematical Statistics and Probability, volume 1, pp. 281–297. University of California Press (1967)

30. Maulik, U., Bandyopadhyay, S.: Performance evaluation of some clustering algorithms and validity indices. IEEE PAMI 24, 1650–1654 (2002)

31. Rendón, E., Abundez, I., Arizmendi, A., Quiroz, E.M.: Internal versus external cluster validation indexes. Int. J. Comp. Comm. 5(1), 27–34 (2011)

32. Ramze Rezaee, M., Lelieveldt, B.B.F., Reiber, J.H.C.: A new cluster validity index for the fuzzy c-mean. Pattern Recogn. Lett. 19(3–4):237–246 (1998)

33. Rousseeuw, P.: Silhouettes: a graphical aid to the interpretation and validation of cluster analysis. J. Comput. Appl. Math. 20(1), 53–65 (1987)

34. Tan, P.N., Steinbach, M., Kumar, V.: Introduction to Data Mining. Addison-Wesley Longman, Inc. Boston (2005)

35. Xie, X.L., Beni, G.: A validity measure for fuzzy clustering. IEEE PAMI 13(8), 841–847 (1991)

## 11

Obstacle detection and warning system for visually impaired people based on electrode matrix and mobile Kinect

Van-Nam Hoang[1] · Thanh-Huong Nguyen[1] · Thi-Lan Le[1] · Thanh-Hai Tran[1] · Tan-Phu Vuong[2] · Nicolas Vuillerme[3,4]

Abstract Obstacle detection and warning can improve the mobility as well as the safety of visually impaired people specially in unfamiliar environments. For this, firstly, obstacles are detected and localized and then the information of the obstacles will be sent to the visually impaired people by using different modalities such as voice, tactile, vibration. In this paper, we present an assistive system for visually impaired people based on the matrix of electrode and a mobile Kinect. This system consists of two main components: environment information acquisition and analysis and information representation. The first component aims at capturing the environment by using a mobile Kinect and analyzing it in order to detect the predefined obstacles for visually impaired people, while the second component tries to represent obstacle's information under the form of electrode matrix.

✉ Van-Nam Hoang
Van-Nam.Hoang@mica.edu.vn

Thanh-Huong Nguyen
Thanh-Huong.Nguyen@mica.edu.vn

Thi-Lan Le
Thi-Lan.Le@mica.edu.vn

Thanh-Hai Tran
Thanh-Hai.Tran@mica.edu.vn

[1] International Research Institute MICA, HUST-CNRS/UMI 2954-Grenoble INP, Hanoi University of Science and Technology, Ha Noi, Vietnam

[2] IMEP-LAHC, Grenoble Institute of Technology (GINP), Grenoble, France

[3] Institut Universitaire de France, LAI Jean-Raoul Scherrer, University of Geneva, Geneva, Switzerland

[4] University Grenoble Alpes, Grenoble, France

Keywords Mobile kinect · Obstacle detection · Point cloud · Assistive system for visually impaired

1 Introduction

Travel activity, even a simple one, consists a long list of travel subtasks. There are two main categories of the subtasks in travel activity that are mobility and environmental access [5]. Mobility itself can be divided in obstacle avoidance and orientation/navigation, while environment access consists of hazard minimization and information/sign. Most of subtasks in travel activity are based on the vision information. For this, sighted people mainly rely on their sense of sight. Visually impaired are only able to use their sense of sight to a limited extent or possibly not at all. Therefore, visually impaired people require support from assistive technology to carry out different travel activity subtasks. In our work, we focus on developing assistive technology for obstacle avoidance for visually impaired people, because it has always been considered a primary requirement for aided mobility. Obstacle avoidance technology needs to address two issues: obstacle detection and obstacle warning. The obstacle detection means the perception of potentially hazardous objects in the environment ahead of time, while the latter one concerns the manner to convey obstacle information to the visually impaired people. White cane can be considered as the first obstacle avoidance assistive tool. However, this tool is generally not used to detect obstacles above knee height. Recently, the advance in sensor technology makes a number of obstacle avoidance technologies available for visually impaired people [19]. However, most researches focus on obstacle detection, obstacle warning is not well studied.

In our previous work, we have proposed an obstacle detection and warning system based on a low-cost device (Kinect)

and electrode matrix [6]. We extend our previous work with three main contributions. Firstly, we improve obstacle detection method in order to decrease the detection miss by using plane segmentation on organized point cloud and eliminating the assumption that obstacles are on the ground. Secondly, instead of using stimulation signal for obstacle warning based on visual substitution as described in [6], we input the obstacle warning by the output of obstacle detection. Finally, we introduce the new patterns on electrode array for mapping information of obstacles and perform different experiments to evaluate the proposed mapping solution.

2 Related works

In the literature, different technologies such as WiFi, RFID, laser, ultrasound, or camera have been used for aiding blind people avoiding obstacles in the environment. In this section, we present only vision-based methods that are relatively close to our work in this paper. Methods for obstacle detection and warning could be categorized depending on how the obstacles are detected and how their information is sent to the user.

2.1 Vision-based obstacle detection

Obstacle detection is a key problem in computer vision for navigation. Existing methods could be categorized into two main approaches. The first approach learns object model then verifies if a pixel or an image patch satisfies the learnt model. In [18], a camera captures grayscale images, then pixels are classified into background or objects based on neural network technique. Then, the pixels belonging to obstacle are enhanced and the background pixels are removed. Joachim et al. [11] detects obstacles utilizing a model of human color vision. Then lens position of the auto-focus stereo camera was used to measure distance of the object center. In [23], a method was proposed for appearance-based obstacle detection. Firstly, color image is filtered, then converted to HSI color space. Then the color histogram on the candidate area is computed and compared with reference histogram.

The second approach is based upon a definition of objectness and detects regions with the highest objectness measures. In [17], authors developed a method for obstacle avoidance based on stereo vision and a simplistic ground plane detection. The obstacle detection relies on the creation of a virtual polar cumulative grid, which represents the area of interest ahead of the visually impaired user.

Approaches using conventional RGB camera draw some inherent limitations such as shadow, occlusion, illumination sensitivity. The use of stereo camera is expensive and requires highly precise calibration. Recently, low-cost RGB-D sensors (e.g., Microsoft Kinect) have been widely used to complement RGB data with depth, helping to improve significantly performance of object detection. In [1], a system reads data from Kinect and expresses it as 3D point cloud then the floor plane and the occupancy of the volume in front of the user are detected. The occupancy represents an obstacle. In [9], the authors proposed a method combining depth and color. First, the depth map is denoised using dilation and erosion morphological operations. Then, least squares method is applied to approximate ground curves and to determine the ground height. The obstacles are decided based on the dramatic change in the depth value. Finally, object labeling is carried out with region-growing technique. Color information is used for edge detection and staircase identification. In [24], Vlaminck et al. presented a method for static obstacle detection consisting of four steps: point cloud registration, plane segmentation, ground and wall detection and obstacle detection. For plane segmentation, the authors employ RANSAC in order to estimate plane. They achieved a state-of-the-art result in obstacle detection using RGB-D data. However, their system is time consuming because of normal estimation and plane segmentation using RANSAC on 3D point cloud takes a lot of time to process. Moreover, the authors assume that the obstacles are on the ground; that assumption is not always satisfied.

2.2 Obstacle warning

Once detected, information of obstacles must be conveyed to the blind. In general, the user could be informed through auditory and tactile sense.

Audio feedback In [11], obstacle information is sent to the user using text-to-speech engine and the loudspeaker. In [25], the vOICe system translates live images into sounds for the blind person to hear through a stereo headphone. The position of visual pattern corresponds to the high pitch, while the brightness is represented by the loudness. In [18], segmented image is divided into left and right parts, transformed to (stereo) sound that is sent to the user through the headphones. In [17], acoustic feedback is in charge of informing the visually impaired users about the potential obstacles in their way. However, to avoid blocking the ears, the authors use audio bone conducting technology which is easy to wear and ears-free.

Tactile feedback Another approach is to transform obstacle information into a vibrotactile or electrotactile stimulations on different parts of the body. Visually impaired users are then trained to interpret the information. This approach allows the hearing sense to be free for the task of precautions or warning dangers. Johnson and Higgins [12] created a wearable device consisted of vibrator motors, each motor is assigned to detected regional obstacles. The value of the closest object in each region is transformed to vibration applied on the skin of abdomen. In [14], obstacle information is transformed to electrical pulses that stimulate the nerves in the skin via electrodes in the data gloves.

Among all the areas on the skin, tongue is very sensitive and mobile since it has the most dense number of receptors. A number of methods conveying electrotactile stimulate on the tongue have been conducted. The first tongue display unit (TDU) [27] translates the optical images captured by a head-mounted camera into electrotactile stimuli that are carried to the tongue by an array of 12 × 12 electrodes via a ribbon cable. This prototype was then commercialized and called Brainport [22]. Tang and Beebe [20] created a two-way touch system to provide directional guidance for blind traveler. It consists of an electrotactile display of 49 electrodes to provide directional cues to the blind users. Recently, [26] has fabricated a matrix of 36 electrodes which sends the electrical impulses to the tongue in order to detect and correct the posture and stability for balance-impaired people.

From these studies, we find that the assistive systems for blind people are various and different from obstacle definition, detection and warning. Kinect sensor has great advantages than conventional RGB camera. This motivates us to use Kinect sensor for obstacle detection. Instead of combining RGB and depth data, we will explore accelerometer information for ground plane detection and remove wall and door planes as possible; thus, false alarms will be reduced. Concerning obstacle warning, we believe that conveying electrotactile pulses on the tongue is an efficient way. We continue our research direction on tongue display unit [14,15] and build a complete system from obstacle detection to obstacle warning.

3 Prototype of obstacle detection and warning for visually impaired people

3.1 Overview

The proposed system is composed of two modules: obstacle detection and obstacle warning (see Fig. 1). The main aim of obstacle detection is to determine the presence of interested obstacles in the scene in front of the users, while the obstacle warning represents and sends this information to the users.

The obstacle detection module takes scene information from a mobile Kinect. In our prototype, the obstacle detection is running on a laptop mounted on a backpack of the visually impaired people and mobile Kinect is the Kinect with battery so that it can be mounted easily on the human body for collecting data and transferring data to the laptop. The scene information, in our case, is the color image, depth image, and accelerometer information provided by Kinect.

Concerning obstacle warning module, we reuse our tactile–visual substitution system which uses the tongue as the human–machine interface, gives a warning to the visually impaired people user to avoid the obstacles on the corridor way. This system is an embedded system that is equipped with an electrode matrix, a microprocessor unit (MCU), a communication module using RF wave [15]. For this module, we have to encode the obstacle information into the electrode matrix.

The prototype of our system is shown in Fig. 2. All the system can be mounted on the human body by backpack which hold the laptop, RF transmitter, and belt to anchor the Kinect. Although the current system is quite bulky and heavy and everything must be mounted on the user body, in the future, where all those things can be miniaturized and integrated into a small, wearable device like Google Glass, this problem can be solved. Especially, with the depth sensor, Microsoft have successful fabricated a device which is similar to the Kinect's depth sensor and can be attached to a normal mobile phone.

In our work, we consider indoor environment where obstacles are defined as objects in front, obstructing or endangering while visually impaired people moving. Specifically, we focus on detecting moving objects (e.g., people) and static objects (e.g., trash, plant pots, fire extinguisher). Staircase

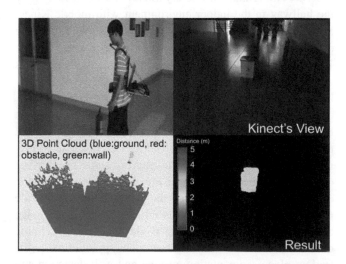

Fig. 2 Prototype system mounted on body (*top left*). *Color* image of the scene captured by Kinect (*top right*). Obstacle detection result in point cloud (*bottom left*). Estimated distance of the detected obstacle (*bottom right*)

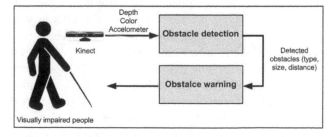

Fig. 1 System flow chart

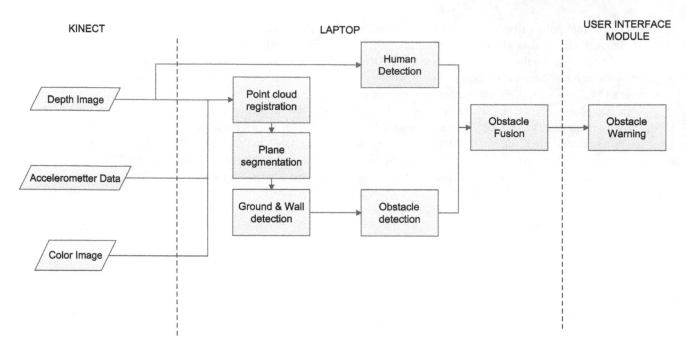

Fig. 3 Static and moving obstacle detection flowchart

has different characteristics and require another approach for detection.

In the following, we will describe in detail the obstacle detection and warning.

3.2 Obstacle detection

With obstacle detection module, we extended the works of Vlaminck in [24] while the objective and all other assumptions are still remained: visually impaired user moving along the hallway in the indoor environment with mobile Kinect and the system will detect an obstacle and give a warning message to the user. For data acquisition, we use mobile Kinect with a laptop as mentioned in Sect. 3.1. Kinect was chosen as the receiver sensor because it can provide many kinds of information such as color data, depth data, audio, etc. Moreover, depth data is the big advantage of Kinect because it is robust under lighting condition and can be used to calculate the distance from the user to obstacle to giving a warning message. The flowchart of static and moving obstacle detection is shown in Fig. 3. Concerning moving obstacle detection, we employ the human detection module provided by Kinect SDK. This module takes depth image as an input and provides a list of detected persons. Static obstacle detection consists of four steps: point cloud registration, plane segmentation, ground and wall detection and obstacle detection. As analyzed in Sect. 2, for static obstacle detection, we improve the work of Vlaminck presented in [24] in-plane segmentation step and ground and wall detec-

tion. First, for plane segmentation step, we use organized point cloud with the segmentation algorithm proposed in [7] instead of using RANSAC as in the work of Vlaminck. This allows us to perform the plane segmentation faster. Second, in [24], the authors base on an assumption that the obstacles are on the ground; therefore, if the ground plane is not detected, the obstacle detection process will terminate. Our work tries to detect ground and wall planes in order to remove that from the point cloud. The obstacle module still works even no ground plane is detected. In the following section, we present in detail the static obstacle detection.

3.2.1 Point cloud registration

Point cloud registration step aims at taking information (color, depth and accelerometer data) from Kinect to build a point cloud. With Kinect, the color and depth image are captured by two different sensors, so they are not aligned. That means that given a pixel in the color image, we cannot get corresponding pixel in depth image directly as well as 3D coordinate. To make a 3D Point Cloud from Kinect data, with each pixel in both color and depth image, we must know exactly the location of this pixel in the 3D coordinate to create an RGB-XYZ point in Point Cloud. To solve that problem, a lot of work has focused on developing a good calibration method in order to transform between color coordinate, depth coordinate and real world coordinate such as Microsoft Kinect SDK, Burrus [8], Tang [21].

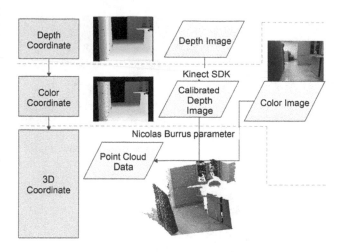

Fig. 4 Coordinate transformation process

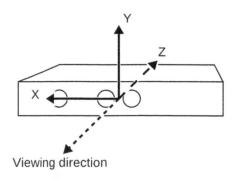

Fig. 5 Kinect coordinate system [3]

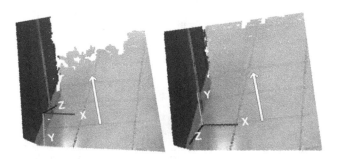

Fig. 6 Point cloud rotation using normal vector of ground plane (*white arrow*): *left* before rotating, *right* after rotating

In our work, we used Microsoft Kinect SDK to convert depth coordinate to color coordinate, then use parameter from [8] to convert to 3D coordinates. Given a depth and color image. For each pixel in the depth image, we can find it is 3D coordinate in meter using the following formula:

$$\text{P3D.x} = (x_c - cx_c) * \text{depth}(x_c, y_c)/fx_c$$
$$\text{P3D.y} = (y_c - cy_c) * \text{depth}(x_c, y_c)/fy_c$$
$$\text{P3D.z} = \text{depth}(x_c, y_c)$$

where x_c and y_c is the pixel coordinate in color image, cx_c, cy_c, fx_c, fy_c is taken from color intrinsic matrix, $\text{depth}(x_c, y_c)$ is the depth value of pixel. This process is illustrated by Fig. 4. Because there are a lot of points in point cloud (about 300.000 points with VGA resolution), so the system becomes time-consuming and cannot run in the real-time. To reduce the execution time, point cloud will be down-sampled using 2×2 block. So that the number of points in the cloud will be reduced by four times.

As mentioned in Sect. 3, our system uses mobile Kinect, which means Kinect mounted on the body. Therefore, while the visually impaired are people moving, Kinect may be shocked and shaking so that the point cloud will be rotated due the changing of Kinect direction. In our project, we used accelerometer data provided by Kinect SDK to rotate point cloud in order to align the ground plane with the xz-plane in reference system.

The accelerometer data is actually a 3-D vector pointing in the direction of gravity with coordinate system centered on the sensor shown in Fig. 5. With the default Kinect configuration (horizontal) represented by the (x, y, z, w), the vector value is (0, −1.0, 0, 0). We use this vector to build rotation matrix and then apply it into point cloud data in order to rotate point cloud. Figure 6 shows the output of this stage.

3.2.2 Plane segmentation

The plane segmentation step is to determine dominant planes from point cloud. For this step, we propose to use the plane segmentation method proposed in [7] that allows to segment point cloud data into multiple planes in real time. The main advantage of this algorithm is that plane segmentation can be done very fast using both information in image structure and point cloud data. For this, the normal vector estimation is performed by using an integral image. The normal vector of a single point is calculated by a cross product of two vectors of four neighbor points: bottom-top and left-right (see Fig. 7a). Based on the normal vector of each single point, first, two maps of tangential vectors, one for x- and the other for y-dimension, are computed. Then, planes are detected by segmentation in normal space (see Fig. 7b). An example of plane segmentation result of the scene illustrated in Fig. 8a is shown in Fig. 8b.

3.2.3 Ground and wall detection

After planes have been segmented, ground and wall planes can be detected easily using some constraints. Because our point cloud has been rotated to align with ground plane in the previous step using gravity vector, so the ground plane must satisfy the following conditions:

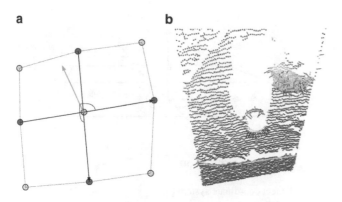

Fig. 7 Normal vector estimation: **a** normal vector of the center point is calculated by a cross product of two vectors of four neighbor points (*in red*); **b** normal vector estimation of a scene

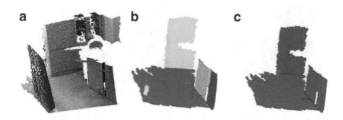

Fig. 8 Plane segmentation and ground and wall detection results: **a** point cloud; **b** segmented planes; **c** detected ground (*in blue*) and wall planes (*in red*)

- The angle between gravity vector and ground plane's normal vector is almost 0 degree;
- Ground plane must be large enough. In our case, we checked the number of points inside a ground plane, if the number of points is larger than 10,000, then we consider it is a ground plane candidate;
- Since Kinect is mounted on the human body, distance between ground plane and Kinect (y-axis coordinates) must be in a range of 0.8−1.2 m.

Wall is considered as perpendicular plane to the ground plane. So, in order to detect wall planes, we use similar constraints with ground plane except that the angle between gravity vector and wall's normal vector is almost 90° and we do not need to check distance between wall plane and the Kinect, because wall plane can appear anywhere in our scene. After ground and wall have been detected, all remaining points will be checked again if they belong to those planes by using distance to detected plane, this step aims to remove the missing points in the plane due to the noise in its normal vector. Then, all the points belonging to ground and wall planes will be removed. Figure 8c shows an example of the ground and wall plane detection for the scene Fig. 8a.

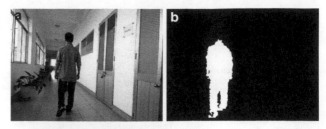

Fig. 9 Example of human detection: **a** color image; **b** human mask

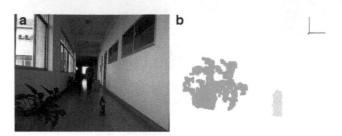

Fig. 10 Example of detected obstacles: **a** *color* image of the scene; **b** detected obstacles represented by *different colors*

3.2.4 Obstacle detection

In this step, we will detect obstacles from the remaining point cloud. There are two kind of obstacle: human and static object. With human detection, Microsoft Kinect SDK also provided human segmentation data. Kinect can track up to six person in a camera field-of-view. This data is encoded as 3 lowest bit for each pixel in depth image and represented index of the person that Kinect has been tracked. Figure 9 shows an example of detected person.

After checking human data in the frame, we remove all points belonging to the detected human and do clustering to find remaining obstacles in the scene. This algorithm is based on the Euclidean distance between neighbor points. From the initial point (seed), the distance between this point and its neighbor will be calculated. Then the points whose distance is smaller than a threshold are kept. This procedure is repeated until all points are checked in the point cloud. And using organized point cloud's structure, the neighbor points will be chosen directly based on 2D coordinate in the depth image. This allows to save a lot of time in comparison with neighbors finding based on the distance between them. Figure 10 illustrates an example of detected obstacle. For obstacles lying on the ground, we calculate the distance to the user to give a warning message.

3.2.5 Obstacle fusion and representation

At this step, all detected obstacles will be checked to give a final warning message. These obstacles include wall, human and static objects. Because there may be more than one obstacle in a frame, so we need to know which obstacle has to

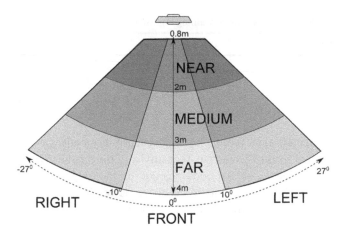

Fig. 11 Obstacle position quantization for sending warning message to visually impaired people

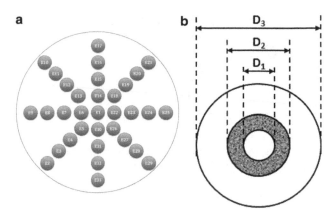

Fig. 12 Design of electrode matrix (**a**) and typical dimension of an electrode pin: $D_1 = 0.2$ mm, $D_2 = 0.4$ mm; $D_3 = 2$ mm (**b**)

be informed to visually impaired people. For this, among detected obstacles, we keep the nearest one whose size is larger than a predefined threshold. Then we quantize the 3D position into three levels of distance (near, medium and far range) and three directions (left, front and right) (see Fig. 11). The encoded information is written in an output file and sent to warning module.

3.3 Obstacle warning

As presented previously, once obstacles have been detected, the second task is to send this information on obstacles to the blind. In our system, the Tongue Display Unit is used for conveying the instructions to the visually impaired users; hence, they will know how to react accordingly. Several methods have been used in literature as the means of transferring the needed information to the users, especially warning signals [2,4,10]. However, the tongue has been investigated by Paul Bach-y-Rita in the context of sensory substitution in which stimulus properties of one sense (e.g., vision) can be converted to stimulation of another sense (e.g., vibrotactile or electrotactile matrix in contact with different parts of human body). We proposed to use the tongue since it is the most sensitive organ of the body with the discrimination threshold of one or two milimeters (the tongue has approximately a million nerve fibers) [27]. Based on this idea, the proposed design of the electrotactile matrix and the representation of obstacle warning will be described in this section.

3.3.1 Design the matrix of electrode

Most of the electrode arrays have the square or rectangular shape in which all the pins are arranged into perpendicular rows and columns. However, the matrix can only be placed on the inner superior part of the tongue in order for all the pins to get in contact with the surface. In our design, we propose

a round matrix of tactile arrays which better conforms to the shape of the tongue. Normally, it is easier for humans to perceive according to directions; therefore, we made use of this feature to arrange electrode pins into 45-degree-difference diameters as shown in Fig. 12a. This arrangement is composed of 2-mm disc-shaped electrode pins with a via of 0.2 mm for connecting to the ground. The distance between two electrodes is 2.7 mm. Figure 12b shows the dimension of an electrode pin.

3.3.2 Information representation

In our TVSS system, the electrotactile stimulation is responsible for informing the visually impaired users about the potential obstacles in their way. Based on the signal in the form of tingles on the tongue, they will obtain information and warning of environment obstacles and react accordingly. The electrotactile stimulation is used to generate tactile sensation on the skin site, specifically the tongue surface. A local electric current is passed through the tongue receptor to stimulate cutaneous afferent nerve fiber. This interface is a good site for electrotactile display, because it does not block the ears of visually impaired users.

After receiving the data of obstacle, we will define the kinds of obstacles into different representation on the electrode matrix. Then, according to the depth information, we will define the degree of warning by changing the level of electrical signal. Actually, the local current is delivered through electrical pulse. A control module is included in the TVSS system to produce these pulses.

For electrotactile stimulus, positive rectangular pulses are chosen to deliver in series to the TDU [13]. According to [16], the pulse period is approximately 100 ms and the duty cycle of each pulse should be 20 % for rather good perception. Since the purpose of informing is in the form of warning, we chose the method of increasing regularly the intensity of electrical stimulation. By doing this, when users come closer

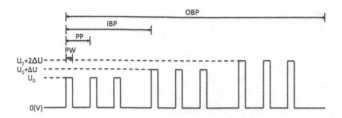

Fig. 13 The stimulation waveform is composed of three levels of pulse groups (bursts) to obtain warning goal. Each burst contains three pulse with period of 100 ms and 20 ms of "on-time"

Table 1 Electrotactile stimulation parameters

Symbol	Meaning	Range	Unit
OBP	Outer burst period	1200–1400	ms
IBP	Inner burst period	400–600	ms
PP	Pulse period	100	ms
PW	Pulse width	20–50	ms
U_0	Lowest voltage level	5–10	V
ΔU	Voltage difference	0.5–3	V

Parameter values are controllable in real time by the control module program

to obstacles, the alert signal becomes stronger and makes them respond and take action to avoid objects. In our scenario, three stimulating voltages were defined: the lowest level, the higher level and highest level. At the lowest level, users can feel clearly the signal. The higher level start to create an uncomfortable feeling and the highest level can cause a strong sensation. Figure 13 and Table 1 display the waveform with three consecutive bursts of pulses. The magnitude of voltage increases steadily.

3.3.3 Obstacle warning representation

To prove the capability of the system to give warning message to the visually impaired individuals, we have to decide what information needs to be conveyed. Not all the objects are defined as an obstacle and after the detection step, the object types or classes and the position of objects need to be distinguished. As a consequence, the electrical stimulation can correspond to the warning of object classes. Besides, the intensity of each stimulation can be leveraged to give the suitable warning message to instruct the users' reaction. In the indoor environment of the experimental part, the object classes will be divided into two, the stationary (e.g., flower pot, fire extinguisher or dustbin) and the moving one (e.g., human or opening door). The object position in front of the users consists of three positions—left, front, right and the warning intensity increases to three levels—near, medium and far. Table 2 demonstrates the division of warning representation.

Table 2 Classification of warning representation

Feature	Type		
Object classes	Stationary	Moving	
Warning level	High	Medium	Low
Position	Left	Center	Right

According to Table 2, a complete feasibility study was performed so as to evaluate the sensitivity of the tongue towards the intensity and electrode position on the tongue as well as the efficiency of this biofeedback device in warning the obstacles on the mobility path of the test subjects.

4 Experimental results

4.1 Material setup

Our prototype device is constructed upon off-the-shelf hardware components including a Kinect sensor which captures the color and depth data, a laptop computer for image processing, a control module and a matrix of electrodes which is arranged on a round substrate. The Kinect sensor is operated by a 12-V source of 8×1.5 V AA batteries (we removed the original adapter and replaced it by the battery source); the control module and the electrode matrix attached to it are powered by a 3-V battery. The Kinect sensor is mounted on the user's belt to record the environment and the matrix of electrodes is placed inside the mouth and attached to the control module through the cable. Figure 14 shows the real prototype of the obstacle detection and warning system.

Fig. 14 Illustration of the warning device. **a** Kinect sensor on user and **b** control module and electrode matrix on user. **a** Kinect sensor mounted on the belt worn by a blind student. Video processing is conducted by a laptop placed on a backpack. **b** The tongue electrotactile device worn on a blind user. The matrix of electrodes is place totally inside the mouth in contact with the dorsal part of the tongue and is controlled by the module through cables

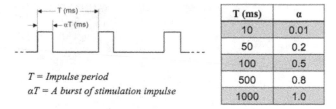

Fig. 15 Testing waveform parameters

T (ms)	α
10	0.01
50	0.2
100	0.5
500	0.8
1000	1.0

T = Impulse period
αT = A burst of stimulation impulse

α T(ms)	<0.01	0.2	0.5	0.8
10	Too fast, Not clear	Too fast, Not clear	Too fast, Strong	Too fast, Strong
50	Fast, Not clear	Fast, Not clear	Fast, Strong	Fast, Strong
100	Good speed, Not clear	Good speed, Good perception	Good speed, Strong	Slow, Strong
500	Slow, Not clear	Slow, Good perception	Slow, Strong	Slow, Too strong
1000	Too slow, Not clear	Too slow, Good perception	Too slow, Too strong	Too slow, Too strong

Fig. 16 Waveform parameters perception

The experiments were conducted with 20 young adults who voluntarily participated. Subjects were recruited at Grenoble University and Hanoi University of Science and Technology. Each volunteer was eager to participate and all provided informed consent to participate. Three main evaluations were implemented: waveform evaluation, intensity evaluation and efficiency evaluation. In each evaluation, all the subjects must be trained for a couple of minutes and then give feedback by their recognition or take part in a real mobility in an indoor environment on one floor.

4.2 Electrical stimulation waveform calibration

In order to have an effective stimulation on the tongue, the waveform was calibrated. As a result, different values of electrical pulse parameters were tested with participants. Five healthy subjects performed this assessment. Their task was to test with one electrode at the front part of the tongue. Different values of impulse period and the duty cycle (the activation duration of the electrode in one impulse) were applied at 3 V and two trials were done with each couple of period and duty cycle. Figure 15 shows the waveform and its testing parameters.

The impulse values were first changed in order for several times and told to the participants. Then the values were generated randomly and each subject was asked about his/her perception. The results are shown in Fig. 16. It seems to give good perception and good speed of recognition at period $T = 100$ ms and dutycycle $= 0.2$. In other cases, if the period is too high, it is too slow for recognition and if the period is low, it is too fast to distinguish. In case of high duty cycle, the electrical stimulation is so strong that it caused pain while in the case of low duty cycle, it is not a clear signal. Giving this timing parameter, the participants were then required to take part in the intensity evaluation.

4.3 Electrical stimulation intensity calibration

The TDU is very variable and may be used with any kind of electrodes, we have designed a particular geometry which is appropriate for the tongue application. The round shape can proliferate the convenience and comfort because it follows the contour of the tongue. This matrix is fabricated on FR4 substrate which is very common for commercial circuit vendor. Each of the electrode has the diameter of over 2 mm and the center–center spacing is 2.34 mm. The overall dimension is 25 mm × 25 mm which fits easily on the tongue. The exposed surface of the electrode is gold-plated to reduce the harm to user's health. Although the tongue electrotactile display has been experimented in many applications, the perception on the electrical stimulation intensity has not yet been studied in detailed. Due to the limited size of the tongue, the electrode diameters must be small and reduce resistance. Aside from this, the region on the tongue determines the intensity. We performed a real test on five different users aging from 25 to 40. The preliminary results show that the contour of the tongue requires much low power than the center and rear part is less perceptive than the front part. A voltage generator produces voltages from 5 to 15 V and the average value is depicted in Fig. 17.

Because the intensity is an important factor for obstacle warning, this result is considered as the average voltage level that users can afford. From the obtained average voltages, the voltage values of different tongue regions are designated based on the lowest average voltage which is defined as V0 in Fig. 18. They are then written in the control program to adjust the voltage level automatically for the next tests. The value of V0 depends on the perception of each participant and is determined prior to the obstacle warning test.

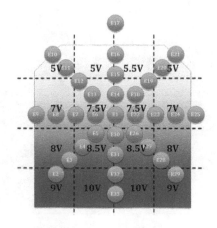

Fig. 17 Average voltage results measured on different regions of the tongue

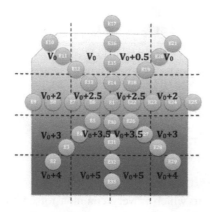

Fig. 18 Voltage-level calculation

4.4 Validation of obstacle detection module

We evaluate the static obstacle detection method with 200 images captured at two different times with visually impaired people in MICA building. We named them dataset 1 and dataset 2. Each dataset contains 100 frames including color image, depth image and accelerometer data. With dataset 1, the ground plane in depth image has a large area; whereas the dataset 2 ground only takes a small area, as can be seen in Fig. 19. We compared our method with the method of Vlaminck et al. [24].

With each dataset, we made two different evaluations: pixel level and object level. Concerning pixel level, for the ground-truth, we apply Watershed algorithm on depth image in order to separate objects from background. The obstacle detection result in point cloud is back projected into 2D image.

For object level, we define manually obstacles of the scene. Each obstacle is determined by a rectangle. A detection result is a true detection if the ratio between the intersection of the

Fig. 19 Example images: **a** and **c** are *color* and depth images in dataset 1; **b** and **d** are *color* and depth images in dataset 2

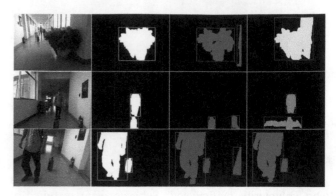

Fig. 20 Obstacle detection result. From *left* to *right* color image, ground truth, detected obstacles of our method and the method in [24]

detected and the ground-truth rectangles and the union of these rectangles is larger than 0.5.

We employ three evaluation measures that are precision, recall and F-measure. These measures are defined as follows:

$$\text{Precision} = \frac{\text{TP}}{\text{TP} + \text{FP}} \tag{1}$$

$$\text{Recall} = \frac{\text{TP}}{\text{TP} + \text{FN}} \tag{2}$$

$$F = 2\frac{\text{Precision} * \text{Recall}}{\text{Precision} + \text{Recall}} \tag{3}$$

Figure 20 illustrates some examples of detection while Table 3 shows the quantitative evaluation. Our algorithm has a slightly higher F-score than method in [24], its has lower precision score but higher recall score, especially in the dataset 2, which has small ground region, the recall is significantly different between two methods (5.6 % higher in pixel level and 12.4 % higher in object level). In overall, our method produces less false alarms with a acceptable rate of true detection. This is because in Vlaminck's method [24] using RANSAC algorithm to segment plane and ground plane must be well identified in order to rotate the point cloud based on normal vector of detected ground plane then detect obstacle. So when the ground plane is wrongly detected or missed, it tends to consider the whole ground plane as a obstacle. That is why the precision with pixel level of method [24] is significantly higher than recall.

Concerning computational time, Fig. 21 shows the detection time of two methods. We tested both of them in same configuration of PC (an Intel Core i7-2720QM processor and 12 GB memory inside) and down-sample rate (2 × 2 block, which produces 76,800 points in point cloud). Both methods operate with average speed of 4–5 Hz (200 ms/frame). In our method, due to plane refinement by calculating distance from all points to detected plane, it occupied most of time while in [24] method, the most time-consuming part is plane segmentation using RANSAC. In general, this processing time is enough to be used in practice.

Table 3 Obstacle detection results comparison with the method in [24]

		Pixel level			Object level		
		P	R	F	P	R	F
Overall	Our	76.9	80	78.4	63.5	73.4	68.1
	[24]	81.9	73.7	77.6	61.9	66.9	64.3
Dataset1	Our	68.3	73.6	70.9	51.7	56.2	53.8
	[24]	69.9	66.9	68.3	46.8	54.9	50.6
Dataset2	Our	85.6	**85.9**	85.8	75	**92.5**	82.8
	[24]	94.9	**80.3**	87	81.8	**80.1**	81

P Precision (%), *R* Recall (%), *F* F-Measure (%)

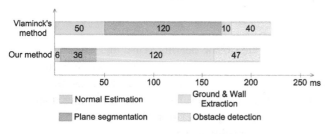

Fig. 21 Detection time of each step of our method and the method in [24]

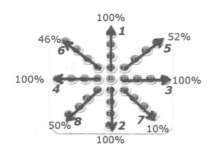

Fig. 22 Average accuracy of eight direction on the tongue

4.5 User perception validation

In order to evaluate the performance of the proposed prototype system, a perception experiment was conducted for users. Based on the design of the electrode matrix and the idea of stimulation pulses, we used a sequence of electrodes to represent eight directions. Each direction corresponds to one radius line and the order of stimulating electrodes is from center to the edge of the tongue. Five participants took part in a training session to adapt to the device then they were asked for randomized directions. Figure 22 shows the average accuracy of perception calculated on five participants. The electrical intensity is generated based on the perception evaluation in Fig. 18.

According to the feedback of users, the edge regions of the tongue often gives good perception. Besides, the left and right-front parts of the tongue achieve higher accuracy than the rear parts. As a result, the obstacle warning representation is suitable for users.

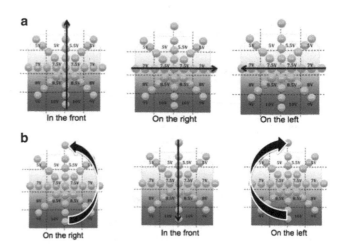

Fig. 23 Electrotactile representation of stationary and moving obstacle warning. **a** stationary object and **b** moving object

The resulted perception for main directions (left, right, forward and backward) are very promising to be used not only for supporting navigation in terms of directivity, but also can further improve the safety by giving detailed information through different representations on electrodes. Several research groups used tongue electrotactile feedback for different purpose for blind people and unbalanced people.

In existing researches [20,26,27], the systems normally have their basic forms of square or rectangular. Our prototype is destined to consume less energy and to be able to change voltage level. It is very important as the warning task requires informing the danger before the user gets very near the obstacle. The experiment and results on warning representation will be described in the next sections. Firstly, we will test with the direction when on the path, there is no obstacle. Then the experiment on obstacle warning will be detailed and discussed.

4.6 Obstacle warning evaluation

The obstacle detection and warning is the major function that we aim at in our research. Based on the output information, the warning signals were generated and the tongue electrotactile system was again used to test this function. Due to the above results on the directions of stimulation impulses on the tongue, we choose the most precise directions: forward, left, right. In addition, the experiment on part 4.5, the edge of the tongue is more sensitive than the interior of the tongue. Figure 23 depicts the representation for stationary and moving obstacle warning for our system.

In Fig. 23, the arrangement of electrodes was made so as to bring the good perception to the users. As a consequence, we made use of the more sensitive regions on the tongue such as the edge of the tongue and the high percentage correction regions on the tongue. The stationary obstacle

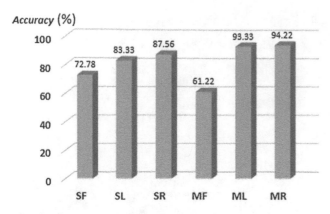

Fig. 24 Distinction accuracy for obstacle warning: *S* stationary object, *M* moving object, *F* on the front, *L* on the left, *R* on the right

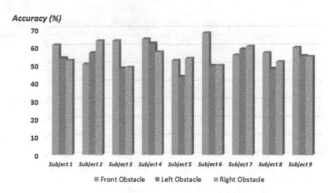

Fig. 25 Obstacle warning result based on the position

was warned by utilizing nine electrodes to indicate its position, while the moving one was alerted by employing the edge electrodes and backward direction. Firstly, the sensitivity test was implemented with nine blindfolded subjects with one voltage level to evaluate their perception capacity towards the position and the kind of object. Each participant performed two stages: the training stage and the perceiving stage.

In training stage, after the V0 value was decided for each participant, they will be trained for adaptation without moving to associate the electrical stimulations with the corresponding command. In perceiving stage, subjects were asked to say the command without knowing in advance. Figure 24 displays the accuracy of distinction of command for indicating position and status of objects. Among six stimulations, the sensitivity results for using the edge of the tongue are higher than using the interior of the tongue. In addition, using nine electrodes can sometimes cause confusion to users about two opposite directions because their stimulating signals use the same electrodes. If the two chains of impulses were struck too close in time, such as two SF impulses, user easily confuses SF for MF. This is also what the test subjects mentioned after the experiment. The same situation happens with the case of SL and SR. That is why the accuracies for SF, SL, SR and MF are below 90 %.

In order to encode the warning signal to tactile representation, electrical stimulating intensity was varied according to the distance to the obstacles. Nine subjects were asked to take part in the obstacle avoidance experiment based on a pseudo-warning signals corresponding to moving and stationary obstacles at different positions while completing a trajectory in a building corridor. Some stationary obstacles such as fire extinguishers, flower pots and dustbins were placed arbitrarily along the way. Each participant must be trained for adaptation with the electrode array during 30 min before conducting the experiment. When the subject got nearer to the obstacle, the intensity of the results are shown in Fig. 25.

Actually due to the hearing sense and the environment perception of the test subjects, the results here could not be totally accounted for the tongue electrotactile system. However, nearly all the subjects obtained higher than 50 % accuracy when they travel in reality. For the case of front obstacle, the capacity of avoidance is really high because the representation on the electrode matrix for the front objects lies in only one region of the tongue, while left and right object can reach from 45 % to around 62 % of avoidance capacity. Not all subjects travelled at normal or low speed to have better perception and they were often curious about the tongue system and did not follow strictly the training stage. That is also why the results were not totally as expected to have higher rate of recognition. However, the accuracy rate can be promisingly improved if more subjects should be required to participate and asked to follow carefully the training stage.

5 Conclusion

In this paper, we proposed a system which is an integration between mobile Kinect with electrode matrix to help visually impaired people from obstacle while moving. Our system is designed to act as a mobility aid and perform the obstacle detection and warning task. Keeping in mind that users are visually impaired people, the information representation is simple, portable, hands and ears-free by using human tongue as the interface. The results indicate that under certain constraints, the imaging technique has so far been able to provide guidance cues, detect both stationary and moving obstacle, calculate rather precisely the depth information in order to give warning information at the right time. Although using tongue as the representation interface requires intensive study on the perception, the preliminary perception results show that it is totally possible to express the alert signal in this form and the electrical stimulation intensity can be adjusted attentively for the users.

The results of our experiment demonstrated that subjects were able to correctly interpret the directional signal provided by the wireless TDU. Interestingly, our results further showed that the tongue behavior is very flexible. Different regions on the tongue adapt to different voltages and recognition also based on the stimulation impulse. Moreover, different users have different levels of stimulation intensity. The outer and front part of the tongue have good perception and low voltage level, while the inner and rear part needs higher voltage activation. It is proved that people can be trained to adapt to a new sense to recover lost information due to impaired sensory modality.

Indeed, not all users can totally get used to this kind of device and the mobility still depends mainly on their natural feeling and instinct. Some visually impaired are not totally blind and they can follow the instruction by light cue. However, our results show that subjects can move independently with the instruction from the TDU but with care. This observation could be relevant for conducting future studies.

Acknowledgements This research is funded by Vietnam National Foundation for Science and Technology Development (NAFOSTED) under Grant Number FWO.102.2013.08.

References

1. Bernabei, D., Ganovelli, F., Di Benedetto, M., Dellepiane, M., Scopigno, R.: A low-cost time-critical obstacle avoidance system for the visually impaired. In: International conference on indoor positioning and indoor navigation (IPIN) (2011)
2. Calder, D.J.: Assistive technology interfaces for the blind. In: 3rd IEEE international conference on digital ecosystems and technologies, pp. 318–323, June (2009)
3. Multi-kinect camera calibration. http://doc-ok.org/?p=295. Accessed 25 July 2016
4. Chen, G., Can, Z., Jun, P.: An intelligent blind rod and navigation platform based on zigbee technology. In: 2011 International conference on E-Business and E-Government (ICEE), pp. 1–4, May (2011)
5. Hersh, M., Johnson, M.A.: Assistive Technology for Visually Impaired and Blind People, 1st edn. Springer, London (2008)
6. Hoang, V.N., Nguyen, T.H., Le, T.L., Tran, T.T.H., Vuong, T.P., Vuillerme, N.: Obstacle detection and warning for visually impaired people based on electrode matrix and mobile kinect. In: 2nd National foundation for science and technology development conference on information and computer science (NICS), pp. 54–59, Sept (2015)
7. Holz, D., Holzer, S., Rusu, R.B., Behnke, S.: Real-time plane segmentation using rgb-d cameras. In: Röfer, T., Mayer, N. M., Savage, J., Saranlı, U. (eds.) RoboCup 2011: robot soccer world cup XV, pp. 306–317. Springer, Berlin (2012)
8. Nicolas Burrus HomePage. http://nicolas.burrus.name. Accessed 25 July 2016
9. Huang, H.C., Hsieh, C.T., Cheng-Hsiang, Y.: An indoor obstacle detection system using depth information and region growth. Sensors **15**, 27116–27141 (2015)
10. Jameson, B., Manduchi, R.: Watch your head: a wearable collision warning system for the blind. In: 2010 IEEE sensors, pp. 1922–1927, Nov (2010)
11. Joachim, A., Ertl, H., Thomas, D.: Design and Development of an indoor navigation and object identification system for the blind. In: Proc. ACM SIGACCESS accessibility, computing, pp. 147–152 (2004)
12. Johnson, L.A., Higgins, C.M.: A navigation aid for the blind using tactile-visual sensory substitution. In: 28th Annual international conference of the IEEE engineering in medicine and biology society, pp. 6289–6292 (2006)
13. Kaczmarek, K.A., Webster, J.G., Bach-y Rita, P., Tompkins, W.J.: Electrotactile and vibrotactile displays for sensory substitution systems. IEEE Trans. Biomed. Eng. **38**(1), 1–16 (1991)
14. Nguyen, T.H., Le, T.L., Tran, T.T.H., Vuillerme, N., Vuong, T.P.: Antenna design for tongue electrotactile assitive device for the blind and visually impaired. In: 7th European conference on antennas and propagation (2013)
15. Nguyen, T.H., Nguyen, T.H., Le, T.L., Tran, T.T.H., Vuillerme, N., Vuong, T.P.: A wearable assistive device for the blind using tongue-placed electrotactile display: design and verification. In: International conference on control, automation and information sciences (ICCAIS), pp. 42–47 (2013)
16. Nguyen, T.H., Nguyen, T.H., Le, T.L., Tran, T.T.H., Vuillerme, N., Vuong, T.P.: A wireless assistive device for visually-impaired persons using tongue electrotactile system. In: Advanced technologies for communications (ATC), 2013 international conference on, pp. 586–591, Oct (2013)
17. Rodrguez, S.A., Yebes, J.J., Alcantarilla, P.F., Bergasa, L.M., Almazan, J., Cela, A.: Assisting the visually impaired: obstacle detection and warning system by acoustic feedback. Sensors **12**, 17476–17496 (2012)
18. Sainarayanan, G., Nagarajan, R., Yaacob, S.: Fuzzy image processing scheme for autonomous navigation of human blind. Appl. Softw. Comput. **7**(1), 257–264 (2007)
19. Solomon, N., Bhandari, P.: Paten lanscape report on assistive devices and technologies for visually and hearing impaired persons. Technical report, Patent lanscape report project (2015)
20. Tang, H., Beebe, D.J.: An oral tactile interface for blind navigation. IEEE Trans. Neural Syst. Rehabil. Eng. **14**(1), 116–123 (2006)
21. Tang, T.J.J., Lui, W.L.D., Li, W.H.: Plane-based detection of staircases using inverse depth. In: Australasian conference on robotics and automation (ACRA) (2012)
22. Brainport Technology. http://www.wicab.com. Accessed 25 July 2016
23. Ulrich, I., Nourbakhsh, I.: Appearance-based obstacle detection with monocular color vision. AAAI (2000)
24. Vlaminck, M., Jovanov, L., Van Hese, P., Goossens, B., Wilfried, P., Aleksandra, P.: Obstacle detection for pedestrians with a visual impairment based on 3d imaging. In: 2013 International conference on 3D imaging (IC3D), pp. 1–7. IEEE (2013)
25. The VOICE. http://www.seeingwithsound.com. Accessed 25 July 2016
26. Vuillerme, N., Pinsault, N., Chenu, O., Fleury, A., Payan, Y., Demongeot, J.: A wireless embedded tongue tactile biofeedback system for balance control. Pervasive Mob. Comput. **5**, 268–275 (2009)
27. Bach y Rita, P., Kaczmarek, K.A., Tyler, M.E., Garcia-Lara, J.: Form perception with a 49-point electrotactile stimulus array on the tongue: a technical note. J. Rehabil. Res. Dev. **35**(4), 427–430 (1998)

## 12

Collaborative Vietnamese WordNet building using consensus quality

Trong Hai Duong[1] · Minh Quang Tran[2] · Thi Phuong Trang Nguyen[3]

Abstract Most ontologies are being developed in an engineering-oriented method: a small group of engineers carefully builds and maintains a presentation of their view of the world. Certainly, there are several tools oriented towards collaborative work: a consensus-building mechanism that allows a large group of people to contribute or annotate a common ontology in a collaborative way to reach consensus among individuals. However, the previous approaches have not yet exploited the most important problem in consensus-based collaboration, when can we get a consensus? The main goal of this research is to investigate an effective methodology for collaborative ontology building in which we apply *consensus quality* and *susceptible to consensus* to reach to the final version of the collaborative ontology building.

Keywords Collaborative ontology · Ontology · Consensus · Ontology building · Ontology engineering

✉ Trong Hai Duong
haiduongtrong@gmail.com

Minh Quang Tran
tranminhquang2209@gmail.com

Thi Phuong Trang Nguyen
phuongtrangict@gmail.com

[1] International University, Vietnam National University-HCMC, Ho Chi Minh City, Vietnam

[2] Institute of Science and Technology of Industry 4.0, Nguyen Tat Thanh University, Ho Chi Minh City, Vietnam

[3] Banking University of Ho Chi Minh City, Ho Chi Minh City, Vietnam

1 Introduction

Human collaboration is an effort among a group of people contributing to a common goal. It can be used as the infrastructure for facilitating the creation of a common and shared understanding. Ontologies can be developed to improve the quantity and quality of communication among participants, who can then benefit from the skills and knowledge of others. Thus, it is very important and necessary for investigating and developing principle approaches and flexible tools to allow individuals to collaboratively build, refine, and integrate existing ontologies.

Most ontologies are being developed in an engineering-oriented method: a small group of engineers carefully builds and maintains a presentation of their view of the world. Maintaining such large ontologies in an engineering-oriented way is a highly complex process: developers need to regularly merge and reconcile their modifications to ensure that the ontology captures a consistent and unified view of the domain. However, conflict can lead to errors in complex ways. These errors may manifest themselves both as structural (i.e., syntactic) mismatches between developers' ontological descriptions, and as unintended logical consequences. Therefore, the tools are unsuitable for ontology construction by large groups of non-experts over the web. In other words, the previous approaches have not yet exploited the most important problem in consensus-based collaboration, which is when we can get a consensus. The main goal of this research is to investigate an effective methodology, which is using the consensus quality to not only ease the collaborative ontology building process by reducing the workload of ontology data integration but also increase the accuracy of the final version of the ontology that is based on a large number of contributors with or without domain experts.

2 Related works

According to our study, there are several tools oriented towards collaborative work [7,8,13,14,16]: a consensus-building mechanism that allows a large group of people to contribute or annotate a common ontology in a collaborative way to reach consensus among individuals. One instance of these tools is Protégé[1] which is established by Stanford University for knowledge acquisition. It provides a graphical and interactive ontology design and knowledge-based development environment. Ontology developers can access relevant information quickly, and navigate and manipulate the ontology. One of the advantages of Protégé is an open, modular design. Tudorache et al. [16] have developed Collaborative Protégé as an extension to the client–server Protégé. Collaborative Protégé allows entire groups of developers who are building an ontology collaboratively to hold discussions, chat, make annotations and make changes as a part of the ontology-development process. One of the advantages of Collaborative Protégé is the ability to create annotations. OntoWiki [2] is a web-based ontology which focuses on an instance editor that provides only rudimentary capabilities as the history of changes and ratings of ontology components. OntoWiki provides different views on instance data (e.g., a map view for geographical data or a calendar view for data containing dates). OntoEdit [15] is a collaborative ontology (CoO) editing environment that integrates numerous aspects of ontology engineering and allows multiple users to develop ontologies in three phases: a requirements specification, refinement, and evaluation/maintenance. KAON [5] focuses on changes of ontology that can cause inconsistencies, a proposed deriving evolution strategy to maintain consistencies. However, the collaborative version of aforementioned approaches may not reach to the consensus among participants since it just accepts the latest modification from any participant on collaborative process. Here, we consider a collaborative ontology building process which allows an entire group to be heard and to participate in the process of ontology building by reaching a consensus and usually aiming at completeness. The goal of collaborative process is to find a common ground and examine these issues in ontology building until mutual agreement between group members has been reached. We agree with previous works [3,4,7,8,10], there are four phases of the collaborative approach to design ontology including: (1) the preparatory phase defines the criteria, specifies boundary conditions for the ontology, and determines standards for assessing its success; (2) the anchoring phase includes the development of an initial version of the ontology which will feed the next phase (evaluation phase) while being aware and complying with the design criteria; (3) the iterative improvement phase enhances ontology until

all participants' points of view reach a consensus through a collaborative building technique. In this phase, the ontology structure will be revised and evolved by collaboration of participants. At each iterative improvement, the ontology is evaluated by aforementioned standards and conditions; (4) the application phase demonstrates the use of collaborative ontology by applying it in various ways. However, the previous approaches have not yet exploited the most important problem in consensus-based collaboration, when can we get a consensus? The main goal of this research is to investigate an effective methodology for collaborative ontology building in which we apply *consensus quality* and *susceptible to consensus* by Nguyen et al. [9] to reach to the final version of the collaborative ontology building.

3 Collaborative algorithm using consensus quality

3.1 Consensus-based collaboration overview

The Nominal Group Technique (NGT) [6] is well known as a method for decision making. It has been used to get the final result among a group whether large or small while considering all opinions and votes from group members. NGT takes into account the participants who join the discussion to choose the result. It is successful when everybody participates and understands the manners, and represents the solution or opinions by themselves without affecting the surroundings around them. NGT is a process where everyone is clearly involved and knows everything while getting the solution without missing anyone in the discussion.

One of the popular consensus-building techniques is the Delphi method [12]. This method is used for normal discussion that does not need complex communication between experts such as meeting face-to-face or having a meeting to talk at a table. It is because this method can be implemented using technology such as email or any other electronic technologies for communication where each question can be sent directly to every group expert. Even though there is a complex problem that needs to be solved, this method can be used to find the solution by sending a series of questionnaires via multiple iterations and getting a solution (data) from experts. The Delphi method is commonly used in education, to estimate forecasts and other fields. The Delphi technique can be done in four steps:

1. The moderator forms a group of experts that participates in the process to solve the problem. However, all of the experts are unidentified.
2. A person will send a questionnaire to the participants via mail or email.
3. Once the person gets the return answer from a participant, the person will analyze the results.

---

[1] http://protege.stanford.edu/.

4. At the last step, if there is no consensus reached, a combination of previous questionnaires and results will be used as a new version of the questionnaire, and the moderator will send this new version again to a participant. Step 2 is repeated until consensus is reached, or the moderator ends the process and makes a final report.

There are some different factors between these two aforementioned methods. As we already know the Delphi method is commonly used without experts needing to meet each other. In Nominal, all participants or experts need to be in one place and doing the process together. The main point of Nominal is all participants are required to meet face-to-face to reach the solution. What they believe in Nominal is, every idea or opinion is strongly agreed upon if experts or participants present their ideas formally and seriously in front of other experts. It means that in Nominal, consensus can be reach if there is real discussion. In contrast to the Delphi methods, they believe that without meeting each other and with believing the anonymous expert, the consensus result is more accurate. It is because without affecting other experts, an individual expert can find the ideas and solution based on expert knowledge, so consensus results are more reliable based on individual expertise.

3.2 Consensus quality

To solve conflicts between participants, a method following [9] has been introduced. Each participant in a collaborative group gives his or her knowledge x to a profile X, which is a set of knowledge that is collected by n participants.

$$X_h = \{x_1, x_2, \ldots, x_n\}$$

where x_i is an annotation of a participant i for the object h which is the set of senses and relations of one word or phrase in Ontology-based Vietnamese WordNet.

For conflicting profiles and their consensuses, a measurement has been used to evaluate these consensuses which follow [9]:

$$\hat{d}(x, X) = 1 - \frac{d(x, X)}{card(X)} \tag{1}$$

where $\hat{d}(x, X)$ is the quality of consensus x in profile X $d(x, X)$ is the sum of all different distances between an element x to the universe. $card(X)$ is the number of participants in X.

For a given distance space(U, d), we define some parameters following [9]:

$$d_{t\_mean}(X) = \frac{\sum_{x, y \in X}(d(x, y))}{k(k+1)} \tag{2}$$

$$d_x(X) = \frac{\sum_{y \in X}(d(x, y))}{k} \tag{3}$$

$$d_{\min}(X) = \min_{x \in U} d_x(X) \tag{4}$$

$$d_{\max}(X) = \max_{x \in U} d_x(X) \tag{5}$$

where $d_{t\_mean}(X)$ is the total average distance of all distances in profile X. $d_x(X)$ represents the average distance of all distances between object x and the elements of profile X. $d_x(X)$ represents the average distance of all distances between object x and the elements of profile X. $d_{\min}(X)$: The minimal value of $d_x(X)$ for $x \in U$

$$card(X) = k.$$

Next, to calculate the distance between two elements of a profile X, *cosine distance* has been used as a measure. Hence, it is required to convert these elements into vectors before applying *cosine distance* function below:

$$d(x_i, x_j) = 1 - \cos(\theta) = 1 - \frac{A \cdot B}{||A|| \, ||B||}$$
$$= \frac{\sum_{k=1}^{n} A_k B_k}{\sqrt{\sum_{k=1}^{n} A_k^2} \sqrt{\sum_{k=1}^{n} B_k^2}} \tag{6}$$

where $d(x_i, x_j)$ is a distance between element x_i and x_j (which $x_i, x_j \in X$), A, B are vectors of element x_i and x_j, respectively. A_k, B_k are respective components of vector A and B. $\cos(\theta)$ represents the similarity of vector A and B.

Example Let X be a profile where $X = \{2 * ab\}$; there are two votes for a and one vote for b. The above-defined values are calculated as follows:

$$d_{t\_mean}(X) = \frac{2 \times (0 + 2 + 0)}{3 \times 4} = \frac{1}{3}$$

$$d_{\min}(X) = \frac{1}{3}$$

To reach an optimal profile, the inequality which follows [9] has been used. The susceptible to consensus of profile X is satisfied if and only if the following inequality takes place

$$d_{t\_mean}(X) \geq d_{\min}(X) \tag{7}$$

X is susceptible to consensus (it is possible to determine a good consensus for X) if the second value is not greater than the first. Satisfying the above inequality means that the elements of profile X are dense enough for determining a good consensus. In other words, opinions represented by these elements are consistent enough for determining a good compromise.

Fig. 1 Collaborative algorithm
using consensus quality

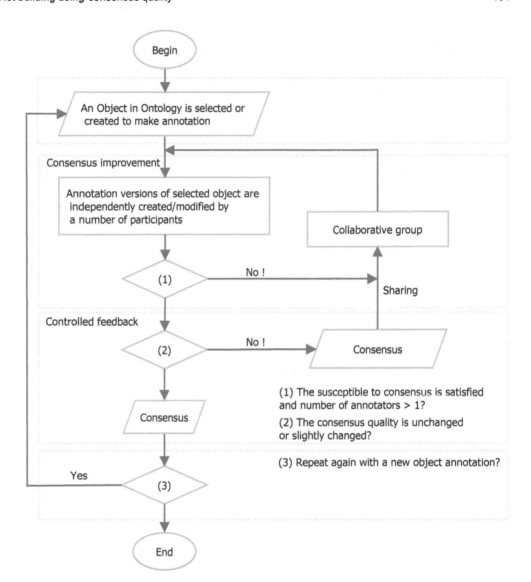

3.3 Collaborative algorithm using consensus quality

The algorithm using consensus quality is expressed in Fig. 1:

Following [4], we present features of a method for collaborative ontology building:

Phase 1 Preparatory: instead of using questionnaires in Delphi we provide criteria for ontology building [3].

Phase 2 Contribution: the changeable ontology is cloned from the original one. Participants can modify their own versions without changing the original version.

Phase 3 Consensus improvement: the annotation versions of an object are independently created/modified by a number of participants. In addition the *Susceptible to Consensus* of this object is calculated using Eqs. (2), (3) and (4). If the result satisfies the inequality (7) and the number of annotators is greater than 1, the process moves to *Phase* 4. Otherwise, the group keeps modifying this object until the inequality (7) occurs.

Phase 4 Controlled feedback: in this phase, the quality of consensus is calculated using Eq. (1). If consensus quality is unchanged or slightly changed, a reconciled ontology that is constructed from the integration of the generated versions will be used as a new version of the ontology. Next, this consensus version will be shared to the group and the process moves back to *Phase* 3. The algorithm will stop until there is no improvement that needs to be done.

Example Assume that there is a laptop which comprises four components such as CPU Memory (RAM) Hard Disk and a model name. To identify the details of this laptop we apply the algorithm as follows:

Step 1: Inviting participant to annotate the object. At the beginning there is only one participant for annotation and the result is collected as shown in Table 1.

Step 2: Calculating all possible *cosine distances* between two different points (participants).

At the moment there is only one point (participant) hence this step is not applicable.

Table 1 1-Participant annotation result

Participants	CPU	Memory	Hard Disk	Model
1	Intel i3	4 GB	500 GB	HP 4230s

Step 3: Calculating the total average distance in this profile which is $d_{t\_mean}(X)$.

In (2) $d_{t\_mean}(X) = 0$ (as we only have one participant)

Step 4: Calculating the minimum distance of this profile.

In (3) and (4), we have $d_{min}(X) = 0$

Step 5: Calculating the quality of consensus if the inequality of susceptible to consensus (7) occurs.

According to steps 3 and 4, the result satisfies the inequality of susceptible to consensus as $dt\_mean(X) = d_{min}(X) = 0$; however, the number of participants is not greater than 1.

Therefore, next, we need to increase the number of participants to 2, which let one more person to annotate the laptop, and go back to **step 1**, the result is as shown in Table 2:

Step 2: Calculating all possible *cosine distances* between two different points (participants).

To convert participants' ideas into vectors, all of the terms are counted as shown in Table 3:

As a result of Table 3, we have 2 vectors for 2 participants:

$P1(1, 0, 1, 0, 1, 1)$

$P2(0, 1, 0, 1, 1, 1)$

In (6),

$d(P1, P2) = 1$
$$-\frac{1 \times 0 + 0 \times 1 + 1 \times 0 + 0 \times 1 + 1 \times 1 + 1 \times 1}{\sqrt{1^2 + 0^2 + 1^2 + 0^2 + 1^2 + 1^2}\sqrt{0^2 + 1^2 + 0^2 + 1^2 + 1^2 + 1^2}} = 0.5$$

Step 3: Calculating the total average distance in this profile which is $d_{t\_mean}(X)$

In (2),

$$d_{t\_mean}(X) = \frac{2 \times 0.5}{2 \times (2 + 1)} = 0.16$$

Step 4: Calculating the minimum distance of this profile.

In (3) and (4), we have $d_1(X) = d_2(X) = d_{min}(X) = \frac{0.5}{2} = 0.25$.

Step 5: Calculating the quality of consensus if the inequality of susceptible to consensus occurs:

According to steps 3 and 4, the result does not satisfy the inequality of susceptible to consensus (7) as $d_{t\_mean}(X) < d_{min}(X)$ (due to 016 < 025).

Therefore, we have to invite one more person to annotate this laptop to reach the consensus back to **step 1** (see Table 4):

Step 2: Calculating all possible *cosine distances* between two different points (participants).

In (6),

$$d(P1, P2) = 1 - \frac{2}{4} = 0.5$$

$$d(P1, P3) = 1 - \frac{0}{4} = 1$$

$$d(P2, P3) = 1 - \frac{1}{4} = 0.75$$

Step 3: Calculating the total average distance in this profile which is $d_{t\_mean}(X)$.

In (2),

$$d_{t\_mean}(X) = \frac{2 \times (0.5 + 1 + 0.75)}{3 \times (3 + 1)} = 0.375$$

Step 4: Calculating the minimum distance of this profile.

Table 2 2-Participant annotation results

Participants	CPU	Memory (GB)	Hard disk (GB)	Model
1	Intel i3	4	500	HP 4230s
2	Intel i5	8	500	HP 4230s

Table 3 Terms frequencies

Participants	Intel i3	Intel i5	4 GB	8 GB	500 GB	HP 4230s
1	1	0	1	0	1	1
2	0	1	0	1	1	1

Table 4 3-Participant annotation results

Participants	CPU	Memory (GB)	Hard disk (GB)	Model
1	Intel i3	4	500	HP 4230s
2	Intel i5	8	500	HP 4230s
3	Intel i5	6	750	HP 4530s

Table 5 4-Participant annotation results

Participants	CPU	Memory (GB)	Hard disk (GB)	Model
1	Intel i3	4	500	HP 4230s
2	Intel i5	8	500	HP 4230s
3	Intel i5	6	750	HP 4530s
4	Intel i5	8	750	HP 4530s

Table 6 5-Participant annotation results

Participants	CPU	Memory (GB)	Hard disk (GB)	Model
1	Intel i3	4	500	HP 4230s
2	Intel i5	8	500	HP 4230s
3	Intel i5	6	750	HP 4530s
4	Intel i5	8	750	HP 4530s
5	Intel i3	8	750	HP 4530s

In (3),

$$d_1(X) = 0.5$$
$$d_2(X) = 0.417$$
$$d_3(X) = 0.583$$

Then following (4), we have $d_{min}(X) = 0.417$.

Step 5: Calculating the quality of consensus if the inequality of susceptible to consensus occurs.

According to step 3 and 4, the result does not satisfy the inequality of susceptible to consensus as $d_{t\_mean}(X) < d_{min}(X)$ (due to 0375 < 0417).

Thus, we increase the number of participants to 4 and back to **step 1** again (see Table 5).

Step 2: Calculating all possible cosine distances between two different points (participants).

In (6),

$$d(P1, P2) = 0.5$$
$$d(P1, P3) = 1$$
$$d(P1, P4) = 1$$
$$d(P2, P3) = 0.75$$
$$d(P2, P4) = 0.5$$
$$d(P3, P4) = 0.25$$

Step 3: Calculating the total average distance in this profile which is $d_{t\_mean}(X)$.

In (2),

$$d_{t\_mean}(X) = 0.4.$$

Step 4: Calculating the minimum distance of this profile.

In (3),

$$d_1(X) = 0.625$$

$$d_2(X) = 0.4375$$
$$d_3(X) = 0.5$$
$$d_4(X) = 0.4375$$

Then following (4), we have $d_{min}(X) = 0.4375$.

Step 5: Calculating the quality of consensus if the inequality of susceptible to consensus occurs.

To be consistent with steps 3 and 4, the result does not satisfy the inequality of susceptible to consensus (7) as $d_{t\_mean}(X) < d_{min}(X)$ (due to 04 < 04375).

As a result, we invite one more participant to annotate this laptop and back to **step 1** (see Table 6).

Step 2: Calculating all possible distances between two different points (participants).

In (6),

$$d(P1, P2) = 0.5$$
$$d(P1, P3) = 1$$
$$d(P1, P4) = 1$$
$$d(P1, P5) = 0.75$$
$$d(P2, P3) = 0.75$$
$$d(P2, P4) = 0.5$$
$$d(P2, P5) = 0.75$$
$$d(P3, P4) = 0.25$$
$$d(P3, P5) = 0.5$$
$$d(P4, P5) = 0.25$$

Step 3: Calculating the total average distance in this profile which is $d_{t\_mean}(X)$.

In (2),

$$d_{t\_mean}(X) = 0.417$$

Step 4: Calculating the minimum distance of this profile. In (3),

Table 7 The relation in Vietnamese WordNet

Property	Domain	Range	Target
hyponymOf	Synset	Synset	Nouns, Adjs
Entails	Synset	Synset	Verbs
similarTo	Synset	Synset	Adjectives
memberMeronymOf	Synset	Synset	Nouns
substanceMeronymOf	Synset	Synset	Nouns
partMeronymOf	Synset	Synset	Nouns
classifiedByTopic	Synset	Synset	Nouns, Adjs, Verbs
classifiedByUsage	Synset	Synset	Nouns, Adjs, Verbs
classifiedByRegion	Synset	Synset	Nouns, Adjectives, Verbs
causes	Synset	Synset	Verbs
sameVerbGroupAs	Synset	Synset	Verbs
attribute	Synset	Synset	Nouns to Adjectives
derivationallyRelated	WordSense	WordSense	Nouns, Verbs, Adjectives, Adverbs
antonymOf	WordSense	WordSense	Nouns, Verbs, Adjectives, Adverbs
seeAlso	WordSense	WordSense	Verbs, Adjectives
participleOf	WordSense	WordSense	Adjectives to Verbs
adjectivePertainsTo	Synset	Synset	Adjectives to Nouns or Adjectives
adverbPertainsTo	Synset	Synset	Adverbs to Adjectives
gloss	WordSense	xsd: string	Synset and Sentence
frame	Verb-WordSense	xsd: string	Synset and a verb construction pattern
partOf	Synset	Synset	Nouns
originalSenseOf	Synset	Synset	Nouns, Verbs
vietEng	Synset	Synset	Nouns, Verbs, Adverbs, Adjectives

$d_1 (X) = 0.65$

$d_2 (X) = 0.5$

$d_3 (X) = 0.5$

$d_4 (X) = 0.4$

$d_5 (X) = 0.5625$

Then following (4) we have $d_{\min} (X) = 0.4$.

Step 5: Calculating the quality of consensus if the inequality of susceptible to consensus occurs.

To be compatible with steps 3 and 4, the result satisfies the inequality of susceptible to consensus (7) as $d_{t\_\text{mean}} (X) > d_{\min} (X)$ (due to 0417 > 04).

Finally, this consensus is shared to everyone who has annotated the laptop. The quality of consensus of the first round is computed as below:

In (1),

$$\hat{d}(x, X) = 1 - \frac{d(x, X)}{card (x)}$$
$$= 1 - \frac{0.65 + 0.5 + 0.5 + 0.4 + 0.5625}{5}$$
$$= 0.4775.$$

4 Experiment

4.1 Vietnamese WordNet

Our proposed approach is assessed by applying for collaborative Vietnamese WordNet building. The structure and relations of Vietnamese WordNet (VW) are initially derived from the English WordNet [1]. VW classifies most of words in Vietnamese language into four main types including Noun–Verb–Adjective and Adverb. These words are put into different type of synsets which stands for synonym sets and interconnected by a number of various relationships. Regarding the structure, VW has three main classes consisting of *Synset*, *Word* and *WordSense*. *Synset* and *WordSense* have subclasses based on the distinction of lexical groups. *Synset* has four subclasses containing *NounSynset*, *VerbSynset*, *AdjectiveSynset*, and *AdverbSynsey*. *WordSense* has four subclasses including *NounWordSense*, *VerbWordSense*, *AdjectiveWordSense*, and *AdverbWordSense*. *Word* has a subclass *Collocation* which is used to store words or phrases in Vietnamese. The class hierarchy of VW is inherited from WordNet [4] and the properties and its significance are shown in Table 7.

Fig. 2 Sample XML dictionary data

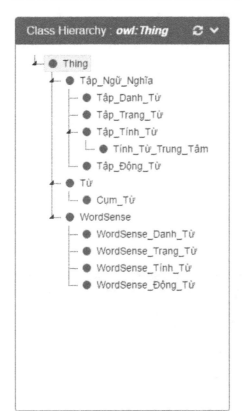

```
<?xml version="1.0"encoding="UTF-8"
standalone="yes"?>
    <dictionary>
        <word>
            <name>a</name>
            <type>dt.</type>
            <definition>Từ thứ nhất trong bản chữ cái.
một nguyên âm: A hoa. a thường.</definition>
        </word>
    </dictionary>
```

Fig. 3 The Vietnamese WordNet's class hierarchy

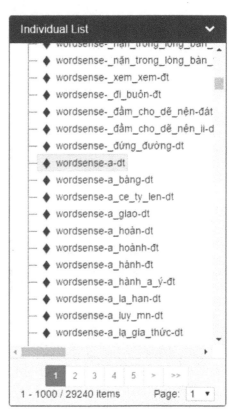

4.2 Demonstration

Creating Vietnamese WordNet Ontology.

To initialize the first version of VW, there are three steps that need to be done as follows:

Step 1—Extracting raw data and converting it to semi-structure data.

We used **Từ Điển Tiếng Việt**, which is according to Vietnamese–Vietnamese dictionary, and extracted all of the words inside the dictionary to an XML formatted file. Basically, there are three details of a word which are extracted such as name, type and definition. The format of this XML looks like the following (see Fig. 2):

Step 2—Cleansing the extracted data.

A cleansing process is performed before adding all of the words in XML file to the ontology as it is not always certain that the extracted data are correct. To be more detailed, sometimes a word name could not be retrieved accurately and a blank or a symbol is returned instead. Therefore, these incorrect words are removed or ignored

Step 3—Matching words with ontology classes and adding them to VW.

This step is to define which types of words match with the classes in Vietnamese Ontology. In the initializing version, the VW is built in a simple way where we only select 4 types of word to be added up to its respective classes: '*Danh từ*' (Noun) will be individualized in '*WordSense_Danh_Từ*', '*Động từ*' (Verb) will be individualized in '*WordSense_Động_Từ*', '*Trạng từ*' (Adverb) will

Fig. 4 Original version of a word

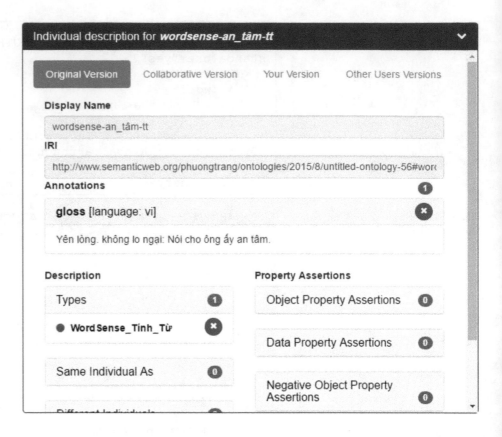

Fig. 5 User version of a word

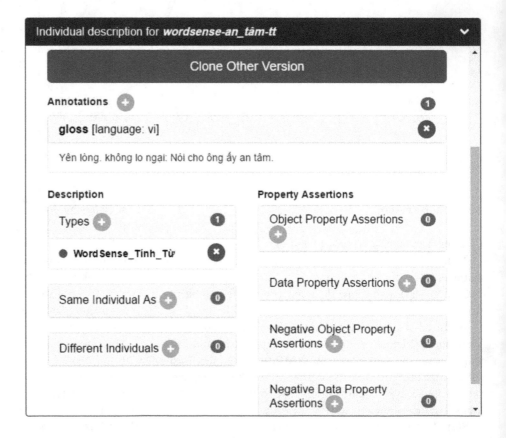

Fig. 6 'Clone' feature options

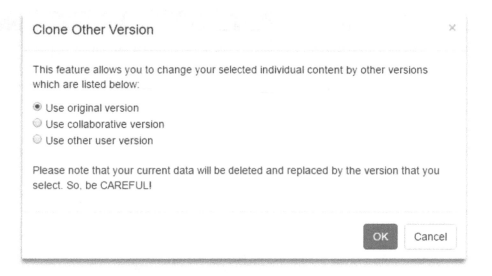

Fig. 7 An example of 'Other User Versions' feature/tab (1)

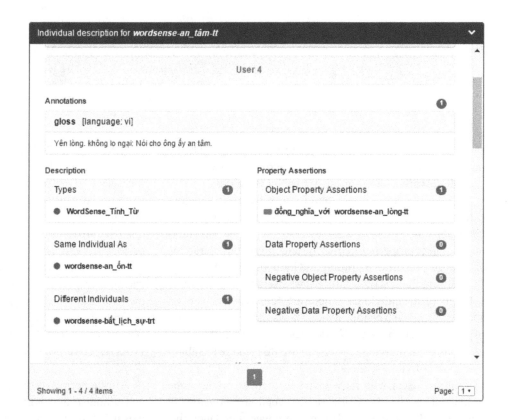

be individualized in '*WordSense_Trạng_Từ*',, and '*Tính từ*' (Adjective) will be individualized in '*WordSense_Tính_Từ*'. Other types of word will be individualized in 'OWL:Thing', which includes cảm từ, số từ, giới từ, đại từ, thán từ. After that the XML file is parsed and the result is added to the Vietnamese WordNet.

The final result—the first Vietnamese Ontology

Finally, the Vietnamese Wordnet Ontology is initialized with 29240 individuals, which '*WordSense_Danh_Từ*' class has 12679 individuals, '*WordSense_Trạng_Từ*' class has 2863 individuals, '*WordSense_Tính_Từ*' class has 4030 individuals, and '*WordSense_Động_Từ*' class has 0 individuals. Other individuals are not classified and by default, they are individuals of 'OWL:Thing' class. Fig. 3 illustrates the initialized version of VW.

However, this version of VW only contains words along with their definitions and there is no connection/or relation-

Fig. 8 An example of 'Other
User Versions' feature/tab (2)

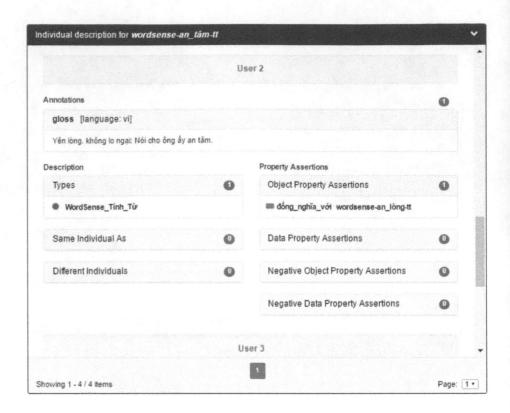

ship between words. As a result, to completely build the
ontology, lots of collaborative work need to be done.

Collaborative Vietnamese WordNet Building

To improve this VW, we build a web-based application,
called Ontology Wiki (OntWiki), to upload and display all
details of VW, by which users are able to view the class hierarchy, object properties hierarchy, data properties hierarchy,
annotation properties hierarchy and individual listed by class.
In addition, the OntWiki also allows users to view multiple
versions of an individual. There are four types of version
such as 'Original Version' which shows the original version
of an individual in the OWL file. 'User Version' is the user's
opinions of an individual, user can use this feature to submit
their point of view. 'Others Users Versions' are the versions
of multiple users who have given their ideas on the same
individual, and finally, 'Collaborative Version' automatically
integrates all versions of all users to create a collaborative
version, which makes use of our proposed collaborative algorithm using consensus quality. In this experiment, we select
500 individuals of '*WordSense_Tính_Từ*' and share them
with thirty participants (collaborative group).

First of all, an administrator of OntWiki created thirty
accounts and gave to this collaborative group. The administrator is the only one who is able to modify the structure of
VW, as well as the original version of individuals (see Fig. 4).
Normal users can only perform personal idea submissions of
individuals, which they can only modify their versions, but
not original version and other users' versions.

Next, to use OntWiki, participants need to login, then
select VW, which is already uploaded by an administrator, select '*WordSense_Tính_Từ*' class in individual page,
and choose a provided list of individuals and start working on it. To ease up the initialization stage of user version,
OntWiki provides a 'clone' feature that allows users to reuse
or copy the original version, collaborative version, or other
user version to their own (see Figs. 5, 6). There are eight
characteristics of an individual that user can modify in their
own version, which includes 'Annotations', 'Types', 'Same
Individual As', 'Different Individuals', 'Object Property
Assertions', 'Data Property Assertions', 'Negative Object
Property Assertions' and 'Negative Data Property Assertions'.

After a period of time, the final results will be collected
and administrators will start to upgrade all of shared individuals using the collaborative versions. By this way, the results
are always transparent between users (see Figs. 7, 8); therefore, the effectiveness goes up very much, time consuming is
reduced due to no meeting conduction, and the effort given
is not high and also has high-quality output.

5 Conclusion

In this work, an effective methodology for collaborative
ontology building is improved from [3,7,8] using quality of
consensus [9] to reach consensus among participants in col-

laborative group. A susceptible to consensus is to answer that when we can have a consensus and the quality of consensus is to determine if the final version of the collaborative ontology has been reached or not. We applied the proposed method for Vietnamese WordNet building. In future work, we will combine trust-based consensus [4] and quality of consensus to solve leading problem in collaboration.

Acknowledgements This research is funded by International University, Vietnam National University, Ho Chi Minh City under grant number T2016-01-IT/HD-DHQT-QLKH.

References

1. Assem, M.V., Gangemi, A., Schreiber, G.: RDF/OWL representation of WordNet. http://www.w3org/TR/wordnet-rdf/

2. Auer, S., Dietzold, S., Riechert, T.: OntoWikia tool for social semantic collaboration. In: The 5th International Semantic Web Conference, pp. 736–749. Springer, ISWC Athens GA (2006)

3. Duong, T.H., Jo, G.S.: Collaborative ontology building by reaching consensus among participants. Int. J. Inf. **13**(5), 1557–1569 (2010)

4. Duong, T.H., Nguyen, N.T., Nguyen, D.C., Nguyen, T.P.T., Selamat, A.: Trust-based consensus for collaborative ontology building. Cybern. Syst. **45**(2), 146–164 (2014)

5. Gabel, T., Sure, Y., Voelker, J.: KAON – ontology management infrastructure. D3.1.1.a, SEKT Project: Semantically Enabled Knowledge Technologies (2004)

6. Gallagher, M., Hares, T., Spencer, J., Bradshaw, C., Webb, I.: The nominal group technique: a research tool for general practice? Fam. Pract. **10**, 76–81 (1993)

7. Holsapple, C.W., Joshi, K.D.: Collaborative approach in ontology design. Commun. ACM **45**, 42–47 (2002)

8. Karapiperis, S.: Consensus building in collaborative ontology engineering processes. J. Univ. Knowl. Manag. **1**, 199–216 (2006)

9. Nguyen, N.T.: Advanced Methods for Inconsistent Knowledge Management. Springer, London (2008)

10. Nguyen, Q.U., Duong, T.H., Kang, S.: Solving conflict on collaborative knowledge via social networking using consensus choice. In: Proceedings of the 4th International Conference on Computational Collective Intelligence: Technologies and Applications, Vol. Part I, pp. 21–30 (2012)

11. Noy, N., McGuiness, D.L.: Ontology development a guide to creating your first ontology. KSL Technical Report KSL-01-05 (2001)

12. Pill, J.: The Delphi method: substance context a critique and an annotated bibliography. Soc. Econ. Plan. Sci. **5**, 57–71 (1971)

13. Ruiz, E.J., Grau, B.C., Horrocks, I., Berlanga, R.: Building ontologies collaboratively using contentCVS. In: Proceedings of the 22nd International Workshop on Description Logics (2009)

14. Ruiz, E.J., Grau, B.C., Horrocks, I., Berlanga, R.: Conflict detection and resolution in collaborative ontology development technical report (2009) Tool and user study available at http://www.kronoactujies/people/Ernsto/contentcvs

15. Sure Y.: OntoEdit: collaborative ontology development for the semantic web. In: International Semantic Web Conference 2002 (ISWC 2002) Sardinia Italia, pp. 221–235 (2002)

16. Tudorache, T., Noy, N.F., Tu, S.W., Musen, M.A.: Supporting collaborative ontology development in Protg. In: Proceedings of 7th International Semantic Web Conference Karlsruhe, pp. 17–32. Springer, Germany (2008)

## 13

Grey clustering in online social networks

Camelia Delcea[1] (ID) · **Ioana-Alexandra Bradea**[1]

Abstract Today's leading businesses have understood the role of "social" in their everyday activity. Online social networks (OSN) and social media have melt and become an essential part of every firm's concern. Brand advocates are the new leading triggers for company's success in online social networks and are responsible for the long-term engagement between a firm and its customers. But what can it be said about this impressive crowd of customers that are gravitating around a certain brand advocacy or a certain community? Are they as responsive to a certain message as one might think? Are they really impressed by the advertising campaigns? Are they equally reacting to a certain comment or news? How they process the everyday grey knowledge that is circulating in OSN? In fact, how impressionable they are and which are the best ways a company can get to them? To give an answer to these questions, the present paper uses grey systems theory for spreading the customer's crowd into groups based on how impressionable they are by commercials, ads, videos and comments in OSN.

Keywords OSN · Grey knowledge · Grey clustering analysis · Strategies in OSN

1 Introduction

A short and easy-to-understand definition of online social networks (OSN) is that they "form online communities among people with common interest, activities, backgrounds, and/or friendships. Most OSN are web based and allow users to upload profiles (text, images, and videos) and interact with others in numerous ways" [1]. As structure, the OSN are usually perceived as a set of nodes—represented by its users, and a set of directed (e.g., "following" activity on Facebook) or undirected (e.g., friendship relationships) edges connecting the various pairs of nodes [2].

Apart from the research and development role played by the OSN mostly through the usage of the customers' feedback to improve and solve problems or even to create and diversify different categories of products/services, the word-of-mouth marketing and targeted advertising are also some of the benefits brought by these networks. In a recent paper about social intelligence and customer experience, Synthesio [3] votes for learning who your customers really are to address them a proper campaign. In addition, by identifying the "army" of product advocates among different communities and getting them closer to a specific brand will give that firm a tremendous opportunity to gain more customers and to extend a real relationship on an individual basis [3].

But before this, it still remains unsolved the question of identifying those particular advocates among the "big crowd" of customers on the OSN. For this, in the following, we are going to use some elements extracted form grey systems theory for spreading the customer's crowd into groups based on how impressionable they are by commercials, ads, videos and comments in OSN.

✉ Camelia Delcea
camelia.delcea@csie.ase.ro

Ioana-Alexandra Bradea
alexbradea1304@yahoo.com

[1] Bucharest University of Economic Studies, Bucharest, Romania

2 An overview of online social networks

The online social networks (OSN) began to capture the attention of more and more scientists with the rise of Web 2.0. After that moment, the virtual world had developed and

Fig. 1 Paper published per year

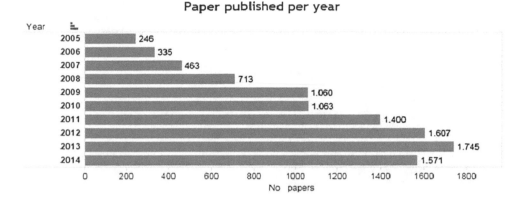

people all over the world began to connect with others, exchanging information. The social networks represent complex networks that contain a lot of people with a specific type of connection or interdependencies between them (friendship, business relations, community, etc.). The study of OSN requires a variety of techniques and methods which can be used to understand and predict the behavior of the components.

The studies in this field treated many research areas such as social issues, e-learning, marketing, communication and reporting, economics and health issues [4–7]. The main social issues that were addressed by the scientific world were aspects regarding confidentiality and privacy [8,9], age gap [10], sentiment analysis [11,12], social activity [13,14], addiction [15] and social assets [16]. The impact of word-of-mouth communication was studied by Brown [17] and the viral marketing by Subramani and Rajagopalan [18]. Economic aspects in OSN were concerning the performance and risks within companies [19], consumers' decisions [20], e-commerce and online public goods [21]. The interest in health issues generated analysis regarding medical professionalism [22,23], patients' communication and patient–doctor relationship in OSN [24].

In 2015, there were recorded 64,672 scientific papers that analyzed the social network area, from which 2687 focused mainly on the study of OSN. The figure below illustrates the evolution of the number of scientific papers published by year. It can be seen that lately, the number of papers have increased, most of them being published in 2013 (Fig. 1).

Most of the papers published in the field of OSN were included in the following areas of interest: computer science, engineering, psychology, business economics, sociology, telecommunications, public environment, education research and information science (see Fig. 2).

Regarding the document type, most of the papers (7050) were articles, followed by proceedings papers (3721), book reviews (728), meeting abstracts (689), editorial materials (370), reviews (217), letters (66), news items (54), corrections (49) and notes (41)—see Fig. 3.

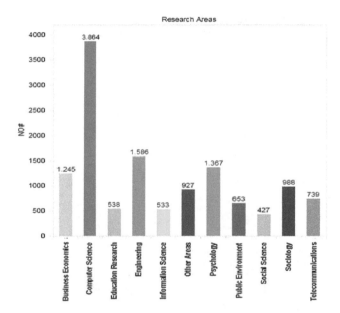

Fig. 2 Research areas for the papers published in OSN field

Most of the papers were from USA (5083), followed by China (1184), England (980), Canada (606), Germany (472), Spain (458), Australia (457), Italy (338), Netherlands (320) and South Korea (304). This geographical distribution is presented in Fig. 4.

Correlated with the geographic distribution of articles published in the field of OSN, most of them were written in English, followed by Spanish, German and French—Fig. 5.

These numerous scientific papers published in this area of interest illustrated the fact that the OSN domain is a continuously growing area, with many aspects that can be analyzed.

3 Grey knowledge

Grey systems theory is one of the newest theories in the field of artificial intelligence and starts from a definition stipulated in the control theory in which an object was considered black when nobody knows anything about its inner structure and

Paper types

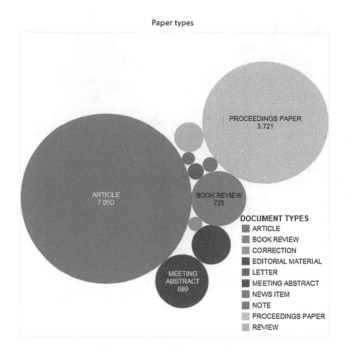

Fig. 3 Document types of OSN papers

Record count for each country

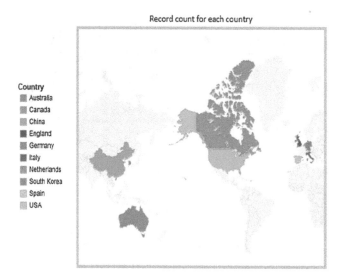

Fig. 4 Record count of papers—a global view

white when this structure was completely known. Therefore, a grey object is that particular entity whose structure is just partially known [25].

By developing its own methods and techniques, the grey systems theory succeeds to extract and bring some new knowledge about a specific object, process or phenomenon. Along with the grey relational analysis, one of the most known and used methods from the grey systems theory, the grey clustering, is also one of the techniques that is bringing some new knowledge regarding a specific community.

In OSN more than in other type of communities and networks, grey systems theory finds its applicability due to the nature of the relationships between its main actors. Forrest

LANGUAGE		
CHINESE	.	31
ENGLISH		12.146
FRENCH	.	72
GERMAN	.	145
ITALIAN	.	9
JAPANESE	.	12
NORWEGIAN	.	9
PORTUGUESE	.	66
RUSSIAN	.	11
SPANISH	.	150

Fig. 5 The language of the papers published on OSN

[26] identifies two main types of relationships in a system: the generative and the non-generative ones. While the generative relationships are due to the interactions among different elements of a system, the non-generative are represented by the inner characteristics of these elements [27,28].

Even though most researches focus mainly on one or another type of these relationships, some advances have been made recently to include both of these aspects, as they are giving more substance about what is really happening at each network's level [26].

Due to these different approaches related to a system, the amount of knowledge extracted is limited and can be easily regarded as grey [29]. Even more, by adding the human component, through the consumers' demands and needs, strictly related to preferences, self-awareness, self-conscience, free-will, etc., the study of the knowledge that can be extracted through OSN is becoming more complicated.

For this, a new type of knowledge can be identified, the grey knowledge, which is lying between the two well-known types of knowledge: the tacit and the explicit one and is continually circulating and transforming within the network. It can be encountered in the internalized and externalized feedback loops that are formed between different network users and it accompanies the external (chatting, e-mails sending, etc.) and internal (listening, watching a commercial, reading a comment, evaluation, observing, etc.) processes. Considering the everyday activities, is can easily be seen that the grey knowledge is the most predominant type of knowledge that can be encountered and, therefore, the study of it can reveal new information that can be used in understanding the OSN's complexity.

4 Grey clustering analysis

Assume that there are n objects to be clustered according to m cluster criteria into s different grey classes [26,30,31] A function noted $f_j^k (\cdot)$ is called the "whitenization" weight function of the kth subclass of the j criterion, with: $i = 1, 2, \ldots, n; j = 1, 2, \ldots, m; 1 \leq k \leq s$ [26]. Consider a typical whitenization function as described by [25,30,31] with four turning points noted as: $x_j^k(1), x_j^k(2), x_j^k(3)$ and $x_j^k(4)$:

$$f_j^k(x) = \begin{cases} 0, & x \notin [x_j^k(1), x_j^k(4)] \\ \frac{x - x_j^k(1)}{x_j^k(2) - x_j^k(1)}, & x \in [x_j^k(1), x_j^k(2)] \\ 1, & x \in [x_j^k(2), x_j^k(3)] \\ \frac{x_j^k(4) - x}{x_j^k(4) - x_j^k(3)}, & x \in [x_j^k(3), x_j^k(4)] \end{cases} \tag{1}$$

or the whitenization weight function of lower measure (a particular case of the typical whitenization function presented above, where the first and the second turning points $x_j^k(1), x_j^k(2)$ are missing):

$$f_j^k(x) = \begin{cases} 0, & x \notin [0, x_j^k(4)] \\ 1, & x \in [0, x_j^k(3)] \\ \frac{x_j^k(4) - x}{x_j^k(4) - x_j^k(3)}, & x \in [x_j^k(3), x_j^k(4)] \end{cases} \tag{2}$$

or the whitenization function of moderate measure (also a particular form of the whitenization function, where the second and the third turning points $x_j^k(2), x_j^k(3)$ coincide):

$$f_j^k(x) = \begin{cases} 0, & x \notin [x_j^k(1), x_j^k(4)] \\ \frac{x - x_j^k(1)}{x_j^k(2) - x_j^k(1)}, & x \in [x_j^k(1), x_j^k(2)] \\ 1, & x = x_j^k(2) \\ \frac{x_j^k(4) - x}{x_j^k(4) - x_j^k(2)}, & x \in [x_j^k(2), x_j^k(4)] \end{cases} \tag{3}$$

or the whitenization weight function of upper measure (another particular form of the whitenization function where the final third and fourth points $x_j^k(3), x_j^k(4)$ are missing):

$$f_j^k(x) = \begin{cases} 0, & x < x_j^k(1) \\ \frac{x - x_j^k(1)}{x_j^k(2) - x_j^k(1)}, & x \in [x_j^k(1), x_j^k(2)] \\ 1, & x \geq x_j^k(2) \end{cases} \tag{4}$$

The grey clustering analysis can be performed by following the below steps: [25,32–34]

Step 1: Determining the form of the whitenization function $f_j^k(\cdot)$, for $j = 1, 2, \ldots, m; 1 \leq k \leq s$.
Step 2: Attributing a cluster weight η_j to each criterion based on external information such as prior experience or qualitative analysis, with $j = 1, 2, \ldots, m$.

Step 3: Calculating all fixed weight cluster coefficients from the whitenization function $f_j^k(\cdot)$ determined at step 1, cluster weights η_j at step 2 and observational values x_{ij} of the object i for the j criterion, with $= 1, 2, \ldots, n; j = 1, 2, \ldots, m; 1 \leq k \leq s$:

$$\sigma_i^k = \sum_{j=1}^{m} f_j^k(x_{ij}) * \eta_j \tag{5}$$

Step 4: If $\sigma_i^{*k} = \max_{1 \leq k \leq s}\{\sigma_i^k\}$, then the object i is belonging to the k^*th grey class.

Let us perform the grey clustering analysis in the case study on the OSN users to determine which of them are being impressed by the marketing campaigns, comments, articles, videos, etc., in the online environment and what conclusions can be drawn from studying their personal and cluster characteristics.

5 Case study on OSN users

For conducting the cluster analysis, a questionnaire was applied to the online social networks' users, 211 persons answering to all the addressed questions. Having the answers, a confirmatory factor analysis was accomplished to validate the construct, validity and reliability of the questionnaire. After proceeding this, the selected factors were passed through the grey clustering method, obtaining three relevant used categories as it will be shown in the following sections.

5.1 Questionnaire and data

The 211 questionnaire's respondents can be divided into five age categories: 104 between 18–25 years old, 76 between 26–35 years old, 20 between 36–45 years old, 7 between 46–55 years old and 4 between 56–65 years old; 61.61 % of them being female and 38.39 % male. Along with the questions regarding the personal characteristics, the respondents were asked to answer the following questions, evaluated through a Likert scale taking values between 1 and 5:

- When I want to buy a product: (DM_1)
  - I buy it immediately without hesitation;
  - I am thinking a while on this opportunity and in a couple of days I decide whether to buy it or not;
  - I am asking for my close friends' advice;
  - I am asking for my friends and family's advice;
  - I am asking for advice from friends and family, I am searching other buyers' comments on internet and on social websites.

- In general: (DM_2)

  - I make my own decision and I stick to it no matter what happens;
  - I make a set of possible decisions, I analyze them a couple of days and after that I take my decision;
  - I have a set of possible decisions and for validation, sometimes, I ask someone else's opinion;
  - I discuss the possible decisions set with close friends/ co-workers/ family;
  - I always discuss the decisions with other people, read news and comments.

- When I cannot identify the product I am looking for: (PL_1)

  - I buy another product from the same producer, but from a different assortment;
  - I am looking for another store where I can buy my product;
  - I buy another product from a similar producer;
  - I am looking for new information that can help me in finding what I need;
  - I cannot evaluate this situation;

- When choosing a particular product/service, I am taking into consideration the following aspects: (please select among: strongly disagree; disagree; undecided; agree; strongly agree)

  - The product and availability term: (P_1);
  - Product's inner characteristics: (P_2);
  - Package characteristics: (P_3);
  - Brand awareness: (P_4);
  - Information received recently about that product: (P_5).

- Which of the following actions have you made on friends' recommendation: (please select the appropriate answer among: never, sometimes, often, usually, always):

  - I have watched a commercial: (INT_1);
  - I have looked for a product promotion campaign: (INT_2);
  - I have informed about an event of a certain company: (INT_3);
  - I have participated on a contest organized by a firm: (INT_4);
  - I have followed that company's activity on social media: (INT_5).

These questions have been divided into three categories, as it can also be observed from the labels attached to them: Decision making and product placement (DM), Product (P) and Interaction with friends on social networks (INT).

5.2 Model fit through a confirmatory factor analysis

Having the answers to the questionnaire above, a confirmatory factor analysis was conducted to validate its main constructions.

The starting construction contained 13 latent factors (Fig. 6a), but due to the poor values obtained for main confirmatory factor analysis's indices such as CMIN/*DF* of 4.612, GFI of 0.836, AGFI of 0.760, CFI of 0.778, NFI of 0.737, RFI of 0.670, IFI of 0.782, RMSEA of 0.131, etc., the construction has been structured as in Fig. 6, holding in analysis just 10 latent factors. For the new latent construct (Fig. 6b), the received results for the mentioned parameters were better than in first case, but still low: CMIN/*DF* dropped to 1.713, GFI of 0.953, AGFI of 0.917, CFI of 0.964, NFI of 0.920, RFI of 0.884, IFI of 0.965, RMSEA of 0.058. Therefore, a new cut in the considered variables was needed.

The P_2 variable has been eliminated due to the low loadings values (see Fig. 7c). As a result, the values of the indicators have received better values: CMIN/*DF* of 1.678, GFI of 0.960, AGFI of 0.926, CFI of 0.970, NFI of 0.930, RFI of 0.895, IFI of 0.970, RMSEA of 0.057.

As improvements still can be made here, the P_3 variable was eliminated (Fig. 8d) conducting to the indicators' values presented and analyzed in the tables (see Tables 1, 2, 3, 4).

Goodness of fit (GOF)

The goodness of fit indicates how well the specified model reproduces the covariance matrix among the indicator variables, establishing whether there is similarity between the observed and estimated covariance matrices.

One of the first measures of GOF is Chi-square statistic through which the null hypothesis is tested so that no difference is between the two covariance matrices, with an acceptance value for the null hypothesis of >0.050. As Table 1 indicates, this value is exceeded. The improved model has a CMIN/*DF* of 1.483 less than the threshold value 2.000 (Table 2).

Moreover, the values of GFI and AGFI are above the limit of 0.900, recording a 0.972, respectively, a 0.940 value, while CFI is exceeding 0.900 (being 0.983—see Table 3) the imposed value for a model of such complexity and sample size. As for the other three incremental fit indices, namely NFI, RFI and IFI, the obtained values are above the threshold value 0.900 for NFI and closely to 1.000 for RFI and IFI.

As Table 4 shows, the root mean squared error approximation (RMSEA) has a value below 0.100 for the default model, showing that there is a little degree to which the lack of fit is due to misspecification of the model tested versus being due to sampling error. The 90 % confidence interval for the RMSEA is between LO90 of 0.000 and HI90 of 0.085, the upper bound being close to 0.080, indicating a good model fit.

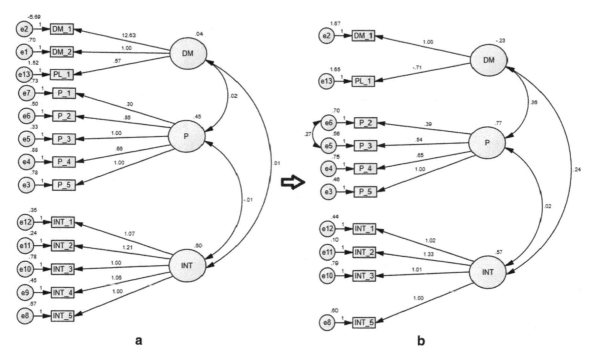

Fig. 6 Latent construct and the measured variables (**a**, **b**)

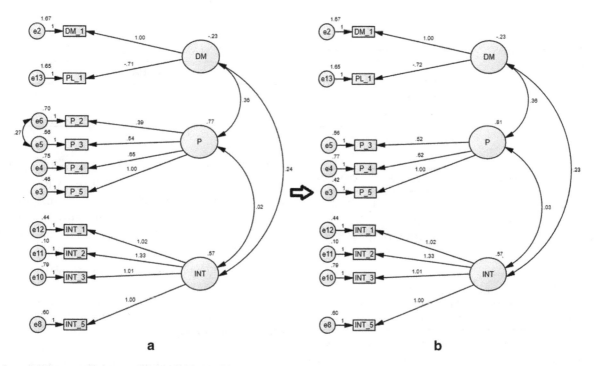

Fig. 7 Latent construct and the measured variables (**a**, **b**)

Validity and reliability

For testing the construct's validity and reliability, first of all, the standardized loadings should be analyzed and should be higher than 0.500, ideally 0.700 or higher. In this case, these values are between 0.634 and 0.953, confirming the validity.

The convergent validity is given by two additional measures: the average variance extracted (AVE) and construct reliability (CR). As these two measures are not computed by AMOS 22, they have been determined using the equations presented in the literature [35].

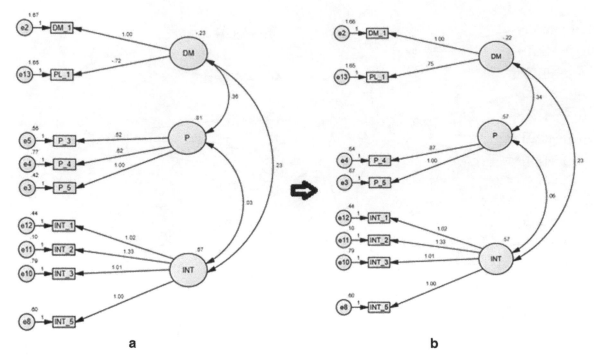

Fig. 8 Latent construct and the measured variables (**a, b**)

Table 1 Result table (AMOS 22 Output)

Minimum was achieved
Chi square = 25.212
Degrees of freedom = 17
Probability level = 0.090

Table 2 CMIN (AMOS 22 Output)

Model	NPAR	CMIN	DF	P	CMIN/DF
Default model	19	25.212	17	0.090	1.483
Saturated model	36	0.000	0		
Independence model	8	514.628	28	0.000	18.380

Table 3 Baseline comparisons (AMOS 22 Output)

Model	NFI Delta1	RFI rho1	IFI Delta2	TLI rho2	CFI
Default model	0.951	0.919	0.983	0.972	0.983
Saturated model	1.000		1.000		1.000
Independence model	0.000	0.000	0.000	0.000	0.000

Table 4 RMSEA (AMOS 22 Output)

Model	RMSEA	LO 90	HI 90	PCLOSE
Default model	0.048	0.000	0.085	0.494
Independence model	0.288	0.266	0.310	0.000

The following values have been obtained for *P*, DM and INT—AVE: 0.431, 0.527 and 0.600, and CR: 0.714, 0.793 and 0.909. An AVE of 0.500 indicates an adequate convergent validity, while a CR of 0.700 or above suggests a good reliability. Having the obtained values, it can be concluded that the overall construct validity and reliability is good and that the considered measures are consistently representing the reality.

5.3 Grey clustering

Using the GSTM 6.0 software, the grey cluster analysis was performed and the results are shown in the following:

```
*****************************Start*********************************
```

(1) Compute coefficients of clustering

(2) Comparison clustering coefficients, and determine the object belongs to which grey class

Objects of belonging to the grey class [1-th]: 2, 3, 7, 8, 9, 10, 12, 13, 26, 34, 38, 39, 42, 44, 45, 46, 47, 54, 55, 56, 57, 60, 73, 75, 78, 79, 80, 81, 88, 96, 97, 100, 101, 102, 103, 104, 107, 119, 122, 123, 124, 128, 129, 137, 141, 142, 143, 145, 146, 156, 159, 160, 161, 173, 174, 179, 180, 181, 188, 190, 191, 198, 199, 204,

Objects of belonging to the grey class [2-th]: 5, 23, 24, 27, 28, 29, 30, 52, 66, 69, 70, 82, 83, 91, 92, 93, 110, 113, 114, 132, 135, 136, 144, 151, 154, 163, 164, 165, 166, 171, 186, 193, 201, 202, 206, 207, 209,

Objects of belonging to the grey class [3-th]: 1, 4, 6, 11, 14, 15, 16, 17, 18, 19, 20, 21, 22, 25, 31, 32, 33, 35, 36, 37, 40, 41, 43, 48, 49, 50, 51, 53, 58, 59, 61, 62, 63, 64, 65, 67, 68, 71, 72, 74, 76, 77, 84, 85, 86, 87, 89, 90, 94, 95, 98, 99, 105, 106, 108, 109, 111, 112, 115, 116, 117, 118, 120, 121, 125, 126, 127, 130, 131, 133, 134, 138, 139, 140, 147, 148, 149, 150, 152, 153, 155, 157, 158, 162, 167, 168, 169, 170, 172, 175, 176, 177, 178, 182, 183, 184, 185, 186, 187, 189, 192, 194, 195, 196, 197, 200, 203, 205, 208, 210, 211,

```
****************************End*********************************
```

Based on the answers received, it can be concluded that the second grey cluster is formed mostly by impressionable persons who are positively reacting to promotion campaigns in an online environment and which are taking into account other's opinions when making a decision.

Considering the members of the second grey cluster, it has been established that they have an average age of 24.1 years, their majority being formed by women, with an average number of friends on OSN of 516, who are accessing the OSN more than once a day. In addition, persons in this category are spending more than four hours per day in online social networks and actively participating in forms and discussions in the online environment.

Having this information about the most impressionable members in OSN, the companies can adapt their strategies to deliver the new pieces of information directly to these users [36]. From here, specific analysis can be done for each new user to determine which group he belongs to.

In addition, another further research direction can be the identification of the most important nodes among the ones that can easily be impressed using a grey approach similar to the one proposed by Wu et al. [37]. In this way, by knowing both the nodes that are easily to be impressed and the ones that have great influence in each network, the companies' strategies can be adapted to better target the OSN audience. Additionally, a storage service [38] can be used to ease the access to such a great amount of stored data.

6 Conclusions

OSN are becoming more and more a reality nowadays. In this context, companies have adapted their strategies to meet the target audience. This paper presents a method for selecting the most impressionable members of a network. For this, a questionnaire has been deployed, applied and validated for better extracting the most impressionable members. Grey clustering was used as the information flowing within the feedback loops in OSN is a grey one.

As further research, a grey relational analysis will be used for identifying the most important and influential node among the most impressionable nodes within an OSN. Having this information, each company can adapt or create a specific strategy that will target this person to increase and strengthen competitive position on the market.

References

1. Schneider, F., Feldmann, A., Krishnamurthy, B., Willinger, W.: Understanding online social network usage from a network perspective. In: Proceedings of the ACM SIGCOMM Conference on Internet Measurement, pp. 35-48 (2009)

2. Heidemann, J., Klier, M., Probst, F.: Online social networks: a survey of a global phenomenon. Comput. Netw. **56**, 3866–3878 (2012)

3. Synthesio: Drive Customer Experience with Social Intelligence (e-book). http://synthesio.com/corporate/en/2014/uncategorized/drive-customer-experience-social-intelligence-ebook/ (2014)

4. Greenhow, C., Robelia, B.: Informal learning and identity information in online social networks. Learn. Media Technol. **34**(2), 119–140 (2009)

5. Delcea, C., Cotfas, L.-A., Paun, R.: Understanding Online Social Networks' Users a Twitter Approach. Computational Collective Intelligence. Technologies and Applications, pp. 145–153. Springer (2014)

6. Yu, A.Y., Tian, S.W., Vodel, D.: Can learning be virtually boosted? An investigation of online social networking impacts. Comput. Educ. **55**(4), 1494–1503 (2010)

7. Delcea, C., Bradea, I., Paun, R., Friptu, A.: A healthcare companies' performance through OSN. New Trends in Intelligent Information and Database Systems, pp. 333–342. Springer (2015)

8. Lewis, K., Kaufma, J., Christakis, N.: The taste for privacy: an analysis of college student privacy settings in an online social network. J. Comput. Med. Commun. **14**, 143–151 (2008)

9. Nosko, A., Wood, E., Seija, M.: Allaboutme: Disclosure in online social networking profiles: the case of Facebook. Comput. Hum. Behav. **26**(3), 406–418 (2010)

10. Pfeil, U., Arjan, R., Zaphiris, P.: Age differences in online social networking—a study of used profiles and the social capital divide among teenagers and older users in My Space. Comput. Hum. Behav. **25**(3), 643–654 (2009)

11. Cotfas, L.A., Delcea, C., Roxin, I., Paun, R.: Twitter ontology-driven sentiment analysis. New Trends in Intelligent Information and Database Systems, pp. 131–139. Springer (2015)

12. Cotfas, L.A., Delcea, C., Segault, A., Roxin, I.: Sentiment Web-Based Social Media Analysis. Transactions on Computational Collective Intelligence XXII, pp. 147–166. Springer (2016)

13. Cheung, C.M.K., Chiu, P.Y., Lee, M.K.O.: Online social networks: Why do students use Facebook? Comput. Hum. Behav. **27**(4), 1337–1343 (2011)

14. Cheung, C.M.K., Lee, M.K.O.: A theoretical model of intentional social action in online social networks. Decis. Support Syst. **49**(1), 24–30 (2010)

15. Benevenuto, F., Rodrigues, T., Meeyoung, C.: Characterizing User Behavior in Online Social Networks. In: Proceeding of the 9th ACM SIGCOMM Internet Measurement Conference, pp. 49–62 (2009)

16. Ellison, N.B., Steinfield, C., Lampe, C.: The benefits of Facebook, friends": social capital and college students' use of online social networks sites. J. Comput. Med. Commun. **12**(4), 23–41 (2007)

17. Brown, J., Broderick, A., Lee, N.: Word of mouth communication within online communities: conceptualing the online social network. J. Interact. Mark. **21**(3), 2–20 (2007)

18. Subrahmanyam, K., Reich, S.M., Waechter, N., Espinoza, G.: Online and offline social networks: use of social networking sites by emerging adults. J. Appl. Dev. Psychol. **29**(6), 420–433 (2008)

19. Schniederjans, D., Cao, E., Schniederjans, M.: Enhancing financial performance with social media: an impression management perspective. Decis. Support Syst. **55**, 911–918 (2013)

20. Delcea, C., Sabau Popa, C.D., Bolos, M.: Consumers' decision in grey online social networks. J. Grey Syst. **27**(4), 12–27 (2015)

21. Wasko, M.M., Teigland, R., Samer, F.: The provision of online public goods: examining social structure in an electronic network of practice. Decis. Support Syst. **47**(3), 254–265 (2009)

22. Thompson, L.A., Dawson, K., Ferding, R.: The intersection of online social networking with medical professionalism. J. Gen. Intern. Med. **23**(7), 954–957 (2008)

23. Guseh, J.S., Brendel, R.W., Brendel, D.H.: Medical professionalism in the age of online social networking. J. Med. Ethics **35**(9), 584–586 (2009)

24. Bosslet, G.T., Torke, A.M., Hickman, S.E.: The patient–doctor relationship and online social networks: results of a national survey. J. Gen. Intern. Med. **26**(10), 1168–1174 (2011)

25. Greene, J., Choudhry, N.K., Kilabuk, E.: Online social networking by patients with diabetes: a qualitative evaluation of communication with Facebook. J. Gen. Intern. Med. **26**(3), 287–292 (2011)

26. Liu, S., Lin, Y.: Grey Systems—Theory and Applications. Understanding Complex Systems Series. Springer, Berlin (2010)

27. Forrest, J.: A Systemic Perspective on Cognition and Mathematics. CRC Press, Boca Raton (2013)

28. Liu, S., Yang, Y., Xie, N., Forrest, J.: New progress of grey system theory in the new millennium. Grey Syst. Theory Appl. **6**(1), 2–31 (2016)

29. Delcea, C.: Not black. Not even white. Definitively grey economic systems. J. Grey Syst. **26**(1), 11–25 (2014)

30. Liu, S., Yang, Y., Fang, Z., Xie, N.: Grey cluster evaluation models based on mixed triangular whitenization weight functions. Grey Syst. Theory Appl. **5**(3), 410–418 (2015)

31. Delcea, C., Cotfas, L.A., Paun, R., Maracine, V., Scarlat, E.: A Grey Approach to Online Social Networks. In: Transactions on Computational Collective Intelligence XXII, pp. 60–79 (2016)

32. Ke, L., Xiaoliu, S., Zhongfy, T., Wenyan, G.: Grey clustering analysis method for overseas energy project investment risk decision. Syst. Eng. Proc. **3**, 55–62 (2012)

33. Wen, K.L.: A Matlab toolbox for grey clustering and fuzzy comprehensive evaluation. Adv. Eng. Softw. **39**, 137–145 (2008)

34. Lin, C.H., Wu, C.H., Huang, P.Z.: Grey clustering analysis for incipient fault diagnosis in oil-immersed transformers. Expert Syst. Appl. **39**, 1371–1379 (2009)

35. Spanos, Y.E., Lioukas, S.: An examination into the causal logic of rent generation: contrasting Porter's competitive strategy framework and the resource-based perspective. Strateg. Manag. J. **22**, 907–934 (2001)

36. Delcea, C., Bradea, I., Paun, R., Scarlat, E.: How impressionable are you? - Grey Knowledge. Groups and Strategies in OSN, Computational Collective Intelligence, pp. 171–180. Springer (2015)

37. Wu, J., Liu, X., Li, Y., Shu, J., Liu, K.: Node importance evaluation in complex networks based on grey theory. J. Inf. Comput. Sci. **10**(17), 5629–5635 (2013)

38. Nguyen, T.T., Nguyen, M.H.: Zing Database: high-performance key-value store for large-scale storage service. Vietnam J. Comput. Sci. **2**(1), 13–23 (2014)

## 14

Towards an uncertainty reduction framework for land-cover change prediction using possibility theory

Ahlem Ferchichi[1] · Wadii Boulila[1,2] · Imed Riadh Farah[1,2]

Abstract This paper presents an approach for reducing uncertainty related to the process of land-cover change (LCC) prediction. LCC prediction models have, almost, two sources of uncertainty which are the uncertainty related to model parameters and the uncertainty related to model structure. These uncertainties have a big impact on decisions of the prediction model. To deal with these problems, the proposed approach is divided into three main steps: (1) an uncertainty propagation step based on possibility theory is used as a tool to evaluate the performance of the model; (2) a sensitivity analysis step based on Hartley-like measure is then used to find the most important sources of uncertainty; and (3) a knowledge base based on machine learning algorithm is built to identify the reduction factors of all uncertainty sources of parameters and to reshape their values to reduce in a significant way the uncertainty about future changes of land cover. In this study, the present and future growths of two case studies were anticipated using multi-temporal Spot-4 and Landsat satellite images. These data are used for the preparation of prediction map of year 2025. The results show that our approach based on possibility theory has a potential for reducing uncertainty in LCC prediction modeling.

Keywords LCC prediction · Parameter uncertainty · Structural uncertainty · Possibility theory · Sensitivity analysis

1 Introduction

LCC is a central issue in the sustainability debate because of its wide range of environmental impacts. Models of LCC start with an initial land-cover situation for a given case study area. Then, they use an inferred transition function, representing the processes of change, to simulate the expansion and contraction of a predefined set of land-cover types over a given period. LCC models help to improve our understanding of the land system by establishing cause-effect relations and testing them on historic data. They help to identify the drivers of LCC and their relative importance. In addition, LCC models can be used to explore future land-cover pathways for different scenarios. However, the performance of the LCC prediction models is affected by different types of uncertainties (i.e., aleatory or/and epistemic uncertainties). These uncertainties can be subdivided into two sources: parameter uncertainty (adequate values of model parameters) [1,2] and structural uncertainty (ability of the model to describe the catchment's response) [3]. These sources contribute with different levels to the uncertainty associated with the predictive model. It is important to quantify the uncertainty due to uncertain model parameter, but methods for quantifying uncertainty due to uncertainty in model structure are less well developed. For quantifying, probability theory is generally used. Moreover, numerous authors conclude that there are limitations in using probability theory in this context. So far, several alternative frameworks based on non-probabilistic theories have been proposed in the literature. By no means do the promoters of theories pretend to replace probability theory; they just

✉ Ahlem Ferchichi
ferchichi.ahlem@gmail.com

Wadii Boulila
wadii.boulila@riadi.rnu.tn

Imed Riadh Farah
riadh.farah@ensi.rnu.tn

[1] RIADI Laboratory, National School of Computer Sciences, University of Manouba, Manouba, Tunisia

[2] ITI Department, Telecom-Bretagne, Brest, France

present different levels of expressiveness that leave room for properly representing the lack of background knowledge [4]. The most common theories that are used from these alternatives are imprecise probabilities [5], random sets [6], belief function theory [7], fuzzy sets [8], and possibility theory [9]. In our context of continuous measurements, the possibility theory is more adapted, because it generalises interval analysis and provides a bridge with probability theory by its ability to represent a family of probability distributions. In summary, the possibility distribution has the ability to handle both aleatory and epistemic uncertainty of pixel detection through a possibility and a necessity measures. In this framework, the possibility distributions of the model outputs are used to derive the prediction uncertainty bounds.

Understanding the impact of parameter and structural uncertainty on LCC prediction models outcomes is crucial to the successful use of these models. On the other hand, model optimization with multiple uncertainty sources is complex and very time-consuming task. However, the sensitivity analysis has been proved to be efficient and robust to find the most important sources of uncertainty that have effect on LCC prediction models output [1,9,10]. Parameter sensitivity analysis allows to examine effects of model parameter on results, whereas structural sensitivity analysis allows to modify the structure of the model and to identify the possible structural factors that affect the robustness of the results (vary structure of model and see impact on results and trade-offs between choices). Several sensitivity analysis methods exist, including screening method [11], differential analysis [12], variance-based methods [13], sampling-based methods [14], and a relative entropy-based method [15]. However, all these require specific probability distribution in modeling both model parameters and model structure. In the literature, previous non-probabilistic methods of sensitivity analysis are developed [16,17]. Several studies have confirmed the robustness of use of Hartley-like measure to apply sensitivity analysis in fuzzy theory framework in numerous fields [33–35]. Minimum value to Hartley-like measure of the model output is considered to be the most sensitive source.

Based on possibilistic approach, this study proposes an approach for reducing parameter and structural uncertainty in LCC prediction modeling. The proposed approach is divided into three main steps: (1) an uncertainty propagation step based on possibility theory is used as a tool to evaluate the performance of the model; (2) a sensitivity analysis step based on Hartley-like measure is used to find the most important sources of uncertainty; and (3) a knowledge base based on machine learning algorithm is built to identify the reduction factors of all uncertainty sources of parameters. Then, values of these parameters are reshaped to improve decisions about future changes of land cover in Saint-Denis city, Reunion Island and Cairo region, Egypt.

The rest of this paper is organized as follows: Sect. 2 presents a description of the proposed approach for reducing uncertainty throughout the model of LCC prediction. Results are given and described in Sect. 3. Finally, conclusion and future works are outlined in Sect. 4.

2 Proposed approach

Modeling LCC helps analyzing causes and consequences of land change to support land-cover planning and policy. In the literature, previous models are proposed for predicting LCC [18–23]. In this study, we use the LCC prediction model described by Boulila et al. in [18]. This model exploits machine learning tools to build predictions and decisions for several remote sensing fields. It takes into account uncertainty related to the spatiotemporal mining process to provide more reliable and accurate information about LCC in satellite images.

In this paper, the proposed approach for reducing parameter and structural uncertainty is applied to model presented in [18] and it has the following steps (Fig. 1): (1) identifying uncertainty related to parameters and model structure; (2) propagating the uncertainty through the LCC prediction model using the possibility theory; (3) performing a sensitivity analysis using the Hartley-like measure; and (4) constructing knowledge base using machine learning algorithm to improve parameters' quality.

2.1 Step 1: identifying parameters and structure of LCC prediction model

2.1.1 Choice of parameters

Input parameters of LCC prediction model describe the objects' features extracted from satellite images which are the subject of studying changes. In this study, we consider 26 features: ten spectral, five texture, seven shape, one vegetation, and three climate features. Spectral features are: mean values and standard deviation values of green (MG, SDG), red (MR, SDR), NIR (MN, SDN), SWIR (MS, SDS), and monospectral (MM, SDM) bands for each image object. Texture features are: homogeneity (Hom), contrast (Ctr), entropy (Ent), standard deviation (SD), and correlation (Cor) generated from gray-level co-occurrence matrix (GLCM). Shape and spatial relationship features are: area (A), length/width (LW), shape index (SI), roundness (R), density (D), metric relations (MR), and direction relations (DR). Vegetation feature is: Normalized Difference Vegetation Index (NDVI) that is the ratio of the difference between NIR and red reflectance. Finally, climate features are: temperature (Tem), humidity (Hum), and pressure (Pre). These features are selected based on previous results, as reported in [18], and are considered as input parameters to the LCC model.

Fig. 1 General modeling proposed framework

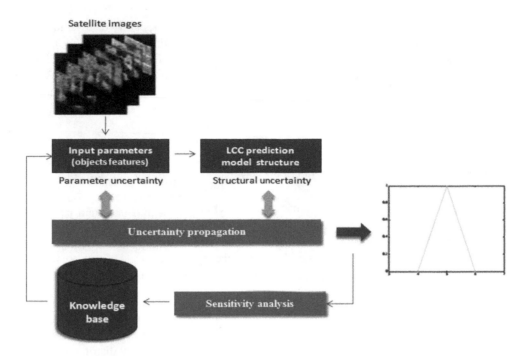

Uncertainties related to these input parameters are very numerous and affect model outputs. In general, these uncertainties can be of two types: epistemic and aleatory. The type of uncertainty of each parameter depends on sources of its uncertainty. Therefore, it is necessary to identify uncertainty sources related to input parameters:

Uncertainty sources of spectral parameters Several studies investigated effects of spectral parameters [28]. Among these effects, we list: spectral reflectance of the surface (S1), sensor calibration (S2), effect of mixed pixels (S3), effect of a shift in the channel location (S4), pixel registration between several spectral channels (S5), atmospheric temperature and moisture profile (S6), effect of haze particles (S7), instrument's operation conditions (S8), atmospheric conditions (S9), as well as by the stability of the instrument itself characteristics (S10).

– *Uncertainty sources of texture parameters* Among these sources, we list: the spatial interaction between the size of the object in the scene and the spatial resolution of the sensor (S11), a border effect (S12), and ambiguity in the object/background distinction (S13).

– *Uncertainty sources of shape parameters* Uncertainty related to shape parameters can rely to the following factors [28]: accounting for the seasonal position of the sun with respect to the Earth (S14), conditions in which the image was acquired changes in the scene's illumination (S15), atmospheric conditions (S16), and observation geometry (S17).

– *Uncertainty sources of NDVI* Among factors that affect NDVI, we can list: variation in the brightness of soil

background (S18), red and NIR bands (S19), atmospheric perturbations (S20), and variability in the sub-pixel structure (S21).

– *Uncertainty sources of climate parameters* According to [29], uncertainty sources related to climate parameters can be: atmospheric correction (S22), noise of the sensor (S23), land surface emissivity (S24), aerosols and other gaseous absorbers (S25), angular effects (S26), wavelength uncertainty (S27), full-width half-maximum of the sensor (S28), and bandpass effects (S29).

2.1.2 Description of model structure

In this study, we use the LCC prediction model described in [18]. This model is divided into three main steps. It starts by a similarity measurement step to find similar states (in the object database) to a query state (representing the query object at a given date). Here, a state is a set of attributes describing an object at a given data. The second step is composed by three substeps: (1) finding the corresponding model for the state; (2) finding all forthcoming states in the model (states having dates superior to the date of the retrieved state); and (3) for each forthcoming date, build the spatiotemporal change tree for the retrieved state. The third step is to construct the spatiotemporal changes for the query state. Each of these steps is based on a number of assumptions as follows:

– Similarity measure step: Distance between states ($d(S_t, S_{t_1}) \geq 0.9$ indicates a higher similarity between the query and the retrieved states). In addition, similarity measure between states is based on time assumption.

– Spatiotemporal change tree building step: The aim of this step is to determine the confidence degrees and the percentage of changes of the model between two dates and for different land-cover types. The confidence degree of changes is achieved by a fuzzy decision tree (fuzzy ID3). This method is based on a number of assumptions such as: the proportion of a data set of land-cover type, the size of a data set, etc. The percentage of changes is achieved by computing the distances between two states and the centroid of the classes.

In this study, we consider structural uncertainty as uncertainty associated with assumptions of model structure, including distance between states, time assumption for similarity measure, assumptions of fuzzy ID3, and distance between states and centroid for changes percentage.

2.2 Step 2: propagating the uncertainty

In this step, we focus on how to propagate parameter and structural uncertainty through the LCC prediction model described in [18] via the possibility theory.

2.2.1 Basics of possibility theory

The possibility theory developed by Dubois and Prade [30] handles uncertainty in a qualitative way, but encodes it in the interval [0, 1] called possibilistic scale. The basic building block in the possibility theory is named possibility distribution. A possibility distribution is defined as a mapping $\pi : \Omega \rightarrow [0, 1]$. It is formally equivalent to the fuzzy set $\mu(x) = \pi(x)$. Distribution π describes the more or less plausible values of some uncertain variable X. A possibility distribution is associated with two measures, namely, the possibility (Π) and necessity (N) measures, which are represented by Eq. (1):

$$\Pi(A) = \sup_{x \in A} \pi(x), \quad N(A) = \inf_{x \notin A}(1 - \pi(x)). \quad (1)$$

The possibility measure indicates to which extent event A is plausible, while the necessity measure indicates to which extent it is certain. They are dual, in the sense that $\Pi(A) = 1 - N(\overline{A})$, with $\overline{A}$ the complement of A. They obey the following axioms:

$$\Pi(A \cup B) = \max(\Pi(A), \Pi(B)) \quad (2)$$
$$N(A \cap B) = \min(N(A), N(B)) \quad (3)$$

An α cut of π is the interval $[\underline{x}_\alpha, \overline{x}_\alpha] = \{x, \pi(x) \geq \alpha\}$. The degree of certainty that $[\underline{x}_\alpha, \overline{x}_\alpha]$ contains the true value of X is $N([\underline{x}_\alpha, \overline{x}_\alpha]) = 1 - \alpha$. Conversely, a collection of nested sets A_i with (lower) confidence levels λ_i can be modeled as a possibility distribution, since the α cut of a (continuous)

possibility distribution can be understood as the probabilistic constraint $P(X \in [\underline{x}_\alpha, \overline{x}_\alpha]) \geq 1 - \alpha$. In this setting, necessity degrees are equated to lower probability bounds and possibility degrees to upper probability bounds.

2.2.2 Propagation of parameter uncertainty

In this section, the procedures of propagating unified structures dealing with parameter uncertainty of LCC prediction model will be addressed. Let us denote by $Y = f(X) = f(X_1, X_2, \ldots, X_j, \ldots, X_n)$ the model for LCC prediction with n uncertain parameters X_j, $j = 1, 2, \ldots, n$, that are possibilistic, i.e., their uncertainties are described by possibility distributions $\pi_{X1}(x_1), \pi_{X2}(x_2), \ldots, \pi_{Xj}(x_j), \ldots, \pi_{Xn}(x_n)$. In more detail, the operative steps of the procedure are the following:

1. Set $\alpha = 0$.
2. Select the α cuts $A_\alpha^{X1}, A_\alpha^{X2}, , A_\alpha^{Xj}, \ldots, A_\alpha^{Xn}$ of the possibility distributions $\pi_{X1}(x_1), \pi_{X2}(x_2), \ldots, \pi_{Xj}(x_j), \ldots, \pi_{Xn}(x_n)$ of the possibilistic parameters X_j, $j = 1, 2, \ldots, n$, as intervals of possible values $[\underline{x}_{j,\alpha}, \overline{x}_{j,\alpha}]$ $j = 1, 2, \ldots, n$.
3. Calculate the smallest and largest values of Y, denoted by $\underline{y}_\alpha$ and $\overline{y}_\alpha$, respectively, letting variables X_j range within the intervals $[\underline{x}_{j,\alpha}, \overline{x}_{j,\alpha}]$ $j = 1, 2, \ldots, n$; in particular, $\underline{y}_\alpha = \inf_{j, X_j \in [\underline{x}_{j,\alpha}, \overline{x}_{l,\alpha}]} f(X_1, X_2, \ldots, X_j, \ldots, X_n)$ and $\overline{y}_\alpha = \sup_{j, X_j \in [\underline{x}_{j,\alpha}, \overline{x}_{l,\alpha}]} f(X_1, X_2, \ldots, X_j, \ldots, X_n)$.
4. Take the values $\underline{y}_\alpha$ and $\overline{y}_\alpha$ found in step 3 as the lower and upper limits of the α cut A_α^Y of Y;
5. If $\alpha < 1$, then set $\alpha = \alpha + \Delta\alpha$ and return to step 2; otherwise, stop the algorithm. The possibility distribution $\pi_Y(y)$ of $Y = f(X_1, X_2, \ldots, X_n)$ is constructed as the collection of the values $\underline{y}_\alpha$ and $\overline{y}_\alpha$ for each α cut.

2.2.3 Propagation of structural uncertainty

The propagation of structural uncertainty is implemented in combination with the propagation of parameter uncertainty. In this section, as parameter uncertainty is modeled by possibility theory, we use this method in this framework.

Suppose that a set of model structures M_k, $1 \leq k \leq K$ represents the uncertainty related to the choice of model. For each model M_k, parameter uncertainty is propagated through this model. Consequently, the output indicator Y is characterized by a set of uncertainty representations according to each model structure. Thus, for all model structures M_k, $1 \leq k \leq K$, we have a set of possibility distributions for output variable Y, noted $\pi_{Y_1}(y), \pi_{Y_2}(y), \ldots, \pi_{Y_K}(y)$. The difference between these representations reflects the variation associated with structural uncertainty of LCC prediction model. These different representations $\pi_{Y_i}(y)$, $1 \leq i \leq K$

can be combined into a single representation. Therefore, the final uncertainty representation of output variable Y can be obtained by the following formulas:

$$\underline{y}^*_\alpha = \inf_{i, Y_i \in [\underline{y}_{i,\alpha}, \overline{y}_{l,\alpha}]} f(Y_1, Y_2, \ldots, Y_i, \ldots, Y_K) \quad (4)$$

$$\overline{y}^*_\alpha = \sup_{i, Y_i \in [\underline{y}_{i,\alpha}, \overline{y}_{l,\alpha}]} f(Y_1, Y_2, \ldots, Y_i, \ldots, Y_K). \quad (5)$$

The possibility distribution $\pi_Y(y)$ of $Y = f(Y_1, Y_2, \ldots, Y_K)$ is constructed as the collection of the values $\underline{y}^*_\alpha$ and $\overline{y}^*_\alpha$ for each α cut. This distribution takes into account both parameter and structural uncertainty in the final output results of the prediction model.

2.3 Step 3: performing the sensitivity analysis

Based on Hartley-like measure, the third step consists to test impact of parameter and structural uncertainties on LCC prediction model output. The Hartley-like measure quantifies the most fundamental type of uncertainty (i.e., aleatory and epistemic uncertainty). This measure is generalized to fuzzy set by Higashi and Klir [31,32]. How to perform sensitivity analysis of both uncertainty sources in the possibilistic framework? The generalized measure H for any non-empty possibility distribution A defined on a finite universal set X has the following form:

$$H(A) = \frac{1}{h(A)} \int_0^{h(a)} \log_2 |A_\alpha| \mathrm{d}\alpha, \quad (6)$$

where A_α denotes the cardinality of the α cuts of the possibility distributions A and $h(A)$ the height of A. For possibilistic intervals or numbers on the real line, the Hartley-like measure is defined as

$$HL(A) = \int_0^1 \log_2(1 + \lambda(A_\alpha)) \mathrm{d}\alpha, \quad (7)$$

where $\lambda(A_\alpha)$ is the Lebesgue measure of A_α [31]. Mathematically, for a possibilistic number $A = [a_L, a_m, a_R]$ given by the possibility distribution

$$\pi_A(x) = \begin{cases} \frac{x - a_L}{a_m - a_L}, & \text{if } a_L \leq x \leq a_m \\ \frac{x - a_R}{a_m - a_R}, & \text{if } a_m \leq x \leq a_R \\ 0, & \text{otherwise} \end{cases} \quad (8)$$

the Hartley-like measure is given by the expression as follows:

$$HL(A) = \frac{1}{(a_L - a_R) \ln(2)} \times ([1 + (a_R - a_L)] \\ \ln[1 + (a_R - a_L)] - (a_R - a_L)). \quad (9)$$

The minimum value of Hartley-like measure of the model output with respect to fixing a particular parameter to the most likely value, for a particular point of observation, leads to finding the most sensitive parameter. We can use the same measure to perform structural sensitivity analysis.

2.4 Step 4: constructing the knowledge base

After performing parameter and structural sensitivity analysis, the main purpose of this step is to identify reduction approaches of all uncertainty sources of LCC model parameters. In general, the knowledge base stores the embedded knowledge in the system and the rules defined by an expert. In this study, we used an inductive learning technique to automatically build a knowledge base. Two main steps are proposed which are training and decision tree generation. The learning step provides examples of concepts to be learned. The second step is the decision tree generation. This step generates the first decision trees from the training data. These decision trees are then transformed into production rules. Then, our knowledge base that contains all uncertainty sources and their reduction approaches is presented in Fig. 2. This knowledge base is used to improve data quality and then reduce in a significant way the uncertainty about future changes of land cover.

3 Experimental results

The aim of this section is to validate and to evaluate the performance of the proposed approach through two case studies for reducing parameter and structural uncertainty in LCC prediction modeling.

3.1 Case study 1

3.1.1 Description of the study area and data

Reunion Island is a French territory of 2500 km^2 located in the Indian Ocean, 200 km South-West of Mauritius and 700 km to the East of Madagascar (Fig. 3). Mean annual temperatures decrease from 24 °C in the lowlands to 12 °C at ca 2000 m. Mean annual precipitation ranges from 3 m on the eastern windward coast, up to 8 m in the mountains and down to 1 m along the south western coast. Vegetation is most clearly structured along gradients of altitude and rainfall [27].

Reunion Island has a strong growth in a limited area with an estimated population of 833,000 in 2010 that will probably be more than 1 million in 2030 [24]. It has been significant changes, putting pressure on agricultural and natural areas. The urban areas expanded by 189 % over the period from 1989 to 2002 [25] and available land became a rare and coveted resource. The landscapes are now expected to fulfil multiple functions, i.e., urbanization, agriculture production,

Fig. 2 Production rules generated from uncertainty sources of input parameters

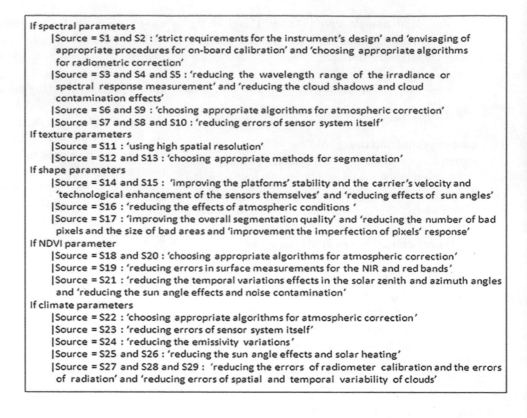

```
If spectral parameters
    |Source = S1 and S2 : 'strict requirements for the instrument's design' and 'envisaging of
        appropriate procedures for on-board calibration' and 'choosing appropriate algorithms
        for radiometric correction'
    |Source = S3 and S4 and S5 : 'reducing the wavelength range of the irradiance or
        spectral response measurement' and 'reducing the cloud shadows and cloud
        contamination effects'
    |Source = S6 and S9 : 'choosing appropriate algorithms for atmospheric correction'
    |Source = S7 and S8 and S10 : 'reducing errors of sensor system itself'
If texture parameters
    |Source = S11 : 'using high spatial resolution'
    |Source = S12 and S13 : 'choosing appropriate methods for segmentation'
If shape parameters
    |Source = S14 and S15 : 'improving the platforms' stability and the carrier's velocity and
        'technological enhancement of the sensors themselves' and 'reducing effects of sun angles'
    |Source = S16 : 'reducing the effects of atmospheric conditions '
    |Source = S17 : 'improving the overall segmentation quality' and 'reducing the number of bad
        pixels and the size of bad areas and 'improvement the imperfection of pixels' response'
If NDVI parameter
    |Source = S18 and S20 : 'choosing appropriate algorithms for atmospheric correction'
    |Source = S19 : 'reducing errors in surface measurements for the NIR and red bands'
    |Source = S21 : 'reducing the temporal variations effects in the solar zenith and azimuth angles
        and 'reducing the sun angle effects and noise contamination'
If climate parameters
    |Source = S22 : 'choosing appropriate algorithms for atmospheric correction'
    |Source = S23 : 'reducing errors of sensor system itself'
    |Source = S24 : 'reducing the emissivity variations'
    |Source = S25 and S26 : 'reducing the sun angle effects and solar heating'
    |Source = S27 and S28 and S29 : 'reducing the errors of radiometer calibration and the errors
        of radiation' and 'reducing errors of spatial and temporal variability of clouds'
```

Fig. 3 Studied area for case study 1

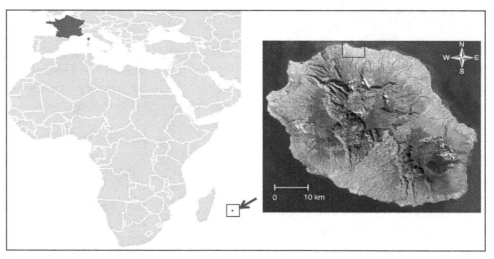

and ecosystem conservation, and this causes conflicts among stakeholders about their planning and management [26].

Saint Denis is the capital of Reunion Island and the city with the most inhabitants on the island (Fig. 3). It hosts all the important administrative offices, and it is also a cultural center with numerous museums. Saint-Denis is also the largest city in all the French Overseas Departments. Available remote sensing data for this research include classified images of land over of Saint Denis from SPOT-4 images for the years 2006 and 2011 (Fig. 4). For this case, satellite data are classified after initial corrections and processing to prepare the data for extracting useful information. Spec-

tral, geometric, and atmospheric corrections of images are conducted to make features manifest, to increase the quality of images, and to eliminate the adverse effects of light and atmosphere. According to the study objective, five categories, including water, urban, forest, bare soil, and vegetation, are identified and classified.

3.1.2 Results of uncertainty propagation

As mentioned perviously, the model parameter and model structure of LCC prediction are marred by uncertainty. Ignoring each of these sources can affect the results of uncertainty

Fig. 4 Land-cover maps

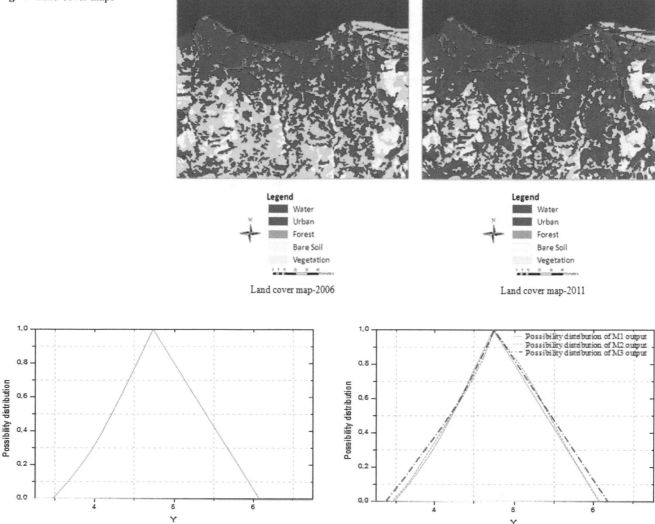

Fig. 5 Possibility distribution of LCC prediction model output for only parameter uncertainty

Fig. 6 Possibility distributions of LCC for three different prediction model structures

propagation. To illustrate the importance of propagating uncertainty related to model parameter and model structure through the LCC prediction model, the analysis with pure parameter uncertainty assumption is conducted. In this case, the possibility distribution of output representing only parameter uncertainty is obtained via possibility theory. Figure 5 shows this distribution based on 10,000 samples. With uncertainty in model parameter, there is uncertainty in model structure. Therefore, it is also import to illustrate the importance of structural uncertainty in LCC prediction modeling by the proposed approach. This is the reason behind using the LCC prediction model described in [18] with three different structures. Then, we obtain three different models (M_1, M_2, and M_3) with different assumptions. To take into account structural uncertainty in the final result, uncertainty related to parameters is first propagated and this for each prediction model.

Figure 5 shows the possibility distribution of the LCC prediction model output, where only parameter uncertainty is propagated.

After propagating uncertainty of parameters through three different model structures, we obtain three uncertain representations of LCC, which are shown in Fig. 6. The difference between these three representations illustrates the impact of structural uncertainty. Compared with the result of the original LCC prediction model (M_1), we can see that these is an important difference between them.

Figure 7 shows possibility distribution representing integrated parameter and structural uncertainty through the LCC prediction modeling. Note that combining parameter and structural uncertainty can be crucially important to enhance the accuracy of the LCC prediction model.

3.1.3 Results of sensitivity analysis

In this paper, the sensitivity analysis based on Hartley-like measure is implemented to estimate the effect of 26 uncertain parameters through three different LCC prediction model structures. Results of the sensitivity analysis are shown in Fig. 8.

The different heights of the bars reveal the various levels of sensitivity, and a long bar indicates high sensitivity

parameter. Parameter variations are illustrated individually for each of the three model structures M_1, M_2, and M_3. The most complex model structure generally shows a higher sensitivity of parameters. M_1 and M_2 have given, almost, the same results. On the other hand, parameters in M_3 are relatively sensitive compared to M_1 and M_2. According to these differences, structural uncertainty plays an important role in the sensitivity analysis and should not be overlooked as part of overall uncertainty reductions. The overall contribution of spectral, shape, and NDVI parameters to the LCC prediction model, which are the highest and the indicative of the most sensitive for the three model structures. After applying the sensitivity analysis process, we will only consider these parameters for preprocessing based on the knowledge base and for optimal parameter estimation. Then, the uncertainty propagation based on possibility theory method is applied to reduce the parameter and structural uncertainty of the LCC prediction model.

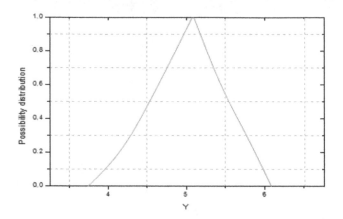

Fig. 7 Possibility distribution of the combined parameter and structural uncertainty of LCC prediction model output

3.1.4 Results of LCC prediction maps

LCC prediction maps are validated based on temporal series of multispectral SPOT images. First, the 2011 LCC was simulated using the 2006 data sets. Then, the simulated changes are compared with the real LCC in 2011 to evaluate the accu-

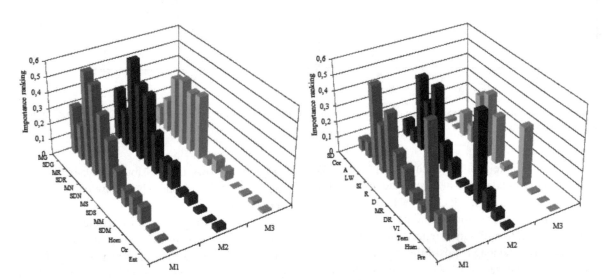

Fig. 8 Comparison between the sensitivity of uncertain parameters in three different LCC prediction model structures based on Hartley-like measure

Table 1 Percentages of LCC of the actual and simulated LCC

	Water (%)	Urban (%)	Forest (%)	Bare soil (%)	Vegetation (%)
Predicted changes in 2025	1.9	37.4	39.31	26.95	26.7
Output of proposed model	1.5	23.18	35.97	22.87	20.08
Real changes in 2011	1.7	21.4	36.1	24.1	16.7

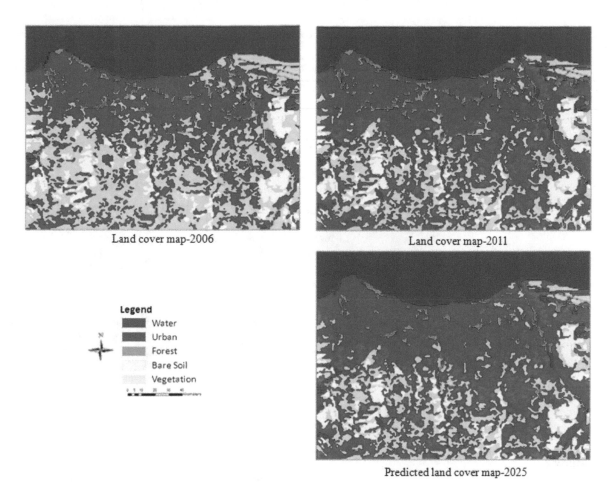

Fig. 9 Comparison between the land-cover maps for years 2006 and 2011 and the predicted land-cover map for 2025

racy and the performance of the proposed approach. Second, the process of LCC is conducted to predict land-cover distributions for forthcoming dates.

Table 1 illustrates a comparison between the actual and simulated percentages occupied by the different land-cover types (water, urban, forest, bare soil, and vegetation) between 2006 and 2011. It shows that the modeled changes generally matched that of the actual changes. These results confirm that the proposed approach can simulate the prediction of LCC with an acceptable accuracy.

After the validation, the next step is to simulate the LCC in 2025, assuming the changes between 2006 and 2011. In this simulation, the LCC and the parameters acquired in 2011 are used as input to simulate the LCC in 2025.

Table 1 shows the simulated changes between 2006 and 2025. Urban expansion is the dominant change process. This can be attributed to the increase in population by increased demands for residential land. There have been significant LCC, where urban land covered 21.4 % of simulated changes in 2011 and 37.4 % in 2025. From these results, it can be found the replacing of the land natural cover (forest and veg-

etation lands) in the study area by residential land (urban land).

Figure 9 depicts the simulated future changes compared with land-cover maps for the years 2006 and 2011.

3.1.5 Evaluation of the proposed approach

To evaluate the proposed approach in improving LCC prediction, we apply the proposed uncertainty propagation approach on the LCC model described by Qiang and Lam in [40] to the Saint-Denis city, Reunion Island. The LCC prediction model proposed in [40] uses the Artificial Neural Network (ANN) to derive the LCC rules and then applies the Cellular Automate (CA) model to simulate future scenarios.

Table 2 depicts the percentages of change of the five land-cover types (water, urban, bare soil, forest, and non-dense vegetation). It shows the difference between real changes, predicted changes of the proposed approach, and changes made by the proposed approach applied to model described in [40].

Table 2 Comparison between real changes, predicted changes of the proposed approach, and changes made by the proposed approach applied to model described in [40]

	Water (%)	Urban (%)	Forest (%)	Bare soil (%)	Vegetation (%)
Proposed approach	1.5	23.18	35.97	22.87	20.08
Approach applied to model in [40]	1.5	25.32	34.98	20.03	16.24
Real changes in 2011	1.7	21.4	36.1	24.1	16.7

Fig. 10 Location of the study area for the case study 2

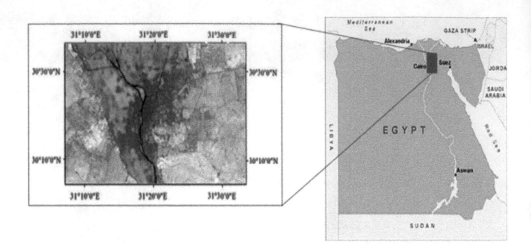

3.2 Case study 2

3.2.1 Description of the study area and data

Cairo, the capital of Egypt, is one of the most crowded cities in Egypt (Fig. 10) and is considered as a world megacity. Mapping LCC is important to understand and analyze the relationships between the geomorphology (highlands and deserts), natural resources (agricultural lands and the Nile River), and human activities. Agricultural lands around Cairo have witnessed severe encroachment practices due to the accelerated population growth. However, adjacent desert plains have also witnessed urbanization practices to encompass the intensive population growth. Different studies have previously been carried out for LCC detection and modeling in the Cairo Region [36–39]. Population of Cairo (Cairo city and Giza) increased from about 6.4 millions in 1976 [36] to about 12.5 million in 2006 according to the Egyptian Central Agency for Public Mobilization and Statistics. The importance of Cairo arises from its location in the mid-way between the Nile Valley and the delta. Main government facilities and services occur at Cairo.

In this case, two Landsat TM5 satellite images are obtained from the United States Geological Survey (USGS) database online resources. These two images acquired in 6 April 1987 and 15 March 2014, respectively, are classified into four land-cover types which are urban, agriculture,

desert, and water to produce LCC maps (Fig. 11). During this time period, Cairo population has increased from an estimated 7 million in 1987 to over 15 million in 2014. The recent population growth has caused the city and its associated urban areas to expand into the surrounding desert, as seen in the right image in Fig. 11. Within the main Nile River Valley, these two images also show an overall increase in developed urban area (red) versus agricultural land (green). As new urban and agricultural areas are being developed in the desert, they require diversion of water supplies from the main Nile River Valley.

In this case study, satellite data are classified after initial corrections and processing to prepare the data for extracting useful information. Spectral, geometric, and atmospheric corrections of images are conducted to make features manifest, to increase the quality of images, and to eliminate the adverse effects of light and atmosphere.

3.2.2 Results of uncertainty propagation

As we mentioned in the first case study, it is necessary to study the effect of both uncertainty sources through LCC prediction model. Figure 12 shows the possibility distribution of output representing only parameter uncertainty based on 10,000 samples. Therefore, it is also import to illustrate the importance of structural uncertainty in LCC prediction modeling by proposed approach. Figure 13 shows

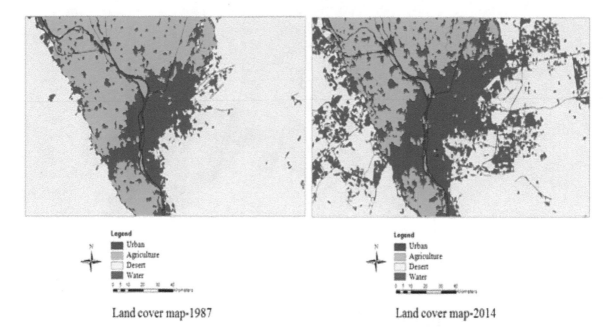

Land cover map-1987   Land cover map-2014

Fig. 11 Land-cover maps

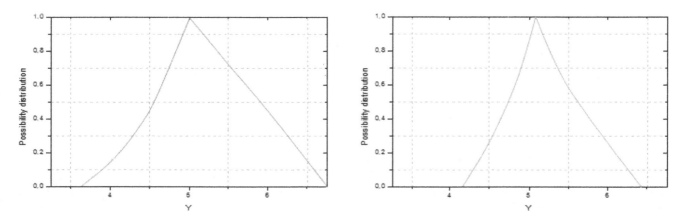

Fig. 12 Possibility distribution of LCC prediction model output for only parameter uncertainty

Fig. 14 Possibility distribution of the combined parameter and structural uncertainties of LCC prediction model output

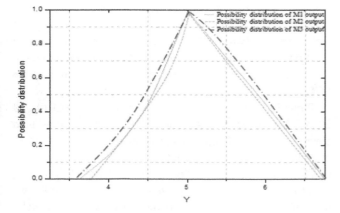

Fig. 13 Possibility distributions of LCCs for three different prediction model structures

the possibility distributions of output representing parameter uncertainty through three different model structures. The difference between these three representations presents the impact of structural uncertainty. In this case study, results of the uncertainty propagation of both parameter and structural uncertainties are shown in Fig. 14.

3.2.3 Results of sensitivity analysis

In this case study, we have also used Hartley-like measure to estimate the 26 uncertain parameters through three different LCC prediction model structures. The main objective is to test the impact of parameter and structural uncertainties. Results of the sensitivity analysis are shown in Fig. 15. In this case, parameters in M_3 are highly sensitive com-

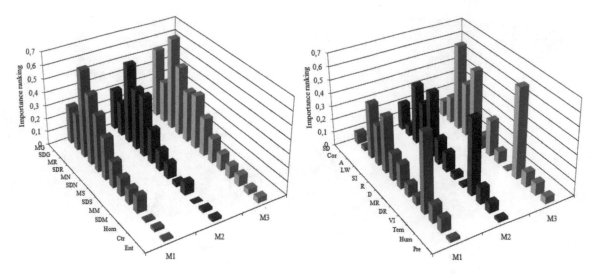

Fig. 15 Comparison between the sensitivity of uncertain parameters in three different LCC prediction model structures based on Hartley-like measure

Table 3 Output of the proposed LCC prediction model in comparison with real changes between 1987 and 2014 in Cairo region

	Urban (%)	Agriculture (%)	Water (%)	Desert (%)
Output of proposed model	15.63	13.80	0.01	4.03
Real changes in 2014	17.32	13.00	0.02	5.00

Table 4 Output of the proposed LCC prediction model of the predicted LCC between 2014 and 2025 in Cairo region

	Urban (%)	Agriculture (%)	Water (%)	Desert (%)
Predicted changes in 2025	20.16	14.72	0.03	6.11
Real changes in 2014	17.32	13.00	0.02	5.00

pared to M_1 and M_2. On the other hand, as in the first case study, the overall contribution of spectral, shape, and NDVI parameters to the LCC prediction model is the highest and represents the most sensitive parameters for the three model structures.

3.2.4 Results of LCC prediction maps

The validation of LCC prediction maps consists of two phases. First, the 2014 LCC is simulated using the 1987 data sets, which is then compared with the real LCC in 2014 to evaluate the accuracy and the performance of the proposed approach. Second, future changes are simulated using the real 2014 data sets.

To check the accuracy of our approach, Table 3 compares actual and simulated percentages occupied by the different land-cover types (urban, agriculture, water, and desert) between 1987 and 2014. According to the proposed model output, the most significant changes in this period are the transitions from agriculture and desert to urban areas (Fig. 11). Over 27 years, from 1987 to 2014, agriculture lost 12 % to urban areas. In addition, 4 % of desert areas became urban between 1987 and 2014, which is equivalent to 24,687

hectares. This percentage results from the application of desert reconstruction strategies to build new communities outside the Nile Valley. The obtained results depict that the proposed approach gives an accurate prediction with about 3.96 % of error through a comparison with the real changes in Cairo region. These results confirm that the proposed LCC prediction model is able to describe the LCC. The proposed approach can simulate the prediction of LCC with an accepT-able accuracy. After the validation of the proposed approach, the next step is to simulate the LCC in 2025, assuming that the changes between 1987 and 2014 will continue during the next 11 years. In this simulation, the LCC and the input parameters acquired in 2014 are used as input to simulate the LCC in 2025.

Table 4 shows the simulated changes between 2014 and 2025. There have been significant LCC, where urban land covered 15.63 % of simulated changes in 2014 and 20.16 % in 2025. This could be attributed to the increase in population by increased demands for residential land. The resulting effect is the decrease in desert land. From these results, we note that the desert land cover in the study area is replaced by residential land (urban land). Knowing the current and estimated urbanization situation will help decision makers to

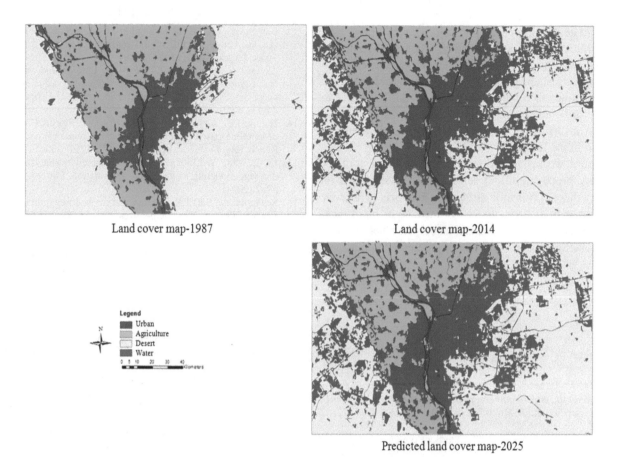

Land cover map-1987

Land cover map-2014

Predicted land cover map-2025

Fig. 16 Comparison between the land-cover maps for years 1987 and 2014 and the predicted land-cover map for 2025

Table 5 Comparaison between real changes and changes prediction for the proposed approach and the proposed approach applied to model described in [40]

	Urban (%)	Agriculture (%)	Water (%)	Desert (%)
Proposed approach	15.63	13.80	0.01	4.03
Approach applied to model in [40]	14.93	13.61	0.01	5.92
Real changes in 2014	17.32	13.00	0.02	5.00

adjust and develop new plans to achieve a sustainable development of urban areas and to protect the historical locations.

Figure 16 depicts the simulated future changes compared with land-cover maps for the years 1987 and 2014. These results indicate usefulness and applicability of the proposed approach in predicting the LCC.

3.2.5 Evaluation of the proposed approach

In this case study, we also apply the proposed uncertainty propagation approach on the LCC model described by Qiang and Lam in [40] to the Cairo region, Egypt.

Table 5 depicts the percentages of change of the four land-cover types (urban, agriculture, water, and desert). This table shows the difference between real changes and changes prediction for the proposed approach and the proposed approach applied to model described in [40].

4 Conclusion

This study has proposed an approach for reducing parameter and structural uncertainty in LCC prediction modeling. The proposed approach herein quantifies uncertainty based on possibility theory. Subsequently, the Hartley-like measure is used to perform the sensitivity of the LCC prediction model parameter and structure. Using the sensitivity analysis, we are able to quantify precisely the effect of each LCC prediction model parameter, and also the effect of model structure. This analysis yields that the spectral, shape, and vegetation parameters are the most sensitive parameters in three different model structures.

To validate the proposed approach, we choose two case studies which are: Saint-Denis city, Reunion Island, and Cairo region, Egypt. We study spectral parameters, texture parameters, shape parameters, vegetation parameter, and climate parameters for three different model structures to simulate forthcoming LCC. Results show that the urban expansion in the two case studies is rapid and should be monitored in the future.

As future work, we propose to put online a tool for uncertainty propagation and sensitivity analysis based on possibility theory. This tool will help researchers to improve the performance of their models. It has also as input parameters of a considered model and as output which of these input parameters that most influence the model output.

References

1. Boulila, W., Bouatay, A., Farah, I.R.: A probabilistic collocation method for the imperfection propagation: application to land cover change prediction. J. Multimed. Process. Technol. **5**(1), 12–32 (2014)
2. Liu, R., Sun, J., Wang, J., Li, X.: Study of remote sensing based parameter uncertainty in production efficiency models. In: IEEE International Geoscience and Remote Sensing Symposium, pp. 3303–3306 (2010)
3. Jacquin, A.P.: Possibilistic uncertainty analysis of a conceptual model of snowmelt runoff. Hydrol. Earth Syst. Sci. **14**, 1681–1695 (2010)
4. Dubois, D., Prade, H.: Formal representations of uncertainty. In: Decision-Making Process: Concepts and Methods, ch. 3, pp. 85–156. ISTE and Wiley, London (2010)
5. Caselton, W.F., Luo, W.: Decision making with imprecise probabilities: Dempster–Shafer theory and application. Water Resour. Res. **28**(12), 3071–3083 (1992)
6. Zhao, X., Stein, A., Chen, X.: Application of random sets to model uncertainties of natural entities extracted from remote sensing images. Stoch. Environ. Res. Risk Assess. **24**(5), 713–723 (2009)
7. Hgarat-Mascle, S.L., Bloch, I., Vidal-Madjar, D.: Application of Dempster–Shafer evidence theory to unsupervised classification in multisource remote sensing. IEEE Trans. Geosci. Remote Sens. **35**(4), 1018–1031 (1997)
8. Gomez, D., Javier, M.: Fuzzy sets in remote sensing classification. Soft Comput. **12**(3), 243–249 (2008)
9. Ferchichi, A., Boulila, W., Farah, I.R.: An intelligent possibilistic approach to reduce the effect of the imperfection propagation on land cover change prediction. Int. Conf. Comput. Collect. Intell. **9330**, 520–529 (2015)
10. Mondal, M.S., Garg, P.K., Sharma, N., Kappas, M.: Cellular automata (ca) markov modeling of LULC change and sensitivity analysis to identify sensitive parameter(s). In: Proceedings of the 27th International Cartographic Conference, vol. 38(818) (2015)
11. Sanchez-Canales, M., Benito, A.L., Passuello, A., Terrado, M., Ziv, G., Acuna, V., Schuhmacher, M., Elorza, F.J.: Sensitivity analysis of ecosystem service valuation in a Mediterranean watershed. Sci. Total Environ. **440**, 140–153 (2012)
12. Bettemier, O.H.: Error estimation of orthorectification of small satellite images by differential sensitivity analysis. J. Aeronaut. Space Technol. **4**(4), 65–74 (2010)
13. Zielinskaa, A.L., Sunb, L.: Applying time-dependent variance-based global sensitivity analysis to represent the dynamics of an agent-based model of land use change. Int. J. Geogr. Inf. Sci. **24**(12), 1829–1850 (2010)
14. Helton, J.C., Johnson, J.D., Sallaberry, C.J., Storlie, C.B.: Survey of sampling-based methods for uncertainty and sensitivity analysis. Reliab. Eng. Syst. Saf. **91**(10–11), 1175–1209 (2006)
15. Li, C., Wang, W., Xiong, J., Chen, P.: Sensitivity analysis for urban drainage modeling using mutual information. Entropy **16**, 5738–5752 (2014)
16. Sengupta, A., Pal, T.K.: Theory and methodology: on comparing interval numbers. Eur. J. Oper. Res. **127**, 28–43 (2000)
17. Ferson, S., Tucker, W.T.: Sensitivity analysis using probability bounding. Reliab. Eng. Syst. Saf. **91**(1011), 1435–1442 (2006)
18. Boulila, W., Farah, I.R., Ettabaa, K.S., Solaiman, B., Ben Ghzala, H.: A data mining based approach to predict spatio-temporal changes in satellite images. Int. J. Appl. Earth Obs. Geoinf. **13**(3), 386–395 (2011)
19. Ballestores, F., Jr., Qiu, Z., Nedorezova, B.N., Nedorezov, L.V., Ferrarini, A., Ramathilaga, A., Ackah, M.: An integrated parcel-based land use change model using cellular automata and decision tree. In: Proceedings of the International Academy of Ecology and Environmental Sciences, vol. 2(2), pp. 53–69 (2012)
20. Razavi, B.S.: Predicting the trend of land use changes using artificial neural network and markov chain model (Case Study: Kermanshah City). Res. J. Environ. Earth Sci. **6**(4), 215–226 (2014)
21. Tayyebi, A., Perry, P.C., Tayyebi, A.H.: Predicting the expansion of an urban boundary using spatial logistic regression and hybrid rastervector routines with remote sensing and GIS. Int. J. Geogr. Inf. Sci. **28**(4), 1–21 (2013)
22. Ralha, C.G., Abreu, C.G., Coelho, C.G., Zaghetto, A., Macchiavello, B., Machado, R.B.: A multi-agent model system for land-use change simulation. Environ. Model. Softw. **42**, 30–46 (2013)
23. Li, X., Yeh, A.G.O.: Neural-network-based cellular automata for simulating multiple land use changes using GIS. Int. J. Geogr. Inf. Sci. **16**(4), 323–343 (2002)
24. INSEE Reunion: Bilan dmographique 2009, Rsultats (40) (2011)
25. Durieux, L., Lagabrielle, E., Andrew, N.: A method for monitoring building construction in urban sprawl areas using object-based analysis of Spot 5 images and existing GIS data. ISPRS J. Photogramm. **63**, 399–408 (2008)
26. van der Valk, A.: The Dutch planning experience. Landsc. Urban Plan. **58**(2), 201–210 (2002)
27. Cadet, T.: La vegetation de l'ile de La reunion, tude phytocologique et phytosociologique. Ph.D. Thesis, University of Aix Marseille (1980)
28. Atanassov, V., Jelev, G., Kraleva, L.: Some peculiarities of the pre-processing of spectral data and images. J. Ship. Ocean Eng. **3**, 55–60 (2013)
29. Jimenez-Munoz, J.C., Sobrino, J.A.: Error sources on the land surface temperature retrieved from thermal infrared single channel remote sensing data. Int. J. Remote Sens. **27**(5), 999–1014 (2006)
30. Dubois, D., Prade, H.: When upper probabilities are possibility measures. Fuzzy Sets Syst. **49**, 65–74 (1992)
31. Klir, G.J., Wiermann, M.J.: Uncertainty Based Information. Elements of Generalised Information Theory. Physica-Verlg, Heidelberg (1998)

32. Hagashi, M., Klir, G.J.: Measure of uncertainty and information based on possibility distribution. Int. J. Gen. Syst. **9**, 43–58 (1983)

33. Chutta, R., Mahanta, S., Datta, D.: Sensitivity analysis of atmospheric dispersion model-Rimpuff using Hartley-like measure. J. Appl. Math. Inform. **31**(1–2), 99–110 (2013)

34. Datta D.: Measures of sensitivity and uncertainty with the fuzzy model of solute transport through groundwater. In: International Conference on Communication and Industrial Application, pp. 1–6 (2011)

35. Ivanov, L.M., Tokmakian, R.T.: Sensitivity analysis of nonlinear models to parameter perturbations for small size ensembles of model outputs. Int. J. Bifurc. Chaos **21**(12), 3589–3609 (2011)

36. Sutton, K., Fahmi, W.: Cairo's urban growth and strategic master plans in the light of Egypt's 1996 population census results. Cities **18**(3), 135–149 (2001)

37. Yin, Z.Y., Stewart, D.J., Bullard, S., Maclachlan, J.T.: Changes in urban built-up surface and population distribution patterns during 1986–1999: a case study of Cairo, Egypt. Comput. Environ. Urban Syst. **29**, 595–616 (2005)

38. Hereher, M.E.: Analysis of urban growth at Cairo, Egypt using remote sensing and GIS. Nat. Sci. **4**, 355–361 (2012)

39. de Noronha, V.E., Caetano, M., Nijkamp, P.: Trapped between antiquity and urbanism—a multi-criteria assessment model of the Greater Cairo Metropolitan Area. J. Land Use Sci. **6**, 283–299 (2011)

40. Qiang, Y., Lam, N.S.N.: Modeling land use and land cover changes in a vulnerable coastal region using artificial neural networks and cellular automata. Environ. Monit. Assess. **187**(57), 1–16 (2015)

## 15

Utilization of nested clustering in VANET to reduce data loss in mobile cloud computing

Erfan Arzhmand[1] ⓘ · Hossein Rashid[2] · Mohammad Javad Fazel Ashrafi[3]

Abstract Over the recent few years, most of network service providers have tried to expand their services all around by newly emerged technologies in network, especially mobile cloud computing. Most emerging cars and vehicles with powerful computers and storages, can be equipped with such new technologies such as vehicular ad hoc network radio, a new wireless technology. These capabilities lead network service providers to use these potentials to expand their network services such as Internet on the roads. It seems there are enough materials and peripherals to design a convenient network but every new architecture will have its limitations and problems, such as data loss, in performance. In this paper at first, we propose a design to find a proper cluster head in a group of vehicles. Then, based on some mathematical and physical methods and criteria, we demonstrate that nested clustering can reduce data loss in real streets and at equipped traffic-light crossroads, noticeably. Finally, we perform the simulation experiments to demonstrate the efficiency of our proposed approach in comparison with other approaches.

Keywords VANET · Nested clustering · Cloud computing · Mobile cloud computing

✉ Erfan Arzhmand
  Erfanarj@gmail.com

  Hossein Rashid
  Hossein.Rashid.IR@ieee.org

  Mohammad Javad Fazel Ashrafi
  St_m.fazel@urmia.ac.ir

[1] Engineering and Technology Department, Shomal University, Amol, Mazandaran, Iran

[2] Computer Engineering Department, Islamic Azad University, Kerman, Iran

[3] Computer Engineering Department, Urmia University, Urmia, Iran

1 Introduction

The ubiquitous requests to be connected to the networks, particularly internet and transferring large-volume data and huge files between internet and consumers, lead us to have more reliable and stronger connections and junctures [1]. Many devices such as smart phones need to be connected to the internet to be online for some applications. Moreover, new internet necessities and new cars and vehicles, equipped with computers and storages enjoying high market penetration rate lead internet service providers to expand their services even through streets. Theoretically, it seems that we can use these resources to design more reliable networks for vehicles on the streets. One of the most emerging technologies to integrate the mobile computer resources for expanding network resources is mobile cloud computing [2].

The mobile cloud computing (MCC) is defined by MCC Forum [3] as a reference to some infrastructures where data processing and storing happen outside the mobile devices and instruments. Based on this definition, Mobile Cloud applications move data storages and processing away from mobile phones to the cloud. This cloud contains not just smart phones resources but broader range of subscribers such as computers and so on.

According to the MCC structure and architecture, Dinh, HT, et al. proposed a categorized form for cloud services [4]. Based on this proposed form, we have three main layers for services in MCC. The first one is Infrastructure as a Service (IaaS). This layer contains hardware and network peripherals. The other layer is Platform as a Service (PaaS) which all operating systems are determined under this category and the last one is Software as a Service (SaaS) which software and applications to serve are enclosed in this field.

Based on above definition for MCC, we can use the other wireless technologies such as Vehicular Ad hoc Network (VANET) for mobile consumers to utilize vehicle resources like using their storages as IaaS [5]. In VANET topology, we have two main parts: the first, Nodes such as vehicles and the second one, Road Side Units (RSU). Nodes can connect together and are called Vehicle-to-Vehicle (V2V) or can connect to the exterior network such as Internet via RSU as a roadside infrastructure and are called Vehicle-to-Infrastructure (V2I) [6,7]. Due to connecting numerous nodes to the RSU, sometimes overhead on RSU occurs and it is not a sufficient state. Because of many solicitations they may collide and fail. To omit or reduce this problem, clustering topology for VANET has been proposed [8]. By this topology, some vehicles gather in a hypothetical cluster and just one member can make dialogue to RSU instead of all of cluster members. We have three kinds of members in a cluster. Cluster Head (CH) which can be the cluster manager, Cluster Gateway (CG) that can connect to other clusters as an interface and (CM) the rest of members, Cluster Member. The important challenge in this topology is to find the most adequate CH in a cluster [9].

The main purpose of clustering method is definitely the reduction of overhead. Therefore, a good clustering algorithm should focus on minimum number of clusters without increasing high communications over the network. It means that according to the clustering approach, we must generate the minimum of packages for V2I and V2V with reducing overhead on CH and RSU concurrently. Besides, we have dissemination at crossroads and intersections which is a significant problem because in cloud services, more stable connection has the highest priority to have the lowest data loss. Based on these problem assumptions, we propose Nested Clustering (NeCl) in our approach as an optimum solution to reduce overhead and data loss. According to NeCl, we can manage CH tasks and shift some of these tasks to Sub Cluster Head (SCH). A SCH is the Cluster Head of a Sub Cluster (SC). One of the most important conditions in a clustering method is to have minimum number of clusters. We definitely observe this condition because managing sub clusters are not on RSUs and their modifying and managing is done only on their cluster heads. It is reasonable to say that NeCl causes remarkable decreasing probability of overhead on CH because of reducing the number of tasks physically. Real streets have their criteria and conditions on intersections and we have some equipped traffic-light crossroads. We have considered these main facts in our proposal, too.

In this paper, we introduce our proposed approach, at first. Then we show how we select the most adequate CH. After that, we use some mathematical criteria and physical conditions to make Nested Clusters and we will show how this proposal works in a real environment theoretically. After that, we propose our simulation results by related diagrams to show efficiency of our proposal in comparison with other approaches in this field. The last section concludes this paper and proposal.

2 Related works

There are very sparse approaches about cloud services on streets and their problems to transfer data from RSU to Vehicles [10]. In the following, we summarize three approaches which try to find suitable and optimum solutions. Then, we enumerate the main drawbacks of each one among all related works in this case.

One of these approaches has been proposed by Yu. Rong et al. [11]. It recommends a cooperative download/upload design with bandwidth sharing. In this approach, when applicant A is going to take a huge file from RSU, there are two steps. The first step is to find some vehicular neighbors such as B and C to set up a vehicular cloud for downloading cooperatively. In the next step, the file is split into some segments (three segments in this example) by RSU and each part is downloaded by vehicles A, B and C concurrently. At last, B and C send the separate file segments to A and A merges the file parts together finally. This proposal will increase the chance of getting a complete file remarkably. But to have an optimum approach there are some drawbacks. First, all of the vehicles should have negotiation with RSU. This is a shortcoming for this design because overhead will occur on RSUs for large amount of vehicles and their several solicitations. On the other hand, this proposal presumes that A, B and C will stay in a same way to complete the task and there is no dissemination among them. But in the real streets, dispersion may occur because of intersections, crossroads or traffic lights.

Arkian et al. [12], have proposed A Fuzzy Clustering-based Vehicular Cloud Architecture (FcVcA) to solve some inherent drawbacks such as overhead on RSUs. According to FcVcA, we should gather vehicles in some separated hypothetical clusters and then find the most proper CH for each cluster using fuzzy logic with some various factors like RSU link quality. By this method, we can see remarkable reduction of overhead on RSUs and because of most proper CH, based on simulation results we build a sufficient cluster to get data with lower data loss in comparison with other similar approaches. This method has some shortcomings, too. FcVcA is much suitable for highways and roads without intersections and any dissemination at crossroads and it has no idea to solve data loss on intersections. Another shortcoming is absolutely overhead on CH. Although we have well reducing overhead on RSUs, most of their tasks are shifted to CH. It is however, better than RSUs because the number of vehicles in a cluster is less than the number of vehicles included in working range of each RSU, but for large amount of requests in the cluster, overhead may occur on CH.

The most similar approach to our proposal has been presented in [13]. In this approach, we use clustering method. Therefore, we select the most proper CH for each cluster using improved FcVcA, at first. Then, by using Genetic algorithm, the most adequate chromosome$_x$ for data applicant X is generated, assisted by CH. After that, data is divided and some parts are moved to chromosome$_x$ and other segments are transferred to X concurrently. The chromosome$_x$ in this approach is a set of vehicles in a same cluster with X which the probability of their behavior at crossroad is almost similar to X. When dissemination occurs among cluster members at a crossroad, the rest segments of files which have not transferred yet will move from chromosome$_x$ to X. By this method, based on its simulation results, data loss for huge files will be reduced at crossroads remarkably. Although this proposal has a sufficient solution for reducing data loss at crossroads, this method has been simulated on the Manhattan model without traffic lights on each intersections and it is a shortcoming for this proposal. Also, because of many processing and calculations, overhead on CH may occur and it includes another shortcoming for this proposal.

3 Proposed design

3.1 Overview

We design our system based on clustering in VANET. The first step to build a cluster is finding an adequate group of vehicles. In this step, we should choose a sufficient method depending on the circumstances and constraints of the problem. For instant, some of the proposed clustering methods are suitable for crowded paths [14,15] or some other ones are convenient for a way with low density of vehicles [16]. On the next step, we should find a sufficient CH. CH is the manager of the cluster and controls the relations between the cluster and RSUs [17].

In this proposed approach, we want to reduce data loss that may occur even at an equipped traffic-light crossroad during file transferring from RSUs to vehicular applicants. For instance, when an applicant asks for a file from internet, RSU will reply. But if the asked file is huge, data loss may occur because of increasing the distance between RSU and applicant. Based on the proposed approach presented in [11], we can split requested file. According to [12], based on MCC, we send all parts of the requested file to the applicant and it seems a good idea to send its cluster concurrently to reduce the effect of increasing distance between RSU and applicant in transferring huge files with high efficiency. But at crossroads we have a different scenario. In this position, dissemination may occur between members of a cluster. To

reduce this, we must look for sufficient members within the cluster whose behavior at crossroad is similar to that of the intended applicants, as in [13].

According to our proposal, we use a pseudo-time division algorithm like the TDMA [18] to make a cluster on the street. When all vehicles between t_0 and t_1 go from a crossroad and enter a related street, RSUs classify them as a cluster and then choose one as an Initiator and send it the prepared list of cluster members and some information about the street like the number of the lanes. Initiator gets the position of each member and calculates the plurality of each lane. Then, Initiator chooses the most replete lane and by the average speed of cluster members, it selects CH among vehicles which are riding in the chosen lane. After that, Initiator takes both the cluster member list and the member position list to the selected CH.

Based on the quantity of the street lanes and following crossroad conditions, CH generates SCs and chooses one member of each SC as SCH. Then, it introduces SCHs to RSU and broadcasts them to own SC and gives the list of SC members to SCH. Also CH is the SCH of its lane. In this state, the cluster seems to be configured hierarchically. Therefore, for instance, when the member x_1 needs to get a file from RSU, it should ask its SCH at first. Then, SCH will ask this file from RSU and also leave own member list to it. RSU splits data in some equal predefined size and sends all parts to SC members with such algorithms as the Greedy Algorithm [19]. When the cluster arrives to the intersection, during unavoidable dissemination there is no data loss theoretically because cluster members which contain the file segments will follow the data applicant.

We consider some usual problems as follows in this proposed approach and have found out adequate solutions for them:

- Traffic lights at crossroad
- Changing the lane.

Although we care about the operating time by reducing the amount of calculations, reducing data loss on intersections during cloud computing and also bringing down the overhead on CH and RSUs are most important to our proposal. In a similar state, we prefer to satisfy these purposes against the operating time considerations.

3.2 Clustering and cluster head

B-1) Creating A Cluster

As mentioned in the overview section, clusters in this proposal are made by RSUs. In this case, RSUs cluster the entering vehicles to the street by specified time interval such as (t_0, t_1). To recognize the entering vehicles, RSUs should calculate the coordinates of each vehicle. There are some

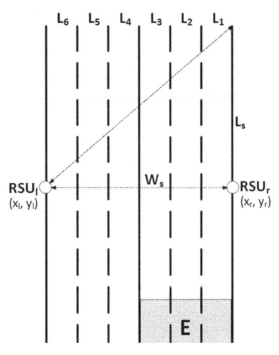

Fig. 1 The position of RSUs

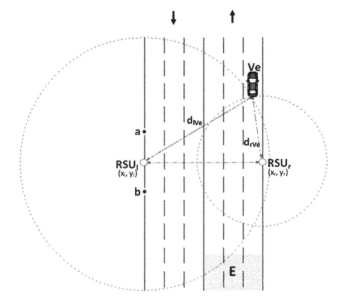

Fig. 2 Coordinating vehicle (Ve)

famous methods to determine the coordinates of each vehicle like Received Signal Strength Indicator (RSSI), but based on some researches and experimental studies [20], RSSI is not reliable for multipath environments. Therefore, we decided to use the scheme of Ou, Chia-Ho [21] and its assumptions. It is GPS-free and most recent approach to calculate the coordinates of vehicles with high reliability and precision.

In this RSU-based localization scheme, we assume all vehicles equipped with VANET transceiver and digital odometer and compass. Based on Fig. 1, we assume that RSU_l and RSU_r with coordinates of (x_l, y_l) and (x_r, y_r), respectively, are installed on either side at the middle position. The coordinates of RSUs are determined by Global Positioning System (GPS). Also the radio range of RSUs (D) covers the width of the road. Therefore,

$$D \geq \sqrt{\left(\frac{L_s}{2}\right)^2 + W_s^2}. \tag{1}$$

In the meantime, the strip l_x (designated in Fig. 1 as l_1 to l_6) is the lane of the street. Also, if RSUs recognize the coordinates of a vehicle in district E, then add it to the list of entrances.

Based on Figs. 1 and 2, we can calculate the coordinates of vehicle $Ve(x_{Ve}, y_{Ve})$ as follows:

$$x_{Ve} = \frac{x_r^2 - x_l^2 + d_{lVe}^2 - d_{rVe}^2}{2x_r - 2x_l} \tag{2}$$

Also

$$y_{Ve} = y_l - \sqrt{-x_{Ve}^2 - x_l^2 + 2x_l x_{Ve} + d_{lVe}^2}, \tag{3}$$

where

$$(x - x_l)^2 + (y - y_l)^2 = d_{lVe}^2 \tag{4}$$
$$(x - x_r)^2 + (y - y_r)^2 = d_{rVe}^2. \tag{5}$$

As shown in Fig. 2, we have two hypothetical circles (4) and (5) which come from the beacon message and vehicle; Ve is exactly on their intersection with the following conditions:

$$y_l = y_r \tag{6}$$
$$x = x_{Ve} \tag{7}$$
$$y = y_{Ve}. \tag{8}$$

Although we can recognize the direction of vehicle Ve using the interior product to find the angle between the current movements vector **Ve** and the road direction **ab** in comparison with the angle between **Ve** and **ba**, we prefer to have a set of points stored in RSUs to recognize the direction of vehicle Ve because the interior product requires more calculations on RSUs. Also, we need more recognition to know which lane vehicle Ve is on. Therefore, it will be better to our proposal to use the sets of points instead of using some methods like the interior product.

RSUs continuously make clusters and get member for them in a specified time interval. When vehicle Ve arrives in the area E, RSUs check if this vehicle is free to join to a cluster; then they make it as a member of a cluster.

```
 1:   Coordinating()
 2:   {
 3:      Coordinate Ve(x_Ve, y_Ve);
 4:      for (s=1; s=n; s++)   //maximum lanes of the street
 5:      {
 6:         if (Ve(x_Ve, y_Ve) ∈ lanes_s)
 7:         {
 8:            return(Ve(x_Ve, y_Ve), lanes_s);
 9:            break;
10:         }
11:      }
12:      return 0;
13:   }
```

Fig. 3 Pseudo-code of coordinating vehicle Ve

```
 1:   Clustering()
 2:   {
 3:      j=0;
 4:      for (t=t_0; t=t_1; t++){   //time interval
 5:         if (Coordinating(Ve) ∈ E[])
 6:            if (Status(Ve)=FreeToJoin)
 7:            {
 8:               ClusterMemberList[][][] ← Ve, Coordinating(Ve);
 9:               j++;
10:            }
11:      }
12:      i=rand() % j+1;
13:      V_init=Ve_i;
14:      send (Ve_init, ClusterMemberList);
15:      send (Ve_init, NumberOfLanes);
16:      return 0;
17:   }
```

Fig. 4 Pseudo-code of clustering

```
 1:   SelectingCH()
 2:   {
 3:      plurality(lane_CH)=0;
 4:      for (i=1; i=n;i++){   //n lanes
 5:         if (plurality(lane_CH)< plurality(lane_i))
 6:            lane_CH=lane_i;
 7:         elseif (plurality(lane_CH)= plurality(lane_i))
 8:            Lane_CH=rand(lane_CH, lane_i);//choose one of two
 9:      }
10:      CH= Lane_CH.member_1;
11:      for (j=2; j=m; j++){   //m members in lane_CH
12:         if (AdS(Lane_CH.member_i)<AdS(Lane_CH.member_i))
13:            CH= Lane_CH.member_i;
14:         elseif (AdS(Lane_CH.member_i)=AdS(Lane_CH.member_i))
15:            CH= rand(CH,Lane_CH.member_i); //choose one of two
16:      }
17:      return 0;
18:   }
```

Fig. 5 Pseudo-code of selecting CH

where

$$Av_{Ve} = \frac{1}{3}\sum_{i=1}^{3} v_i \tag{10}$$

$$Av_c = \frac{1}{n}\sum_{j=1}^{n} v_j \tag{11}$$

$$\sigma_c = \sqrt{\frac{1}{n}\sum_{j=1}^{n}\left(Av_{Ve}\text{-}v_j\right)^2}. \tag{12}$$

As Eq. (10) shows, we need only three samples of velocity for each vehicle to calculate the average speed, without more calculating and computing such as acceleration because we assume that we are in the urban area which contains vehicles with totally constant velocity. Av_c is the average speed of cluster in (11) and at last, σ_c is the standard deviation of average speed of Ve among n member of cluster. In (12) we omit Bessel's correction because we have included whole members of the cluster [22].

To select the adequate CH, V_{init} calculates the number of members on each lane of the street (plurality), at first. Then, using the values of plurality and adjacency to average speed (AdS), it selects the most adequate CH of this cluster (Fig. 5).

Lines 8 and 15 in Fig. 5 indicate that if we stay on a point to prefer one of two equal variables, then we choose randomly.

When CH is selected, V_{init} sends the list of cluster members and their information, at first. Then, it broadcasts CH to all members of cluster and introduces it to RSUs.

3.3 Nested clustering

The next phase of our proposed approach is NeCl. Cluster Head (CH), based on the coordinates of cluster members and Next Crossroad Conditions (NCC), builds nested clusters as

In Fig. 3, line 6 tries to find the lane of Ve(x_{Ve}, y_{Ve}). It must be compared with the set of points for each lane. These sets for each street are calculated and stored in RSUs previously.

As Fig. 4 shows, every vehicle being in a time interval and included in area E, and not being a member of other cluster, must join the new created cluster. After getting members at t_1, RSUs select one of the members as initiator (lines 12 and 13). At last, RSUs send the list of cluster members and the number of the street lanes to Ve$_{init}$.

B-2) Selecting The Cluster Head

Ve$_{init}$, based on the information of members, should select the most adequate CH for this hypothetical cluster. It has the coordinates and exact lane of each vehicle as the basic information, but it needs the average speed of each vehicle to select CH precisely. In fact, it needs to know the value of adjacency of each vehicle to the average speed of cluster members.

To measure this adjacency, we ought to use Eq. (9) as follows:

$$AdS_{Ve} = \frac{(Av_{Ve} - Av_c)}{\sigma_c}, \tag{9}$$

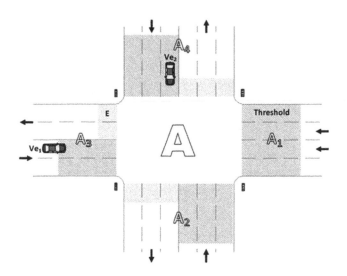

Fig. 6 Crossroad A

```
1:   CreatingSC()
2:   {
3:     for (j=1;j=street.lane; j++){
4:       if (purpose(lane_j.member)=purpose(lane_(j-1).member))
5:         SC_(i-1)[]←lane_j.member;
6:       else{
7:         SC_i[]←lane_j.member;
8:         counter+=;}}
9:     for (i=1;i=counter; i++){
10:    if (CH∉SC_i[]){
11:      r=rand() % SC_i[].quantity+1
12:      SCH_i=SC_i.member_r;}
13:    elseif (CH∈SC_i[])
14:        SCH_i=CH;
15:    }
16:   return 0;
17:  }
```

Fig. 7 Pseudo-code of creating SC

the Sub Cluster (SC). Then, it selects one of SC members as the Sub Cluster Head (SCH). It is clear that CH is one of SCHs in this procedure.

As Fig. 6 shows, we have crossroad A for instance. Crossroad A has four branches: A_1, A_2, A_3 and A_4. Each branch of crossroad A has its conditions. For instance, A_3 has two ways and each way has two lanes or A_1 has one way and four lanes. Vehicle Ve_1 is coming to crossroad A from A_3 and it has just two choices: turning right on intersection A to A_2 or turning left to A_4. Also, vehicle Ve_2 has two choices: turning right to A_3 and going straight to A_2. In the meantime, there is no choice to turn to A_1 at crossroad A.

At some urban crossroads, we have traffic lights and, therefore, this is another condition for a crossroad that we should consider. In addition, as we can see in Fig. 6, each branch has a threshold near the crossroad. In threshold field, vehicles cannot change their lanes. This fact is salutary during NeCl calculations.

Another condition for a crossroad is the weight of each branch. Based on previous gathered information, we know how many vehicles at a crossroad have been detected by RSUs in a time arrival. In Fig. 6, if RSUs detects x_1, x_2, x_3 and x_4 vehicles corresponding on branches A_1, A_2, A_3 and A_4, then we can calculate the weight of A_a as follows:

$$We\,(A_a) = 100 \left(\frac{x_a}{x_A} \right), a = 1, 2, 3, 4, \tag{13}$$

where

$$x_A = \sum_{a=1}^{4} x_a. \tag{14}$$

The condition of weight and its proportion for each branch at a crossroad is sufficient for our proposal to distinguish and prefer more probable one among some similar choices.

Cluster Head (CH), based on NCC and the number of lanes, creates SCs. As Fig. 7 shows, CH creates SC based on the number of the lanes, at first. Also, the function Purpose() checks the destination of vehicles on lane$_j$ based on NCC. If destinations are the same, then both member lanes will be in a same SC. The function Purpose() also recognizes the vague purposes as unequal state.

If vehicle Ve changes its lane after clustering, it should tell its related SCH to remove it from the list of SC and tell CH. Then, CH asks the new coordinates of Ve from RSUs and RSUs reply CH using Coordinating (). After that, based on the new coordinate, CH introduces it to the related SC.

For instance, if Vehicle Ve needs a file, it asks from the related SCH. SCH asks this file from RSUs and gives the list of its SC to RSUs simultaneously. RSUs split the file in presumed size if needed. After that, they send the parts of requested file to members of SC containing the name of applicant Ve. Then, SC members transfer those segments to Ve.

When CH touches the Threshold Area, as depicted on Fig. 8, it asks the state of traffic light from RSUs (C_{sl}, t_{sl}). C_{sl} is the color of traffic light and t_{sl} is the remaining time of being C_{sl}. As Pseudo-code of Fig. 8 shows, if CH arrives in green light, then it broadcasts to SCHs.

According to Fig. 8, t_{CH} is the required time for CH to arrive crossroad and it is calculated follows:

$$t_{CH} = \frac{y_{th}}{Av_{CH}}. \tag{15}$$

As Fig. 9 depicts, we can see the SCs of Cluster A. Also during t_{sl}, if each SCH recognizes that dissemination in SC at crossroad will occur, then it creates Sub SC (SSC) and defines a member of SSC as SSC Head (SSCH). If applicant

```
1:  TrafficLight()
2:  {
3:     Coordinate (Ve_CH);
4:     if (Ve_CH(x_CH, y_CH)∈ThresholdArea[])
5:        AskTrafficLight(C_sl, t_sl);
6:     if (C_sl=Green)
7:        if (t_CH<t_sl)
8:           Broadcast(t_sl);
9:     return 0;
10: }
```

Fig. 8 Pseudo-code of traffic light

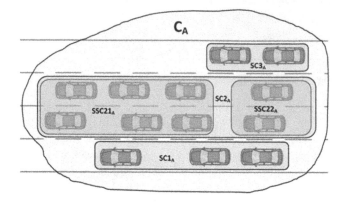

Fig. 9 Cluster and sub clusters

```
1:  CreatingSSC()
2:  {
3:     SSC_1[]=0;
4:     for (i=1; i=SC.quantity; m++){
5:        if (t_i≥t_sl)
6:           SSC_1[]+=member_i;
7:     }
8:     if (SSC_1[]≠0){
9:        SSC_2[]=SC[]-SSC_1[];
10:       if (SCH∈SSC_1[]){
11:          SSCH_1=SCH;
12:          r=rand() % SSC_2.quantity+1;
13:          SSCH_2=SSC_2[].member_r;}
14:       else{
15:          SSCH_2=SCH;
16:          r=rand() % SSC_1.quantity+1;
17:          SSCH_1=SSC_1[].member_r;}
18:       Broadcast (SSCH_1 & SSCH_2);
19:    }
20:    return 0;
21: }
```

Fig. 10 Pseudo-code of creating SSC

Ve is in SSC_1, then all parts of data which SSC_2 members are carrying should be transferred to SSC_1 members. Figure 10 presents the Pseudo-code of creating SSCs and selecting SSCHs, respectively. Figure 10 also shows the method of selecting SSCH.

By NeCl, transferring big files to its applicant is done by reducing data loss at crossroads because NeCl predicts the causes of data loss and gives some solutions to have more reliable data transferring.

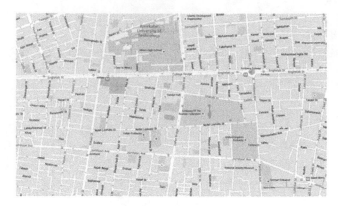

Fig. 11 Jomhouri and Enqelab avenue

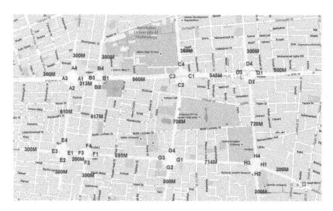

Fig. 12 Simulation area

4 Performances and simulations

To simulate our proposed approach, we have considered the reality. Therefore, we simulated our proposal in such real plan with the real scales. As depicted in Fig. 11, the simulation area is in zone eleven of Tehran city which contains a part of Jomhouri and Enqelab Avenue and also some other related streets and roads [23]. Both of Jomhouri and Enqelab Avenue are the famous roads in the middle of Tehran.

For simulating our proposed approach, we use both OMNet++ [24] as a network simulator and SUMO [25] as a traffic simulator. These tools connect and work together using VEINS [26].

As Fig. 12 shows, our simulation area contains 8 crossroads and their 22 related roads and also the length of each one. There are more intersections and crossroads but we use main roads. Also, our proposal needs crossroads to be equipped with traffic lights for possible evaluation. The table of branches of each crossroads and related lanes has been sorted in the Table 1.

Table 1 shows the main part of Crossroad Conditions for the simulation area. For instance, at crossroad A, there are two lanes for going out from A via A_1 and two lanes for coming into A via A_1 and also, at crossroad G, there are

Table 1 Conditions of the crossroads branches

Branch	Out	In	Branch	Out	In
A_1	2	2	E_1	3	0
A_2	1	0	E_2	1	0
A_3	2	2	E_3	0	3
A_4	0	1	E_4	0	1
B_1	2	2	F_1	3	0
B_2	2	2	F_2	2	2
B_3	2	2	F_3	0	3
B_4	2	2	F_4	2	2
C_1	2	2	G_1	3	0
C_2	3	0	G_2	3	0
C_3	2	2	G_3	0	3
C_4	0	3	G_4	0	3
D_1	2	2	H_1	3	0
D_2	0	3	H_2	0	3
D_3	2	2	H_3	0	3
D_4	3	0	H_4	3	0

Table 2 Simulation parameters and their values

Parameter	Value
Simulation time	300 s
Road length	200–960 m
Number of vehicles	550–1350
Number of roads	22 (68 lanes)
Number of crossroads	8
Number of Traffic lights	22
Red light	15–45 s
Green light	15–45 s
Yellow light	3s
Speed of vehicles	10–45 km/h
Transmission ratio	5 Mbps
Size of message	100 Bytes
Safe distance between vehicles	2 m
Vehicle length	3 m
D_{th}	150 m

three lanes for going out from G via G_2 and there is no lane for coming into G via G_2.

According to Table 1 and this simulation area, we have 22 roads and 68 lanes of which 18 lanes are for the input of the vehicles in this simulation scenario. Also it contains 8 equipped traffic-light crossroads. We presume all vehicles are equipped with transmitter radio that supports IEEE 802.11p and IEEE 1609 [27] standards. In addition, we assume Poisson distribution in traffic ratio [28]. The total time of simulation is 300s and we repeat each level of simulation for 1000 times and increase the certainty of the results using Monte Carlo method [29]. The assumptions and parameters of our simulation are sorted in Table 2.

Our simulation is focused on the content of the transferring file. We choose three contents for the mentioned file as 2MB, 4MB and 8MB to compute the probability of getting whole of file successfully. Also, we consider both factors of the total number of vehicles and the average speed of vehicles in the roads. Then, we compare our results with the similar results of FcVcA and Genetic method.

To calculate the probability of getting file (P_{get}), we use equation (16) as follows:

$$P_{get}(f_{suc}|f_{sent}) = \frac{P(f_{suc} \cap f_{sent})}{P(f_{sent})} \quad (16)$$

Since f_{suc} and f_{sent} are not the independent events, we use equation (16) which f_{suc} is the set of taken files successfully and f_{sent} is the set of sent files totally [30].

For the first level of simulation, presuming the velocity of all vehicles 40 km/h, we consider the number of vehicles in the roads. Theoretically, when the quantity of vehicles

increases as a resource, the total successful transferred files will increase [31]. Our results depicted in Fig. 13 show this fact. When the total vehicles increase, the probability of getting file is increased but, based on our results, we can see some differences between the results of our proposed approach and the others. The main reason is absolutely vulnerable of FcVcA and Genetic method at equipped traffic-light crossroads. Although Genetic method has a solution at crossroads to reduce data loss, we should consider that Genetic method has not any solution for traffic lights and, therefore, dissemination may occur in clusters because of traffic lights. On the other side, FcVcA has not any solution even at crossroads and fragmented clusters. Therefore, it is reasonable if we see data loss in this proposal.

Our explanations for Fig. 13 can explain Figs. 14 and 15. But with a closer look, we can see if the size of packet increases, the diagram of our proposed approach and genetic method will take some more distance with FcVcA diagram. Although the Genetic method has vulnerability at equipped traffic-light crossroads, FcVcA has not seen crossroads in its proposed approach and this is the main reason for this meaningful distance between FcVcA diagram and the others when the size of file increases.

The next level of our simulation is focused on the velocity of vehicles. It is reasonable if the total velocity of vehicles increases, then data loss in vehicular cloud computing would increase. It is sufficient for us that we reduce data loss concurrently when the total speeds of vehicles increases. Figures 16, 17 and 18 declare our simulation results about the probability of getting file successfully when the total velocity of vehicles increases. As we can see in these diagrams, when the total velocity increases, data loss increases on all

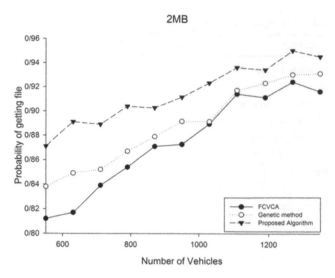

Fig. 13 Probability of getting file vs. number of vehicles (2MB)

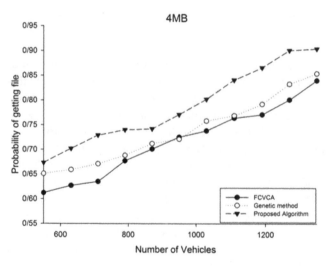

Fig. 14 Probability of getting file vs. number of vehicles (4MB)

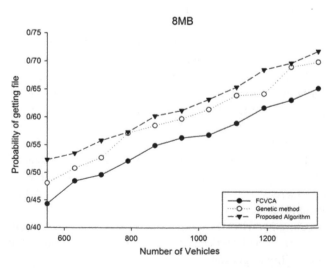

Fig. 15 Probability of getting file vs. number of vehicles (8MB)

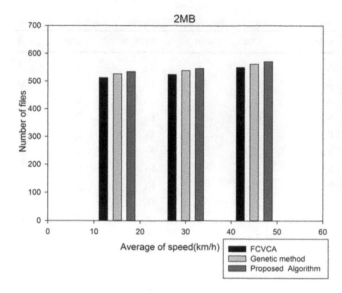

Fig. 16 Number of files vs. average of speed (2MB)

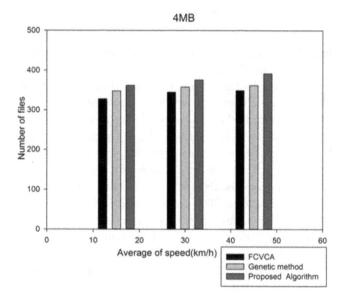

Fig. 17 Number of files vs. average of speed (4MB)

compared methods. Although data loss is increased totally, the probability of data loss in our proposed approach is less than others remarkably. When a file is divided, each part is smaller. Therefore, the chance of getting it is increased. On the other hand, gathering all split parts of a file among some vehicles and merging them is difficult and it causes data loss to increase even when a part of a file is missed. All compared methods support this solution. But at crossroads the probability of data loss is increased because we have disseminations among vehicles. Hence, our proposed approach increases the probability of getting a file successfully because it can reduce data loss in comparison with other similar compared methods.

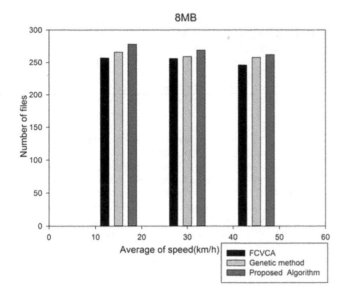

Fig. 18 Number of files vs. average of speed (8MB)

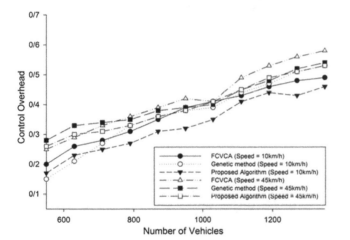

Fig. 19 Control overhead

Based on our proposed approach, having the adequate overhead is questionable in comparison with FcVcA and Genetic Method because we have many calculations and V2V and V2I negotiations to find sufficient CHs and cluster vehicles adequately.

To calculate and compare this factor, we should define the Control Overhead. Control Overhead is defined as the ratio of the total number of control messages to the total number of packets to make a cluster.

Figure 19 shows the comparison of this ratio among our proposed approach, FcVcA and Genetic method. As we can see, even though all three diagrams are really close together, the control overhead of NeCl has fewer ratios. Based on the control overhead for 10 and 45 km/h, although our proposed approach has many calculations and V2I and V2V dialog to perform the clusters, sub clusters and CHs, many calculations of Fuzzy logic increase the Control overhead of FcVcA

and Genetic method. This is one of our main reasons to use the other method to calculate instead of Fuzzy logic in our proposed approach.

5 Conclusion

At first, we defined MCC and VANET and also, detailed them and their relations. After that, we introduced and described some related woks in this field. Then, based on clustering method in VANET, we introduced NeCl in VANET. Furthermore, using NeCl, we presented our proposed approach to reduce MCC data loss at crossroads, especially the equipped traffic-light crossroads using nested clusters, their adequate CHs and the crossroad conditions based on NeCl. Finally, we depicted and detailed the diagrams and schemes of our simulation results in comparison with two other similar methods.

References

1. Gantz, J., Reinsel, D.: The digital universe in 2020: big data, bigger digital shadows, and biggest growth in the Far East. IDC iView: IDC Anal. Futur. **2012**, 1–16 (2007)
2. Whaiduzzaman, Md, et al.: A survey on vehicular cloud computing. J. Netw. Comput. Appl. **40**, 325–344 (2014)
3. MCC-forum. Discover the world of Mobile Cloud Computing. London: mobile cloud computing forum (2011)
4. Dinh Hoang, T., et al.: A survey of mobile cloud computing: architecture, applications, and approaches. Wirel. Commun. Mob Comput. **13.18**, 1587–1611 (2013)
5. Mershad, K., Artail, H.: Finding a STAR in a vehicular cloud. Intell. Transp. Syst. Mag. IEEE **5**(2), 55–68 (2013)
6. Bordley, L., Cherry, CR., Stephens, D., Zimmer, R., Petrolino, J.: Commercial motor vehicle wireless roadside inspection pilot test, Part B: Stakeholder perceptions. In: 91st annual meeting of the transportation research board (2012)
7. Yang, X., Liu, L., Vaidya, NH., Zhao, F.: "A vehicle-to-vehicle communication protocol for cooperative collision warning". In: Proceedings of the 1st annual international conference on mobile and ubiquitous systems, networking and services, pp. 114–23. MOBIQUITOUS'04. IEEE (2004)
8. Yu, J.Y., Chong, P.H.J.: A survey of clustering schemes for mobile ad hoc networks. In: Communications Surveys and Tutorials, vol. 7, no. 1, pp. 32–48. IEEE, First Qtr. (2005)
9. Fernando, Niroshinie, Loke, Seng W., Rahayu, Wenny: Mobile cloud computing: a survey. Futur. Gen. Comput. Syst. **29**(1), 84–106 (2013)
10. Bali, R.S., Kumar, N., Rodriguez, J.J.P.C.: Clustering in vehicular ad hoc networks: taxonomy, challenges and solutions. Veh Commun **1**(3), 134–152 (2014)
11. Yu, Rong, et al.: Toward cloud-based vehicular networks with efficient resource management. Netw IEEE **27.5**, 48–55 (2013)
12. Hamid Reza., A., Reza Ebrahimi., A., Saman, K.: FcVcA: a fuzzy clustering-based vehicular cloud architecture. In: Communication Technologies for Vehicles (Nets4Cars-Fall), 2014 7th International Workshop, pp. 24–28. IEEE (2014)

13. Erfan, A., Hossein, R.: Expansion of vehicular cloud services on crossroads using fuzzy logic and genetic algorithm. In: Computer Science and Software Engineering (JCSSE), 2015 12th International Joint Conference on. IEEE (2015)

14. Tian, D., Wang, Y., Lu, G., Yu, G.: A VANETs routing algorithm based on Euclidean distance clustering. In: 2nd IEEE International Conference on Future Computer and Communication, Wuhan, pp. V1-183–V1-187 (2010)

15. Salhi, I., Cherif, M., Senouci, S.: Data collection in vehicular networks. ASN symposium. pp 20–21 (2008)

16. Chang, W., Lin, H., Chen, B.: "TrafficGather: an efficient and scalable data collection protocol for vehicular ad hoc networks". In: 5th IEEE Conference on Consumer Communications and Networking, Las Vegas, NV, pp. 365–369 (2008)

17. Peng, F., et al.: Cluster-based framework in vehicular ad-hoc networks. Ad-hoc, mobile, and wireless networks, pp. 32–42. Springer, Berlin (2005)

18. Almalag, Mohammad S., Olariu, S., Weigle, M.C.: TDMA cluster-based mac for vanets (tc-mac). In: World of Wireless, Mobile and Multimedia Networks (WoWMoM), 2012 IEEE International Symposium on a IEEE (2012)

19. Kuzmanovic, A., Knightly, E.W.: TCP-LP: A distributed algorithm for low priority data transfer. INFOCOM 2003. Twenty-Second Annual Joint Conference of the IEEE Computer and Communications. IEEE Societies, vol. 3. IEEE (2003)

20. Parameswaran, Ambili T., Husain, Mohammad I., Upadhyaya, S.: Is rssi a reliable parameter in sensor localization algorithms: an experimental study. In: Field Failure Data Analysis Workshop (F2DA09) (2009)

21. Ou, Chia-Ho: A roadside unit-based localization scheme for vehicular ad hoc networks. Int. J. Commun. Syst. 27(1), 135–150 (2014)

22. McLachlan, Norman William: Bessel functions for engineers. Clarendon Press, Oxford (1961)

23. Website: http://map.tehran.ir, (2015)

24. Varga, A.: OMNeT++ Discrete Event Simulation System User Manual. 4.2.2. (2011)

25. Behrisch, M., Bieker, L., Erdmann, J., Krajzewicz, D.: SUMO—simulation of urban mobility: an overview. SIMUL 2011, The Third International Conference on Advances in System Simulation, pp. 63–68 (2011)

26. Sommer, C.: Vehicles in network simulation (VEINS) Project. Website: http://veins.car2x.org. (2012)

27. Al-Sultan, S., Moath, M., Al-Bayatti, Ali, Zedan, H.: A comprehensive survey on vehicular ad hoc network. J. Netw. Comput. Appl. 37(1), 380–392 (2014)

28. Gerlough, Daniel L.: Simulation of traffic flow. Highway Research Board Special Report 79 (1964)

29. Fishman, G.S.: Monte Carlo: Concepts, Algorithms, and Applications. Springer Verlag, New York (1995)

30. Feller, W.: An introduction to probability theory and its applications, vol. I (1950)

31. Hassan, A., et al.: V-Cloud: vehicular cyber-physical systems and cloud computing. In: Proceedings of the 4th International Symposium on Applied Sciences in Biomedical and Communication Technologies. ACM (2011)

## 16

Autonomic fine-grained replication and migration at component level on multicloud

Linh Manh Pham[1] · Tuan-Minh Pham[2]

Abstract Although migration and replication of applications in a distributed environment have been discussed by many researchers, the implementations of these features are rarely focused when deployed in the cloud. The cloud enterprises usually have to migrate or replicate partly or fully their services because of economical or disaster preventing reasons. Because the cost of copying the whole virtual machines is too high due to their big size, the replication at application level is a possible approach. This work proposes an autonomic replication and migration mechanism integrated in an implementation of a fine-grained deployment framework which enables ability to migrate and replicate-service components on the clouds. We formulate the deployment problem of replicated components to optimize the system performance as a quadratic program. Our proposed framework ensures the high availability and scalability of services, and complies with the service-oriented architecture. Our experiments conducted in real scenarios of elastic demands demonstrate that the proposed fine-grained migration and replication is more efficient than the coarse-grained ones when an autonomic system responds to fluctuation of webapp's workload. We also show the influence of adding servers and upgrading server connections on the system performance.

✉ Tuan-Minh Pham
minhpt@hnue.edu.vn

Linh Manh Pham
linh-manh.pham@imag.fr

[1] Laboratoire d'Informatique de Grenoble, University of Grenoble Alpes, Grenoble, France

[2] Faculty of Information Technology, Hanoi National University of Education, Hanoi, Vietnam

Keywords Autonomic computing · Cloud computing · Application migration · Application replication · Network virtualization

1 Introduction

Cloud computing is a recent trend of information technology, with its application distributed in every field. With minimal effort or service provider interaction, the configurable computing resources can be rapidly provisioned and released on demand with a pay-as-you-go style [1]. Ideally, all things a cloud user needs are a machine with an enabled web browser. In terms of service model, there are three well-discussed layers known as IaaS for Infrastructure as a Service, PaaS for Platform as a Service, and SaaS for Software as a Service. Many other XaaS terms are used nowadays to name different provided services in the cloud.

Cloud environments can be used to host service-based applications following a service-oriented architecture (SOA). SOA is a collection of self-contained services which communicate with each other using provided interfaces [2]. Management of service-based applications in cloud environments is a challenging task in the aspects of fault tolerant, performance and security. Cloud service management plays an important role to respect the service-level agreement (SLA) between the service consumers and providers. In this context, one of the solutions to ensure the SLA is the ability to support mobility services which allows the migration and replication of services between virtual machines (VM) or among different containments. Many attempts to provide migration and replication of service-based applications in the cloud exist. They can be classified into three categories: application-centric migration, image-based migration and migration to a virtualized container. The application-centric migration such as [3,4] extracts and migrates application arti-fact, resources and configuration from the source to a new provisioned application deployment environment on the tar-get. The image-based migration such as [5,6] converts source into VM images and imports them into target cloud after some adjustment. The migration to virtualized container technique, such as [7] migrates the source VM to run in a virtual-ized container inside the target without any modifications. All of the mentioned approaches do not offer an autonomi-cally fine-grained solution at service component level. Such a solution helps cloud users mitigate manual effort which is tedious and error-prone. Furthermore, much research so far pay attention to migration of legacy applications to the cloud, but cloud-to-cloud (i.e. C2C) migration/replication is rarely focused [8].

As mentioned, migration/replication can help cloud ser-vices to keep functioning in case of failure and respond to environmental changes on time. This increases the system reliability and scalability, two of non-functional require-ments frequently described in the SLA in terms of service-level objectives (SLO). Migration and replication, migrates or replicates the critical software components, so that if one of components fails, the others can be used instead, or if one is not enough, others can be created to share workload. With a high level of component abstraction, these issues can be optimized by providing fine-grained granularity. Granularity refers to the unit of sharing in the cloud that can be an entire VM or a tiny file [9]. Granularity needs to be considered if multiple choices in moving or replicating a service in the specific conditions exist. We would not need to migrate or replicate an entire VM if partly migration or replication can solve the problems better.

The major contributions of this paper are as follows. First, we propose an autonomically fine-grained service migra-tion and replication mechanism at component level, which is implemented on a multicloud distributed deployment frame-work. We also make a contribution in the development of a hierarchical DSL (domain-specific language) of the frame-work. The DSL helps not only to describe structure of component-based application naturally but also to demon-strate replicating/migrating rules in an intuitive and friendly way. Our first result was presented at the 2nd Nafosted Con-ference on Information and Computer Science [10]. Second, we complement our framework with the optimal deploy-ment problem of replicated components. More specifically, we tackle the online optimization problem of component placement on multicloud regarding to the communication cost under constraints on system resources and a hierarchical structure of component-based applications. We formulate the placement problem as a quadratic program. Third, we vali-date our proposed mechanism by an experiment conducted in the context of an elastic scenario, and provide useful insights for cloud providers to decide if they should add servers or

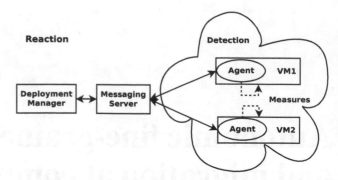

Fig. 1 Autonomic framework for migration and replication of cloud applications

upgrade server connections to improve the average respon-sive time of the system.

The rest of this paper is organized as follow: Sect. 2 gives an overview of architecture of the framework in the aspects of deployment manager, fine-grained hierarchical DSL and autonomic management. We introduce the migration and replication mechanism in Sect. 3. We present the formulation of the optimal deployment problem in Sect. 4. The validating experiments are presented in Sect. 5. Section 6 reviews the related work. Conclusions are stated in Sect. 7.

2 The autonomic framework

To support the autonomic migration and replication of cloud applications, we need a framework which satisfies the follow-ing requirements: (1) supports for describing components of cloud applications naturally at design time; (2) provides auto model parsing as well as dependencies and constraints resolv-ing at runtime; (3) implements IaaS coordination which distributes service components into multiclouds, thereby avoiding the vendor lock-in problem, provides runtime exe-cution as well; (4) advocates autonomic management to detect and respond to changes in runtime environments. Such a framework is depicted in Fig. 1, which is made up of several modules:

- The Deployment Manager (DM) is an application in charge of managing VMs and the agents (see below). It acts as a coordination interface to the set of VMs or devices on premises and on clouds. It is also in charge of instantiating VMs in the IaaS and physical machines such as embedded boards. It includes core modules of a MAPE-K autonomic model [11] such as Monitoring, Analysis, Planning, Execution and Knowledge exchange, which help the DM response to changes from surround-ing environment.
- The Agent is a software component that must be pre-installed and bootstrapped on every VM and device which

are managed. Agent probes the status of both hardware and software components and send these data to the DM periodically. These agents communicate with the DM and each other through an asynchronous messaging server.

- The Messaging Server is the key component acting as a distributed registry of import/export variables that enable communications between the DM and the agents and among agents themselves.

More details in these modules can be found in [12]. We have proposed and developed a deployment platform, which satisfies the requirements (1), (2) and (3) in [13]. In that paper, an open-source platform is designed to deploy complex distributed applications on multiclouds, which fosters deployment automation a step further by distributing virtual resources with pre-installed software (i.e. virtual appliances). It allows to describe distributed applications and handle deployment of the entire or a part of them. The platform is improvable and adaptable with a lightweight kernel which implements all necessary mechanisms to plug new behaviors for addressing new applications and a new execution environment. Moreover, the platform supports scaling and dynamic (re)configuration natively. This provides flexibility and allows elastic deployments.

With regards to SOA principle, the platform sees a complex application as a combination of "components" and "instances". While each component is a self-contained service that is homologous with the "object" definition, instances are obviously embodiment of these objects. In addition, the platform is designed to see an application also as a hierarchy of components. It means some components may be a containment to host or provide execution environment for other ones such as VM or container. All components derive from an abstract "root" component. Instances inherit all properties derived from its corresponding component. The main motivation of hierarchy is to keep track of exactly where instances were implemented in the system. It helps the system to make right decisions in autonomic deployment. The parent/children relationship of components is depicted naturally in an example about OSGi-based [14] application in Fig. 2. It is a cloud application providing Java message service (JMS) through its software components as Joram [15] and JNDI [16]. These components are containerized as bundles complying to the OSGi specification. A Karaf [17] component is also needed serving as OSGi container for the Joram and JNDI bundles.

In Fig. 2, there is an important field: children which lists other components that can be instantiated and deployed over this component. In the OSGi example, it means we can deploy Karaf over a VM instance. In turn, Joram and JNDI can be deployed over instances of Karaf. The hierarchical model resolves the containment relations (i.e. vertical relationship)

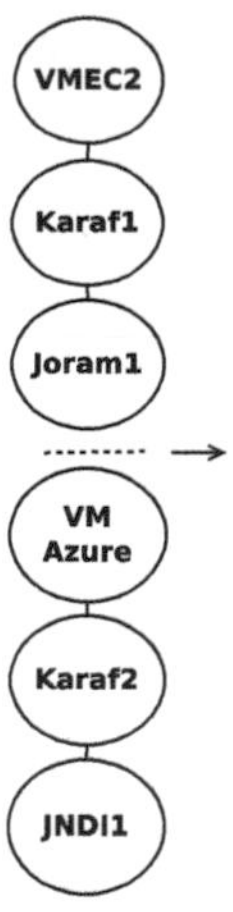


```
# EC2 VM
VM_EC2 {
installer: iaas;
children: Karaf;
}

# Azure VM
VM_Azure {
installer: iaas;
children: Karaf;
}

# Karaf: OSGi Container
Karaf {
installer: bash;
exports: ip, agentID = 1;
children: Joram, JNDI;
}

# Joram: OSGi Application Srv
Joram {
installer: osgi-bundle;
exports: portJR = 16001;
imports: Karaf.agentID, Karaf.ip;
}

# JNDI: OSGi-based Java naming
JNDI {
installer: osgi-bundle;
exports: portJNDI = 16401;
imports: Karaf.agentID, Karaf.ip;
}
```

```
# A VM EC2 with Karaf & Joram
instanceof VM_EC2 {
    name: vmec2;

    instanceof Karaf {
        name: karaf1;

        instanceof Joram {
            name: joram1;
        }
    }
}

# A VM Azure with Karaf & JNDI
instanceof VM_Azure {
    name: vmazure;

    instanceof Karaf {
        name: karaf2;

        instanceof JNDI {
            name: jndi1;
        }
    }
}
```

Fig. 2 An OSGi-based JMS service described by the framework's DSL (the graph in the middle and the initial instances description in the right)

amidst components at disparate layers. At runtime, the Graph and the Initial Instances Description are used to determine which components can be instantiated, and how they can be deployed. Abstracted components include the deployment roots (e.g. VMs, containers, devices, remote hosts), databases, application servers and application modules (e.g. WAR, ZIP, etc.). They list what the deployers want to deploy or possibly deploy. What is modeled in the graph is really a user choice. Various granularity can be described. It can either dig very deeply into the hierarchical description or bundle things together such as associating a given bundle with an OSGi container. Multi-IaaS is supported by defining several root components. Each one will be associated with various properties (e.g. IaaS provider, VM type, etc.). It is worth noting that an instance in a hierarchy can be located using an absolute path in the framework's DSL. For example, the "Joram1" instance can be referred to by the path "/vmec2/karaf1/joram1".

From these descriptions, the platform then takes the burden of launching the VMs, deploying software on them, resolving dependencies dynamically among software components, updating their configuration and starting the whole stuff when ready. The monitoring of each component after launching is also taken into consideration. Our continuous works to bring forward autonomic features to this platform, which satisfies the requirement (4), are discussed as our contributions in the next sections.

3 The autonomic replication and migration mechanism

We apply the autonomic management as an integrated feature of the platform in [13], which consists of two parts. On one side, agents retrieve measures on their local node. These measures are compared against some values given in the agent's configuration. If they exceed, equal or are lower than the given values, depending on the configuration rules, agents send a notification to the DM. On the other side, when the DM receives such a notification, it checks its configuration to determine which actions to undertake. These actions can range from a single log entry, to e-mail notification or even replicating a service on another machine. Figure 1 also sums up the way autonomic management works. While detection is delegated to the agents, reactions are managed by the DM.

The autonomic configuration is in fact defined in application projects. It means every project has its own rules and reactions. In this perspective, the project structure is enriched with a new directory, called autonomic. The autonomic directory expects two kinds of files. Measures files include a set of measures to perform by the agent. Such a file is associated with a given component in the graph. Hence, we can consider the autonomic rules as an annotation on a component in the graph. Rules files define the actions to undertake by the DM when a measure has reached a given limit or a particular condition has met. Such a file is associated with the whole application. Both types of files consume a part of the DSL language of the platform. This DSL part is specific to fine-grained migrating and replicating actions detailed as follows.

Measures files indicate measures an agent will have to perform regularly on its machine. An agent can use several options to measure something. The option or extension used to perform the measure is declared explicitly along with the measure name. Each measure is performed independently of the others. It means every measure matching the rule results in a message sent to the DM. The agent measures and notifies when needed and it has not to interpret these measures. This is responsibility of the autonomic modules of the DM. Here is the syntax for the declaration of a measure:

[EVENT measure−extension measure−name]

The measure-extension includes LiveStatus, REST and File. The LiveStatus [18], which is the protocol used by Nagios [19] and Shinken [20], allows to query a local Nagios or Shinken agent. We simply write a LiveStatus request:

```
# A simple query for Live Status.
[EVENT nagios myRuleName−80]
GET hosts
Columns: host_name accept_passive_checks
         acknowledged
Filter: accept_passive_checks = 1
```

An agent can query a REST service. The result can be interpreted as an integer or as a string.

```
# Check the result returned by a
# REST HTTP service.
```

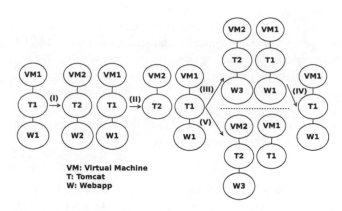

Fig. 3 Illustration of using five replicating/migrating reactions

```
[EVENT rest myRuleName−1]
Check http://google.fr THAT value > 0
```

An agent can also check the local file system. Depending on the existence of a file or a directory, or based on the absence of a given file, a notification will be sent to the DM.

```
# Notify the DM if a file exists
# and delete it.
[EVENT file myRuleName−1]
Delete if exists /opt/tmp
```

Rules files contain the reactions to undertake by the DM when a measure verified by a given rule on the agent side. These files use a custom syntax as following one.

```
[REACTION measure−name reaction−handler]
Optional parameters for the handler
```

There are four available handlers. Log is to log an entry without any parameters. Mail is to send an e-mail. It accepts only one parameter which is an e-mail address. Replicate-Service is to replicate a component on a new machine. It takes a chain of component names as parameters. Delete-Service is to undeploy and remove a component that was replicated. It takes a component name as parameter. To demonstrate for utility of the mentioned rules, we use an example about a J2EE application with three tiers including web (Apache), application (Tomcat) and database (MySQL) servers. The Apache uses "mod_jk" to provide load-balancing mechanism for Tomcat servers which host instances of a Webapp. The autonomic events which can affect to such system are going to be discussed carefully in Sect. 5. In this section, we describe five basic reactions usually used in autonomic replication/migration as follows. The illustration of these five reactions are shown in Fig. 3.

I To replicate the entire stack of
  "/VM1/Tomcat1/Webapp1" (all three instances):

  ```
  [REACTION high−RT−1 Replicate−Service]
  /VM1/Tomcat1/Webapp1  /VM2/Tomcat2/Webapp2
  ```

It is worth noting that if an empty VM2 already exists, it will be reused and "filled" with a new Tomcat2 containing a new Webapp2. Otherwise, a totally new entire stack will be created.

II To remove a specific instance Webapp2 of the stack "/VM2/Tomcat2/Webapp2", we need to provide the absolute path of this instance:

[REACTION low−RT−1 Delete−Service]
/VM2/ Tomcat2 /Webapp2

III To replicate a specific instance Webapp1 of the stack "/VM1/Tomcat1/Webapp1" to under the Tomcat2 (/VM2/Tomcat2/) and name it Webapp3:

[REACTION high−RT−2 Replicate−Service]
/VM1/ Tomcat1 /Webapp1 /VM2/ Tomcat2 /Webapp3

IV To remove the entire stack "/VM2/Tomcat2/Webapp3", we only need to provide the absolute path of the root instance which is VM2 in this case:

[REACTION low−RT−2 Delete−Service]
/VM2

It is also worth noting that the VM2 and its children (Tomcat2, Webapp3) will be gracefully stopped, undeployed and removed from the system orderly and automatically. In the case of migration, we combine both "Replicate-Service" and "Delete-Service" rules. For instance, after [III]:

V To migrate a specific instance Webapp1 of the stack "/VM1/Tomcat1/Webapp1" to under the Tomcat2 (/VM2/Tomcat2/) and name it Webapp3:

Replicate the Webapp1 first
[REACTION low−RT Replicate−Service]
/VM1/ Tomcat1 /Webapp1 /VM2/ Tomcat2 /Webapp3
Then remove the Webapp1
[REACTION low−RT Delete−Service]
/VM1/ Tomcat1 /Webapp1

These five basic reactions are reusable by any adaptive engines of any cloud platforms as long as they own modules supporting the description and distribution of fine-grained components.

4 Optimal deployment of components

The previous section introduces the mechanism of the autonomic replication and migration in which the agents notify the DM of measures collected on their local nodes, and the DM interprets these measures into actions. In this section, we study the optimization of DM's actions. More specifically,

we determine an application server to which a component should be deployed to optimize the application performance under constrains on computing resources and the structure of components.

The DM decides the replication or undeployment of a component, depending on metrics on local nodes and the autonomic configuration defined in application projects. These changes in the deployment of components are represented by the current network of components of all applications and the new network of components. Let $P_1 = (C, G)$ be the current network of components of all applications where C is a set of components, and G is a set of links among components, called c-links. $g_{ij} \in G$ ($i, j \in C$) is the c-link between component i and component j, where i and j are components of the same application and they exchange data if $g_{ij} = 1$, or not if $g_{ij} = 0$. Similarly, we denote the new network of components by $P_1' = (C', G')$.

We consider a network of server instances $P_2 = (S, E)$ where S is a set of servers and E is a set of links among server instances, called s-links. Several server instances can be deployed in the same physical server. $w_{ij} \in E$ ($i, j \in S$) is the communication cost between server instances i and j. We denote by u_{cs} ($c \in C$, $s \in S$) the current deployment state of P_1, where component c is deployed on server s if $u_{cs} = 1$, or not if $u_{cs} = 0$. Let $\tilde{C} = C' \backslash C$ be new components that the DM decides to replicate. Let d_i ($i \in S$) be the total computing resource of server i. We define r to be an amount of computing resource required to deploy component i to a server. Let $x = (x_{cs})$ ($c \in \tilde{C}$, $s \in S$) be a candidate solution of deployment of new components where component c is deployed on server s if $x_{cs} = 1$, or not if $x_{cs} = 0$.

The system performance of a deployment solution is measured by the total cost of the communication among new components $c_1 \in \tilde{C}$, the communication among components $c_2 \in C \cap C'$ that are components appearing in both the current deployment and the new one, and the communication between c_1 and c_2. Since the cost of the communication among c_2 in different solutions is similar, the cost of a deployment solution is given by

$$\varphi(x) = \sum_{c_1 \in \tilde{C}} \sum_{s_1 \in S} \sum_{s_2 \in S} x_{c_1 s_1} w_{s_1 s_2}$$
$$\times \left(\sum_{c_2 \in \tilde{C}} x_{c_2 s_2} g'_{c_1 c_2} + \sum_{c_2 \in C \cap C'} u_{c_2 s_2} g_{c_1 c_2} \right) \quad (1)$$

The low cost of a deployment solution results in the improvement of average responsive time (ART). Therefore, the objective of the DM is to optimize the deployment so that the communication cost added by new components are minimized. Specifically, given the current network of components $P_1 = (C, G)$, the new network of components

$P'_1 = (C', G')$, the network of server instances $P_2 = (S, E)$, the current deployment state (u_{cs}) where $c \in C$ and $s \in S$, find a deployment solution $x = (x_{cs})$ where $c \in C' \backslash C$ and $s \in S$ to minimize the communication cost subject to constraints on computing resources. This can be formulated as the following quadratic programming problem:

$$\text{Min} \quad \varphi(x)$$

$$\text{s.t.} \quad \sum_{c \in \tilde{C}} x_{cs} r_c + \sum_{c \in C \cap C'} u_{cs} r_c \leq d_s \quad \forall s \in S \tag{2}$$

$$\sum_{s \in S} x_{cs} = 1 \quad \forall c \in \tilde{C} \tag{3}$$

$$x_{cs} \in \{0, 1\} \quad \forall c \in \tilde{C}, s \in S \tag{4}$$

The optimization problem of service placement has been studied in several areas of future Internet, and the integer programming has been considered as a potential approach for solving the problem [21,22]. The complexity of the service placement problem is NP-hard [23]. A quadratic program can be solved by several optimization tools such as the CPLEX Optimizer [24]. In the following section, we are going to study the system performance of a deployment solution using the CPLEX Optimizer to solve the problem in various system configurations.

5 Evaluation

We first conduct an experiment to validate the proposed framework in context of an elasticity scenario. Then, we answer the question of whether we should add more server or upgrade server connection to improve the system performance.

5.1 Experiment setup

The elasticity context applies to the aforementioned J2EE application. With application tier, we use in initials two Tomcat servers dedicating to serve two different webapps: Webapp1 and Webapp2. We use the "mod_proxy" to build a cluster of Apache servers to avoid yet another bottleneck. Each of Apache server implements the "mod_jk" serving as a load balancer in front of these Tomcat ones. This experiment focuses on elasticity of application tier, thus without loss of generality, the database one is shared among webapps and hosted on a single MySQL server. All the VM used in this system are Microsoft Azure Standard_A2 instances with 2 cores and 3.5 GB memory. Each Tomcat created in the elastic reactions is a Amazon EC2 m3.medium with 1 core and 3.75 GB memory. The managed system is called System Under Test (SUT) that we use CLIF server [25], an distributed load injector, to create load profile and generate workload for the

SUT to observe how the system reacts to changes of average response time (ART). These reactions are empowered by autonomic mechanisms aforementioned in Sect. 3. The topology of this scenario is depicted in Fig. 4.

5.2 Test scenario

The loads are injected into an entrance of the Apache cluster which is a virtual IP. Then this cluster distributes the loads to the corresponding webapps through the Tomcat servers. In this particular situation, the Webapp2 often gets low load, thus has a load profile as in Fig. 5 with 50 virtual users who try to send HTTP GET requests to the Webapp2 and then "think" a couple of time randomly. The virtual servers are threads created simultaneously by the CLIF server while the experiment was being performed according to the load profile of the Webapp2 (pre-defined also using CLIF server). Behaviors of the virtual users are captured from real-world operations using a capturing tool of the CLIF server.

The owner of the Webapp2 need not any elastic mechanisms provided by the cloud PaaS provider due to the low load of the Webapp2. On the other hand, the Webapp1 usually receives high load and thus has a load profile as in Fig. 5, which is also designed by the CLIF server. The Webapp1 usually takes the burden of about 450 virtual users who have similar behaviors as in the case of Webapp2. The owner of Webapp1 requires the cloud PaaS provider to ensure an acceptable performance for his webapp. Therefore, he demands an elastic load-balancing solution to guarantee an ART as low as possible as stated in an SLA established between him and the provider. When the ART varies, this solution includes provisioning a whole new Tomcat/Webapp1 server (reaction [I]) or replicating only the Webapp1 instances (reaction [III]) while scaling out as well as removing the servers (reaction [IV]) or migrating the webapps (reaction [V]) while scaling in with minimum side effects to overall system.

The polling periods is set to 10 s that means the ART of all requests from all users are collected each 10 s. These gathered data are sent to the framework's analysis module to be aggregated and further analyzed. The analyzed information then is delivered to the planning module to generate new configuration for the system based on ECA (event-condition-action) rules.

The ECA rules decide whether the system should create an entire application server or only replicate a webapp instance using the set of reactions. One of the rules is to prevent multiple creating of new VMs or a new instance in a short period of time. At least the system needs to wait until it gets knowledge about the new one before another can be created automatically. It is called synchronization time which includes the VM provisioning, Tomcat installation, Webapp deployment and reconfiguration time for the existing Apache

Fig. 4 Topology of J2EE test case using CLIF load injector

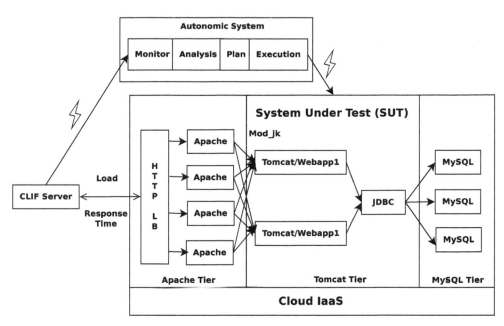

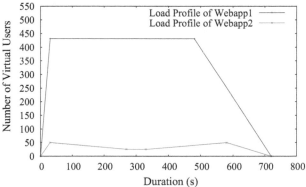

Fig. 5 CLIF load profiles of Webapp1 and Webapp2

(to know the attendance of the new Tomcat) in the case of creating a new Tomcat/Webapp server. With replicating or migrating a Webapp instance, the synchronization time only contains the two latter ones. Another rule is to prohibit the migration/replication of an instance to hosts where also are on-peak times. The very first 10-min snapshot of this experiment is shown in Fig. 6 and results are discussed deeply in the next section.

5.3 The efficiency of the fine-grained mechanism

Figure 6 shows the ART of both webapps and the corresponding reflections from the autonomic system to fluctuations of the response time. In addition, the figure also reports the changes in number of Tomcat servers while running the test case. The max response time of Webapp1 is set to 800 ms, it means if the ART goes over this limitation, creating new Tomcat server or replicating the Webapp request should be made. In contrast, if the ART goes under min response time

(200 ms), a removing or migrating decision should be triggered.

We see that the ART of Webapp1 peaked at the 40th second because of aggressive accesses of the 450 virtual users simultaneously. At point "A1", a command to create a new Tomcat server was triggered instead of a replication due to a peak (≈400 ms) happening in Webapp2. The max and min response times of Webapp2, which are not shown in Fig. 6, were set to 400 and 100 ms, respectively. After this request, the framework observed the SUT silently without any further requests until it gets knowledge about the new server. This synchronization time finished at the 180th second (point "A2"), thus the Webapp1 users continued experiencing slow accesses during 2 min 20 s more. At point "B1", once again the ART of Webapp1 was larger than the max limitation whereas the ART of Webapp2 was getting low. It is suitable to make a replication Webapp1 (/VM1/Tomcat1/Webapp1) to under Tomcat2 and name it Webapp1_2 (/VM2/Tomcat2/Webapp1_2). The synchronization time for creating the Webapp1_2 was about 20 s which offered about 2 min better than the case of creating a new Tomcat server. Moreover, the system avoided creating a totally new server resulting in saving resources for PaaS provider and money for both PaaS user and provider. In reverse, the system performed two times of the scaling in: a request to remove a Tomcat3 server at "C1" (which had been created at "A2") and a request to remove the Tomcat1 server at "D1" (which had been there from the beginning). The synchronization in both cases were almost the same (more or less than 20 s, finish at "C2" and "D2") because we do not care about the shutting down time of a VM. In spite of that, the result of this elasticity is the saving of two VMs (from 3 VMs at "C1" to 1 VM at "D2") while the system were in low-load period.

Fig. 6 Autonomic responses
with fluctuation of average
response time of Webapps

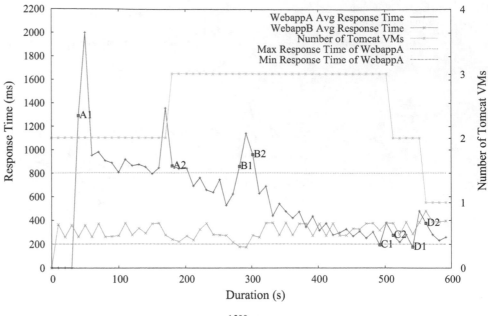

Because the changes in load of a website usually happen, applying the fine-grained migrating/replicating mechanism to an autonomic system brings significant performance improvement as well as cost saving.

5.4 The improvement on the system performance

We consider a baseline scenario in which a total of 100 components of 10 applications are deployed to 20 server instances. The computing resource of one server represented as a number of CPU cores, and the resource required to deploy a component to a server are uniformly distributed in [10, 100] and [1, 5], respectively. The communication cost among servers and the relation between components of an application are chosen uniformly in [1, 9] and [0, 1], respectively. A server is chosen uniformly in the set of servers whose resources are available for deploying a component.

We compare the performance cost of the system in three scenarios including the baseline scenario and two modified scenarios of the baseline scenario. In the first modified scenario, we add 4 servers to the baseline scenario. The resource of the new servers, the communication cost among new servers, and that between a new server and an old server are generated by the same rule described in the baseline scenario. In the second modified scenario, the communication cost between servers deceases by 1 in comparison with that in the baseline scenario. For the three scenarios, the number of new components replicated by the DM is varied between 5 and 45. We use the CPLEX Optimizer [24] to solve the optimal deployment of the new components in each setting, and compute the communication cost of the system. As one can see from Fig. 7, the communication cost of the system in a scenario of upgrading server connections is lower than that in a scenario of adding servers. This occurs because the

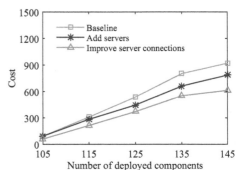

Fig. 7 The impact of adding servers and improving server connections

communication cost between two components is very small if they are deployed to the same server. The results suggest that it is better for a cloud provider to upgrade a server connection to improve the average responsive time of the system rather than add more servers.

5.5 The overhead of the framework

We evaluated the overhead introduced by the framework by doing experiments in two cases: (1) application deployed without the framework and (2) application deployed with the framework. The experiments are conducted on the VMAzure Standard A2 instances (2 cores and 3.5 GB memory). In the experiments, 1000 requests were generated. The requests sent were executed 20 times in both scenarios. Table 1 presents the results of the average execution time of each scenario as well as the additional costs introduced by the framework itself.

From the results presented in Table 1 , we can see that the overhead introduced by the framework is only 1.84 %. This

Table 1 Execution time and additional cost

Scenario	Average execution time	Overhead introduced by the framework
Application	10.85	–
Application with the framework	11.05	1.84 %

additional cost is generated mainly by the monitoring module which collects information for the elasticity autonomic mechanism. This module is integrated into the Deployment Manager. In summary, the overhead introduced by the framework is negligible given the discussed advantages.

6 Related work

Horizontal scaling action broadly supported by current cloud providers. They usually allow fixed-size VMs to be scaled out depending on current workload demand. On the contrary, vertical scaling, which obtains the elasticity by changing VM configuration (i.e. redimension), is offered scarcely by the providers. Even if redimension is supported, resizing VM resources on the fly is prohibited. GoGrid [26] allows its customers to increase RAM of VMs, but requires a VM reboot. Although Amazon EC2 introduces a wide range of VM instances with different sizes and configurations to simulate vertical scaling when needed (i.e. VM replacement or substitution), VM restart is still a must. The coarse-grained scaling with fixed-size VMs often leads to resource provisioning overhead resulting in the over-provisioning. Research on elastic VM of Rodero-Merino et al. [27] about VM substitution and Dawoud et al. [28] about fine-grained scaling to simulate the resizing have partly resolved this challenge. However, cloud providers is most likely prefer providing horizontal scaling with fatty VMs, thus research on combination of scaling actions on multiple levels of resource granularity as our work is really essential.

There have been several studies on the migration and replication of applications on cloud environments [29–33]. In [29], Ferrer et al. proposed the Optimis offering a chain of tools consisting of a Service Builder, an Administration Controller, a Deployment Engine, a Service Optimizer and a Cloud Optimizer. Service providers use these components to develop, deploy and execute applications on different clouds. Moreover, the SLA parameters are monitored and the services are migrated to another cloud if needed. Satzger et al. [30] developed the Meta-Cloud with existing standardizations that provides an API for web applications, recipes for migration/replication and deployment, resource templates

for defining requirements and offerings, resource monitoring for checking QoS properties, etc. In [31], Reich et al. proposed a solution to migrate stateful Web Services on basis of SLA violations. The services are hosted by Web Service Resource Framework (WSRF) containers. These containers monitor the SLA parameters and detect violations. If an SLA condition is violated, a proper migration destination is searched over the P2P network for a service picked randomly by a particular container. The SLAs are defined for each service using WS-Agreement, an SLA description language. However, these solutions lack a DSL to abstract the complex services.

So far, there has been little discussion about the use of abstracted representations of component-based applications for the migration and replication of applications on cloud environments. In [32], Hao et al. introduced a General Computing Platform (GCP) which hosts different kinds of services, from infrastructure to application services. This system uses a workflow model for service composition and a cost model for making migration decision. The system is similar to our approach because services used in the workflow model are also the abstracted representations of real ones and then the abstracted ones are replaced with concrete instances. However, the hierarchical description of multi-tier applications is not feasible with this system. Our work is different as it proposes a DSL to describe a hierarchical structure of component-based application.

A model-driven approach for the design and execution of applications on multiple clouds is proposed by Ardagna et al. [33]. For the abstracted clouds, the code is semi-automatically translated and applications have to be implemented only one time. Then the best cloud for a service is selected regarding non-functional criteria such as the costs, the risks by a DSS (decision support system). Eventually, the dynamic migration/replication of services between clouds is provided by a runtime management API. However, with this approach, the autonomous factor is not taken into account. Our proposed framework provides an autonomic management mechanism in which the decision of migration and replication is controlled by the deployment manager responding to rapid fluctuations of demands. In addition, no research has been found that surveyed the online optimization problem of component placement on multicloud regarding the communication cost under constraints on system resources and a hierarchical structure of component-based applications. Most studies on the placement problem in cloud computing have been carried out in either the placement of virtual machines or an application component without considering the online solution with regard to both a structure of component-based applications and constraints on cloud infrastructure [34–37]. Our study was designed to fill the gap.

7 Conclusion

In the era of cloud computing, the trend which enterprises choose to deploy their software on hybrid and multicloud is indispensable. The flexible choice among cloud providers helps enterprises to save the cost due to which they can select the best services to install different software parts. This leads to demands of service migration and replication across the clouds. Our proposed framework supports service migration/replication mechanism to fulfill the need at component level. It allows deployers to describe software using a hierarchical DSL, deploy it using an implementation of a multicloud distributed deployment framework, and provide autonomic rules to respond to fluctuations of environment, thereby ensuring availability and scalability. In our framework, we also address the optimal deployment problem of components replicated by the DM. While the cost of copying the whole virtual machines is too high due to their big virtualization overhead, the fine-grained service replication/migration at component level is a possible solution. The experiments were conducted to prove the advantage of our partial approach in comparison to full migration and replication of an entire server stack. The numerical results also provide a suggestion of improving the system performance for a cloud provider.

Although componentized implementation improves scalability, our framework requires an application to follow a service-oriented architecture. It will be a future direction to study an application re-hosting pattern to integrate a monolithic legacy application with service-based applications in the framework for improving consistency and reducing cost through consolidation and sharing across cloud environments. Other possible future directions include the more detailed analysis of system performance in a large deployment scenario taking into account elastic demands and network fluctuations, or a deep analysis of comparison between different replication and migration approaches.

Acknowledgements This work was partially supported by Microsoft Research Europe, and project B2016-SPH-17 from the Vietnam Ministry of Education and Training.

References

1. Final version of NIST cloud computing definition published. http://www.nist.gov/itl/csd/cloud-102511.cfm. Visited on March 2015

2. Thanh, D.V., Jrstad, I.: A service-oriented architecture framework for mobile services. In: Proceedings of the advanced industrial conference on telecommunications/service assurance with partial and intermittent resources conference/e-learning on telecommunications workshop, pp. 65–70 (2005)

3. AppZero. https://www.appzero.com. Visited on March 2015

4. CliQr. http://www.cliqr.com/platform/. Visited on March 2015

5. Racemi. http://www.racemi.com. Visited on March 2015

6. CohesiveFT. https://cohesive.net. Visited on March 2015

7. Ravello. http://www.ravellosystems.com. Visited on March 2015

8. Lloyd, W., Pallickara, S., David, O., Lyon, J., Arabi, M., Rojas, K.: Migration of multi-tier applications to infrastructure-as-a-service clouds: An investigation using kernel-based virtual machines. In: Proceedings of the 12th IEEE/ACM international conference on grid computing (GRID), pp. 137–144 (2011)

9. Vardhan, M., Yadav, D., Kushwaha, D.: A transparent service replication mechanism for clouds. In: Proceedings of the sixth international conference on complex, intelligent and software intensive systems (CISIS), pp. 389–394 (2012)

10. Pham, L.M., Pham, T.M.: Autonomic fine-grained migration and replication of component-based applications across multi-clouds. In: Proceedings of the 2nd Nafosted conference on information and computer science (NICS), pp. 5–10 (2015)

11. Huebscher, M.C., McCann, J.A.: A survey of autonomic computing - degrees, models, and applications. ACM Comput. Surv. **40**(3), 7:1–7:28 (2008)

12. Pham, L.M., Tchana, A., Donsez, D., Zurczak, V., Gibello, P.Y., de Palma, N.: An adaptable framework to deploy complex applications onto multi-cloud platforms. In: Proceedings of the IEEE RIVF international conference on computing communication technologies - Research, Innovation, and vision for the future (RIVF), pp. 169–174 (2015)

13. Pham, M.L.: Roboconf : an autonomic platform supporting multi-level fine-grained elasticity of complex applications on the cloud. Theses, Université Grenoble Alpes (2016). https://tel.archives-ouvertes.fr/tel-01312775

14. OSGI. http://www.osgi.org/Main/HomePage. Visited on March 2015

15. JORAM: Java (TM) Open reliable asynchronous messaging. http://joram.ow2.org. Visited on June 2016

16. Java Naming and Directory Interface (JNDI). http://docs.oracle.com/javase/8/docs/technotes/guides/jndi/index.html. Visited on June 2016

17. Apache Karaf. http://karaf.apache.org/. Visited on June 2016

18. Livestatus. https://mathias-kettner.de/checkmk_livestatus.html. Visited on March 2015

19. Nagios. http://www.nagios.org. Visited on March 2015

20. Shinken. http://shinken-monitoring.org. Visited on March 2015

21. Pham, T.M., Fdida, S.: DTN support for news dissemination in an urban area. Comput. Netw. **56**(9), 2276–2291 (2012)

22. Pham, T.M., Minoux, M., Fdida, S., Pilarski, M.: Optimization of content caching in content-centric networks. Tech. Rep. hal-01016470, UPMC Sorbonne Universités (2014). http://hal.upmc.fr/hal-01016470/en/

23. Baev, I., Rajaraman, R., Swamy, C.: Approximation algorithms for data placement problems. SIAM J. Comput. **38**(4), 1411–1429 (2008)

24. IBM ILOG CPLEX Optimizer. http://www.ibm.com/software/integration/optimization/cplex-optimizer/. Visited on November 2015

25. CLIF server. http://clif.ow2.org. Visited on March 2015

26. GoGrid. http://www.gogrid.com/. Visited on April 2016

27. Rodero-Merino, L., Vaquero, L.M., Gil, V., Galán, F., Fontán, J., Montero, R.S., Llorente, I.M.: From infrastructure delivery to service management in clouds. Futur. Gen. Comput. Syst. **26**(8), 1226–1240 (2010)

28. Dawoud, W., Takouna, I., Meinel, C.: Elastic vm for cloud resources provisioning optimization. In: Proceedings of the first international conference on advances in computing and communications, pp. 431–445 (2011)

29. Ferrer, A.J., Hernández, F., Tordsson, J., Elmroth, E., Ali-Eldin, A., Zsigri, C., Sirvent, R., Guitart, J., Badia, R.M., Djemame, K., Ziegler, W., Dimitrakos, T., Nair, S.K., Kousiouris, G., Konstanteli, K., Varvarigou, T., Hudzia, B., Kipp, A., Wesner, S., Corrales, M., Forgó, N., Sharif, T., Sheridan, C.: Optimis: A holistic approach to cloud service provisioning. Futur. Gener. Comput. Syst. **28**(1), 66–77 (2012)

30. Satzger, B., Hummer, W., Inzinger, C., Leitner, P., Dustdar, S.: Winds of change: from vendor lock-in to the meta cloud. IEEE Intern. Comput. **17**(1), 69–73 (2013)

31. Reich, C., Bubendorfer, K., Banholzer, M., Buyya, R.: A SLA-oriented management of containers for hosting stateful web services. In: Proceedings of the IEEE international conference on e-science and grid computing, pp. 85–92 (2007)

32. Hao, W., Yen, I.L., Thuraisingham, B.: Dynamic service and data migration in the clouds. In: Proceedings of the 33rd annual IEEE international computer software and applications conference (COMPSAC)., vol. 2, pp. 134–139 (2009)

33. Ardagna, D., di Nitto, E., Mohagheghi, P., Mosser, S., Ballagny, C., D'Andria, F., Casale, G., Matthews, P., Nechifor, C.S., Petcu, D., Gericke, A., Sheridan, C.: Modaclouds: A model-driven approach for the design and execution of applications on multiple clouds. In: Proceedings of the 4th international workshop on modeling in software engineering (MiSE), pp. 50–56 (2012)

34. Dong, J., Jin, X., Wang, H., Li, Y., Zhang, P., Cheng, S.: Energy-saving virtual machine placement in cloud data centers. In: Proceedings of the 13th IEEE/ACM international symposium on cluster, cloud and grid computing (CCGrid), pp. 618–624 (2013)

35. Li, K., Zheng, H., Wu, J.: Migration-based virtual machine placement in cloud systems. In: Proceedings of the 2nd international conference on cloud networking (CloudNet), pp. 83–90. IEEE (2013)

36. Zhu, X., Santos, C., Beyer, D., Ward, J., Singhal, S.: Automated application component placement in data centers using mathematical programming. Int. J. Netw. Manag. **18**(6), 467–483 (2008)

37. Zhang, Q., Cheng, L., Boutaba, R.: Cloud computing: state-of-the-art and research challenges. J. Intern. Serv. Appl. **1**(1), 7–18 (2010)

## 17

A computationally lightweight and localized centrality metric in lieu of betweenness centrality for complex network analysis

Natarajan Meghanathan[1]

Abstract The betweenness centrality (BWC) of a vertex is a measure of the fraction of shortest paths between any two vertices going through the vertex and is one of the widely used shortest path-based centrality metrics for the complex network analysis. However, it takes $O(|V|^2 + |V||E|)$ time (where **V** and **E** are, respectively, the sets of nodes and edges of a network graph) to compute the BWC of just a single node. Our hypothesis is that nodes with a high degree, but low local clustering coefficient, are more likely to be on the shortest paths of several node pairs and are likely to incur a larger BWC value. Accordingly, we define the local clustering coefficient-based degree centrality (LCCDC) for a node as the product of the degree centrality of the node and one minus the local clustering coefficient of the node. The LCCDC of a node can be computed based on just the knowledge of the two-hop neighborhood of a node and would take significantly lower time. We conduct an exhaustive correlation analysis and observe the LCCDC to incur the largest correlation coefficient values with BWC (compared to other centrality metrics under three different correlation measures) and to hold very strong levels of positive correlation with BWC for at least 14 of the 18 real-world networks analyzed. Hence, we claim the LCCDC to be an apt metric to rank the nodes or compare any two nodes of a real-world network graph in lieu of BWC.

Keywords Betweenness centrality · Degree centrality · Local clustering coefficient · Correlation coefficient · Complex network graphs

✉ Natarajan Meghanathan
natarajan.meghanathan@jsums.edu

[1] Department of Computer Science, Jackson State University, Jackson, USA

1 Introduction

Network science (a.k.a. complex network analysis) is an emerging area of interest in the data science discipline and corresponds to analyzing complex real-world networks from a graph theory point of view. Among the various metrics used for complex network analysis, node centrality is a prominently used metric of immense theoretical interest and practical value. The centrality of a node is a link statistics-based quantitative measure of the topological importance of the node with respect to the other nodes in the network [1]. Applications for node centrality metrics could be, for example, to identify the most influential persons in a social network, the key infrastructure nodes in an internet, the super-spreaders of a disease, etc. The existing centrality metrics could be broadly classified into two categories [1]: neighbor-based and shortest path-based. Degree centrality (DegC) and eigenvector centrality (EVC) [2] are well-known metrics for neighbor-based centrality, while Betweenness centrality (BWC) [3] and closeness centrality (ClC) [4] are well-known metrics for shortest path-based centrality. Throughout the paper, the terms 'node' and 'vertex', 'link' and 'edge', and 'network' and 'graph' are used interchangeably. They mean the same.

The degree centrality of a vertex is the number of neighbors connected to the vertex and can be determined just based on the one-hop neighborhood knowledge. The eigenvector centrality of a vertex is a measure of the degree of the vertex as well as the degree of its neighbors. The betweenness centrality of a vertex is a measure of the fraction of the shortest paths between any two vertices that go through the vertex; whereas the closeness centrality of a vertex is a measure of the shortest path distances to every other vertex in the network. Other than degree centrality, all the above three centrality metrics require the global knowledge of the network for their computation.

With respect to the running time of the algorithms to compute the centrality metrics, for an arbitrary network graph of $|V|$ vertices and $|E|$ edges: the EVC of all the vertices en masse can be computed in $O(|V|^3)$ time, whereas it would take $O(|V|+|E|)$ and $O(|V|^2+|V||E|)$ time, respectively, to compute the closeness centrality and betweenness centrality of an individual vertex. The BWC, thus, incurs the longest running time to be computed for just a single node. As the BWC for a node u is defined as the sum of the fraction of shortest paths between any two nodes i and j ($i \neq j \neq u$) that go through node u, one would have to run the shortest path algorithm on every node in the graph to compute the BWC of even a single node. Even though the BWC of all the vertices could be determined once the shortest path algorithm is run on every node in a network graph, it is still too much of a computation overhead on network graphs with a larger number of nodes and/or edges (especially, if one is interested in just knowing the relative importance of a selected few vertices with regards to their location on the shortest paths among any two vertices in the network graph). Thus, the motivation of this research is to explore the possibility of using a computationally lightweight localized centrality metric that is highly correlated to the BWC and could be used to rank the vertices or compare selected vertices in a network graph in lieu of the BWC.

Our high-level contribution in this paper is the proposal of a local clustering coefficient-based degree centrality (LCCDC) metric as a computationally lightweight centrality alternative for the betweenness centrality (BWC). The local clustering coefficient of a node in a graph is the fraction of the pairs of its neighbors that are directly connected to each other. The underlying theoretical basis for the proposed LCCDC metric is that if none of the neighbors of a vertex go through the vertex for shortest path communication, and then none of the other vertices in the graph go through the vertex for shortest path communication. Accordingly, we define the LCCDC of a vertex as the product of the degree of the vertex and one minus the local clustering coefficient of the vertex. The LCCDC metric, thus, quantifies the extent, to which the degree centrality of a vertex facilitates shortest path communication through the vertex and could be at most the degree centrality of the vertex. If a vertex has a high degree, but a low local clustering coefficient, it implies that though the vertex has several neighbors—a very few of these neighbors are directly connected to each other. Hence, a high-degree vertex with a low local clustering coefficient is likely to be on the shortest path for several pairs of vertices in the network (at least for the neighbors of the node). On the other hand, a vertex with a higher clustering coefficient (even if it has a higher degree) is not likely to be on the shortest paths connecting its neighbors and thereby not likely to be on the shortest paths between any two vertices in the graph. All of the

above arguments form the basis of our hypothesis that a high-degree vertex with a low local clustering coefficient is more likely to exhibit a larger value for the betweenness centrality.

We explore the level of correlation between LCCDC and BWC through extensive experimental studies involving a suite of 18 real-world networks, whose degree distribution ranges from Poisson to Power-law [5] under three different correlation measures [5]. We observe the LCCDC to exhibit highest values for the correlation coefficient with BWC (compared to DegC, EVC, and ClC under all the three correlation measures). In addition to the quantitative values, we also qualitatively classify the level of correlation for BWC with the other centrality metrics studied in this paper, and observe the newly proposed LCCDC metric to exhibit strong-very strong levels of positive correlation with BWC for at least 16 of the 18 real-world networks analyzed. High levels of positive correlation between time-efficient LCCDC and time-consuming BWC are an indicator that if two vertices are to be compared based on their BWC values, it would be more likely sufficient to just compare their LCCDC values. Similarly, the ranking of the vertices in a real-world network graph based on their BWC values is more likely to be the same as the ranking of the vertices based on the LCCDC metric. Thus, we claim that the LCCDC could be used to compare vertices in lieu of their BWC.

The rest of the paper is organized as follows: Sect. 2 reviews the classical centrality metrics (DegC, EVC, BWC, and ClC) and the calculation of the BWC metric with an example. Section 3 introduces the local clustering coefficient-based degree centrality (LCCDC) metric and justifies its proposal as an alternate for BWC with a motivating example. Section 4 introduces the three measures of correlation used in the experimental studies on real-world networks. Section 5 presents the 18 real-world network graphs and discusses the results of correlation coefficient analysis for BWC with each of LCCDC, DegC, EVC, and ClC as well as ranks the five centrality metrics on the basis of the execution time incurred to compute them on these graphs. Section 6 reviews related work on correlation studies involving the centrality metrics. Section 7 concludes the paper and explores directions for future research.

2 Node centrality metrics

We now review the centrality metrics that are used for the correlation coefficient analysis studies in this paper. These are the neighbor-based degree centrality (DegC) and eigenvector centrality (EVC) metrics and the shortest path-based betweenness centrality (BWC) and closeness centrality (ClC) metrics.

The degree centrality (DegC) of a vertex is the number of neighbors for the vertex in the graph and can be easily computed by counting the number of edges incident on the vertex. If $\mathbf{A}$ is the $n \times n$ adjacency matrix for a graph, such that $\mathbf{A}[i, j] = 1$ if there is an edge connecting v_i to v_j (for undirected graphs) and $\mathbf{A}[i, j] = 0$ if there is no edge connecting v_i and v_j. The degree centrality of a vertex v_i is quantitatively defined as follows: $\text{DegC}(v_i) = \sum_{j=1}^{n} A[i, j]$. It would take $O(|V|)$ time to determine the degree centrality of a vertex, as there would be $n = |V|$ entries in the row corresponding to each vertex in the adjacency matrix.

The eigenvector centrality (EVC) of a vertex is a quantitative measure of the degree of the vertex as well as the degree of its neighbors. A vertex that has a high degree for itself as well as located in the neighborhood of high-degree vertices is likely to have a larger EVC. The EVC values of the vertices in a graph correspond to the entries for the vertices in the principal eigenvector of the adjacency matrix of the graph. An $n \times n$ adjacency matrix has n eigenvalues and the corresponding eigenvectors. The principal eigenvector is the eigenvector corresponding to the largest eigenvalue (principal eigenvalue) of the adjacency matrix, $\mathbf{A}$. Moreover, if all the entries in a square matrix are positive (i.e., greater than or equal to zero), the principal eigenvalue as well as the entries in the principal eigenvector are also positive [6]. We determine the EVC of the vertices using the power-iteration method [6] of complexity $O(|V|^3)$ in a graph of $|V|$ vertices, as there are $O(|V|^2)$ multiplications in each iteration of the power-iteration method, and there could be at most $|V|$ iterations before the normalized value of the eigenvector converges to the principal eigenvalue (typically, the number of iterations needed for the convergence to happen would be far less than the number of vertices in the graph).

The betweenness centrality (BWC) of a vertex is the sum of the fraction of shortest paths going through the vertex between any two vertices, considered over all pairs of vertices. In this paper, we determine the BWC of the vertices using the breadth first search (BFS)-variant of the well-known Brandes algorithm [7]. We run the BFS algorithm [8] on each vertex in the graph and determine the level of each vertex (the number of hops/edges from the root) in each of these BFS trees. The root of a BFS tree is said to be at level 0 and the number of shortest paths from the root to itself is 1. On a BFS tree rooted at vertex r, the number of shortest paths for a vertex i at level l ($l > 0$) from the root r is the sum of the number of shortest paths from the root r to each the neighbors of vertex i (in the original graph) that are at level $l-1$ in the BFS tree. Since we are working on undirected graphs, the total number of shortest paths from vertex i to vertex j (denoted sp_{ij}) is simply the number of shortest paths from vertex i to vertex j in the shortest path tree rooted at vertex i or vice-versa. The number of short-

est paths from a vertex i to a vertex j that go through a vertex k (denoted $\text{sp}_{ij}(k)$) is the maximum of the number of shortest paths from vertex i to vertex k in the shortest path tree rooted at i and the number of shortest paths from vertex j to vertex k in the shortest path tree rooted at vertex j. Thus, $\text{BWC}(k) = \sum_{\substack{k \neq i \\ k \neq j}} \frac{\text{sp}_{ij}(k)}{\text{sp}_{ij}}$. With regard to the run-time complexity of the Brandes algorithm, it would take $O(|V| + |E|)$ time to run the BFS shortest path algorithm on a particular vertex and a total of $O(|V|*(|V|+|E|))$ time on the $|V|$ vertices of a network graph. In addition, for each vertex: one has to trace through the $|V|$ shortest path trees to determine the number of shortest paths from the root vertices of these shortest path trees to the particular vertex for which we want to find the BWC. This could take another $|V||E|$ time for all the vertices in the graph. Thus, the computation time incurred to determine the BWC values of all the vertices in a graph would be: $O(|V|^2 + |V||E| + |V||E|)$, which for all theoretical purposes is written simply as: $O(|V|^2 + |V||E|)$.

Figure 1 illustrates an example to calculate the BWC of the vertices on a sample graph that is used as a running example in Figs. 1, 2, 3, 4, 5, and 6. We can observe the betweenness values for vertices 0, 6, and 7 are zero each, because no shortest path between any two vertices go through them. We observe that even though vertices 4 and 5 have the same larger degree, the average degree of the neighbors of vertex 5 is slightly lower than the average degree of the neighbors of vertex. As a result, vertex 5 is more likely to occupy a relatively larger fraction of the shortest path between any two vertices and incur a relatively larger BWC value compared to vertex 4 (even though vertex 4 has a larger EVC value). In addition, even though vertex 3 has a larger degree than vertex 1, the BWC of vertex 1 is significantly larger than that of vertex 3. This could be attributed to vertex 1 lying on the shortest path from vertices 0 and 2 to vertices 4, 5, 6, and 7; on the other hand, vertex 3 lies only on the shortest path between 2 and 5.

The closeness centrality (ClC) of a vertex is the inverse of the sum of the number of shortest paths from the vertex to every other vertex in the graph. We determine the ClC of the vertices by running the BFS algorithm on each vertex and summing the number of shortest paths from the root vertex to every other vertex in these BFS trees. It would take $O(|V| + |E|)$ time to run the BFS algorithm once and determine the shortest path tree rooted at a particular vertex. To determine the closeness centrality of all the vertices in a graph, one would have to run the BFS algorithm on each of the vertices: thus, incurring an overall time complexity of $O(|V|*(|V| + |E|)) = O(|V|^2 + |V||E|)$. However, unlike the BWC metric, there is no additional computation overhead incurred to determine the ClC values of the vertices.

Fig. 1 Example to illustrate the calculation of betweenness centrality

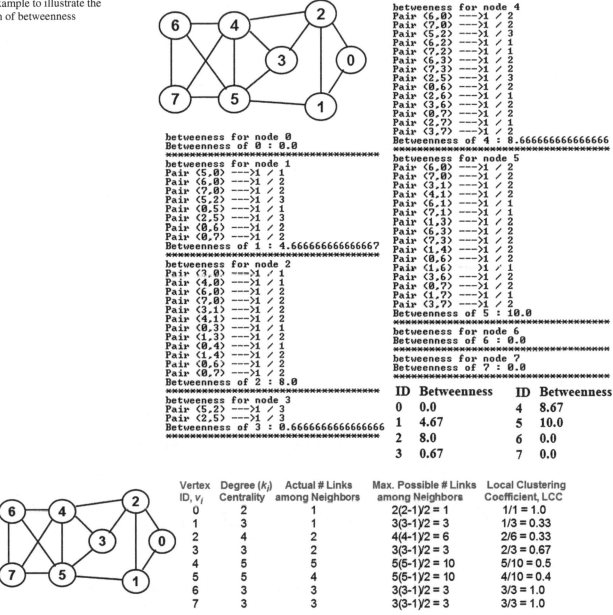

```
betweeness for node 0
Betweenness of 0 : 0.0
********************************************
betweeness for node 1
Pair (5,0) --->1 / 1
Pair (6,0) --->1 / 2
Pair (7,0) --->1 / 2
Pair (5,2) --->1 / 3
Pair (0,5) --->1 / 1
Pair (2,5) --->1 / 3
Pair (0,6) --->1 / 2
Pair (0,7) --->1 / 2
Betweenness of 1 : 4.666666666666667
********************************************
betweeness for node 2
Pair (3,0) --->1 / 1
Pair (4,0) --->1 / 1
Pair (6,0) --->1 / 2
Pair (7,0) --->1 / 2
Pair (3,1) --->1 / 2
Pair (4,1) --->1 / 2
Pair (0,3) --->1 / 1
Pair (1,3) --->1 / 2
Pair (0,4) --->1 / 1
Pair (1,4) --->1 / 2
Pair (0,6) --->1 / 2
Pair (0,7) --->1 / 2
Betweenness of 2 : 8.0
********************************************
betweeness for node 3
Pair (5,2) --->1 / 3
Pair (2,5) --->1 / 3
Betweenness of 3 : 0.6666666666666666
********************************************
```

```
betweeness for node 4
Pair (6,0) --->1 / 2
Pair (7,0) --->1 / 2
Pair (5,2) --->1 / 3
Pair (6,2) --->1 / 1
Pair (7,2) --->1 / 1
Pair (6,3) --->1 / 2
Pair (7,3) --->1 / 2
Pair (2,5) --->1 / 3
Pair (0,6) --->1 / 2
Pair (2,6) --->1 / 1
Pair (3,6) --->1 / 2
Pair (0,7) --->1 / 2
Pair (2,7) --->1 / 1
Pair (3,7) --->1 / 2
Betweenness of 4 : 8.666666666666666
********************************************
betweeness for node 5
Pair (6,0) --->1 / 2
Pair (7,0) --->1 / 2
Pair (3,1) --->1 / 2
Pair (4,1) --->1 / 2
Pair (6,1) --->1 / 1
Pair (7,1) --->1 / 1
Pair (1,3) --->1 / 2
Pair (6,3) --->1 / 2
Pair (7,3) --->1 / 2
Pair (1,4) --->1 / 2
Pair (0,6) --->1 / 2
Pair (1,6)     >1 / 1
Pair (3,6) --->1 / 2
Pair (0,7) --->1 / 2
Pair (1,7) --->1 / 1
Pair (3,7) --->1 / 2
Betweenness of 5 : 10.0
********************************************
betweeness for node 6
Betweenness of 6 : 0.0
********************************************
betweeness for node 7
Betweenness of 7 : 0.0
********************************************
```

ID	Betweenness	ID	Betweenness
0	0.0	4	8.67
1	4.67	5	10.0
2	8.0	6	0.0
3	0.67	7	0.0

Vertex ID, v_i	Degree (k_i) Centrality	Actual # Links among Neighbors	Max. Possible # Links among Neighbors	Local Clustering Coefficient, LCC
0	2	1	2(2-1)/2 = 1	1/1 = 1.0
1	3	1	3(3-1)/2 = 3	1/3 = 0.33
2	4	2	4(4-1)/2 = 6	2/6 = 0.33
3	3	2	3(3-1)/2 = 3	2/3 = 0.67
4	5	5	5(5-1)/2 = 10	5/10 = 0.5
5	5	4	5(5-1)/2 = 10	4/10 = 0.4
6	3	3	3(3-1)/2 = 3	3/3 = 1.0
7	3	3	3(3-1)/2 = 3	3/3 = 1.0

Fig. 2 Example to illustrate the calculation of local clustering coefficient

3 Local clustering coefficient-based degree centrality

The local clustering coefficient (LCC) of a vertex is the ratio of the actual number of links between the neighbors of the vertex to that of the maximum possible number of links between the neighbors of the vertex [1]. For a vertex v_i with degree k_i (i.e., k_i neighbors), the maximum possible number of links between the neighbors of the node is $k_i(k_i-1)/2$. Figure 2 illustrates the computation of the LCC values of the vertices on the example graph used in Fig. 1. We see that a vertex having high degree need not necessarily have a higher LCC, as it would be difficult to expect direct

links between any two neighbors of the vertex. In Fig. 2, we observe that both vertices 4 and 5 that have a degree of 5 each incur LCC values that are lower than the LCC of vertices 6 and 7 that have a degree of 3 each. In addition, vertices with the same degree need not have the same LCC, as the connectivity among the neighbors of each vertex could be different from that of the others. We notice that though vertices 3, 6, and 7 have a degree of 3 each, the LCC of vertex 3 is only 0.33, whereas vertices 6 and 7 have an LCC of 1.0 each.

Our hypothesis behind the proposed local clustering coefficient-based degree centrality (LCCDC) metric is as follows: a high-degree vertex with a lower clustering coefficient is essential to at least connect the neighbors (that are not

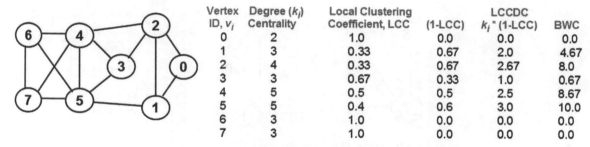

Vertex ID, v_i	Degree (k_i) Centrality	Local Clustering Coefficient, LCC	(1-LCC)	LCCDC k_i*(1-LCC)	BWC
0	2	1.0	0.0	0.0	0.0
1	3	0.33	0.67	2.0	4.67
2	4	0.33	0.67	2.67	8.0
3	3	0.67	0.33	1.0	0.67
4	5	0.5	0.5	2.5	8.67
5	5	0.4	0.6	3.0	10.0
6	3	1.0	0.0	0.0	0.0
7	3	1.0	0.0	0.0	0.0

Fig. 3 Example to illustrate the calculation of local clustering coefficient-based degree centrality

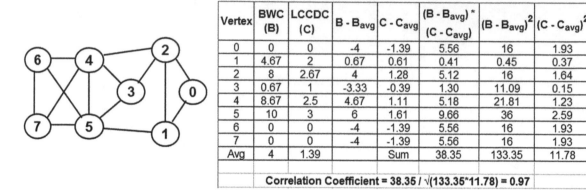

Vertex	BWC (B)	LCCDC (C)	B - B_{avg}	C - C_{avg}	(B - B_{avg}) * (C - C_{avg})	(B - B_{avg})^2	(C - C_{avg})^2
0	0	0	-4	-1.39	5.56	16	1.93
1	4.67	2	0.67	0.61	0.41	0.45	0.37
2	8	2.67	4	1.28	5.12	16	1.64
3	0.67	1	-3.33	-0.39	1.30	11.09	0.15
4	8.67	2.5	4.67	1.11	5.18	21.81	1.23
5	10	3	6	1.61	9.66	36	2.59
6	0	0	-4	-1.39	5.56	16	1.93
7	0	0	-4	-1.39	5.56	16	1.93
Avg	4	1.39		Sum	38.35	133.35	11.78

Correlation Coefficient = 38.35 / √(133.35*11.78) = 0.97

Fig. 4 Example to illustrate the computation of Pearson's correlation coefficient (betweenness centrality: B and local clustering coefficient-based degree centrality: C)

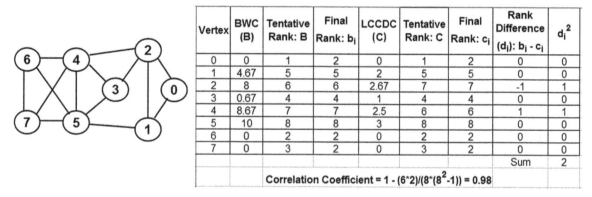

Vertex	BWC (B)	Tentative Rank: B	Final Rank: b_i	LCCDC (C)	Tentative Rank: C	Final Rank: c_i	Rank Difference (d_i): $b_i - c_i$	d_i^2
0	0	1	2	0	1	2	0	0
1	4.67	5	5	2	5	5	0	0
2	8	6	6	2.67	7	7	-1	1
3	0.67	4	4	1	4	4	0	0
4	8.67	7	7	2.5	6	6	1	1
5	10	8	8	3	8	8	0	0
6	0	2	2	0	2	2	0	0
7	0	3	2	0	3	2	0	0
							Sum	2

Correlation Coefficient = 1 - (6*2)/(8*(8^2-1)) = 0.98

Fig. 5 Example to illustrate the computation of Spearman's correlation coefficient (betweenness centrality: B and local clustering coefficient-based degree centrality: C)

directly connected to each other) of the vertex on a shortest path. In addition, such a high-degree vertex with a lower LCC might be on the shortest path of several other pairs of vertices (especially, for those vertices that are in the 2-hop and 3-hop neighborhood), eventually contributing to a higher BWC for the vertex. On the other hand, a vertex in a connected graph incurs a BWC of zero if none of the neighbors of the vertex go through it for their shortest path(s) to any other vertex in the graph. In other words, a vertex sustains a BWC value of zero if it is either a stub vertex (has a degree of 1: that is connected to only one other vertex) or there exists a link between any two neighbors of the vertex. In both the cases, the LCC of the vertex is 1 and the BWC value for the vertex will be

zero. Considering all of the above, we propose to calculate the LCCDC metric for a vertex as the product of the degree centrality of the vertex and one minus the local clustering coefficient of the vertex. That is, LCCDC(v_i) = k_i * (1 − LCC(v_i)). The proposed formulation also sets up meaningful upper bound and lower bound for the LCCDC metric. With the above formulation, the maximum possible value for the local clustering coefficient-based degree centrality of a vertex is the degree centrality of the vertex itself (if the LCC of the vertex is 0) and the minimum possible value for the LCCDC of a vertex is 0 (if the LCC of the vertex is 1). Thus, the proposed formulation for LCCDC of a vertex captures the extent to which the degree centrality of a vertex is useful

Fig. 6 Example to illustrate the computation of Kendall's correlation coefficient (betweenness centrality: B and local clustering coefficient-based degree centrality: C)

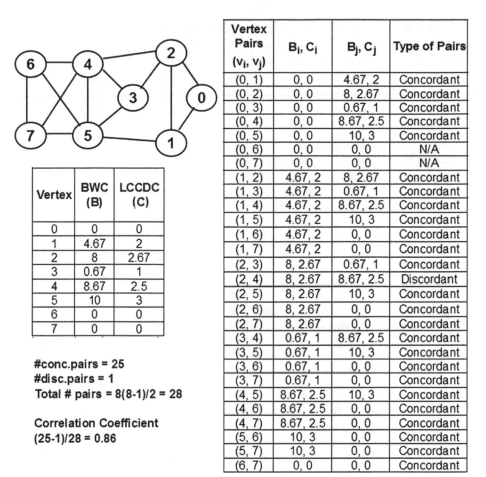

Vertex	BWC (B)	LCCDC (C)
0	0	0
1	4.67	2
2	8	2.67
3	0.67	1
4	8.67	2.5
5	10	3
6	0	0
7	0	0

#conc.pairs = 25
#disc.pairs = 1
Total # pairs = 8(8-1)/2 = 28

Correlation Coefficient
(25-1)/28 = 0.86

Vertex Pairs (v_i, v_j)	B_i, C_i	B_j, C_j	Type of Pairs
(0, 1)	0, 0	4.67, 2	Concordant
(0, 2)	0, 0	8, 2.67	Concordant
(0, 3)	0, 0	0.67, 1	Concordant
(0, 4)	0, 0	8.67, 2.5	Concordant
(0, 5)	0, 0	10, 3	Concordant
(0, 6)	0, 0	0, 0	N/A
(0, 7)	0, 0	0, 0	N/A
(1, 2)	4.67, 2	8, 2.67	Concordant
(1, 3)	4.67, 2	0.67, 1	Concordant
(1, 4)	4.67, 2	8.67, 2.5	Concordant
(1, 5)	4.67, 2	10, 3	Concordant
(1, 6)	4.67, 2	0, 0	Concordant
(1, 7)	4.67, 2	0, 0	Concordant
(2, 3)	8, 2.67	0.67, 1	Concordant
(2, 4)	8, 2.67	8.67, 2.5	Discordant
(2, 5)	8, 2.67	10, 3	Concordant
(2, 6)	8, 2.67	0, 0	Concordant
(2, 7)	8, 2.67	0, 0	Concordant
(3, 4)	0.67, 1	8.67, 2.5	Concordant
(3, 5)	0.67, 1	10, 3	Concordant
(3, 6)	0.67, 1	0, 0	Concordant
(3, 7)	0.67, 1	0, 0	Concordant
(4, 5)	8.67, 2.5	10, 3	Concordant
(4, 6)	8.67, 2.5	0, 0	Concordant
(4, 7)	8.67, 2.5	0, 0	Concordant
(5, 6)	10, 3	0, 0	Concordant
(5, 7)	10, 3	0, 0	Concordant
(6, 7)	0, 0	0, 0	Concordant

in facilitating shortest path communication through the vertex, and we claim it to be lightweight alternative to the BWC metric (as verified in Sect. 4).

Figure 3 illustrates the computation of the LCCDC values of the vertices of the example graph used in Figs. 1 and 2. We observe that larger the LCCDC value for a vertex, the larger the BWC value for the vertex and vice-versa. We observe that vertices 0, 6, and 7 that do not lie on the shortest path for any two vertices in the graph have a BWC of zero each and also have LCCDC value of zero each. Notice that for each of these 3 vertices 0, 6, and 7: the neighbors of the vertex have direct links to each other and are not required to go through the vertex (this is one of the two scenarios for which the BWC value of a vertex will be zero, as explained above). We also notice that though both vertices 4 and 5 have a degree of 5 each, vertex 5 has relatively larger values for both the LCCDC and BWC metrics owing to relatively fewer fraction of direct links among its neighbors. Likewise, though both vertices 1 and 3 have a degree of 3 each, vertex 1 has relatively larger BWC and LCCDC values due to a relatively fewer fraction of direct links among its neighbors.

The local clustering coefficient of a vertex can be computed by checking whether the neighbors of the vertex are directly connected to each other. For a vertex i with k_i neighbors, there is a possibility of $k_i(k_i-1)/2$ edges among the neighbors of vertex i. This could be efficiently done in O(1) time for each pair of neighbors by checking their corresponding entry in the adjacency matrix, leading to a time complexity of O(k_i^2) for a vertex i of degree k_i. Thus, the time complexity incurred to compute the local clustering coefficient of the vertices in a graph narrows down to the problem of determining an upper bound for the sum of the squares of the degrees of the vertices in a graph. This has been derived to be $O(|E| * (\frac{2*|E|}{|V|-1} + |V| - 2))$ for a graph of $|V|$ vertices and $|E|$ edges [36]. It would take O($|V|^2$) time to compute the degree centrality of the vertices in a graph. Hence, the time complexity incurred to compute the LCCDC of the vertices in a network graph of $|V|$ vertices and $|E|$ edges can be written as: $O(|V|^2 + |E| * (\frac{2*|E|}{|V|-1} + |V| - 2))$.

4 Correlation coefficient measures

We now discuss the three well-known correlation coefficient measures that are used to evaluate the correlation between BWC and LCCDC as well as the correlations between BWC and each of the other three centrality metrics (DegC, EVC and ClC) presented in Sect. 2. These are the product moment-based Pearson's correlation coefficient, Rank-based Spearman's correlation coefficient, and Concordance-based Kendall's correlation coefficient. The Spearman's and Kendall's correlation measures are rank-based and the Pearson's correlation measure is a measure of the linear relationship between two variables (in our case, the LCCDC and BWC metrics) [6]. The Pearson's measure captures the correlation between the two metrics as follows: If we were to list the vertices in the monotonically increasing order of their BWC values, are the LCCDC values of these vertices are also in the monotonically increasing order or decreasing order or neither. The Spearman's measure captures the correlation as follows: How close is the ranking of the vertices based on the increasing order of their BWC values and in the increasing order of their LCCDC values? Kendall's measure captures the correlation between the two metrics as follows: Consider any two vertices v_i and v_j. If $BWC(v_i) > BWC(v_j)$, is the $LCCDC(v_i) > LCCDC(v_j)$ or $LCCDC(v_i) < LCCDC(v_j)$ or $LCCDC(v_i) = LCCDC(v_j)$? All the three correlation measures are independent of each other. We use three different and independent correlation measures to more rigorously validate our hypothesis that the time-efficient LCCDC metric can be used to rank the nodes or compare any two nodes in a real-world network graph in lieu of the time-consuming BWC metric.

The correlation coefficient values obtained for all the three measures range from −1 to 1. Correlation coefficient values closer to 1 indicate a stronger positive correlation between the two metrics considered (i.e., a vertex having a larger value for one of the two metrics is more likely to have a larger value for the other metric too), while values closer to −1 indicate a stronger negative correlation (i.e., a vertex having a larger value for one of the two metrics is more likely to have a smaller value for the other metric). Correlation coefficient values closer to 0 indicate no correlation (i.e., the values incurred by a vertex for the two metrics are independent of each other). We will adopt the ranges (rounded to two decimals) proposed by Evans [9] to indicate the various levels of correlation, shown in Table 1. The color code to be used

for the various levels of correlation are also shown in this table.

For simplicity, we refer to the two data sets as B and C, respectively, corresponding to the betweenness centrality and each of the other four centrality metrics (including the LCCDC). We will use the results from Fig. 3 to illustrate examples for the computation of the correlation coefficient under each of the three correlation measures.

4.1 Pearson's product moment-based correlation coefficient

The Pearson's product moment-based correlation coefficient for two data sets is defined as the covariance of the two data sets divided by the product of their standard deviation [5]. Let B_{avg} and C_{avg} denote the average values for the BWC and the LCCDC centrality metric for a graph of n vertices and let B_i and C_i denote, respectively, the values for the BWC and LCCDC incurred for vertex v_i. The Pearson's correlation coefficient (indicated PCC) is quantitatively defined as shown in Eq. (1). The term product moment is associated with the product of the mean (first moment) adjusted values for the two metrics in the numerator of the formulation. Figure 4 presents the calculation of the PCC for the betweenness centrality (B) and local clustering coefficient-based degree centrality (C) values obtained for the example graph used in Figs. 1, 2, 3. We obtain a correlation coefficient value of 0.97 (see Fig. 4) indicating a very strong positive correlation between the two metrics for the example graph.

$$PCC(B, C) = \frac{\sum_{i=1}^{n} (B_i - B_{avg})(C_i - C_{avg})}{\sqrt{\sum_{i=1}^{n} (B_i - B_{avg})^2 \sum_{i=1}^{n} (C_i - C_{avg})^2}} \dots$$

(1)

4.2 Spearman's rank-based correlation coefficient

Spearman's rank correlation coefficient (SCC) is a measure of how well the relationship between two data sets (variables) can be assessed using a monotonic function [5]. To compute the SCC of two data sets B and C, we convert the raw scores B_i and C_i for a vertex i to ranks b_i and c_i and use formula (2)

Table 1 Range of correlation coefficient values and the corresponding levels of correlation

Range of Correlation Coefficient Values	Level of Correlation	Range of Correlation Coefficient Values	Level of Correlation
0.80 to 1.00	Very Strong Positive	-1.00 to -0.80	Very Strong Negative
0.60 to 0.79	Strong Positive	-0.79 to -0.60	Strong Negative
0.40 to 0.59	Moderate Positive	-0.59 to -0.40	Moderate Negative
0.20 to 0.39	Weak Positive	-0.39 to -0.20	Weak Negative
0.00 to 0.19	Very Weak Positive	-0.19 to -0.01	Very Weak Negative

shown below, where $d_i = b_i - c_i$ is the difference between the ranks of vertex i in the two data sets. We follow the convention of assigning the rank values from 1 to n for a graph of n vertices, even though the vertex IDs range from 0 to $n-1$. To obtain the rank for a vertex based on the list of values for a centrality metric, we first sort the values (in ascending order). If there is any tie, we break the tie in favor of the vertex with a lower ID; we will thus be able to arrive at a tentative, but unique, rank value for each vertex with respect to the centrality metric. We determine a final ranking of the vertices as follows: For vertices with unique value of the centrality metric, the final ranking is the same as the tentative ranking. For vertices with an identical value for the centrality metric, the final ranking is assigned to be the average of their tentative rankings. Figure 5 illustrates the computation of the tentative and final ranking of the vertices based on their betweenness centrality and local clustering coefficient-based degree centrality values in the example graph used in Figs. 1, 2, 3, 4 as well as illustrates the computation of the Spearman's rank-based correlation coefficient.

$$\text{SCC}(B, C) = 1 - \frac{6 \sum_{i=1}^{n} d_i^2}{n(n^2 - 1)} \ldots \quad (2)$$

In Fig. 5, we observe ties among vertices with respect to both BWC and LCCDC. The tentative ranking is obtained by breaking the ties in favor of vertices with lower IDs. In the case of BWC (B), we observe the 3 vertices 0, 6, and 7 to have an identical BWC value of 0 each and their tentative rankings are, respectively, 1, 2, and 3 (ties for tentative rankings are broken in favor of vertices with lower IDs); the final ranking (2) of each of these 3 vertices is thus the average of 1, 2, and 3. A similar scenario could be observed for LCCDC: vertices 0, 6, and 7 have an identical LCCDC value of 0 each and the final ranking of each of these three vertices is 2, based on their tentative rankings of 1, 2, and 3. The Spearman's rank-based correlation coefficient (SCC) computed for maximal clique size and degree centrality for the example graph used from Figs. 1, 2, 3, 4 is 0.98. We observe the SCC value to be slightly larger than the PCC value obtained in Fig. 4 for the same graph and the level of correlation for both the measures falls in the range of very strong positive correlation.

4.3 Kendall's concordance-based correlation coefficient

The Kendall's concordance-based correlation coefficient (KCC) for any two centrality metrics (say, B and C) is a measure of the similarity (a.k.a. concordance) in the ordering of the values for the metrics incurred by the vertices in the graph [5]. We define a pair of distinct vertices v_i and v_j as concordant if $\{B_i > B_j \text{ and } C_i > C_j\}$ or $\{B_i < B_j \text{ and } C_i < C_j\}$. In other words, a pair of vertices v_i and v_j are concordant if either one of these two vertices strictly have a larger value

for the two metrics B and C compared to the other vertex. We define a pair of distinct vertices v_i and v_j as discordant if $\{B_i > B_j \text{ and } C_i < C_j\}$ or $\{B_i < B_j \text{ and } C_i > C_j\}$. In other words, a pair of vertices v_i and v_j are discordant if a vertex has a larger value for only one of the two centrality metrics. A pair of distinct vertices v_i and v_j are neither concordant nor discordant if either $\{B_i = B_j\}$ or $\{C_i = C_j\}$ or $\{B_i = B_j \text{ and } C_i = C_j\}$. The Kendall's concordance-based correlation coefficient is simply the difference between the number of concordant pairs (denoted #*conc.pairs*) and the number of discordant pairs (#*disc.pairs*) divided by the total number of pairs considered. For a graph of n vertices, KCC is calculated as shown in formulation (3).

$$\text{KCC}(B, C) = \frac{\#conc.pairs - \#disc.pairs}{\frac{1}{2}n(n-1)} \ldots \quad (3)$$

Figure 6 illustrates the calculation of the Kendall's correlation coefficient between BWC and LCCDC for the example graph used in Figs. 1, 2, 3, 4, 5. For a graph of 8 vertices, the total number of distinct pairs that could be considered is $8(8-1)/2 = 28$, and out of these, 25 pairs are classified to be concordant and just 1 pair as discordant (this itself is a direct indication of the very strong positive correlation between BWC and LCCDC). The remaining 2 pairs are neither concordant nor discordant (denoted as N/A) in the figure. We get a correlation coefficient of 0.86: still falling in the range of very strong positive correlation, though the absolute value of the correlation coefficient is lower than the correlation coefficient values obtained with the Pearson's and Spearman's measures. The KCC is also observed to return the lowest correlation coefficient values for all our experiments with the real-world networks (Sect. 5). Thus, the KCC could be construed to provide a lower bound for the correlation coefficient values and the level of correlation between BWC and the centrality metrics considered.

5 Real-world network graphs

We consider a suite of 18 real-world network graphs for our correlation analysis. We list below and identify these graphs in the increasing order of their variation in node degree, captured in the form of a metric called the spectral radius ratio for node degree (denoted λ_{sp}) [10]. The spectral radius ratio for node degree for a graph is the ratio of the principal eigenvalue of the adjacency matrix of the graph to that of the average node degree. The λ_{sp} values are always greater than or equal to 1.0. The larger the value, the larger the variation in node degree. The λ_{sp} values of the real-world networks considered in this paper range from 1.01 to 3.48 (i.e., from random networks to scale-free networks). Random networks exhibit a Poisson-style degree distribution and have a lower

Table 2 Fundamental properties of the real-world network graphs used in the correlation studies

#	Net.	λ_{sp}	#nodes	#edges	k_{avg}	G_c	D	PL_{avg}	G_a	G_m	CC_{avg}	#comps
1	FON	1.01	115	613	10.7	1.46	4	2.51	0.191	0.604	0.403	1
2	EAN	1.12	77	1549	40.2	10.6	2	1.47	−0.040	0.211	0.770	1
3	FTC	1.21	48	170	7.1	0.68	5	2.40	−0.014	0.455	0.438	1
4	RFN	1.27	217	1839	16.9	1.71	4	2.40	0.097	0.431	0.363	1
5	SJF	1.29	75	155	4.1	0.29	7	3.49	0.030	0.595	0.322	1
6	UKF	1.35	81	577	14.2	1.33	4	2.10	0.039	0.449	0.574	1
7	PBN	1.42	105	441	8.4	0.32	7	3.08	−0.023	0.521	0.488	1
8	BJN	1.45	198	2742	27.7	0.57	6	2.24	0.031	0.444	0.633	1
9	TFF	1.49	50	122	3.3	0.10	8	2.65	0.363	0.741	0.599	4
10	HCN	1.66	74	302	7.9	0.67	4	2.14	0.030	0.546	0.854	4
11	KFP	1.70	39	85	4.3	0.10	10	3.23	0.241	0.448	0.361	5
12	LMN	1.82	77	254	6.6	0.21	5	2.64	−0.077	0.553	0.736	1
13	CFN	1.83	87	407	9.1	0.98	3	1.95	−0.166	0.372	0.777	2
14	MTB	1.95	70	295	9.2	0.33	2	1.85	0.029	0.380	0.794	1
15	FBN	2.29	187	939	10.0	0.10	7	3.07	0.349	0.687	0.631	21
16	AKN	2.48	138	494	7.1	0.33	5	2.45	−0.081	0.371	0.798	2
17	ERN	3.00	472	1314	6.1	0.05	11	4.02	0.182	0.534	0.347	3
18	SJC	3.48	475	625	2.6	0.03	17	6.49	0.350	0.945	0.818	104

variation in node degree; their λ_{sp} values are typically closer to 1.0. Scale-free networks have a larger variation in node degree (especially those like the airline networks that have a few hubs—high degree nodes, and the rest of the nodes are of relatively much lower degree)—incurring a larger λ_{sp} value.

The real-world network graphs are briefly introduced below, in the increasing order of their λ_{sp} value. We also identify these networks with their ID (ranging from 1 to 18 as listed below) as well as with a three-character abbreviation—listed along with the λ_{sp} value. Table 2 lists the values for the following fundamental properties for each of these networks: average degree (k_{avg}), algebraic connectivity (G_c) [11], diameter (D), average path length (PL_{avg}), assortativity (G_a) [12], modularity (G_m) [13], average clustering coefficient (CC_{avg}) [1], and number of components (#comps). The values for each of the above properties for the real-world network graphs were obtained using our own implementation of the algorithms to determine these properties and their validity is verified using the Gephi [14] tool. We restrict ourselves to networks of moderate size due to the excessive computation time involved in computing the betweenness centrality for larger networks. In addition, we restrict ourselves to undirected network graphs (i.e., those that have a symmetric adjacency matrix) for the analysis conducted in this paper. Note that betweenness centrality is a symmetric centrality metric (i.e., unlike in-degree and out-degree, there do not exist in and out versions of BWC).

1. US Football Network (FON; $\lambda_{sp} = 1.01$) [15]: this is a network of 115 football teams (nodes) of US universities that played in the Fall 2000 season; there is an edge between two nodes if the corresponding teams have played against each other in the league games.

2. Employee Awareness Network (EAN; $\lambda_{sp} = 1.12$) [16]: this is a network of 77 employees (nodes) from a research team in a manufacturing company; there exists an edge between two nodes if the two employees are aware of each other's knowledge and skills.

3. Flying Teams Cadet Network (FTC; $\lambda_{sp} = 1.21$) [17]: this is a network of 48 cadet pilots (vertices) at an US Army Air Forces flying school in 1943, and the cadets were trained in a two-seated aircraft; there exists an edge between two vertices if at least one of the two corresponding cadet pilots have identified the other pilot among his/her preferred partners with whom she/he likes to fly during the training schedules.

4. Residence Hall Friendship Network (RFN; $\lambda_{sp} = 1.27$) [18]: this is a network of 217 residents (vertices) living at a residence hall located on the Australian National University campus. There exists an edge between two vertices if the corresponding residents are friends of each other.

5. San Juan Sur Family Network (SJF; $\lambda_{sp} = 1.29$) [19]: this is a network of 75 families (vertices) in San Juan Sur, Costa Rica, 1948. There exists an edge between two vertices if at least one of the two corresponding

families have visited the other family's household at least once.

6. UK Faculty Friendship Network (UKF; λ_{sp} = 1.35) [20]: this is a network of 81 faculty (vertices) at a UK university. There exists an edge between two vertices if the corresponding faculty are friends of each other.

7. US Politics Books Network (PBN; λ_{sp} = 1.42) [21]: this is a network of books (vertices) about US politics sold by Amazon.com around the time of the 2004 US presidential election. There exists an edge between two vertices if the corresponding two books were co-purchased by the same buyer (at least one buyer).

8. Jazz Band Network (JBN; λ_{sp} = 1.45) [22]: this is a network of 198 Jazz bands (vertices) that recorded between the years 1912 and 1940; there exists an edge between two bands if they shared at least one musician in any of their recordings during this period.

9. Teenage Female Friendship Network (TFF; λ_{sp} = 1.49) [23]: this is a network of 50 female teenage students (vertices) who studied as a cohort in a school in the West of Scotland from 1995 to 1997. There exists an edge between two vertices if the corresponding students reported (in a survey) that they were best friends of each other.

10. Huckleberry Coappearance Network (HCN; λ_{sp} = 1.66) [24]: this is a network of 74 characters (vertices) that appeared in the novel Huckleberry Finn by Mark Twain; there is an edge between two vertices if the corresponding characters had a common appearance in at least one scene.

11. Korea Family Planning Network (KFP; λ_{sp} = 1.69) [25]: this is a network of 39 women (vertices) at a Mothers' Club in Korea; there existed an edge between two vertices if the corresponding women were seen discussing family planning methods during an observation period.

12. Les Miserables Network (LMN; λ_{sp} = 1.81) [24]: this is a network of 77 characters (nodes) in the novel Les Miserables; there exists an edge between two nodes if the corresponding characters appeared together in at least one of the chapters in the novel.

13. Copperfield Network (CFN; λ_{sp} = 1.83) [26]: this is a network of 87 characters in the novel David Copperfield by Charles Dickens; there exists an edge between two vertices if the corresponding characters appeared together in at least one scene in the novel.

14. Madrid Train Bombing Network (MTB; λ_{sp} = 1.95) [27]: this is a network of suspected individuals and their relatives (vertices) reconstructed by Rodriguez using press accounts in the two major Spanish daily newspapers (El Pais and El Mundo), regarding the bombing of commuter trains in Madrid on March 11, 2004. There existed an edge between two vertices if the correspond-

ing individuals were observed to have a link in the form of friendship, ties to any terrorist organization, co-participation in training camps and/or wars, or co-participation in any previous terrorist attacks.

15. Facebook Network (FBN; λ_{sp} = 2.29): this is a network of the 187 friends (vertices) of the author in the well-known social media network, Facebook [28]. There exists an edge between two nodes if the corresponding people are also friends of each other.

16. Anna Karnenina Network (AKN; λ_{sp} = 2.47) [24]: this a network of 138 characters (vertices) in the novel Anna Karnenina; there exists an edge between two vertices if the corresponding characters have appeared together in at least one scene in the novel.

17. Erdos Collaboration Network (ECN; λ_{sp} = 3.00) [29]: this is a network of 472 authors (nodes) who have either directly published an article with Paul Erdos or through a chain of collaborators leading to Paul Erdos. There is an edge between two nodes if the corresponding authors have co-authored at least one publication.

18. Social Journal Network (SJN; λ_{sp} = 3.48) [30]: this is a network of 475 authors (vertices) involved in the production of 295 articles for the Social Networks Journal, since its inception until 2008; there is an edge between two vertices if the corresponding authors co-authored at least one paper published in the journal.

We measured the execution time incurred (measured in milliseconds) to compute each of the 5 centrality metrics: LCCDC, DegC, BWC, EVC, and ClC for the above 18 real-world networks. The executions were conducted on a computer with Intel Core i7-2620M CPU @ 2.70 GHz and an installed main memory (RAM) of 8 GB. We ran the procedures for each of these 5 centrality metrics on each of the real-world networks for 20 iterations and averaged the results. Table 3 lists the raw values for the average execution time (in milliseconds) for each of the 5 centrality metrics on the 18 real-world networks. Figure 7 plots the natural logarithm of the average execution time (for the values to be plotted on a comparable scale) incurred for the centrality metrics on each of the real-world networks. While the networks are listed in Table 3 and Fig. 7 in the increasing order of their spectral radius ratio for node degree (the same order as in Table 2); for each network, the centrality metrics are shown in the decreasing order of the execution times. Overall, we observe that networks with a larger number of nodes incur a larger execution time; for networks with comparable number of nodes, the execution time for the centrality metrics increases with increase in the edge-node ratio (ratio of the number of nodes to the number of edges), especially to compute the time-consuming centrality metrics, such as the

Table 3 Average execution time to compute the centrality metrics for the real-world network graphs

#	Net.	# nodes	Edge-node ratio	Average execution time to compute the centrality metrics (ms)				
				BWC	EVC	ClC	LCCDC	DegC
1	FON	115	5.33	166149.5	6229.7	1403.8	136.5	26.2
2	EAN	77	20.12	61915.4	3203.2	582.8	459.2	17.5
3	FTC	48	3.54	9694.8	921.4	136.8	25.8	10.6
4	RFN	217	8.47	2,198,077.4	54,264.1	8925.4	472.1	50.6
5	SJF	75	2.07	33,514.1	1924.1	407.1	36.9	17.1
6	UKF	81	7.12	56,355.1	2321.3	507.5	133.0	18.2
7	PBN	105	4.20	1,16,321.7	4802.3	992.1	94.3	24.3
8	BJN	198	13.85	1,970,503.6	74,771.2	17,774.7	12,137.8	56.3
9	TFF	50	2.44	4527.5	548.1	109.5	13.7	9.5
10	HCN	74	4.08	25,299.1	1520.1	347.8	62.3	17.1
11	KFP	39	2.18	3782.5	318.9	76.8	13.3	7.2
12	LMN	77	3.30	35,168.4	1361.2	470.2	42.2	17.1
13	CFN	87	4.68	56,355.1	2321.3	507.5	133.0	18.2
14	MTB	70	4.21	23,998.0	1170.4	308.7	52.8	16.7
15	FBN	187	5.02	8,17,865.3	24,435.9	5166.5	184.4	40.3
16	AKN	138	3.58	3,96,377.5	1,54,722.5	27,190.2	1270.7	33.8
17	ERN	472	2.78	23,106,718.9	5,38,524.0	81,444.4	1238.4	100.7
18	SJC	475	1.32	14,564,978.3	3,49,242.1	82,584.8	181.3	89.7

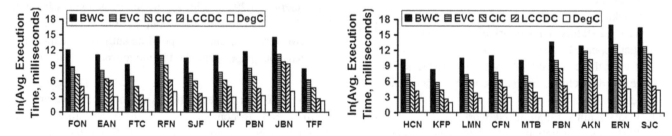

Fig. 7 Average execution time to compute the centrality metrics for the real-world network graphs (natural logarithm scale)

BWC and EVC. Table 3 and Fig. 7 display a clear ranking of the centrality metrics with respect to the execution time: BWC and DegC incur, respectively, the largest and smallest values for the average execution time for each real-world network analyzed. As the LCCDC values are computed by making use of the DegC values, it is natural to expect the execution time of the procedure to compute the LCCDC values to be larger than that of the DegC values. The execution time of the degree centrality metric appears to be anywhere from 0.4–69 % of the execution time of the LCCDC metric.

From Table 3 and Fig. 7, we could clearly observe the LCCDC metric to consistently incur a lower execution time compared to the BWC, EVC, and ClC metrics for each of the real-world networks analyzed. We observe the execution time incurred to compute the LCCDC metric to be significantly smaller than that of the BWC metric. The ratio of the average execution time for computing the BWC and LCCDC values for the real-world networks ranges from 117 to 80,330. The

ClC metric incurs an execution time that is at least 25 % larger than the execution time of the LCCDC metric and appears to be even significantly larger for several real-world networks evaluated. The EVC metric incurs an execution time that is 6 to 1926 times larger than the execution time of the LCCDC metric. Considering all of the above, our claim that LCCDC is a computationally lightweight metric is well justified.

Table 4 presents the raw values for the correlation coefficient obtained for the Betweenness centrality metric and each of the four centrality metrics: LCCDC, DegC, EVC, and ClC based on the PCC, SCC, and KCC measures. We color code the levels of correlation in Table 4 according to the color codes listed in Table 1. Under all the three correlation measures, we observe the proposed LCCDC metric to demonstrate significantly larger correlation coefficient values with BWC vis-a-vis the correlation coefficient values incurred by the other centrality metrics. Among the three correlation measures, the Spearman's rank-based correla-

Table 4 Correlation coefficient values between betweenness centrality and the other centrality metrics for real-world network graphs

#	Net.	Pearson Correlation Coeff.				Spearman Correlation Coeff.				Kendall's Correlation Coeff.			
		LCC DC	Deg C	ClC	EVC	LCC DC	Deg C	ClC	EVC	LCC DC	Deg C	ClC	EVC
1	FON	0.67	0.28	0.82	0.15	0.61	0.40	0.84	0.17	0.44	0.20	0.65	0.12
2	EAN	0.94	0.89	0.95	0.74	1.00	0.83	0.83	0.68	0.95	0.69	0.69	0.57
3	FTC	0.92	0.78	0.79	0.54	0.92	0.73	0.80	0.41	0.77	0.55	0.61	0.30
4	RFN	0.90	0.84	0.76	0.65	0.93	0.84	0.86	0.62	0.79	0.66	0.67	0.45
5	SJF	0.86	0.81	0.79	0.53	0.85	0.73	0.77	0.41	0.66	0.52	0.57	0.29
6	UKF	0.91	0.78	0.71	0.63	0.95	0.79	0.75	0.60	0.82	0.61	0.57	0.45
7	PBN	0.78	0.71	0.78	0.44	0.86	0.68	0.81	0.37	0.69	0.49	0.61	0.26
8	BJN	0.76	0.61	0.48	0.40	0.86	0.74	0.73	0.57	0.71	0.57	0.56	0.42
9	TFF	0.68	0.22	0.36	0.14	0.88	0.46	0.47	-0.19	0.61	0.29	0.34	-0.11
10	HCN	0.94	0.83	0.06	0.67	0.92	0.70	0.69	0.65	0.55	0.41	0.41	0.37
11	KFP	0.70	0.47	0.28	0.28	0.80	0.51	0.61	0.40	0.62	0.35	0.46	0.26
12	LMN	0.93	0.75	0.63	0.42	0.88	0.77	0.68	0.72	0.60	0.48	0.43	0.43
13	CFN	0.90	0.81	0.82	0.58	0.95	0.83	0.77	0.77	0.73	0.60	0.55	0.53
14	MTB	0.87	0.73	0.15	0.55	0.91	0.76	0.68	0.56	0.64	0.53	0.46	0.35
15	FBN	0.54	0.26	0.18	-0.12	0.86	0.58	0.70	-0.22	0.67	0.40	0.52	-0.14
16	AKN	0.95	0.89	0.66	0.72	0.88	0.78	0.66	0.69	0.54	0.49	0.39	0.41
17	ERN	0.83	0.78	0.15	0.62	0.92	0.86	0.72	0.64	0.69	0.63	0.51	0.44
18	SJC	0.59	0.39	0.34	0.03	0.78	0.65	0.56	0.16	0.29	0.22	0.19	-0.08

tion measure yields the largest values for the correlation coefficient between LCCDC and BWC, such that the level of correlation is very strongly positive for 16 of the 18 networks analyzed and strongly positive for the remaining two networks. Similarly, with respect to the Pearson's product moment-based correlation measure, we observe the LCCDC metric to exhibit correlation levels of strongly to very strongly positive for 16 of the 18 networks (11 networks exhibit very strongly positive correlation and 5 networks exhibit strongly positive correlation). The Kendall's concordance-based correlation measure yields the lowest values for the correlation coefficient between BWC and the other centrality metrics. Nevertheless, even under the Kendall's correlation measure: we observe the LCCDC metric to exhibit strong to very strong positive correlation with BWC for 14 of the 18 real-world networks analyzed. Overall, considering all the three correlation measures, we could say that the LCCDC metric exhibits strong to very strong levels of positive correlation for at least 14 of the 18 real-world networks analyzed. Such a high level of correlation with BWC is not observed for the other three centrality metrics analyzed in this paper, as well as for any other network analysis metric in the literature.

Figures 8, 9 and 10 compare the relative magnitude of the values for the correlation coefficient (based on the proximity of the data points to the diagonal line in these figures) obtained for BWC-LCCDC with each of the other three combinations of centrality metrics: BWC-DegC, BWC-ClC, and BWC-EVC under each of the three correlation measures.

Each data point in these figures corresponds to a particular real-world network. If a data point is below the diagonal line, it implies the correlation coefficient incurred for BWC-LCCDC is larger than the correlation coefficient incurred for the BWC-centrality metric combination for the real-world network that the data point represents. If a data point lies above the diagonal line, it implies the BWC-LCCDC correlation coefficient is lower than the BWC-centrality metric combination for the corresponding real-world network. If a data point lies on the diagonal line, it implies the correlation coefficient values are almost equal. Among the other three centrality metrics analyzed (see Figs. 8, 9, 10 for a comparison), the degree centrality metric exhibits relatively higher levels of correlation with BWC. Nevertheless, when compared to the correlation coefficient values incurred for BWC-LCCDC, the BWC-DegC correlation coefficient values are at least lower by 0.05 (in a scale of −1 to 1) for all the 18 real-world networks and lower by at least 0.10 for at least 10 of the 18 real-world networks under each of the three correlation measures.

The only centrality metric which exhibits correlation coefficient values (with BWC) matching or exceeding to that incurred for LCCDC-BWC for at least one of the real-world networks under at least one of the three correlation measures is the closeness centrality (ClC) metric. The best case scenario for ClC is that there exists just one real-world network (among the 18 networks analyzed) for which the BWC-ClC correlation coefficient is larger than the BWC-LCCDC correlation coefficient under all the three correlation measures;

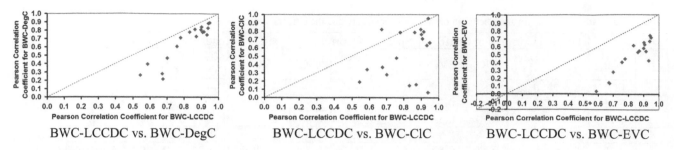

Fig. 8 Distribution of the correlation coefficient values for real-world networks under the Pearson's product moment-based correlation measure (from the centrality metrics viewpoint)

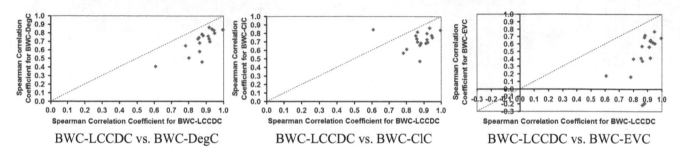

Fig. 9 Distribution of the correlation coefficient values for real-world networks under the Spearman's Rank-based correlation measure (from the centrality metrics viewpoint)

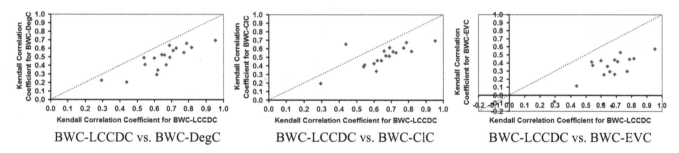

Fig. 10 Distribution of the correlation coefficient values for real-world networks under the Kendall's concordance-based correlation measure (from the centrality metrics viewpoint)

in addition, under the Pearson's and Spearman's correlation measures: the correlation coefficient values incurred for ClC with BWC equal to those incurred for LCCDC with BWC for two of the 18 real-world networks. Note that the closeness centrality metric is relatively more computation-intensive (a shortest path algorithm needs to be run at every vertex), as is also vindicated by the results in Table 3 and Fig. 7. The Eigenvector centrality (EVC) metric exhibits relatively lower levels of correlation with BWC among all the centrality metrics analyzed and under all the three correlation measures. This could be attributed to the relatively larger clustering coefficient values incurred for vertices with higher EVC. A node *i* with a higher EVC is more likely surrounded by nodes having higher degree: a majority of these nodes could be directly connected to each other and there would be no need to go through node *i*. As a result, vertices with higher EVC are very less likely to lie on the shortest path for their neighbor nodes.

Among the three correlation measures used to evaluate the correlation of BWC with LCCDC and the other centrality metrics, we observe the Spearman's measure to yield correlation coefficient values that are relatively more closer to that of the Pearson's measure. This could be deduced by observing the relative proximity of the data points to the diagonal line in Fig. 11: the data points corresponding to the Spearman's and Pearson's correlation measures are relatively more closer to the diagonal line when compared to the data points corresponding to the Kendall's and Pearson's correlation measures. Overall, for a majority of the real-world networks analyzed, the Spearman's and Kendall's correlation measures appear to, respectively, provide the upper bound and lower bound for the values of the correlation coefficient (and the correlation levels) incurred between BWC and each of the other four centrality metrics.

With respect to the impact of the variation in node degree on the correlation levels, overall: we observe the level of cor-

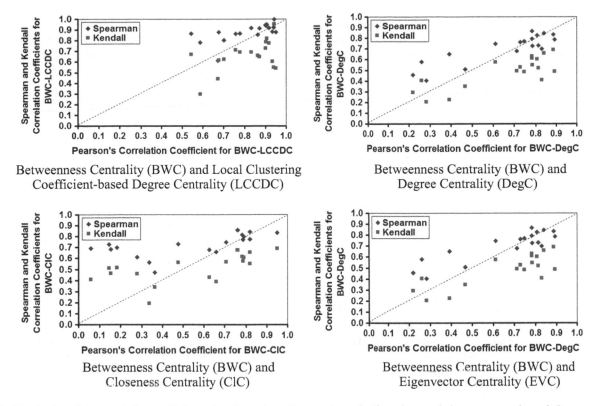

Betweenness Centrality (BWC) and Local Clustering Coefficient-based Degree Centrality (LCCDC)

Betweenness Centrality (BWC) and Degree Centrality (DegC)

Betweenness Centrality (BWC) and Closeness Centrality (ClC)

Betweenness Centrality (BWC) and Eigenvector Centrality (EVC)

Fig. 11 Distribution of the correlation coefficient values for real-world network graphs (from the correlation measures viewpoint)

relation between BWC and each of the four centrality metrics to decrease with increase in the spectral radius ratio for node degree (more predominantly observed with the Kendall correlation measure and to a certain extent with the Pearson's and Spearman's correlation measures). A high-level view of the results in Table 4 indicates that the correlation level tends to reduce from a higher positive level to a relatively lower level as the spectral radius ratio for node degree of the real-world network graphs increases. As the networks become increasingly scale-free (i.e., the variation in node degree in the network increases), the trend we could deduce is a decrease in the correlation coefficient values between BWC and each of the four centrality metrics (especially in the case of Eigenvector centrality under all the three correlation measures).

6 Related work

Several centrality metrics have been proposed for the complex network analysis. UCINET 6 [31] employs the following eight of these centrality metrics: degree, betweenness, closeness, eigenvector, power, information, flow, and reach. As mentioned earlier, the most frequently used centrality metrics are: degree, closeness, betweenness, and eigenvector. In one of the first studies on correlations among central-

ity metrics, Bolland [32] observed that degree centrality and closeness centrality are highly correlated, while the betweenness centrality is relatively uncorrelated with degree, and closeness and eigenvector centralities. Rothenberg et al. [33] observed the information centrality and distance metrics (eccentricity, mean, and median of the path length between any two vertices) to be not so strongly correlated with the degree and betweenness centrality metrics. Rotherberg et al. [33] observed the degree centrality to be the most strongly correlated metric with betweenness centrality: we also observe that next to LCCDC, the degree centrality could be claimed as the centrality metric that exhibits stronger correlation with BWC. With respect to the impact of symmetry in the adjacency matrix on the correlation levels observed, Valente et al. [34] observed that the disparity between symmetric centrality metrics (like betweenness) and asymmetric centrality metrics (like degree) increases when computed on the undirected instances of directed network graphs.

For scale-free networks [35], the distribution of the betweenness centrality of the vertices has been observed to follow a power-law pattern (similar to that of the degree centrality) [37]. It was also observed in [38] that for scale-free networks that are either dissortative [12] or neutral with respect to node degree, the average of the betweenness centralities of the neighbors of a vertex is proportional to the betweenness centrality of the vertex considered; whereas, for assortative scale-free networks, the betweenness centralities of the neighbors of a vertex is independent of the betweenness centrality of the vertex considered.

Among the various localized centrality metrics proposed in the literature, the "leverage" centrality metric proposed by Joyce et al. [39] for brain networks has gained prominence. Leverage centrality of a node is a measure of the extent of connectivity of the node relative to the connectivity of its neighbors. For a node i with degree k_i and set of neighbors N_i, the leverage centrality of node i, $\text{LVC}(i) = \frac{1}{k_i} \sum_{j \in N_i} \frac{k_i - k_j}{k_i + k_j}$ [39]. Leverage centrality is based on the notion that a node with degree higher than the degree of its neighbors is likely to be more influential on its neighbors and vice-versa. The above formulation for LVC restricts its use only for vertices with degree 1 or above and not applicable for isolated vertices. On the other hand, our proposed LCCDC metric (also a localized centrality metric) could be computed for any vertex and the entire network graph need not be just one single connected component. Moreover, the above formulation for leverage centrality metric compares the degree of a node with the degree of an individual neighbor node, and fails to take into consideration the connectivity among the neighbor nodes themselves (without involving the node in consideration). Hence, the leverage centrality metric cannot be a suitable alternate for the betweenness centrality (BWC) metric, as is also evidenced in the correlation studies of [39]: the correlation between leverage centrality and BWC is lower than the correlation between degree centrality and BWC. On the other hand, we observe that the correlation between LCCDC and BWC is even stronger than the correlation between degree centrality and BWC that has been observed in the literature until now. Thus, our proposed LCCDC metric is significantly different from that of the leverage centrality, closeness centrality, and the other centrality metrics.

Li et al. [40] conducted an extensive correlation study for the centrality metrics on 34 real-world network graphs as well as the theoretical graphs generated from the Erdos-Renyi (ER; for random networks) [41] and Barabasi-Albert (BA; for scale-free networks) [36] models. It has been observed in [40] that the degree centrality metric exhibits the strongest levels of correlation with the betweenness centrality metric for both the ER and BA networks. Likewise, for about two-thirds of the 34 real-world network graphs, the BWC-DegC correlation coefficient values were observed to be the largest incurred compared to the correlation coefficient values incurred for BWC-ClC, BWC-LVC, and BWC-EVC. Unlike our paper, the correlation study in Li et al. [40] has been conducted only with the Pearson's product moment-based correlation measure. We observe from the results of this paper that the Kendall's concordance-based correlation

measure gives a lower estimate for the levels of correlation between any two centrality metrics. The LCCDC metric withstands the test with respect to all the three correlation measures and consistently incurs larger values for the correlation coefficient with BWC compared to the correlation coefficient values incurred for any other centrality metric with BWC.

7 Conclusions

The high-level contribution of this paper is the proposal of a localized, computationally lightweight alternate centrality metric for the computation-intensive betweenness centrality (BWC) metric that is widely used for the complex network analysis. We effectively magnify the importance of a node to connect its neighbors on the shortest path (evaluated through the local clustering coefficient) with the node's degree to assess its importance to connect any two nodes in the network on a shortest path. Our hypothesis is that nodes with higher degree, but lower local clustering coefficient, are more likely to be part of several shortest paths between any two node pairs in the network. Accordingly, we propose the local clustering coefficient-based degree centrality (LCCDC) for a vertex as the product of the degree of the vertex and one minus the local clustering coefficient. We observe the LCCDC to exhibit a strong-very strong positive correlation with BWC (under all the three correlation measures used) for a majority of the real-world network graphs analyzed. Even with the Kendall's concordance-based correlation measure (that is observed to return lower values for the correlation coefficient among the three correlation measures considered), we observe the LCCDC metric to exhibit strong-very strong levels of correlation with BWC for 14 of the 18 real-world networks analyzed (whereas the degree centrality and closeness centrality metrics could at most exhibit strong correlation with BWC for at most 4–5 of the 18 real-world networks analyzed). Under the Spearman's rank-based correlation measure, we observe the LCCDC to be very strongly correlated to BWC (correlation coefficient values of 0.80 or above) for 16 of the 18 real-world networks. Thus, we confidently claim that the LCCDC could effectively serve as an alternate metric for ranking the vertices of a graph in lieu of the BWC. To the best of our knowledge, we have not come across such a computationally lightweight centrality metric that is highly correlated with betweenness centrality. As part of future work, we will explore extending the application of the LCCDC metric (with appropriate modifications) for directed real-world network graphs as well as conduct a correlation study between LCCDC and BWC for network graphs generated from theoretical models (like the ER and BA models).

References

1. Newman, M.: Networks: an introduction, 1st edn. Oxford University Press, Oxfrod (2010)
2. Bonacich, P.: Power and centrality: a family of measures. Am. J. Sociol. **92**(5), 1170–1182 (1987)
3. Freeman, L.: A set of measures of centrality based on betweenness. Sociometry **40**(1), 35–41 (1977)
4. Freeman, L.: Centrality in social networks conceptual clarification. Soc. Netw. **1**(3), 215–239 (1979)
5. Triola, M.F.: Elementary statistics, 12th edn. Pearson, NY (2012)
6. Lay, D.C.: Linear algebra and its applications, 4th edn. Pearson, NY (2011)
7. Brandes, U.: A faster algorithm for betweenness centrality. J. Math. Sociol. **25**(2), 163–177 (2001)
8. Cormen, T.H., Leiserson, C.E., Rivest, R.L., Stein, C.: Introduction to algorithms, 3rd edn. MIT Press, Cambridge (2009)
9. Evans, J.D.: Straightforward Statistics for the Behavioral Sciences, 1st edn, Brooks Cole Publishing Company (1995)
10. Meghanathan, N.: Spectral radius as a measure of variation in node degree for complex network graphs,. In: Proceedings of the 7th international conference on u- and e- service, science and technology, pp. 30–33, Haikou, China (2014)
11. Maia de Abreu, N.M.: Old and new results on algebraic connectivity of graphs. Linear Algebra Appl. **423**(1), 53–73 (2007)
12. Newman, M.E.J.: Assortative mixing in networks. Phys. Rev. Lett. **89**(2), 208–701 (2002)
13. Newman, M.E.J.: Modularity and community structure in networks. J. Natl. Acad. Sci. USA **103**(23), 8557–8582 (2006)
14. Cherven, K.: Mastering Gephi network visualization. Packt Publishing, UK (2015)
15. Girvan, M., Newman, M.E.J.: Community structure in social and biological networks. Proc. Natl. Acad. Sci. USA **99**(12), 7821–7826 (2002)
16. Cross, R.L., Parker, A., Cross, R.: The hidden power of social networks: understanding how work really gets done in organizations. 1st edn. Harvard Business Review Press, NY (2004)
17. Moreno, J.L.: The sociometry Reader, pp. 534–547, The Free Press, Glencoe (1960)
18. Freeman, L.C., Webster, C.M., Kirke, D.M.: Exploring social structure using dynamic three-dimensional color images. Soc. Netw. **20**(2), 109–118 (1998)
19. Loomis, C.P., Morales, J.O., Clifford, R.A., Leonard, O.E.: Turrialba social systems and the introduction of change, pp. 45–78, The Free Press, Glencoe (1953)
20. Nepusz, T., Petroczi, A., Negyessy, L., Bazso, F.: Fuzzy communities and the concept of bridgeness in complex networks. Phys. Rev. E **77**(1), 016107 (2008)
21. Krebs, V.: Proxy networks: analyzing one network to reveal another. Bulletin de Méthodologie Sociologique **79**, 40–61 (2003)
22. Geiser, P., Danon, L.: Community structure in Jazz. Adv. Complex Syst. **6**(4), 563–573 (2003)
23. Pearson, M., Michell, L.: Smoke rings: social network analysis of friendship groups, smoking and drug-taking. Drugs Educ. Prev. Policy **7**(1), 21–37 (2000)
24. Knuth, D.E.: The Stanford GraphBase: a platform for combinatorial computing, 1st edn. Addison-Wesley, Reading (1993)
25. Rogers, E.M., Kincaid, D.L.: Communication networks: toward a new paradigm for research, Free Press, USA (1980)
26. Newman, M.E.J.: Finding community structure in networks using the eigenvectors of matrices. Phys. Rev. E **74**(3), 036104 (2006)
27. Hayes, B.: Connecting the dots. Am. Sci. **94**(5), 400–404 (2006)
28. Facebook Netvizz Application. https://apps.facebook.com/netvizz/
29. Pajek Datasets. http://vlado.fmf.uni-lj.si/pub/networks/data/
30. Freeman, L.: Datasets. http://moreno.ss.uci.edu/data.html
31. Borgatti, S.P., Everett, M.G., Johnson, J.C.: Analyzing social networks. 1st edn. SAGE Publications, UK (2013)
32. Bolland, J.M.: Sorting out centrality: an analysis of the performance of four centrality models in real and simulated networks. Soc. Netw. **10**(3), 233–253 (1988)
33. Rothenberg, R.B., Potterat, J.J., Woodhouse, D.E., Darrow, W.W., Muth, S.Q., Klovdahl, A.S.: Choosing a centrality measure: epidemiologic correlates in the colorado springs study of social networks. Soc. Netw. **17**(3-4), 273–297 (1995)
34. Valente, T.W., Coronges, K., Lakon, C., Costenbader, E.: How correlated are network centrality measures? Connections **28**(1), 16–26 (2008)
35. Barabasi, A.L., Albert, R.: Emergence of scaling in random networks. Science **286**(5439), 509–512 (1999)
36. de Caen, D.: An upper bound on the sum of squares of degrees in a graph. Discret. Math. **185**(1–3), 245–248 (1998)
37. Goh, K., Oh, E., Jeong, H., Kahng, B., Kim, D.: Classification of scale-free networks. J. Natl. Acad. Sci. USA **99**(20), 12583–12588 (2002)
38. Goh, K., Oh, E., Kahng, B., Kim, D.: Betweenness centrality correlation in social networks. Phys. Rev. E **67**(1), 017101 (2003)
39. Joyce, K.E., Laurienti, P.J., Burdette, J.H., Hayasaka, S.: A new measure of centrality for brain networks. PLoS One **5**(8), e12200, 1–13 (2010)
40. Li, C., Li, Q., Van Mieghem, P., Stanley, H.E., Wang, H.: Correlation between centrality metrics and their application to the opinion model. Eur. Phys. J. B **88**(65), 1–13 (2015)
41. Erdos, P., Renyi, A.: On random graphs I. Publ. Math. **6**, 290–297 (1959)

Permissions

The contributors of this book come from diverse backgrounds, making this book a truly international effort. This book will bring forth new frontiers with its revolutionizing research information and detailed analysis of the nascent developments around the world.

We would like to thank all the contributing authors for lending their expertise to make the book truly unique. They have played a crucial role in the development of this book. Without their invaluable contributions this book wouldn't have been possible. They have made vital efforts to compile up to date information on the varied aspects of this subject to make this book a valuable addition to the collection of many professionals and students.

This book was conceptualized with the vision of imparting up-to-date information and advanced data in this field. To ensure the same, a matchless editorial board was set up. Every individual on the board went through rigorous rounds of assessment to prove their worth. After which they invested a large part of their time researching and compiling the most relevant data for our readers.

The editorial board has been involved in producing this book since its inception. They have spent rigorous hours researching and exploring the diverse topics which have resulted in the successful publishing of this book. They have passed on their knowledge of decades through this book. To expedite this challenging task, the publisher supported the team at every step. A small team of assistant editors was also appointed to further simplify the editing procedure and attain best results for the readers.

Apart from the editorial board, the designing team has also invested a significant amount of their time in understanding the subject and creating the most relevant covers. They scrutinized every image to scout for the most suitable representation of the subject and create an appropriate cover for the book.

The publishing team has been an ardent support to the editorial, designing and production team. Their endless efforts to recruit the best for this project, has resulted in the accomplishment of this book. They are a veteran in the field of academics and their pool of knowledge is as vast as their experience in printing. Their expertise and guidance has proved useful at every step. Their uncompromising quality standards have made this book an exceptional effort. Their encouragement from time to time has been an inspiration for everyone.

The publisher and the editorial board hope that this book will prove to be a valuable piece of knowledge for researchers, students, practitioners and scholars across the globe.

List of Contributors

Tung Pham, Hang Dang and Thai Hoang Le
Faculty of Information Technology, VNUHCM-University of Science, Ho Chi Minh City, Vietnam

Trung Le
Faculty of Information Technology, HCMc University of Pedagogy, Ho Chi Minh City, Vietnam

Nguyen-Tuan-Thanh Le
IRIT Laboratory, University Paul Sabatier Toulouse III, Toulouse, France
University of Science and Technology of Hanoi, Hanoi, Vietnam

Chihab Hanachi
IRIT Laboratory, University Toulouse Capitole I, Toulouse, France

Serge Stinckwich
IRD, UMI 209, UMMISCO, IRD France Nord, 93143 Bondy, France
Sorbonne Universités, Univ. Paris 06, UMI 209, UMMISCO, 75005 Paris, France
Université de Caen Basse-Normandie, Caen, France

Tuong-Vinh Ho
IRD, UMI 209, UMMISCO, IRD France Nord, 93143 Bondy, France
Sorbonne Universités, Univ. Paris 06, UMI 209, UMMISCO, 75005 Paris, France
Institute Francophone International, Vietnam National University, Hanoi, Vietnam

Khai T. Huynh,Tho T. Quan and Thang H. Bui
Faculty of Computer Science and Engineering, Ho Chi Minh City University of Technology, Ho Chi Minh City, Vietnam

Wafa Wali and Bilel Gargouri
MIR@CL Laboratory FSEGS, Sfax, Tunisia

Abdelmajid Ben Hamadou
MIR@CL Laboratory ISIMS, Sfax, Tunisia

Umang Aggarwal and Maria Trocan
Institut Superieur d'Electronique de Paris, 28 Rue Notre Dame des Champs, Paris, France

Francois-Xavier Coudoux
IEMN (UMR CNRS 8520) Department OAE, Valenciennes University, 59313 Valenciennes Cedex 9, France

Kristína Machová and Jaroslav Štefaník
Department of Cybernetics and Artificial Intelligence, Technical University, Letná 9, 04200 Košice, Slovakia

Mirjana Ivanović, Zoran Budimac and Dejan Mitrović
Department of Mathematics and Informatics, Faculty of Sciences, University of Novi Sad, Novi Sad, Serbia

Milan Vidaković
Faculty of Technical Sciences, University of Novi Sad, Novi Sad, Serbia

Hidenao Abe
Department of Information Systems, Bunkyo University, 1100 Namegaya, Chigasaki, Kanagawa 2538550, Japan

Hai Quang Hong Dam
University of Information Technology, Ho Chi Minh City, Vietnam

Sven Nordholm
Curtin University of Technology, Perth, Australia

Marwan Hassani
Architecture of Information Systems Group, Eindhoven University of Technology, Eindhoven, The Netherlands

Thomas Seidl
Database Systems Group, LMU Munich, Munich, Germany

Van-Nam Hoang, Thanh-Huong Nguyen,Thi-Lan Le and Thanh-Hai Tran
International Research Institute MICA, HUST-CNRS/UMI 2954-Grenoble INP, Hanoi University of Science and Technology, Ha Noi, Vietnam

Tan-Phu Vuong
IMEP-LAHC, Grenoble Institute of Technology (GINP), Grenoble, France

Nicolas Vuillerme
Institut Universitaire de France, LAI Jean-Raoul Scherrer, University of Geneva, Geneva, Switzerland University Grenoble Alpes, Grenoble, France

Trong Hai Duong
International University, Vietnam National University-HCMC, Ho Chi Minh City, Vietnam

Minh Quang Tran
Institute of Science and Technology of Industry 4.0, Nguyen Tat Thanh University, Ho Chi Minh City, Vietnam

Thi Phuong Trang Nguyen
Banking University of Ho Chi Minh City, Ho Chi Minh City, Vietnam

Camelia Delcea and Ioana-Alexandra Bradea
Bucharest University of Economic Studies, Bucharest, Romania

Ahlem Ferchichi
RIADI Laboratory, National School of Computer Sciences, University of Manouba, Manouba, Tunisia

Wadii Boulila and Imed Riadh Farah
RIADI Laboratory, National School of Computer Sciences, University of Manouba, Manouba, Tunisia ITI Department, Telecom-Bretagne, Brest, France

Erfan Arzhmand
Engineering and Technology Department, Shomal University, Amol, Mazandaran, Iran

Hossein Rashid
Computer Engineering Department, Islamic Azad University, Kerman, Iran

Mohammad Javad Fazel Ashrafi
Computer Engineering Department, Urmia University, Urmia, Iran

Linh Manh Pham
Laboratoire d'Informatique de Grenoble, University of Grenoble Alpes, Grenoble, France

Tuan-Minh Pham
Faculty of Information Technology, Hanoi National University of Education, Hanoi, Vietnam

Natarajan Meghanathan
Department of Computer Science, Jackson State University, Jackson, USA

Index